TRADE LIBERALIZATION AND POVERTY: A HANDBOOK

Centre for Economic Policy Research

Centre for Economic Policy Research
90–98 Goswell Road
London EC1V 7RR
UK

Tel: +44 20 7878 2900
Fax: +44 20 7878 2999

Email: cepr@cepr.org
Website: http:\\www.cepr.org

British Library Cataloguing in Publication Data
A catalogue record for this book is available from the British Library

ISBN: 1 898128 62 6

Printed and bound in the UK

TRADE LIBERALIZATION AND POVERTY:
A HANDBOOK

Neil McCulloch
Institute of Development Studies, Sussex

L Alan Winters
University of Sussex, Centre for Economic Performance, London School of Economics and CEPR, London

Xavier Cirera
Institute of Development Studies, Sussex

This Handbook is an output from a project funded by the UK Department for International Development (DfID) for the benefit of developing countries. The views expressed are not necessarily those of DfID or other parts of the UK Government.

Contents

List of Tables

List of Figures

List of Boxes

Preface and Acknowledgements

The connection between trade liberalization and poverty in developing countries has been on the policy agenda for several years and has recently become a matter of intense public debate. There are many views and anecdotes about the links, but not much careful analysis. In particular, there is little work that is simultaneously rigorous and accessible to a wide range of people. This Handbook starts to fill that gap.

The origins of the Handbook lie in research on trade and poverty initiated by the UK Department for International Development in 1998, which was subsequently to provide background material for both the World Bank's World Development Report 2001, *Attacking Poverty*, and the UK Government's White Paper *Eliminating World Poverty: Making Globalisation Work for the Poor*, 2000. These exercises revealed not only the paucity of evidence on trade and poverty but also the absence of any kind of framework for thinking about the issue. In response, a framework was developed by one of the authors of this Handbook, and it has since become the basis for several explorations up to and including *The Global Poverty Report 2001* produced by the International Financial Institutions for the G8 meeting in Genoa in July 2001.

But a framework is only a start in understanding the links between trade liberalization and poverty. To be useful in the fight against poverty, not only does it need to be coupled with empirical work to test its relevance and robustness, but it must also be turned into a practical tool for policy-makers analysing their own countries. Original empirical work based on the framework is currently underway at the University of Sussex (funded again by the Department for International Development under its Economic and Social Research mandate, ESCOR), but it is too early to know its results. This Handbook does the rest of the job. It explains the framework in some detail, discusses how it can be implemented in practice, collects evidence on the various effects of trade liberalization on poverty, and explores the implications for trade and anti-poverty policy in developing countries. It then discusses ten specific aspects of trade liberalization that are likely to be relevant in the next few years and shows how to analyse their implications for poverty.

One of our major conclusions is that the links between trade liberalization and poverty are very country-specific. So while the Handbook assembles a broad range of empirical information on parts of the relationship and sometimes infers some robust rules of thumb for thinking about the problem, it espouses no universal answers or even universal methodologies for finding them. What we do set out, however, is a way of identifying key considerations and a series of ten practical cases showing how to think through and predict the effects of trade liberalization in particular economies.

In the course of a project of this length and complexity, the authors accumulate a huge debt to fellow scholars who contribute directly or indirectly to the ideas presented. Among those whose comments, discussion and input we would like to acknowledge are Max Corden, Jamie de Melo, David Dollar, Tricia Feeney, Subir Gokarn, Stephen Golub, Duncan Green, Bernard Hoekman, Peter Holmes, Kate Jordan, Ravi Kanbur, Caroline Lequesne, Jim Levinsohn, Michael Lipton, Julie Litchfield, Andrew McKay, Nick Mabey, Will Martin, Keith Maskus, Pradeep Mehta, Oliver Morrissey, Raghav Narsalay, Martin Ravallion, Robert Read, Dani Rodrik, Jim Rollo, Nevin Shaw, Isidro Soloaga, Chris Stevens, Zhen Kun Wang, Sally-Ann Way, Howard White and Adrian Wood.

We are also grateful to participants in events at which some of the contents of the Handbook have been discussed. These were organized by the Bertil Ohlin Liberalisation Seminar, CEPR, the ESRC Development Economics Study Group, the Development Studies Association, the Department for International Development, the EU-LDC Network, the European Commission, the ESRC International Economics Study Group, the International Labour Organization, the London School of Economics, the North American Association for Economics and Finance, the Royal Economic Society, the University of Sussex, the World Bank and the World Trade Organization.

Thanks are due to Rosie Bellinger, Jenny Edwards, Janet Ellis, Diane Jordan, Vicki MacLean, Julia Meacham and Shoshana Ormonde for logistical help.

Romesh Vaitilingam provided excellent and indispensable editorial help and Lisa Moss of CEPR and Linda Machin managed the publication process. We are grateful to all.

We owe a huge debt to the staff of the Department for International Development, especially the International Trade Department, which initiated, funded, managed and contributed vastly to our efforts. Their conventions preclude our naming them personally, but our gratitude is deep nonetheless.

Of course, none of these people is responsible for the Handbook's remaining shortcomings, and none of the views expressed in it should be attributed to them or their employers.

Finally, are grateful to our friends, partners and families for their patience and support while this project has been underway: respectively, Rosaleen Cunningham and Euan McCulloch; Zhen Kun Wang and Oliver Winters; and Alexandra Hughes, Alicia Carril and Miquel Cirera.

Neil McCulloch
L Alan Winters
Xavier Cirera

August 2001

Executive Summary

Openness to trade has long been seen as an important element of sound economic policy – and trade liberalization as a necessary step for achieving it. At the same time, continuing extreme poverty in developing countries is perhaps the biggest blemish on the contemporary global economic canvas. This Handbook examines how our concerns about the latter should affect our attitude towards and implementation of the former.

In general, trade liberalization is an ally in the fight against poverty: it tends to increase average incomes, providing more resources with which to tackle poverty. And while it will generally affect income distribution, it does not appear to do so in a systematically adverse way. Nevertheless, it is important to recognise that most trade reforms will hurt someone, possibly pushing them into, or deeper into, poverty, and that some reforms may increase overall poverty even while they boost incomes in total. Thus, despite the general presumption in favour of trade liberalization, there remain important public policy questions of how to implement it in a way that maximizes its benefits for poverty alleviation and what to do about any poverty that it does create or exacerbate.

The Handbook considers the matter both from a general perspective and by exploring specific types of trade liberalization. It draws on economic analysis, empirical evidence and practical experience to construct a broad framework to explain links between trade liberalization and poverty. It shows how countries and liberalizations are likely to vary from case to case, and how to use the framework to identify the critical features of specific cases in practice. It then discusses the sort of effects that liberalization may have on the ground and the appropriate policy responses to problems that might arise.

The framework outlines three pathways through which trade liberalization can have a direct effect on poverty:

- *Price transmission.* The first effect of trade liberalization is to change the prices of the liberalized goods. If these price changes are translated into changes in the prices actually faced by poor households, then the direct impact on poverty depends on whether poor households are net consumers or net producers of the product whose price has changed – a price increase benefits net producers and hurts net consumers. It is important to note, however, that some of the most dramatic gains from liberalization are associated not with changes in prices, but with the creation or destruction of markets – where goods start or cease to be traded.

It is also critical to know whether the price changes at the border arising from trade liberalization are actually transmitted to the poor. This depends on several factors, notably the structure of the distribution sector; the way in which government institutions such as marketing organizations operate; and whether the goods are traded at a local, regional, national or international level. If price changes are not transmitted to the poor, complementary policies may be needed to establish markets, improve competition and deepen market integration.

- *Enterprises*. Trade liberalization also affects households through its impact on profits and hence on employment and wages. There are two opposite ways in which this may occur. First, if wages are flexible and labour is fully employed, then price changes caused by trade liberalization will be reflected in wage changes, with employment staying the same. But alternatively, if there is a large pool of workers who move in or out of jobs when circumstances change, then trade liberalization will cause changes in employment. In reality, there will be a combination of these effects. How this affects poverty depends not only on how employment changes, but also on the types of labour that poor households supply and where the various wage rates lie relative to the poverty line.

- *Taxes and spending*. Trade liberalization may also affect poverty through changes in the government's fiscal position, particularly if trade taxation is an important source of revenue. But trade liberalization does not always cut revenue (if non-tariff barriers and tariff exemptions are also tackled); alternative sources of revenue do not have to target the poor; and social and anti-poverty programmes can be at least partially protected even if expenditure does decline. Moreover, good macroeconomic management is far more important for maintaining social spending than trade taxation.

Four further issues are fundamental to the overall impact of trade liberalization on poverty. The first and most important is **economic growth**. The weight of evidence is that openness to trade is good for growth and that growth benefits the poor. There may be exceptions, which need to be addressed by specific policy interventions, but there is no evidence that openness or growth systematically harm the poor. For its full benefits, however, trade liberalization should be accompanied by sound policies in areas such as transport and communications infrastructure, market facilitation, competition, education and governance; otherwise it will fail to generate the investment and productivity improvements needed for growth.

The second issue is the short- and medium-term **costs of adjustment**. The reason why trade liberalization generates so much public controversy is often concern about these costs – most notably job losses in formerly protected sectors, but also potential loss of government revenue. The size of the adjustment costs created by trade reform varies greatly from country to country, but empirical evidence suggests that they are not always large. Nevertheless, trade reform does tend to force governments to split their anti-poverty efforts among the chronically poor, the productive poor and those who are transitorily poor as a result of the reform. The key is to take account of the ability of poor households to cushion themselves against the costs of adjustment without at the same time undermining their incentives to adjust. And it is important to protect social expenditure and ensure appropriate targeting of the poor.

Third, trade liberalization can change the nature of the **risk and uncertainty** that poor households face, although not always for the worse. It can also affect their ability to cope with risk and uncertainty. Policies such as improving access to credit markets can help a great deal here along with improvements in asset distribution and in the flexibility of local labour markets.

Finally, there is the issue of **supply response**: the ability of poor households to respond to the new opportunities presented by trade liberalization. Much of this will be influenced by their location and demographic structure, and the gender, health status, education and assets of their members. But for long-run benefits to accrue in terms of poverty alleviation, reasonable supply responses are essential. These will be aided by complementary public policy in such areas as: investment in infrastructure (irrigation and rural roads) to ensure that agricultural production can be connected to world markets; property rights to encourage investment in the land; appropriate agricultural extension and mechanisms for the dissemination of market and technical information; and the development of markets for credit, agricultural inputs and services.

Having laid out the framework for analysing the links between trade and poverty, the Handbook explores ten specific aspects of trade liberalization – key sectors, policy instruments and issues. All of these are likely to be on the agenda in future rounds of negotiations in the World Trade Organization (WTO) and some are already under discussion. Equally, all offer scope for unilateral liberalization quite independent of the WTO. In each of these cases, the Handbook identifies the most important links so that policy-makers can assess their significance in the context of their own countries, make decisions on the key domestic policy requirements, implement unilateral reform and/or prepare their negotiating positions for multilateral talks.

- *Trade in agriculture.* Agriculture is the key sector for nearly all poverty analysis: the poor are predominantly rural; food accounts for a major share of all poor people's expenditure; agriculture is their major source of income; and farm incomes have large spillovers to others in the rural economy. The markets in this sector are among the most distorted in the world, with both developed and developing countries maintaining high levels of protection. Reforms, both unilateral and multilateral, have the potential for considerable poverty alleviation, although particular groups of poor people may suffer from liberalization.

To predict the effects of agricultural liberalization, governments need to know each poor group's net consumption of the goods to be liberalized – whether they buy more of them than they sell – as well as details of rural labour markets and demand patterns. And to increase the reform's pro-poor effects, governments must establish complementary policies to ensure that increased agricultural incomes filter through to the poor, such as extension services and communications infrastructure.

- *Trade-related intellectual property rights (TRIPs).* The protection of intellectual property rights through the WTO's TRIPs Agreement gives temporary monopolistic rents to innovative companies, which are mainly located in developed countries. The implications for developing countries depend on their market size and capacity for innovation. At best, the poor are likely to suffer small losses from any strengthening of the protection as increased prices precede any substantial diffusion of technology. To ensure an ultimately pro-poor effect, developing countries will need to adopt industrial and educational policies that foster the adoption and diffusion of technology.

- *Trade in services.* The General Agreement on Trade in Services (GATS) provides a framework for trade liberalization in services, which account for the bulk of world output. But progress has been slow with myriad trade restrictions significantly reducing supply and raising prices. Prominent among the service export interests of developing countries is the temporary movement of labour to provide services. If the movement of relatively unskilled workers was allowed, there could be very positive effects on poverty alleviation. In addition, some service reforms aid the poor directly – for example, those in health and education. And others may increase unskilled employment – such as tourism – or boost local efficiency and competitiveness – such as financial services. But liberalizing some inefficient services may eliminate unskilled jobs while offering their main benefits to the relatively rich.

- *Trade in manufacturing.* Liberalizing trade in manufactured goods is an important goal for the next round of multilateral trade talks and for countries acting unilaterally. Developing countries protect manufacturing much more than do developed countries. Liberalization can clearly foster poverty alleviation by enhancing growth and productivity and improving resource allocation. But the conditions have to be in place for firms to respond to new threats and opportunities; and some workers might lose so safety nets may be necessary. Abolition of the Multi-Fibre Arrangement will benefit developed countries that liberalize and potential exporters of clothing, but those countries with no comparative advantage in the sector will lose.

- *Export and domestic subsidies.* In theory, subsidies provide a way to address market failure and hence increase aggregate incomes. But it is very difficult to ensure that they are not captured by interest groups. Export subsidies will generally raise the domestic prices of the subsidized goods; depending on the circumstances, production subsidies may do so too. The effect of this on poverty will depend on the net consumption of the subsidized goods by poor households. Subsidies can also affect factor prices, with subsidies to industrial sectors favouring returns to capital and skilled labour over those to the unskilled. The cost of financing subsidies can also have adverse effects on the poor.

- *Anti-dumping*. Anti-dumping duties have become the most popular tool of protectionism in the developed countries, and the ease with which they can be imposed has a deterrent effect well beyond the set of exports that actually face them. What is more, developing countries are starting to use anti-dumping more frequently themselves – and the effects are generally damaging for the poor. Anti-dumping duties favour profits over wages and the jobs they preserve are unlikely to involve the poor. The price increases they induce, on the other hand, are likely to hurt the poor. And by absorbing skilled labour, anti-dumping regimes also reduce the productivity and wages of unskilled labour.

- *Labour standards*. Despite the economic and moral arguments for supporting the adoption of labour standards, the rationale for linking them to trade is weak. While they can certainly benefit developing countries and the poor, they must be consistent with a country's level of development. If they are too ambitious, they are likely to harm the poorest, who will be left out of the regulated sectors. Non-trade measures provide more efficient ways to improve labour conditions than trade sanctions. These include educational programmes and the promotion of civil society institutions, some of which may require developed countries to provide resources and technical assistance.

- *Environmental standards*. The poor are commonly very vulnerable to environmental degradation. But in general, correcting the problem is a matter of domestic policy that should be quite independent of international trade. While trade liberalization can exacerbate poverty through its environmental effects, if domestic environmental policy is sound, there is no presumption that it will do so. But policy-makers need to consider the possible linkages and pre-empt extreme problems by using compensatory and complementary policies. Genuinely international environmental issues are better handled by multilateral environmental agreements than by trade policy and sanctions.

- *Competition policy*. Competition is one of the best allies in the fight against poverty, because it constrains the exercise of market power. And while openness to trade generates strong competition in some sectors, an effective competition policy might be needed in others. But competition policy is costly and building the necessary institutions may slow down poverty alleviation by diverting skilled labour from productive activities. Governments should focus on appropriate regulation for natural monopolies and ensuring the 'contestability' of the domestic market. A multilateral agreement on competition policy may provide assistance – and would be pro-poor if it disciplined hard-core cartels (though these are relatively few). But again the potentially high costs must be weighed against any potential benefits.

- *Investment and trade-related investment measures (TRIMs).* The ultimate goal of policy interventions like TRIMs, which seek to influence the behaviour of foreign companies, is to stimulate economic growth. Insofar as they are effective, they may help poverty alleviation, but in reality, their direct effects are more likely to be negative than positive for the poor. So unilateral reductions in TRIMs, or a multilateral agreement to limit their use, would not increase poverty. At the same time, developing countries do need to devise policy and institutional regimes that encourage foreign direct investment (FDI) since it can be a powerful force for growth and poverty alleviation.

Finally, the Handbook contains two key messages for policy-makers. First, the impact of trade liberalization on poverty is very country-specific; although the Handbook presents the pathways through which each aspect of liberalization might affect poverty, policy-makers themselves will have to identify which of these pathways are the most important in their particular circumstances.

Second, although the range and complexity of the potential linkages between trade liberalization and poverty may appear daunting, the most important effects in any given country are likely to be relatively simple and reasonably obvious. In short, it *is* possible for policy-makers to develop suitable responses to ensure that the poor gain from trade liberalization.

PART 1: Linking Trade Liberalization and Poverty

1 About this Handbook

Openness to trade has long been seen as an important element of sound economic policy – and trade liberalization as a necessary step for achieving it. At the same time, continuing extreme poverty in developing countries is perhaps the biggest blemish on the contemporary global economic canvas. This Handbook asks how concerns about the latter should affect our attitude towards and implementation of the former. It considers the matter first from a general perspective, using economic analysis and experience to construct a framework for exploring the links between trade liberalization and poverty. It then goes on to consider ten specific aspects of trade liberalization, identifying the links that are most likely to be important and showing how policy-makers can assess their significance in the context of their particular countries.

In general, trade liberalization is an ally in the fight against poverty: it tends to increase average incomes, providing more resources with which to tackle poverty; and while it will generally affect income distribution, it does not appear to do so in a systematically adverse way. It should be recognized, however, that most trade reforms will hurt someone, possibly pushing them into, or deeper into, poverty, and that some reforms may increase overall poverty even while they boost incomes in total. Thus, despite the general presumption in favour of trade liberalization, there remain important public policy questions of how to implement it in a way that maximizes its benefits for poverty alleviation and what to do about any poverty that it does create or exacerbate.

If trade liberalization and poverty were both easily measured, and if we had plenty of data on both, we might be able to derive simple empirical regularities linking them. This would allow us to define broad policy positions and provide a base from which to consider the details of specific cases. Unfortunately, however, neither of these conditions is met, so we are thrown back on case-by-case analysis based on fragmentary evidence on parts of the argument. The key to collecting and interpreting this evidence and designing policies to alleviate any ill effects of a liberalization is to design a framework for identifying the channels through which such effects might operate. Thus, after discussing the background issues behind trade policy and poverty in Chapters 2 and 3 (for example, how we define and measure them and how economists have thought about these two issues in the past), we present such a framework in Chapter 4.

3

Following that, we discuss how previous researchers have attempted to link trade and poverty (Chapter 5), show how our framework may be implemented (Chapter 6) and examine its implications for the connection between trade policy and anti-poverty policy (Chapter 7). The remaining chapters explore ten specific aspects of trade liberalization: agriculture, trade-related intellectual property rights (TRIPs), services, manufactures, export and domestic subsidies, anti-dumping duties, labour standards, environmental standards, competition policy and investment and trade-related investment measures.

The analysis described here is based on a major research effort undertaken by the University of Sussex with funding from the Department for International Development. But the book is not a research monograph. Neither, however, is it a 'cookbook' or user manual, walking the reader through a well-specified series of steps that ultimately reveal a precise estimate of the effect of a trade reform on the number of people in poverty. Rather, it is a handbook to help policy-makers analyse (and debate) their own circumstances and formulate their own views about the opportunities and dangers entailed in their own policy packages. It aims to be concrete, quoting specific examples where possible, but it recognizes that every country and every liberalization is unique. Hence, there is no alternative to policy-makers collecting their own information and undertaking their own analysis.

The Handbook is primarily aimed at policy-makers in ministries that are concerned with trade policy and poverty, and the people who interact with them, such as members of civil society and officials from donor organizations. It is likely to be particularly useful to those who are conducting their countries' discussions with the Bretton Woods organizations – the World Bank and the International Monetary Fund (IMF) – and other donors, as well as those responsible for formulating positions for international trade talks at regional or global – World Trade Organization (WTO) – levels. But as we emphasize, trade policy involves far more than just international negotiations, so the Handbook should also be used in finance and commerce ministries where the day-to-day business of unilateral trade policy is discussed. Naturally, we also hope that the book will be of interest to students and researchers in economics and other disciplines and to people who are interested in poverty *per se*.

Much of the Handbook will be accessible to readers with little or no experience in economics. But the precision and detail with which certain issues have to be discussed means that, in places, we assume a small amount of experience or training in the discipline. We have sought to keep the discussion as clear as possible, however, and to help the reader along with a glossary and some appendices.

1.1 Why poverty matters

That poverty matters is self-evident. More than one in five of the world's population, well over one billion people, live on less than US$1 per day, and more than half of the world's people make do on less than US$2 per day. Extremely low incomes are matched by deprivation in numerous other areas: more than 110 million primary-school-age children in developing countries do not attend school; infant and under-five mortality rates remain appallingly high in many countries, with over two million infants dying each year before their first birthday; and millions are forced to live in marginal or polluted environments. Poverty is a human catastrophe, and in a world with sufficient resources to meet the basic material needs of all, the persistence of such widespread poverty is shocking. Its elimination should be the single greatest challenge to international and domestic public policy.

The fact that poverty matters has led the international donor community to refocus their efforts on poverty over the last 20 years: the reduction of poverty is now the central overarching objective of most donors. Thus, poverty also 'matters' in a policy sense, since understanding the causes of poverty and the way in which public policy can help to reduce poverty is key to achieving the International Development Target of halving poverty by 2015. This Handbook contributes to this effort by showing how one particular aspect of public policy – trade reform – affects poverty.

Saying that poverty matters has another implication: it suggests that other things matter less. We do not mean to imply that access to health care, improving education, building better roads and so on are less important than 'poverty alleviation' in some abstract sense. On the contrary, we see these issues as part and parcel of the efforts needed to reduce poverty in its broadest sense. But we do mean to make clear that our focus is on poverty and not on inequality. Inequality may be important politically and may help to explain some economic behaviour, but we shall touch on it only in so far as certain forms of inequality prevent the poor from benefiting from trade reform.

1.2 Why trade liberalization matters

Why trade liberalization matters is perhaps less evident than why poverty matters. Trade liberalization has been a central part of mainstream policy advice for at least 20 years and one of the most prominent characteristics of recent globalization. Although the process of globalization encompasses much more than trade liberalization, reducing the barriers to international trade in goods and services will remain one of the main drivers of globalization.

There has been a dramatic growth in world trade in the last 50 years as successive rounds of multilateral negotiations have progressively reduced barriers to trade. This has made international trade one of the most important engines of growth in the world economy, underpinning the unprecedented increases in living standards in so many countries since the Second World War.

Nonetheless, very high barriers to trade remain. Agricultural markets are still heavily protected in both rich and poor countries, while the international market for most services is still strongly biased towards domestic providers, and the international mobility of most types of labour is extremely restricted.

Consequently, further trade liberalization has the potential to deliver further gains in efficiency and higher rates of growth for the world economy. Trade liberalization therefore matters in its own right. But given the central role of growth in long-term poverty reduction, it particularly matters for the poor.

As with poverty, saying that trade liberalization matters prompts the suggestion that other things matter less. Our intention is certainly not to imply that other policies are unimportant. Indeed, we would argue the very opposite: economic growth and development require effectiveness over a huge range of policies and institutions. For example, closest to our subject matter, the improved regulation of international capital and investment flows is important both in its own right and as a complement to the liberalization of goods and services markets. But given that our subject is trade liberalization and that our book is already very long, we will only touch on investment issues in so far as they affect trade.

1.3 Why the links matter

The most obvious answer to the question of why the links matter is that poverty and trade liberalization matter individually. Poverty is the greatest challenge to public policy – and reducing it the most fundamental objective. Trade liberalization is believed to be an important part of the policy package for prosperity and growth and potentially for poverty alleviation. Thus, it is only common sense to ask whether they complement or hinder each other and how they can be jointly optimized. Only if poverty and trade policy were known to be wholly independent would there be no case for thinking about the links – and that is manifestly not the case.

But we must not jump from this observation to the conclusion that the links between trade and poverty are always of critical importance. Poverty is not a direct result of international trade. Rather, it arises from such phenomena as lack of assets, poor access to communal resources and public services, geographical isolation, poor health and education, powerlessness and vulnerability. Thus, the important policy problem is how to alleviate poverty, not the link between poverty and the international trade regime or trade policy. The link with trade policy matters only to the extent:

- first, that trade liberalization affects the direct determinants of poverty;
- second, that trade liberalization is a significant contributor to reducing poverty – that is, relative to the whole range of other possible policies, trade policy offers an efficient route to poverty alleviation, or compared with alternative policies for poverty alleviation, trade policy offers more poverty bang per buck of forgone opportunities.

In many cases, in fact, we shall see that the links are rather weak. Thus, concerns about poverty should not fundamentally alter attitudes towards trade liberalization nor should open trade policies fundamentally affect the portfolio of anti-poverty policies. But the strength or weakness of this link is useful to know; indeed, it is one of our principal conclusions that it will sometimes be quite legitimate to separate consideration of the two policies.

The relative independence of trade and poverty policies is an important normative conclusion of our whole research programme. It suggests that although it may be desirable to sequence a trade liberalization through time in order to reduce its impact on poverty, it will rarely be desirable to abandon it altogether. Rather, policy-makers should analyse where the adverse poverty effects may fall and prepare for them by introducing complementary and sometimes compensatory policies to alleviate their effects – a policy of 'predicting and pre-empting' poverty effects. The broad policy implication of our analysis is that where trade liberalization is likely to yield aggregate gains to a country, it should generally proceed and that analysis of its poverty consequences should be used to determine how the aggregate gains can be used to ensure that the poor benefit.

In Part 2 of the Handbook, we discuss some of the complementary policies that are likely to be necessary to underpin particular liberalizations. Some of these are general – for example, ensuring that safety nets are in place or that the poor have opportunities to improve their skill levels. Others, however, are quite specific – for example, ensuring that rural infrastructure will allow farmers to export newly liberalized export crops or that procedures for implementing competition policy are not bureaucratic and expensive.

But there is another important reason for considering carefully the links between trade liberalization and poverty. The public debate about 'trade policy and poverty' has become, as Kanbur (2001) argues, emblematic of the broader debate about the role of markets in development. Kanbur identifies two groups of commentators who ostensibly agree on the objective of reducing poverty, but who appear to disagree profoundly about the means of doing so:

- type-As – archetypally from finance ministries and international financial institutions, who take a rather 'economistic' and analytical approach; and
- type-Bs – archetypally from civil society and non-governmental organizations (NGOs), who are more broadly social scientific in their thinking.[1]

Kanbur argues that these groups ostensibly agree on much of the development agenda and that as a result, their differences over trade policy have become exaggerated and extreme. Certainly, the disagreements are widely and loudly aired. But if the trade and poverty issue has become the arena for conflict between two contrasting approaches to development, it becomes doubly important to take the links seriously. First, impassioned debate is not always the best way of exploring the subtleties of a real economic problem – there are likely to be a lot of myths around, which can only complicate policy-making in the real world. Second, if this is the basis on which policy-makers, commentators and academics will choose between paradigms, a great deal is at stake and we had better get the answers right.

<u>1.4</u> **What economists bring to the debate**

Kanbur locates the differences between the type-As and type-Bs over trade policy and poverty in three dimensions. The first is the level of aggregation, with type-As focusing on apparently objective measures of poverty defined at high levels of aggregation, and type-Bs relying on broader concepts of poverty using less quantitative measures and much more dependent on personal experience on the ground.

The second is the time horizon, with type-As stressing the medium run, in which economic adjustment has occurred and dynamic forces have played out, whereas type-Bs focus more on the short run, in which adjustment costs and temporary poverty loom large.[2]

Kanbur's third dimension of difference concerns assumptions about market structure. Type-As, he states, broadly come from a 'perfect markets' tradition, in which information flows freely and incentives for efficiency work well. In contrast, type-Bs believe markets function rather poorly and are dominated by the interests of powerful corporations and elites: reform, therefore, is as likely to give elites new opportunities to exploit the poor and weak as it is to liberate the latter and allow them to improve their lot. In fact, to characterize type-As as believing in perfect markets is not quite correct since much of the traditional policy case for trade liberalization is based on its ability to expose local oligopolists to international competition. But they probably do have greater faith than type-Bs in the competitive properties of the global market. In particular, they believe that in the longer run, international markets are, for the most part, reasonably open to entry and competition and, in the absence of interference, work pretty well.

Kanbur concludes with a plea for dialogue: for each of the two archetypes to understand what the other can bring to the table. This Handbook and its associated research are an attempt to do just that, at least as far as the economics of trade policy and poverty are concerned.[3] Our analysis does take seriously the issues of aggregation and time horizons, recognizing that changes in these dimensions will change the conclusions that can be reached about the effects of trade reform on poverty. We have also considered cases where market structure is critical to the results, and have analysed the case for trying to control global market power more closely. But overall, our analysis probably has a stronger presumption than some others might choose that global markets are reasonably contestable – that they do allow for entry and competition – and hence, that extreme exploitation is not the normal state of affairs.

The present work is strongly grounded in economics and economic concepts of poverty. We certainly do not believe that other approaches to, and aspects of, poverty are irrelevant, but we do believe that the economic ones are central and quite enough for one handbook. If this Handbook helps policy-makers to formulate and carry out their economic analyses better, the whole of their poverty and trade policies will be better informed and we will be amply pleased.

Economics brings five particular elements to the analysis of trade liberalization and poverty. First, it stresses the importance of measurement and quantification. We argue in Chapter 3 that the quantitative analysis of poverty is extremely useful. Poverty is indeed an absolute evil, but it is not realistic or useful to proceed as if it had no gradations. It is important for at least some purposes to know the depth of poverty that poor people experience, and it certainly matters whether one hundred or one million families become poor because of some policy choice. Many policy choices will help some families and harm others, and so public decisions must ultimately be based on trade-offs between these groups.

Second, economists bring powers of abstraction to the debate. Abstraction is frequently criticized for floating free of the real world; indeed, this is a danger in any analysis and characteristic of much second-rate work. But the functioning of a society – even in its simplest commercial dimensions – is immensely complex, and without simplifying in order to lay bare the fundamentals of an argument, there is no hope of identifying rigorously what are the crucial factors and steps. Thus, we make no apology for working with simple models – representations of reality – rather than claiming to be able to deal with reality itself.

Of course, abstraction is a means to an end: a trade-off has to be made between the artificiality of a model and its reach in terms of providing answers to pressing questions. And abstract models must be constantly tested to check that they retain the essence of the problem in hand. Such trade-offs and testing are often rather imprecise and subjective processes and can give rise to great disagreement. So we do not claim that our models are self-evidently the best way of representing a problem, only that we find them sufficiently useful ways of organizing our thoughts to recommend them to others. To help readers make their own judgements on this matter, we try to spell out the basic structures and assumptions of our models in fairly accessible terms.

Abstraction and modelling can also impose consistency on our thinking, helping to ensure that the same assumptions are used to assess both sides of a case. So the third contribution from our economics-based approach is that we specify a single analytical framework within which to conduct all our work. The framework is not particularly tight or formal by the standards of economic theory, and different aspects of it are emphasized in different places. Nevertheless, the discipline that operating within a single framework imposes on the study is useful in ensuring consistency and comparability across cases. Consistency, in turn, is useful in building up readers' familiarity with the elements of the framework so that it becomes easier to apply to their own cases when the need arises.

The fourth characteristic of the economist's approach to trade liberalization and poverty is to recognize that individual agents respond to incentives not only in their decisions about where to work and what to buy, but also in their political decisions. In other words, political economy is a fundamental part of economics. Thus, for example, economics teaches that when governments evince a willingness to intervene in an economy, private agents will exploit that fact by seeking to influence the interventions in ways that benefit themselves. Thus, a policy action not only influences the particular case in which it is applied, but may also have systemic effects, which can have very widespread consequences. Put concretely, economics generally teaches that simple non-discretionary policy rules have the advantage of discouraging lobbying activity.

Of course, trade liberalization is a political act and implementing it in particular ways or even at all requires a good deal of political skill. But we, as economists, and by extension this Handbook, have nothing to add on this issue, not because it does not matter, but because it is an area in which we claim no particular expertise. Much of what follows will identify likely winners and losers from particular policy actions and, hence, will be important inputs to the calculations that politicians have to make. But how those benefits are sold to stakeholders and how interests are combined into viable coalitions is not something that we discuss.

The final, unique and critically important contribution of economics to this analysis is the notion of 'general equilibrium'. Economists have taken the trite observation that everything depends on everything else and turned it into a powerful analytical tool. Central to many of our views is the argument that if labour is used for one activity it cannot simultaneously be used for another activity: if we expand sector A, unless the sum total of inputs increases, we must reduce something else.

So, for example, if we extract highly skilled labour from the production sector of a developing economy in order to staff an anti-dumping investigation office, we will pay the price in terms of lower production. Moreover, as the production sector loses skilled labour, its ratio of skilled to unskilled labour falls, so that each unskilled labourer has slightly fewer skilled resources to work with. This, in turn, makes him or her slightly less productive, which, in turn, tends to cut the wage. Similar considerations arise from the facts that a pound spent on good X cannot be spent on good Y and that in the long run, a country cannot export if it does not import.

The importance of general equilibrium is that in predicting the impact on poverty, we need to consider not only policies that affect the poor directly, but also any that influence the overall structure of the economy. Similarly, we need to consider the consequences of a policy not just for the sector in which it is applied but for other sectors too. Of course, in some cases the 'spillovers' between sectors will be sufficiently small for us to ignore, allowing us to work sector-by-sector or market-by-market – in what economists refer to as 'partial equilibrium'. This is intuitively and computationally much easier and so is very attractive, and economists have devised heuristic rules to identify cases where this is legitimate. Nonetheless, the fundamental fact remains that the effects of policy can be very widespread indeed.

1.5 Main lessons

The Handbook contains a number of lessons for policy-makers, both general in terms of the broad potential linkages between trade liberalization and poverty, and specific in terms of the linkages in relation to particular sectors and instruments of trade policy. The main lessons can be summarized as follows:

- The weight of evidence is that openness to trade is good for growth and that growth benefits the poor. But to enjoy the full benefits of trade liberalization, it should be accompanied by sound policies in areas such as transport and communications infrastructure, market facilitation, competition, education and governance.
- There are three broad pathways through which trade liberalization can have a direct effect on poverty: through its impact on the prices of liberalized goods, through its impact on profits and hence on employment and wages, and through its impact on the government's fiscal position. The outcome depends on whether the poor are net consumers or producers of liberalized goods, what types of labour they supply, and where their wages lie relative to the poverty line.
- Although it is possible to describe the pathways through which each aspect of liberalization might affect poverty, the impact of trade liberalization on poverty is very country-specific. This means that policy-makers themselves will have to identify which of these pathways are the most important in their particular circumstances.
- The range of potential linkages between trade liberalization and poverty is wide, but the most important effects in any given country are likely to be relatively simple and obvious. Hence policy-makers *can* develop suitable policy responses to help the poor gain from trade liberalization.
- For many dimensions of trade liberalization, the direct effects on poverty will be negligible. Where they are not, the appropriate response is not to stop liberalizing but to proceed while pursuing complementary policies to help the poor gain from liberalization and to provide social protection to support those who may lose. Trade-related compensation packages will not generally be feasible or desirable in developing countries.
- Trade liberalization almost inevitably involves costs of adjustment, notably job losses in formerly protected sectors. The best way to ease the pain of transition is to protect social expenditure and ensure appropriate targeting of the poor, offering a cushion without undermining their incentives to adjust.
- Trade liberalization can change the nature of the risk and uncertainty that poor households face although, not always for the worse. It can also affect their ability to cope with risk and uncertainty. Policies such as improving access to credit markets can help a great deal here, along with improvements in asset distribution and in the flexibility of local labour markets.
- For the long-term benefits of the trade liberalization to accrue to the poor, supply responses by poor households to the new opportunities are essential. These will be influenced by their location and demographic structure and the gender, health status, education and assets of their members. Complementary policies in such areas as infrastructure and market development are likely to be necessary.

- Agriculture is the key sector for poverty alleviation: despite rising urban poverty, the poor are still predominantly rural, agriculture is their major source of income, and farm incomes have large spillovers to others in the rural economy. Moreover, food accounts for a major share of all poor people's expenditure. Liberalizing agricultural trade, both unilaterally and multilaterally and by both developed and developing countries, has the potential for considerable poverty alleviation, although particular groups of poor people may suffer.

- Trade in manufactured goods still faces significant barriers in developed countries (on products like clothing and footwear) and to a greater extent in developing countries. Liberalization will foster poverty alleviation by enhancing growth and productivity and improving resource allocation. But the conditions have to be in place for firms to respond to new threats and opportunities and, even so, some manufacturing jobs may be lost. Safety nets may be necessary if alternative forms of employment are not rapidly available for displaced workers.

- Trade liberalization in services offers particularly promising opportunities for poverty alleviation, especially if temporary movements of relatively unskilled workers were to be allowed. Some service reforms can aid the poor directly – for example, those in transport, health and education – and others may increase unskilled employment – such as tourism – or boost local efficiency and competitiveness – such as financial services.

- The long-term effects of strengthening protection for intellectual property rights are uncertain, but in the short to medium term, although such moves may benefit some middle-income countries, they are almost bound to hurt small and poor economies.

- Specific interventions in international trade, such as export subsidies, anti-dumping duties and local content requirements, will rarely be to the advantage of the poor, who have too little power to prevent the transfers from being captured by other groups. Hence poverty concerns will rarely justify resisting liberalization in those areas.

- Strengthening domestic labour or environmental standards may help the poor, but linking higher standards to trade agreements is much more likely to hurt them.

Notes

1   Kanbur recognizes that these descriptions are caricatures.
2   And for those concerned with environmental implications, the very long run too.
3   Indeed, it was Kanbur's challenge to take seriously these two positions in policy analysis that sparked one of the present authors' (Winters) interest in trade and poverty when both he and Kanbur worked at the World Bank.

2   The Debate over Trade Liberalization

This chapter reviews the debate over the costs and benefits of openness to trade. In particular, it explores:

- The difficulty of measuring openness.
- The costs and benefits of openness.
- How domestic competition determines the impact of openness on prices.
- Whether openness to trade increases economic growth.
- The impact of openness on the volatility of output and the terms of trade.
- The political economy of openness.

During the last decade, there has been a major public debate over the costs and benefits of economic openness. Before turning to discuss poverty (in Chapter 3) and the linkages between trade liberalization and poverty (in Chapter 4), this chapter reviews that debate. Of course, the continuing controversy over globalization ranges far wider than merely openness to trade: in particular, it includes openness to capital and the free movement of labour. But in the hope of being able to say something more concrete and useful, we restrict our attention here (as elsewhere in the Handbook) to the issue of trade liberalization.

We start with a discussion of the difficulty of measuring openness and an overview of the many different measures that have been used. This is followed by an elaboration of the principal benefits and costs of openness to trade. We then examine the theory and evidence for four key debates over openness:

- *Openness, prices and competition*: whether openness actually reduces prices and how this depends on the nature of domestic competition.
- *Openness and growth*: the long-running and controversial debate over the relationship between openness to trade and economic growth.

- *Openness and volatility*: whether openness increases the volatility of output and the terms of trade.
- *Openness and politics*: the main political economy reasons for the existence of protection.

2.1 What is openness?

Clarifying the precise meaning of openness is a far from trivial matter, even when only considering openness to goods and service, rather than broader concepts of openness entailing the free movement of capital, labour and culture across borders. The problem hinges on the two different approaches to measuring openness:

- *Openness in practice*, which focuses on the importance of trade in a country's economic activities and the existence of actual price

Table 2.1 Measures of openness

Measure	Definition
Trade dependency ratio	The ratio of exports and imports to GDP
Growth rate of exports	The growth rate of exports over the specified period
Tariff averages	A simple or trade-weighted average of tariff levels
Collected tariff ratios	The ratio of tariff revenues to imports
Coverage of quantitative restrictions	The percentage of goods covered by quantitative restrictions
Black market premium	The black market premium for foreign exchange, a proxy for the overall degree of external sector distortions
Heritage Foundation index	An index of trade policy that classifies countries into five categories according to the level of tariffs and other (perceived) distortions
IMF index of trade restrictiveness	A composite index of restrictions on a scale of 0 to 10
Trade bias index	The extent to which policy increases the ratio of importable goods' prices relative to exportable goods' prices compared to the same ratio in world markets.
The World Bank's outward orientation index	An index that classifies countries into four categories depending on their perceived degree of openness
Sachs and Warner index	A composite index that uses several trade-related indicators: tariffs, quota coverage, black market premia, social organization and the existence of export marketing boards
Leamer's openness index	An index that estimates the difference between the actual trade flows and those that would be expected from a theoretical trade model

distortions regardless of the reason for their presence. This is an outcome that may not be controlled by government.
* *Openness in policy*, which focuses on the existence and extent of policy measures designed to control or curb trade. This is controllable by government.

Countries that are open in practice may not be open in policy and *vice versa*. For example, trade is typically a much larger share of GDP for small countries than for large countries. Thus, mere size may make a small country open in practice, even though it may apply numerous policy distortions to trading activities. Conversely, a country may have few restrictions on trade but may operate an exchange rate policy that creates large price distortions in practice. The real issue is the extent to which international trade determines local prices.

Table 2.1 shows a selection of measures of openness that have been used by researchers. Unfortunately, the various measures of trade openness are quite weakly correlated – see Harrison (1996) and Pritchett (1996). Consequently, when statements are made about the links between openness and prices, growth, inequality and so on, it is important to be clear which measure is being used and whether the statements' validity depends on the choice of openness measure.

2.2 The costs and benefits of openness

Notwithstanding the problems of measuring openness, the debate over trade liberalization is, in essence, a debate about the costs and benefits of openness. This section outlines the principal costs and benefits of openness, of which there are four on each side of the debate.

2.2.1 Benefits of openness

Among the benefits claimed for openness are:

Cheaper consumption
Liberalization, by definition, reduces the barriers to trade. In general, when markets are functioning effectively, this will result in a reduction in the domestic price of the liberalized good, by either making cheaper foreign goods available or reducing the rents that may have previously been captured by domestic producers.

More efficient production and allocation of resources
Increasing openness increases the degree of competition faced by domestic producers. This may result in closures and consequent unemployment. But openness can increase welfare in the longer term by allowing a country to improve its efficiency of production in three ways:

* increasing the efficiency with which existing resources are used;

- encouraging specialization and the re-allocation of resources towards those activities that reflect the country's comparative advantage;
- allowing economies of scale through exports to the world market.

New ideas and technology
Even if openness only refers to the goods market, liberalization allows improved access to the ideas and technologies embodied in foreign goods. Such access can, in principle, enhance a country's technological capability and assist productivity improvement. But this is a subject of considerable controversy – see Rodrik (1995b) for a review of the literature.

Political trade-offs
Individual countries are free to liberalize as much or as little as they want unilaterally, but much trade liberalization actually occurs within the framework of multilateral and plurilateral trade agreements. One of the reasons for this is that governments may be under strong domestic political pressure not to liberalize certain sectors. They may be able to resist such pressures by obtaining equivalent 'concessions' of market access for their exporters. Thus, one benefit of participation in multi-country negotiations on trade liberalization may be improved access to other markets as well as the construction of counterbalancing domestic political constituencies. This is not so much a benefit of openness as a benefit of the manner in which openness is generally achieved.

2.2.2 Costs of openness

The main objections that have been raised against openness to international trade are:

Anti-competitive behaviour
Some sectors are dominated internationally by a relatively small number of large multinational enterprises. Many developing-country governments fear that trade liberalization will enable large foreign companies to eliminate small domestic rivals through anti-competitive behaviour, even when those domestic companies are efficient. After domestic rivals have been removed, such companies could then be in a position to charge monopoly prices. It is not clear, however, how well grounded these fears are. First, the argument requires that the multinationals are able to prevent entry into the developing-country market even after they have raised prices. Second, such anti-competitive behaviour could be prevented through effective domestic competition policy or anti-dumping actions, although many developing countries have weak regulatory capacity for such initiatives.

Reduced opportunities for learning by doing
Increased openness precludes the possibility of trade measures to protect strategic industries. Many East Asian economies used trade protection to stimulate investment and productivity improvements in industries with

strong potential for technological capability building (see Singh, 1994; and Lall, 1998). Trade liberalization could, in principle, prevent other countries adopting a similar approach (although it could equally be argued that trade liberalization provides different opportunities for such learning).

Increased volatility
In the same way as some commentators argue that capital market liberalization played a role in facilitating the large and rapid capital outflows that precipitated the Asian crisis of 1997–8, it is sometimes claimed that trade liberalization may increase terms-of-trade volatility and, as a consequence, the volatility of GDP. Furthermore, long-term changes in the structure of the economy resulting from trade liberalization could increase the concentration of economic activity, making countries more vulnerable to changes in world prices.

Loss of sovereignty
Finally, several countries oppose participation in multi-country trade agreements (rather than openness itself) because of the loss of sovereignty involved. Of course, all multi-country agreements inevitably involve the sacrifice of some measure of sovereignty in return for the benefits of cooperation. But it is important to recognize that acceptance of the mutual constraints imposed by multi-country trade agreements is considered a political cost in many countries. Openness can thus present an 'economic integration trilemma' between the pursuit of greater economic integration, proper public economic management and national sovereignty (see Summers, 1999).

2.3 Openness, prices and competition

The first and most obvious advantage of trade liberalization is that it should reduce the domestic price of importable goods. In general, this is the case: lower tariffs will translate one-for-one into lower domestic prices, assuming that an individual country's trade reforms do not change the world price – see Box 2.1 on the so-called 'small country assumption'.

Clearly, then, the extent to which domestic prices change depends on the size of the distortions that are removed. In many sectors in many countries, the main price distortions result from indirect policies, such as inappropriate exchange rate valuation or administrative or institutional constraints on prices, rather than through commodity taxes, such as tariffs and export taxes (see Schiff and Valdés, 1992). Insofar as trade reform incorporates the liberalization of such indirect measures, it may induce large price changes, even if the liberalization of tariffs is in itself rather modest.[1]

Assuming that reforms do not affect world prices, the extent to which trade liberalization will reduce domestic prices depends on two factors:

The costs of domestic production relative to the tariff-inclusive price
If the 'benefits' of protection have been absorbed primarily by increasing

Box 2.1 The small country assumption

In analysing the impact of trade liberalization on domestic prices, it is common to assume that the developing country in question is small relative to the rest of the world. This means that the country is unable to affect world prices, but simply takes them as a 'given'.

Most countries in most markets are too small to influence prices on their own so this assumption is broadly correct. And if it is true, then the domestic price of imported goods changes by the exact amount of any tariff change.

But there are two situations in which the small country assumption may not apply:

- **When the country is not small**
  For example, Brazil, China and India are much more likely to be able to influence international prices than Bolivia, Singapore and Sri Lanka. In such situations, an 'optimal' tariff imposed by the large country can in theory reduce world demand sufficiently to lower the world price.
- **When the country's share of production is not small**
  Even small countries can have significant market power in particular goods if they are a major world producer of this good. In this case, an 'optimal' export tax can reduce world supply by enough to raise the world price.

If the small country assumption does not hold, then it is important to take into account how liberalization will affect the world price.

local costs – that is, by inefficient local production – then liberalization can have little immediate effect on the price of domestically produced goods. Imports will be cheaper, however, and will doubtless expand their share of the market, and this will put pressure on local firms. The latter will then have either to increase their efficiency or contract their output sufficiently to reduce costs if they are to survive. These changes may take time.

The extent of competition within the domestic market
If there is strong competition within the domestic market and the domestic cost of production is less than the world price plus the tariff, then it will not be possible for domestic producers to raise their prices up to this level. Consequently, trade liberalization will not give rise to significant reductions in the prices of domestic goods. On the other hand, if competition at any part of the chain between the producer and the retailer is limited, then it is likely that domestic margins will have been increased, raising the price towards the tariff-inclusive price of imports, and liberalization will have scope to reduce domestic prices directly.

In addition, it is necessary to consider:

The extent of competition and product differentiation within the world market
Competition in the world market may also affect the price reductions caused

by trade liberalization. For example, if production of a good is dominated by a small number of firms, then these firms may be in a position to 'price to market'; that is, to set prices above marginal costs according to what the market will bear. This situation is most likely to arise for goods that are strongly differentiated so that only one or two firms make a particular variety, for example, different types of cars or consumer goods. Any trade liberalization in these markets is likely to be partly captured by increased company profits rather than being passed onto consumers.[2] The same is true of goods whose world markets are truly monopolized by multinationals earning monopoly profits, though in reality, there are relatively few of these.

In addition to the factors that determine whether a unilateral liberalization will result in changes in domestic prices, it is important to recognize that there may be significant changes in world prices resulting from multilateral liberalization. Thus, if a country reduces its trade barriers, it may indeed reduce the domestic price of imported goods, but this effect could be swamped by the price effects of a multilateral trade liberalization. This is most likely where the multilateral liberalization affects goods in which the international market is already highly distorted. For example, a large part of production and trade in agricultural goods occurs under a range of distortionary policies. Consequently, the 'world' price refers only to the relatively small residual trade not subject to these distortions. In these cases, significant multilateral reforms that affect output and consumption taking place under the distortions could have a proportionately very large effect on the quantities traded in the residual markets and thus have a strong impact on world agricultural prices.

Economists' estimates of the direct benefits from trade liberalization associated with changes in prices are typically quite small. Table 2.2 shows a typical estimate of the benefits of multilateral liberalization, in this case the Uruguay Round. The second column of Table 2.2 estimates that the global benefit from the commitments made is quite small: US$93 billion or 0.4% of global GDP. Even when the model is extended to take account of possible increasing returns to scale in certain industries and imperfect competition, the estimated global benefits rise only to US$96 billion (the third column). Only when the potential impact of rising prices on investment in the capital stock is taken into account do the estimates rise substantially (the fifth column), but even here the global benefit only reaches US$171 billion or 0.7% of global GDP, although the effects are larger (and smaller) for individual countries.

But these results only paint a partial picture of the benefits of liberalization. In particular, the welfare gains associated with the ability to obtain goods that were simply unobtainable before tend to be much larger than the gains associated with changes in the relative prices of existing goods (see Romer, 1994).

Furthermore, the dynamic benefits of liberalization are thought to be several orders of magnitude larger than the static benefits. These dynamic benefits come from the re-allocation of resources to reflect comparative advantage, as

Table 2.2 Estimated gains and losses from Uruguay Round liberalization for different countries and regions (1992 US$ billions)

Region	Base-model impacts on welfare gains and losses annually		Static IRTS model impacts on welfare gains and losses		IRTS steady-state model impacts on welfare	
	Complete reform package	*As % of GDP*	*Complete reform package*	*As % of GDP*	*Complete reform package*	*As % of GDP*
Austria	1.135	0.4	1.2	0.2	3.3	1.0
New Zealand	0.381	1.0	0.4	1.0	1.4	3.5
Canada	1.160	0.2	1.3	0.2	2.6.	0.4
United States	12.842	0.2	13.3	0.2	26.7	0.4
Japan	16.692	0.5	16.9	0.5	22.7	0.6
Korea	4.574	1.5	4.8	1.6	7.5	2.4
European Union (12)	38.845	0.6	39.3	0.6	49.9	0.7
Indonesia	1.301	1.1	1.3	1.1	2.6	2.0
Malaysia	1.864	3.3	1.8	3.2	5.0	8.8
Philippines	0.890	1.6	0.9	1.7	2.4	4.2
Singapore	0.918	2.1	0.9	2.1	0.7	1.7
Thailand	2.435	2.1	2.5	2.2	12.6	10.7
China	1.170	0.3	1.3	0.3	2.0	0.4
Hong Kong	−1.267	−1.4	−1.2	−1.3	−1.1	−1.2
Taiwan	0.404	0.2	0.4	0.2	1.1	0.5
Argentina	0.645	0.3	0.7	0.3	2.3	1.0
Brazil	1.310	0.3	1.4	0.4	4.3	1.0
Mexico	0.145	0	0.2	0	2.3	0.6
Rest of Latin America	1.198	0.4	1.3	0.5	4.7	1.6
Sub-Saharan Africa	− 0.418	− 0.2	− 0.3	− 0.2	− 0.7	− 0.5
Middle East & N Africa	− 0.388	− 0.1	− 0.3	0	1.5	0.2
Eastern Europe and former Soviet Union	− 0.421	− 0.1	− 0.2	0	1.2	0.1
South Asia	3.286	1.0	3.7	1.1	6.7	1.8
Other European	4.154	0.3	4.2	0.3	8.8	0.7
Developing countries (total)	17.651	0.4	19.4	0.4	55.2	1.1
Industrialized countries (total)	75.208	0.4	76.6	0.4	115.4	0.6
World	92.859	0.4	96.0	0.4	170.6	0.7

Source: Harrison, Rutherford and Tarr (1996).

well as the efficiency gains resulting from increased competition. It is precisely these dynamic gains that are argued to spur economic growth. Consequently, a great deal of attention has been paid to the relationship between openness and growth, the issue to which we now turn.

2.4 Openness, growth and technology

Perhaps the most important benefit claimed by proponents of openness is its positive effect on economic growth. Economic growth is the key to permanent poverty alleviation. It is also strongly related to contemporaneous reductions in poverty (see, for example, Bruno et al., 1996; or Roemer and Gugerty, 1997). Unless growth seriously worsens income distribution, the proportion of the population living in absolute poverty will fall as average incomes increase. The balance of the evidence seems to be that although growth can be associated with growing inequality (or economic decline with narrowing inequality), the effects on poverty tend to be dominated by the advantageous direct effects of growth (see, for example, Demery and Squire, 1996, on Africa).

This effect also appears to generalize to the very poor, defined as those who live on less than US$1 per day (see Chen and Ravallion, 1996; or Bruno et al., 1996). But at such very low levels of income, small shocks can be very important, and Demery and Squire (1996) find hints of contrary evidence in Africa. In recent work, Dollar and Kraay (2001) found that on average, the incomes of the poorest fifth of the population grew proportionately with GDP per head in a sample of 80 countries over four decades.[3] This was as true of growth induced by openness to trade as that due to other stimuli.

The result that growth tends on average to reduce poverty is not really that surprising. In general, it will be easier for governments to raise the resources for poverty-alleviating policies if incomes are growing. Equally, the idea that recessions (that is, negative growth) are associated with worsening poverty is hardly controversial. Nonetheless, it is useful to remember that the relationship between non-income indicators of poverty (such as infant mortality, maternal mortality, educational levels, discrimination, social exclusion and so on) and economic growth is much less direct. Thus, while economic policies will have an important bearing on how much economic growth increases the incomes of the poor, government policy will also be critical in determining how growth is translated into reduction in other dimensions of poverty (see Chapter 3 for a more detailed discussion of the different dimensions of poverty).

Given the strong connection between economic growth and income poverty, the linkage between openness and economic growth is of vital importance in the debate over the impact of trade liberalization on poverty.

2.4.1 Openness and growth in theory

The theoretical links between openness and growth are strong. First, the presence of an import duty or restriction creates an anti-export bias by raising the price of importable goods relative to exportable goods. Removal of this bias through trade liberalization will encourage a shift of resources from the production of import substitutes to the production of exports, which will generate growth in the short to medium run as the country adjusts to a new allocation of resources more in keeping with its comparative advantage.

Furthermore, the traditional Heckscher–Ohlin theory of trade states that under certain assumptions, countries will export the goods that make intensive use of their most abundant factor. Thus, if developing countries are characterized as 'labour-abundant' and developed countries as 'capital-abundant', then trade liberalization should encourage a shift of resources towards the production of labour-intensive exports by developing countries. This in turn should increase the demand for labour, generating growth and reducing poverty.

Unfortunately, the very powerful results associated with the traditional Heckscher–Ohlin model are based on a number of quite restrictive assumptions. In particular, the model assumes:

- *Two factors* (capital and labour): in particular, it makes no distinction between skilled and unskilled labour, neither does it include land or natural resources. Extensions to the model that include more factors produce far less clear-cut results.
- *Two countries*: whereas in reality there are many. This may matter because the previous actions of some countries (for example, in forming trade blocs or obtaining a lead in certain sectors) may affect the benefits from trade liberalization for subsequent countries.
- *Two goods*: but in fact there are at least thousands of individual goods. In addition, services are of growing importance in international trade.
- *Immobile factors*: but capital in particular is now highly mobile and labour can be too in certain circumstances.
- *Perfect competition*: but in fact, world trade in some sectors is dominated by a small number of very large multinationals, suggesting that monopolistic and oligopolistic behaviour is likely.
- *Constant returns to scale*: but some industries, such as software, exhibit strong increasing returns to scale. This tends to encourage the formation of large global companies to exploit these economies of scale.

Models that incorporate some or all of these elements produce weaker results on the relationship between a country's factor endowments, preferences, technology and the direction of trade. But they virtually all suggest that liberalization will favour the factors used intensively by export industries and display a presumption that these will be the abundant factors of production. Even defining an abundant factor can be difficult though, once we move beyond two factors, and working out what it will be in practice is more complicated. Identifying the factors used intensively in exporting can be similarly difficult in practice. Thus, while trade liberalization is likely to favour abundant factors, actually translating this into clear predictions requires caution.

Nonetheless, theoretical models of 'endogenous growth' have been constructed that suggest that openness should be positively associated with growth (see Grossman and Helpman, 1991; Romer, 1992; Barro and Sala-i-Martin, 1995; and Obstfeld and Rogoff, 1996). Such models suggest that openness spurs growth through numerous channels, including:

- *Embodied technology*: greater availability of imports enables domestic producers to have access to and benefit from the technology embodied in imports. In addition, it enables domestic technologists to 'reverse engineer' imports, thereby enhancing technological knowledge.
- *Availability of inputs*: openness can improve the availability of key inputs, enabling activities that may not have been possible before.
- *Associated technical assistance and learning*: technology imports often come with technological services attached, in the form of technical assistance or product support. Again, these may enhance technological capacity.
- *Reduction of networking costs*: the identification of suitable business partners and import and export linkages is costly. Openness may reduce such costs for firms already involved in international trade and encourage others to get involved.

The following section describes the evidence for some of these linkages in practice.

2.4.2 Openness and growth in practice

Although theoretical models generally produce a positive relationship between openness and growth, what matters is whether this relationship is borne out in practice. There is quite strong evidence that even allowing for adjustment strains, trade liberalization typically boosts growth in the relatively near term (see, for example, World Bank, 1992; and Greenaway et al., 1998). The important long-run issue, however, is not whether a single act of liberalization boosts growth, but whether its outcome – the state of greater openness – does so.

Numerous studies have examined the relationship between different measures of openness and economic growth. Typically, these studies construct a measure of the openness of trade policy and then see if it is statistically related to growth across a large number of countries. Over the 1990s, there was a growing conviction that openness was good for growth due to the results of some visible and well-promoted cross-country studies (for example, Dollar, 1992; Sachs and Warner, 1995; and Edwards, 1998), all of which found openness to be strongly positively associated with growth.

Recently, however, these studies have been strongly criticized by Rodríguez and Rodrik (1999), who argue, among other things, that the measures of openness used in these papers are flawed and their econometrics weak. This adds to earlier concerns that the results are dependent on the chosen measure of openness and the specification used (see Harrison, 1996; and Harrison and Hanson, 1999a, who claim that the measure of openness introduced by Sachs and Warner 'fails to establish a robust link between more open trade policies and long-run growth').

Among the most convincing of recent studies advancing the view that openness does indeed promote growth is that of Frankel and Romer (1999). Their analysis also tackles the difficult issue of the direction of causality between openness and growth. Many previous studies suffer from the disadvantage that it is not possible to say whether the correlation between openness and growth is because openness causes growth, or because countries that grow faster tend to open up at the same time.

Frankel and Romer (1999) deal with this by looking only at the effect of that component of openness caused by populations, land areas, borders and distances – in other words, by factors that economic growth cannot influence (at least in the short term). This component explains a significant proportion of the differences in income levels and growth performance between countries, and from this might be inferred a general relationship running from increased trade to increased growth. The effect is not very precisely defined numerically, but is quite significant economically: for example, at the conservative end of their range, an increase of one percentage point in the openness ratio increases both the level of income and subsequent growth by around 0.5%.

Of course, the effect of 'natural' openness on growth may not be the same as the effect of policy-induced openness on growth. But it is difficult to think of reasons why this should not be so when 'policy' amounts to the absence of trade barriers and that has a clear parallel with the absence of 'natural' barriers. It is not difficult, on the other hand, to imagine that artificially stimulated trade, perhaps through export subsidies or discriminatory trade policies, is less beneficial for growth. This point chimes with Vamvakidis' (1999) results: using panel data for over 100 countries, he concludes that multilateral liberalizations over the period 1950–89 were associated with increases in rates of growth, while regional (discriminatory) ones were not.[4]

Overall, the fairest assessment is that liberalized trade alone has not yet been unambiguously and universally linked to subsequent economic growth. The difficulty of establishing an empirical link between liberal trade and growth almost certainly arises in part from two difficulties:

- First, it is difficult to measure accurately the trade stance of a country, particularly when countries are relatively closed. For example, tariffs need to be aggregated, quantitative restrictions assessed and then aggregated and the level of enforcement measured (see Winters, 2000d).
- Second, although liberal trade policies are beneficial because they enlarge the set of opportunities, a long-term effect on growth almost certainly requires such policies to be combined with other good policies as well. For example, investment in public goods, such as transport and communication infrastructure, can greatly enhance the ability of firms and individuals to take advantage of the opportunities that may be created by liberalization. Furthermore, Krueger (1990b) argued that openness is likely to be correlated with better policy in a number of dimensions, and there is some evidence for this from Ades and Di Tella (1997, 1999) on corruption and from Romer (1993) on inflation.

It is also important to note that although trade openness has not been unequivocally linked to higher growth, it has certainly not been identified as a hindrance. Moreover, liberal trade has a positive role as part of a package of measures promoting greater use of the market, more stable and less arbitrary policy intervention, stronger competition and macroeconomic stability. With the exception of the last, an open trade regime is probably essential to the long-run achievement of these stances, and it probably helps with the last as well (see Krueger, 1990b). Thus, taken as a whole, trade liberalization is likely to be a major contributor to economic development.

2.4.3 Pathways of influence

Even if trade liberalization does have a positive effect on growth, it is not clear precisely how this effect operates. But it is likely that any link from openness to growth operates at least partly by enhancing technical progress. There are a number of ways in which this might occur, although their relative weights will differ from case to case.

Access to imports
Better access to imports makes new inputs, new technologies or new management techniques available to local producers. The evidence that access to imports enhances performance is quite strong (see Esfahani, 1991; and Feenstra et al., 1997).

Exporting and economic performance
The evidence on a link from exporting to technology is rather weaker than that for the value of access to imports. While macro studies and case studies have suggested links, detailed and formal work based on enterprise data is doubtful: Bigsten et al. (1998) find links for Africa, while Kraay (1998) is ambiguous for China, and Tybout and Westbrook (1995) find nothing for Latin America.

Foreign direct investment and efficiency
Similarly, it is quite difficult to prove that foreign direct investment (FDI) boosts efficiency (see, for example, Haddad and Harrison, 1993).
   The general problem in linking exporting, FDI and efficiency is one of causation: efficiency and exporting are linked because efficient firms export, not necessarily because exporters become efficient. And FDI and efficiency are linked because investors choose efficient firms and sectors in which to invest, not necessarily because FDI makes them efficient.

Improved competition
In most cases, reduced protection will increase competition in the domestic market, making it more difficult for producers to benefit from anti-competitive practices and forcing them to focus efforts on improving technical efficiency. Thus, by enhancing the 'contestability' of markets, trade liberalization may be able to improve efficiency too.

Business contacts and networks
One somewhat neglected area is the idea that openness may encourage growth through supporting the development of international business contacts and networks. In other words, openness may improve the flow of information and technical skills. Although the manner in which contacts and networks influence international trade has been investigated (see Rausch and Feenstra, 1999), their impact on growth is not known.

Although all of these pathways of influence between trade liberalization and growth will be important in some cases, their relative importance is likely to be country-specific.

Another very sensitive issue in the area of openness and the diffusion of technology is intellectual property. The Uruguay Round Agreement on this issue certainly entails developing countries having to pay more to use certain technologies and, in those cases, it will both reduce income and curtail the use of the technologies. On the other hand, the increased rewards may stimulate the flow of technology to developing countries, although to date, firm evidence to that effect is lacking. The commercialization of intellectual property may also have biased it away from meeting the needs of the poor, since collectively they represent such a small market. The critical examples of this are, perhaps, South Africa's difficulties in acquiring anti-AIDS cocktails at reasonable cost and the failure of pharmaceutical companies to work seriously on malaria.[5]

2.4.4 A tentative conclusion

The debate over the link between openness and growth is important. As shown above, while they are of course useful, the static benefits of trade liberalization are small and completely dwarfed by any potential impact on long-term growth rates. Consequently, there is a debate about the importance of openness relative to other factors influencing growth.

While some authors argue that openness (in combination with sound macroeconomic management) is an extremely important component of successful development (see World Bank, 1993), others claim that openness has played a relatively minor role. Indeed, some researchers argue that the high levels of trade protection and interventionist industrial policies adopted by some East Asian economies promoted an environment conducive to investment and technological learning and that these, rather than openness, have been the real reasons for growth (see Wade, 1990; and Rodrik, 1999a).[6]

Overall, it may be fair to say that openness, by providing lower prices, better information and newer technology has a useful role to play in promoting growth. But it must be accompanied by appropriate complementary policies (most notably, education, infrastructure, financial and macroeconomic policies) to yield strong growth. The precise mix of trade and other policies that is needed will be strongly dependent on the specific circumstances of each country.

2.5 Openness and volatility

It is often claimed that liberalization increases volatility. Volatility is normally assumed to be harmful because of its negative effects on investment. For example, Pindyck (1991) reviews how uncertainty and 'irreversability' affect investment behaviour. And Guillaumont et al. (1999) show how terms-of-trade instability negatively affects growth in Africa through its influence on investment and the real exchange rate. But the statement 'liberalization increases volatility' needs to be clarified in two respects:

What type of liberalization?
It is important to make a distinction between capital market liberalization and goods market or trade liberalization. Explanations for the Asian crisis of 1997–8 have typically focused on the role of capital flows rather than the efforts of those countries to liberalize trade. The issues of capital and trade liberalization are linked, particularly in developing countries that are pursuing simultaneous macroeconomic stabilization and adjustment policies that contain elements of many forms of liberalization. But conceptually and often practically, the issues are quite separate, and in this Handbook we focus explicitly on trade liberalization rather than the wider issue of its linkages to the capital account.

Volatility of what?
It is important to make a distinction between volatility of the terms of trade, volatility of output and volatility of consumption. Trade liberalization may increase one type of volatility but not another.

2.5.1 Theoretical linkages

In theory, there are two ways in which trade liberalization will affect the volatility of output and the volatility of the terms of trade:

Specialization
The international integration of goods markets allows national economies to specialize in goods in which they have a comparative advantage. Although such specialization may raise the average income of a country, if its economy subsequently experiences a set of random industry-specific shocks, this can lead to erratic shifts in the demand for the country's exports. Whether this shows itself in increased volatility of output or increased volatility of the terms of trade (that is, increased price volatility) depends on the nature of the goods in which the country has specialized.

The traditional Prebisch–Singer argument here is that developing countries that export primary products face a long-term deterioration in their terms of trade as demand for these products fails to keep pace with rising incomes and new material-replacing technologies reduce the demand for some commodities. But this only affects the trend of the terms of trade rather than their volatility. More relevant is the general assumption that the supply of primary products is not particularly sensitive to price changes, with the result that shifts in demand give rise to large price fluctuations. Insofar as increased openness gives rise to greater specialization in the production of such primary products, greater terms-of-trade volatility would be expected. On the other hand, if the supply of exports is reasonably sensitive to changes in prices, then shocks in demand caused by specialization will result in more volatile output (see Razin and Rose, 1992).

Risk diversification

Trade liberalization increases a country's exposure to foreign shocks and therefore increases the weight of foreign, relative to domestic, shocks experienced by a country. The effect that this has on the overall level of risk faced by the country will depend on the relative size of foreign and domestic shocks and the extent to which these shocks are correlated – that is, whether the occurrence of a shock to the foreign economy affects the chances of a *different* shock happening to the domestic economy.[7]

Overall, at low levels of trade, trade liberalization will tend to reduce overall risk because it is very unlikely that international and domestic conditions would be either both very good or both very bad together. In addition, world markets are usually more stable than local ones, because they already aggregate a lot of offsetting shocks from around the world. Thus, if a crop is transformed by trade liberalization from a non-tradable good into a tradable one, the overall risk faced by the country is likely to fall. If trade levels are very high or foreign shocks are much greater than domestic ones, however, overall risk could increase. Similarly, if foreign and domestic shocks are strongly positively correlated, the risk-spreading effect will be rather weak.

Thus, theory suggests that the overall effect of trade liberalization on the volatility of output and the terms of trade will depend on the relative strength of the specialization and risk diversification effects. If the specialization effect dominates, then either output or the terms-of-trade volatility will increase; the same will be true if linking to global markets actually increases rather than reduces risk. But if trade liberalization allows a country to diversify risks by more than specialization increases risk, then it may result in lower output or terms-of-trade volatility.

2.5.2 Empirical evidence

The empirical evidence on the links between trade liberalization and output and terms-of-trade volatility is remarkably limited and surprisingly inconclusive. We report results in four areas:

Openness and output volatility

A study by Razin and Rose (1992) combines national accounts data for 138 countries between 1950–88 with IMF data on trade and capital restrictions and a set of other measures of trade openness in an attempt to estimate the impact of openness on volatility. They fail to find significant correlations between openness and volatility, mainly because shocks may be common across a number of countries.

Openness and terms-of-trade shocks

If openness encourages specialization, it would be expected that the net barter terms of trade (the ratio of import to export prices) would be more volatile for open economies than for closed economies. But work by Lutz and Singer (1994) refutes this. It might also be expected that small economies (which tend to be more specialized) will experience greater terms-of-trade volatility than larger economies. But Easterly and Kraay (2000) find that this too is not borne out by the evidence.

Terms-of-trade volatility and income volatility

Lutz (1994) finds a negative relationship between terms-of-trade volatility and output growth, but only for the income terms of trade (the *total value* of exports divided by the import price) and for developed countries. The relationship appears not to hold for low-income countries and primary-product exporters. Theoretically, a given volatility in the terms of trade implies a greater volatility in national income the more open the economy. Thus, we would expect the volatility of national income to be greater in more open economies. This also receives empirical support from Rodrik (1998) and Easterly and Kraay (2000).

Openness and domestic shocks

An important related question is whether more open economies generate larger or smaller *domestic* shocks. Krueger (1990b) argues that openness encourages better policy positions in general, suggesting that openness will generate smaller domestic shocks. Rodrik (1998), on the other hand, suggests that more open economies have greater volatility in total income, implying that the terms-of-trade element dominates the local shocks elements. But income volatility does not necessarily imply greater consumption volatility, for open economies may be better able to smooth consumption (and investment and government spending) by importing.

Thus, not only is it not possible to say definitively that trade liberalization causes greater output or terms-of-trade volatility, it is also not clear from the evidence to date that terms-of-trade volatility negatively affects growth in poorer countries. But it should be emphasized that these results stem from cross-country studies with widely varying experience for individual countries. Although it may not generally be the case that trade liberalization increases output or terms-of-trade volatility, it may be possible to indicate the likely impact on volatility in the context of a particular country.

2.6 Openness and politics

Much of the economic literature on trade focuses on the question of what trade policy 'should' be in order to maximize the welfare of a country's citizens. But a country's policy stance towards the rest of the world is fundamentally a political choice. Consequently, it is important to understand why a country adopts a particular trade policy stance. Research on the political economy of trade policy attempts to answer the question 'why is trade policy the way it is?' by analysing policy as the outcome of a political bargaining game with several competing players.[8]

2.6.1 Who are the players?

The players in political economy models of trade policy fall into two groups:

Demand-side players
These are individuals or groups who are attempting to influence trade policy outcomes – the 'demand' side of trade policy. Demand-side players typically include import-competing domestic industry, organized labour, exporters, consumers and/or the median voter.

Import-competing domestic industries are generally considered to be opponents of trade liberalization since greater openness erodes the rents that they currently enjoy. And they are often supported by organized labour, which tends to be most concerned with the potential loss of employment resulting from greater competition.

Exporters, by contrast, are generally concerned with cheaper access to inputs and intermediate goods and to some extent with redressing the anti-export bias associated with protection. Consumers are generally assumed to prefer cheaper goods, as well as greater product diversity from liberalization. But, occasionally, consumers may also be assumed to have a bias towards domestic goods, making them less hostile to trade protection.

Supply-side players
These are individuals or groups responsible for formulating and implementing trade policy – the 'supply' side of trade policy. Supply-side players usually include government bureaucrats, politicians and political parties.

Assumptions about the motivations of bureaucrats dealing with trade policy vary: they might be concerned with maximizing social welfare or with maximizing their personal gain through the corrupt implementation of trade policy. Similarly, politicians are usually assumed to be concerned principally with ensuring their re-election. But they may also be partial to particular sectors or industry or income groups or be swayed by financial (or other) contributions to their political campaigns.

The precise manner in which different players are chosen and their incentives specified determine the trade policy results obtained from political economy models of trade policy. Although current models have contributed to an understanding of why protection may exist, several questions remain unanswered. Two stand out: first, why is protection the norm; and second, why is trade policy rather than other means used for protection?

2.6.2 Why is protection the norm?

Most models of political economy are attempts to explain protection. But why is trade policy biased against trade instead of in favour of it? Given the substantial advantage to consumers in terms of lower prices and higher quality and diversity, along with the interests of exporters, it is not clear why political economy solutions almost invariably result in more protection rather than less. There may be several reasons but we explore four:

Ease of taxation
Trade protection is not a new phenomenon; it has existed at least since nation states have been in a position to tax foreign trade. One of the reasons why trade protection has been popular historically is because the taxation of foreign trade is administratively easier than taxation of domestic goods. This is because foreign trade typically has a limited number of points of entry into the country. Consequently, focusing taxation efforts on the goods passing through these places can yield considerable revenue for relatively little administrative cost. Alternative forms of taxation, such as sales tax, income tax or property taxes, may entail the identification and taxation of large numbers of firms or individuals with resulting high administrative costs.

Nevertheless, dependence on trade taxation has generally declined over recent years as the administrative capacity to apply more broad-based and sophisticated forms of taxation has developed.[9] Thus, although administrative ease may explain the historical preference for trade taxation (and this remains an issue for some countries with limited administrative capacity), it does not provide a good explanation of why so many countries continue to use high levels of trade protection.

Economic ignorance
A simple reason for the existence of trade protection is economic ignorance. Populist arguments often portray imports as an economic threat (and exports as an economic boon), dismissing entirely the potential benefits of imports in terms of lower prices, product diversity, improved efficiency, and so on. Such views are held by many politicians in all countries. Thus, trade protection may simply be a reflection of the economic ignorance of political leaders being reflected in national trade policy.

Again, this argument is unconvincing. The benefits (as well as the costs) of trade have been known for centuries and all countries have intellectuals and academics capable of advising governments on the basic economics of trade. Thus, economic ignorance is not a plausible explanation for the widespread use of trade protection.

Non-economic objectives

Another factor explaining trade protection is the existence of so-called non-economic objectives. For example, the leadership of a country may wish to promote a particular social structure (for example, family rather than commercial farms) or to use trade policy as an instrument of foreign policy, rather than to maximize the welfare of their citizens.

It is clear that there is some truth in this argument: most nations see trade policy in the wider context of their foreign relations rather than as merely as a component of their economic policies. But with the majority of trading nations now democracies, it seems likely that the preferences of at least a sizeable minority of citizens in most countries will have a bearing on the trade policy chosen. Since democratic regimes have to balance the competing interests of many different groups, they are more likely to yield outcomes favourable to a larger part of the country's population than regimes in which popular representation plays a smaller role. Consequently, the mere existence of non-economic objectives does not provide a convincing explanation for the widespread use of trade protection.

Concentration of interests

Perhaps the most plausible explanation for the prevalence of trade protection is that the individuals and groups who benefit from protection are often strongly concentrated whereas those who stand to benefit from liberalization are usually highly diffuse. Thus, if a small number of domestic firms are involved in a protected sector, then they will have a strong interest in ensuring continued protection. Lobbying for protection costs resources. Consequently, it is only worth investing these resources if the potential gains exceed these costs. The potential beneficiaries of liberalization are millions of consumers, who are unconnected and spread throughout the country. Consequently, the coordination costs of organizing the beneficiaries are high relative to the benefits that any individual consumer is likely to receive. The concentration of producer interests combined with the dispersion of consumer interests can result in a bias towards protection.

But this argument also has its weaknesses. First, the export sector typically stands to gain from liberalization and is often as concentrated in structure as any import-substituting industry: why do producers in the export sector appear to be less influential in forming trade policy than producers in the import sector? Second, the aggregate gains to consumers are large even if the individual gains are small. Consequently, we might expect enterprising individuals to set up consumer associations to press the case for consumers collectively. Of course this does happen, but again the voice of consumer associations appears to count for less than that of key importers.[10]

The nature of competition in the import-competing sector can be another key determinant of the political acceptability of trade liberalization. Rents from protection are largest and most easily captured in situations where a very small number of domestic firms are active in an industry. Consequently, when competition is weak and the gains from lobbying are large, there are strong incentives for firms to lobby. Conversely, when competition is strong (either because there are a large number of firms or because market entry is relatively easy), then firms are reluctant to invest substantial resources in lobbying. This is because the gains are small and likely to be captured by all of the firms in the industry – the free-rider problem (see Panagariya and Rodrik, 1993). Thus, the extent of domestic competition within an industry can have an important bearing on the willingness of firms to lobby against liberalization.

Finally, it is important to note that the poor do not feature at all in the above factors determining the existence of protection. This matters because opposition to trade liberalization is sometimes justified on the grounds that it may hurt the poor. Such opposition would have greater force if protection existed because the poor had lobbied for it. In reality, the poor play virtually no role in determining the level of protection while the voices that are heard most loudly are among the least likely to be poor. While this does not mean that trade liberalization will necessarily be good for the poor, it should encourage a certain scepticism about the claims of those non-poor groups who may be adversely affected by liberalization to represent the interests of the poor.

2.6.3 Why are trade restrictions used for protection rather than other means?

Even if the above arguments can collectively explain the protection of particular industries, it is not clear why that protection should take the form of trade policy. Rodrik (1995a) provides a useful example of this point. Assume that a government wishes to protect garment workers by increasing their lifetime income by $x over that which would have occurred under free trade. Consider five possible ways of achieving this:

- a lump-sum grant of $x to every worker employed in the garment industry presently;
- the same lump-sum grant, but to future as well as present garment workers;
- a permanent employment subsidy to the garment industry;
- a permanent production subsidy to the garment industry;
- or a permanent tariff on imported foreign garments.

Economic theory suggests that that these measures are increasingly costly ways of achieving the stated objective, with the tariff being the mostly costly of all. Why then is the worst of these options typically the one chosen?

The simple answer is that the first four options all cost money from the government budget whereas a tariff raises revenue for the government. Psychologically, this may be important within government, but as before, it is not an entirely satisfactory answer. Governments could both compensate for any lost revenue from the trade liberalization[11] and raise the necessary funds for the subsidy options by imposing a non-discriminatory tax such as an excise tax, a sales tax or VAT. This would still be welfare-improving overall.

The true reason for the reluctance of governments to pursue such a path may lie more with the political costs associated with making subsidies explicit, imposing new forms of taxation and the administrative costs of switching to new systems.

2.6.4 Implications for trade liberalization

Political economy models of trade policy have been extremely valuable because they explicitly model the processes of influence and decision-making. For future policy design, it is clearly important that models should characterize the actual political processes in order to recommend appropriate policies. As Leidy (1994) writes, 'we must step back from analysing the social-welfare consequences of alternative trade policies. We must identify instead an institutional design, a legal framework, that best harnesses these political-influence incentives to the public interest'. This is particularly important since it is perfectly possible for a political majority to vote against reform, even where a majority of the population would gain from such reform (see Fernandez and Rodrik, 1991).[12]

In particular, it is important for policy-makers to think through the implications of trade liberalization for different groups. If a trade liberalization is deemed to be beneficial, then it will be necessary to think carefully about how to build the necessary coalitions of interest behind the chosen reform, so that it is not derailed by the actions of vested interests. Furthermore, it may sometimes be helpful for policy-makers to use the political apparatus of multilateral negotiations to secure 'concessions' from trading partners and thereby make their own trade liberalization more politically acceptable domestically. In addition, the multilateral framework can provide a useful way of enhancing the credibility of commitments to future liberalization. This credibility in itself can make liberalization easier since firms and individuals are more likely to act on the assumption that such liberalizations will take place.[13]

But it is important to end by stressing that the political economy of trade liberalization is the means rather than the end in itself. Whether or not a trade liberalization should take place should depend on the economic analysis presented in the previous sections. Openness has both benefits and costs. The presumption is that the benefits will outweigh the costs, but it must be recognized that there may be difficulties to face and that some people may lose overall.

Summary

- Measuring openness to trade is complex and controversial. It is therefore important that relationships between openness and other variables should hold for a wide variety of different measures of openness.
- The potential benefits of openness to trade are cheaper consumption, more efficient production and better allocation of resources, new ideas and technology, and political gains from openness.
- The possible costs of openness to trade are anti-competitive behaviour, reduced opportunities for learning by doing, increased volatility and loss of economic sovereignty.
- Trade liberalization tends to reduce domestic prices unless domestic production is already particularly efficient and competitive.
- Most theory and much empirical evidence suggest that openness to trade encourages economic growth – but debate continues as to how confident we should be of this result. There is certainly no evidence that it does the reverse.
- Theory suggests that openness to trade may increase terms-of-trade or output volatility, but the empirical evidence for this is weak. But terms-of-trade volatility tends to result in higher income volatility the more open the economy.
- Trade policy can be viewed as the outcome of a political economy bargaining game between lobbyists and policy-makers.
- Trade protection exists for many reasons, including ease of taxation, economic ignorance, non-economic objectives and concentration of interests. But ultimately, trade policy should be determined by the economic costs and benefits.

Notes

1   Of course, tariff changes can be very significant, as, for example, with the liberalization of tariff peaks, which may induce a qualitative shift from no trade in a good to trade, effectively reducing the price of the good from infinity to some finite level.

2   In such differentiated markets, increased profits are eventually eroded away to zero by the new entry (of new and better differentiated varieties) that they encourage. To the extent that new varieties are valuable, consumers (including poor ones) gain through this process too.

3   White and Anderson (2000) stress that this is only an 'average' result. They show that in a quarter of the countries, an adverse change in inequality offsets the benefits to the poor of the change in mean incomes. Of course, the 'average'-ness of the result means that there is a corresponding number of cases in which the benefits of growth are supplemented and increased by favourable distributional shifts.

4 Vamvakidis (1999) considers only liberalizations up to 1989 in order to leave enough post-reform data to identify growth effects.

5 Chapter 10 takes up this issue in more detail.

6 The fact that several East Asian economies employed substantial state intervention does not mean that they were not open or that they had strong anti-export biases. Indeed, most commentators agree that export incentives served to offset the biases towards import-competing firms stemming from protection and that governments promoted a one-sided form of openness by making support dependent on fulfilling export quotas. See, for example, Rhee et al. (1984) on the rigour of the export incentives in Korea.

7 For example, a fall in the price of some international commodity does not affect whether there is a good harvest so these shocks are uncorrelated.

8 Rodrik (1995a) provides a useful survey of research in this area.

9 See Chapter 4 for an indication of the countries that still have a high dependence on trade taxation.

10 The main reason why consumer associations may be less prominent than producer associations is the so-called 'free-rider' problem. Since the individual gain to any consumer from setting up such an association is bound to be less than the individual cost of doing so, each consumer would rather 'free ride' on somebody else setting up the association. But if everyone behaves like this, then the association will not be set up.

11 See Chapter 4 for a discussion of whether trade liberalization does lead to revenue reductions in general.

12 This can occur because individuals may be uncertain about whether they will win or lose from the reform.

13 Chapter 7 discusses the process of trade policy reform in more detail.

3   Poverty and the Poor

> **This chapter** reviews the latest thinking and data on poverty world-wide, including:
>
> - An overview of the many different concepts of poverty.
> - A description of the different ways of measuring poverty.
> - An indication of the extent of poverty world-wide.
> - An elaboration of the International Development Targets.
> - A review of the characteristics of the poor emerging from Poverty Assessments.
> - A framework for understanding the causes of income poverty.

Chapter 2 described the debate over the costs and benefits of openness. Before moving on to discuss a framework for analysing the ways in which trade liberalization might affect the poor, it is important to consider poverty and the poor themselves. This chapter therefore begins by asking 'what is poverty?' and outlining some of the ways in which poverty is measured. This is followed by a brief overview of where the poor live and the global trends in poverty and in meeting the International Development Targets. The diverse characteristics of the poor revealed in numerous 'poverty assessments' are the focus of the following section. We conclude with a discussion of the causes of poverty and the interaction between shocks and household endowments.

3.1 What is poverty?

The traditional economic approach to measuring poverty is to calculate either the income or consumption expenditure of a household over the period of time under consideration (usually a year) and then to identify as poor the households or individuals who fall below some minimally acceptable level (the poverty line). Thus, poverty is defined simply as a lack of income or consumption.

The advantage of simple income- or consumption-based poverty measures is that they allow poverty comparisons to be made across countries and across time. But although simple measures of individual or household income or consumption continue to be the mainstay of much poverty analysis, it is clear that poverty is a broader concept than merely having an income or consumption expenditure that lies below a poverty line. In other words, poverty is inherently *multidimensional*. The many dimensions of poverty can include:

- *Income*: having low income or consumption.
- *Assets*: having little or poor-quality land, housing, livestock or other productive assets.
- *Environmental*: having to live in a polluted or hazardous environment or having to work on poor-quality land.
- *Education*: having little or no education.
- *Health*: having illnesses of various kinds.
- *Powerlessness*: being excluded from decisions that have an impact on one's life.
- *Discrimination*: being subject to arbitrary discrimination on the basis of gender, ethnicity or any other reason.
- *Vulnerability*: being susceptible to a wide range of 'shocks', such as harvest failure, illness, price changes, violence, etc.

It would be possible to add many more dimensions to the concept of poverty: there is no definitive list. Each of these dimensions can be considered a form of poverty in its own right, but the word poverty is generally used to refer to an overarching concept that involves the combination of the many different dimensions of poverty. Thus, a household that has a low income, but whose members are healthy, well educated and live in a pleasant area with good access to services might not generally be considered poor by many people. Alternatively, a household whose income rises above the poverty line but which has few assets, lives in an environmentally degraded area and is subject to constant discrimination might reasonably be regarded as poor. The problem of defining poverty, therefore, is a problem of finding a suitable synthesis of the many different dimensions of poverty. In other words, when does deprivation in one or more dimensions result in poverty?

3.1.1 Sen's concept of poverty

One of the best known approaches to answering this question is that of Nobel Laureate Amartya Sen, who describes poverty in terms of:

- *Functionings*, which represent the various things that people can do or be in their lives (see Sen, 1993). Basic functionings might include 'being well nourished' or 'escaping avoidable disease', while more complex functionings might include 'being able to take part in the life of the community'.

Figure 3.1 Sen's entitlements, capabilities and functionings approach

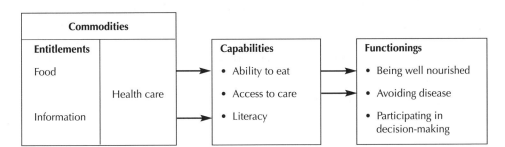

- *Capabilities*, which represent the ability to convert the 'entitlements' people have – that is, the commodities over which they have control within the existing legal framework – into functionings that they value. Thus, in Figure 3.1, which provides a diagrammatic description of Sen's approach, food lies within these people's entitlement set and they have the capability of being able to eat; therefore, they can achieve the functioning of being well nourished.

Sen's framework helps to explain how individuals may fail to achieve important functionings. For example, disabled people, who may have substantial command over commodities because of their income, may still be unable to translate this into a capability that they might value, such as being able to walk. Alternatively, as Figure 3.1 shows, information in the form of a newspaper might be available to people, but they may not be able to translate this into a valuable functioning if they cannot read; this is an example of 'capability failure', indicated by the lack of an arrow between the capability and the functioning.

There might also be 'entitlement failure': for example, Figure 3.1 shows a situation in which people are capable in principle of accessing health but health care is not available (it is not within the set of commodities to which they are entitled; there is therefore no arrow from the entitlement set to the capability). Sen describes poverty as a combination of 'entitlement failure' (the loss of command over resources) and 'capability failure' (the loss of the ability to convert resources into useful functionings).

Although Sen's work has provided an important conceptual advance in thinking about poverty, putting his framework into practice can prove difficult. This is because it is necessary to decide precisely which functionings are of most importance and to characterize precisely how people's entitlements are translated into functionings. In practice, poverty analysis tends to try and incorporate the multidimensional nature of poverty by broadening out from simple income and consumption measures through the inclusion of wider indicators of well-being and 'ill-being'.[1]

3.1.2 **The World Bank's concept of poverty**

The World Bank's World Development Report 2001, 'Attacking Poverty', provides another important description of poverty (World Bank, 2001). This calls for a focus of anti-poverty efforts in three key areas: opportunity, security and empowerment. Underlying this is a concept of poverty based on:

*   lack of opportunity;
*   insecurity and vulnerability; and
*   powerlessness.

3.1.3 **Lack of opportunity**

Lack of opportunity includes the traditional concept of income and consumption poverty, but it is broader than this. In particular, it includes the lack of key assets necessary to attain basic necessities. These assets are of several kinds:

*   *Human assets*: such as the capacity for basic labour, skills and good health.
*   *Natural assets*: such as land and livestock.
*   *Physical assets*: such as access to infrastructure, housing, roads, irrigation etc.
*   *Financial assets*: such as access to credit.[2]
*   *Social assets*: such as networks of contacts and reciprocal obligations that can be called on in time of need.

In addition, lack of opportunity includes the inability of poor people to use the assets they have to obtain their basic needs. For example, market failures may prevent people from buying key goods or from obtaining employment.

3.1.4 **Insecurity and vulnerability**

One critical aspect of poverty arises particularly strongly from studies that ask poor people how they define poverty: the importance of security. Poor households often suffer severe insecurity because of risks from a wide variety of different sources. Table 3.1 provides an overview of these risks.

Many of the negative shocks experienced by poor households are idiosyncratic, that is, specific to the household and its members. These include illness, injury, disability, old age, death, crime and domestic violence. Other shocks are 'covariate', experienced by many households simultaneously either regionally or nationally, for example, natural disasters, epidemics, civil war and social upheaval, and macroeconomic, terms-of-trade and other price shocks. The poor place a high value on mechanisms to protect themselves against such shocks since if an already poor household receives even a relatively small further negative shock, it can have potentially devastating consequences.

In general, there are three mechanisms though which households can improve their security and reduce their vulnerability:[3]

Table 3.1 The main sources of risk to households, communities, regions and countries

Type of Risk	Idiosyncratic	Covariant	
	Risks affecting an individual or household (micro)	*Risks affecting groups of households or communities (meso)*	*Risks affecting regions or nations (macro)*
Natural		Rainfall Landslide Volcanic eruption High winds	Earthquake Flood Drought
Health	Illness Injury Disability Old age Death	Epidemic	
Social	Crime Domestic violence	Terrorism Gang activity	Civil strife War Social upheaval

Economic		Unemployment
		Resettlement
		Harvest failure
			Changes in food prices
			Growth collapse
			Hyperinflation
			Balance of payments,
			  financial or
			  currency crisis
			Technology shock
			Terms-of-trade shock
			Transition costs of
			  economic reforms

Political		Riots	Political default on social programmes Coup d'état
Environmental		Pollution Deforestation	Nuclear disaster

Source: World Bank (2001).

Risk reduction

The best way to deal with a negative shock is not to experience it in the first place. Risk reduction mechanisms attempt to improve security by reducing the risk of a negative shock in the first place. Some of these mechanisms are undertaken by individuals and households, such as preventative health practices, migration, seeking out more secure income sources and diversifying from existing sources, and investing in physical and human capital. Others require complementary public policy in the form of sound policies for the management of the macroeconomy, the environment, education, public health, infrastructure, provision of financial services, active labour market policies and agricultural extension policies.

In particular, it should be noted that trade liberalization (both internal and external) can have both a risk-increasing and a risk-reducing effect. It may increase risk if it removes formerly fixed, managed producer or consumer prices. But it may also reduce risk if it allows greater competition in the markets of most importance to the poor, since this will mean that poor households are less vulnerable to decisions made by individual traders or employers. More immediately, it may also allow households to import goods that may have been subject to large price swings in the past due to the limited size of the local market.

Insurance
Households may also take steps to insure themselves against a bad outcome. Individual and household efforts in this category include the creation of marriage and extended family ties, entering into sharecropping tenancy arrangements, and maintaining buffer stocks of key goods. Groups and communities may also invest in building social capital through networks, associations, rituals and reciprocal gift-giving. In addition, markets may provide pensions, accident and disability insurance, though these are often inaccessible to the poor. Similarly, state-provided pensions, and unemployment, illness and disability insurance may be available to some, but these are often linked to employment in the public service and are therefore inaccessible to most of the poor in developing countries.

Coping
The difficulty faced by many poor households in reducing risk and insuring themselves against negative shocks means that many must rely on adaptation or 'coping' mechanisms to mitigate the worst aspects of a shock once it has already occurred. These mechanisms include:

- *Increasing output or greater involvement in the labour market*: households will often increase the number of hours they work, both by working longer hours and by putting additional household members into income-generating activities. This can mean removing children from school in order to help households make ends meet. See Kochar (1995) for an analysis of the importance of the labour market in smoothing incomes.[4]
- *Running down savings and assets*: households will run down savings in times of difficulty and may start to sell household assets.[5] But poor households often have an acute understanding of the intertemporal trade-offs between consumption during the current difficult period and keeping productive assets to maintain future production. For example,

farming households rarely sell bullocks and ploughs except in times of extreme distress (see Devereux, 1993).

- *Accessing credit*: if households have access to credit then this can be used to smooth consumption when faced with negative shocks. But poor households often have limited access to credit. Even micro-credit programmes do not always reach the poor and loans are typically given only for productive investment rather than to support consumption in times of distress (see Hulme and Mosley, 1996).
- *Migration*: poor households will often send one or more members to another part of the country as a response to a negative shock. This includes productive members who migrate to urban areas in search of employment, as well as the outplacement of children and other dependents with wealthier relatives during times of distress (see Serra, 1997).

Despite the three mechanisms – risk reduction, insurance and coping – poor households often remain extremely vulnerable. For example, poor households are generally much less well insured against negative shocks than wealthier households (see, for example, Jalan and Ravallion, 1999, on insurance in rural China).[6] Almost by definition, they have fewer savings and assets on which to call than richer households (and the collapse of asset prices during distress selling makes this form of protection of limited value during covariate shocks – see Sen, 1981). Often as a consequence of their low asset position, the poor also have little access to credit, particularly for consumption purposes.

This means that the poor must often rely on income diversification through migration and increased participation in the labour market to cushion shocks. But increased labour market participation of children comes at the cost of investment in their education and can therefore help to reinforce intergenerational poverty. Furthermore, labour markets may not be able to absorb the large increases in labour supply resulting from a covariate shock. Hence the importance of food-for-work and employment guarantee schemes to the poor. Similarly, poor households with few assets or high dependency ratios may not be in a position to relinquish current income for possibly higher future income by sending a productive member of the household away to find employment. For all these reasons, insecurity and vulnerability are central to the poor's perception of poverty.

3.1.5 Empowerment

No discussion of the meaning of poverty would be complete without mentioning empowerment. Participatory research shows that poor people constantly highlight their sense of 'disempowerment' as central to their experience of poverty (see Narayan et al., 2000). This disempowerment can take many forms. For example, households or individuals may be discriminated against because of their gender, caste, race or ethnic group. Gender inequality in particular is widespread: indeed, the more extreme manifestations of power inequality between men and women constitute a gross violation of human rights. Domestic violence is startlingly prevalent around the world and in some societies; the lower value assigned to women and girls translates into excess mortality (see World Bank, 2001). Furthermore, the empowerment and income dimensions of poverty are linked. For example, discrimination based on caste, race or ethnicity can reinforce social barriers and perpetuate inequalities in access to the resources necessary to move out of income poverty.

Poor households often face bad treatment by those in positions of authority. Teachers may not bother turning up to teach in schools in poor areas; nurses and doctors may refuse or delay treatment; and government officials may dismiss the views of the poor as ignorant or irrelevant. Equally, market traders may exploit the illiteracy and innumeracy of the poor while some landlords can effectively control the lives of their poor tenants.

There is, therefore, a growing recognition of the empowerment dimension of poverty and the need for anti-poverty initiatives to tackle the social and political barriers to poverty alleviation. These include:

- positive measures to reduce and eliminate discrimination;
- efforts to make state institutions more responsive to the needs of the poor;
- support for social mobilization of the poor to press for political policies more aligned with their interests.

Although economic analysis of political decision-making is commonplace, the economic analysis of empowerment is virtually non-existent. So although trade liberalization could, in principle, have some impact on the empowerment of the poor (and it may be important in certain circumstances to take this into account), it is not at all clear how to reach any general conclusions about the link between trade liberalization and the empowerment dimension of poverty. Therefore, while noting the importance of this dimension of poverty, we do not discuss it further in this Handbook.

3.2 Measuring poverty[7]

How poverty is measured is clearly determined by the concept of poverty being used. Consequently, there are many different approaches to the measurement of poverty. We outline two of the most commonly used approaches and then provide a way of classifying different poverty measures according to a set of criteria. These criteria can be applied to almost any poverty measures used in practice.

3.2.1 Measures of income poverty

The most common approach to measuring poverty is to calculate a measure of household or individual income or consumption expenditure based on data from household surveys. If the survey is representative of the national population, then it is possible to use such data to calculate the number of people whose income or consumption falls below a national poverty line.

Nationally representative surveys and the technology for processing them quickly and cheaply have greatly improved since the beginning of the 1990s. Consequently, assessments of income poverty are relatively easy to undertake. Furthermore, if enough households are surveyed, it can be possible to calculate poverty at a regional or sub-regional level and, if surveys are repeated, to make comparisons over time.

Despite these strengths, the use of income poverty measures has some weaknesses. People's experience of poverty is multidimensional and may include dimensions such as powerlessness, which are poorly captured by focusing only on income or consumption. Furthermore, there are problems associated with collecting accurate income and consumption expenditure information from household surveys, and it is often difficult to account for the value of common property resources or of services provided by the government. For example, if there are two otherwise identical households but one is near a government health clinic and the other is not, it is hard to reflect in an income measure the greater accessibility of health care.[8]

3.2.2 Participatory approaches

Recent years have seen an enormous expansion in the use of participatory methods of research, planning, management and monitoring of poverty (see Chambers, 1997). These methods emphasize the active involvement of the poor themselves in defining the concepts of poverty that are relevant to them. The list below shows such a set of concepts or criteria used by local people in Asia and sub-Saharan Africa for 'ill-being' (see Chambers, 1995):

- disabled (for example, blind, crippled, mentally impaired, chronically sick);
- widowed;
- lacking land, livestock, farm equipment, grinding mill;
- cannot decently bury their dead;
- cannot send their children to school;
- having more mouths to feed and fewer hands to help;
- lacking able-bodied members who can fend for their families in the event of crisis;
- with bad housing;
- having vices (such as alcoholism);
- being 'poor in people', lacking social supports;
- having to put children in employment;
- single parents;
- having to accept demeaning or low-status work;
- having food security for only a few months each year;
- being dependent on common property resources.

The participatory approach explores poor people's perceptions of poverty, tries to understand the resources at their disposal and the ways in which these are used and the ways in which they cope with hardship – see Box 3.1.

Box 3.1 **The tools of participatory poverty assessments**

A variety of participatory tools have been devised to work on different issues and in different contexts. These are mostly group exercises based on local information. The ones often used in participatory assessments are:

- **Wealth or well-being rankings**: assigning households to well-being or wealth categories on the basis of criteria identified by the group.
- **Seasonal calendars**: graphical depiction of seasonal trends and events.
- **Maps**: drawing a map of the community identifying structure, institutions or community facilities that are important in the group members' lives.
- **Matrix scoring**: scoring events or preferences on the basis of criteria agreed by the group.
- **Oral life histories**: a record of people's lifetime experiences.

A combination of these tools can be used to provide a qualitative assessment of such issues as: who the poor are in a village; when are the times of greatest seasonal stress; the extent of access to key facilities; the priorities and preferences of the community; and the ways in which natural and policy-induced shocks have affected people's lives.

3.2.3 Classifying measures of poverty

Given such a wide range of possible definitions of poverty, it is helpful to have some means of classifying different poverty measures. Most of the measures of poverty in common use can be categorized according to differences along four different dimensions:

Internal/external
One critical distinguishing characteristic among alternative definitions of poverty is determined by who it is that decides on the definition. Many external researchers construct their own definitions of poverty based on the information they obtain from poor households and communities; thus, the definition of poverty is 'external'. But increasingly, participatory techniques have been used to facilitate a definition of poverty by the poor households with whom the researcher is engaged, an 'internal' definition. Often this distinction is described as objective versus subjective, though strictly speaking *all* definitions of poverty are subjective (even if they are quantitative): the key distinction is *who* is responsible for determining the concept of poverty used.

Input/outcome
Many measures of poverty focus on inputs to the individual or household. These include income and consumption measures. Conversely, some researchers prefer outcome-based measures such as morbidity, mortality and nutritional status. The distinction is important since some individuals with high inputs, however defined, may not be able to exploit them to achieve acceptable outcomes; while others with low inputs may achieve acceptable outcomes.[9]

Box 3.2 **Where to draw the poverty line?**

Absolute poverty lines: these are usually based on the cost of a basket of basic goods and services. Often the basket may consist only of the food necessary to reach a given calorific intake per day. The cost of this 'food only' basket is sometimes used as an extreme poverty line. When the cost of other basic non-food goods, such as housing and clothing, is added, this gives an upper poverty line. The methodology for the construction of poverty lines can become complex: see Ravallion and Bidani (1994) for an example of best practice.

Relative poverty lines: these are defined by reference to the general standard of living in a given country. The line may be drawn as a fraction of average income or the average wage. For example, in Europe, half the median income is often used as a relative poverty line. Because relative poverty lines are relative to the general standard of living rather than being based on a minimum set of basic goods, they are higher in richer countries than in poor countries. Furthermore, relative poverty lines reflect the general distribution of income, so more equal societies will tend to have higher relative poverty lines than less equal ones.

Absolute/relative

'Absolute' poverty measures calculate poverty based on a set of measurable quantities, such as food consumption: a person or household is poor if the overall value of, say, their consumption lies below the poverty line. Others argue that poverty is fundamentally a relative concept. There are two different senses in which this may be meant. Most commonly, this means that the threshold below which a household is considered to be poor is determined with reference to the welfare of other households. This is the distinction between absolute and relative poverty lines – see Box 3.2. But some argue that the concept of poverty is inherently relative – that is, that an individual or household's poverty cannot be measured on its own, but only relative to the welfare of other households. For example, the extent to which a household is excluded from the society in which it lives is an inherently relative concept of poverty (see de Haan and Maxwell, 1998, for a review of poverty and social exclusion in developing and developed countries).

Static/dynamic

Static poverty measures assess poverty at a single point in time or during a single period. Such measures are more common, particularly among external poverty measures, since they are easier to collect, involving only one visit to the poor household or community. But there is considerable evidence that household welfare varies greatly over time. This is true during the course of any given year (see Chambers, 1989, who points out the importance of seasonality to poor households); from year to year, because of weather, health and other shocks to well-being; and over many years, because of demographic and social shifts. Dynamic measures of poverty attempt to capture the impact of such variability on well-being.[10] Similarly, measures of vulnerability attempt to account for the possibility of disaster rather than merely looking at the current welfare status of the household (see Pritchett et al., 2000).

The choices made along these four dimensions give rise to quite different measures of poverty. For example, the Foster–Greer–Thorbecke class of poverty measures described in Box 3.3 are external in that they are defined by outsider researchers; input-based since they tend to use income or consumption as the measures of household welfare; absolute since they tend to use an absolute poverty line and focus on indicators that are measurable for each household separately from others within its community; and static since they look at poverty at one point in time (although see Jalan and Ravallion, 1998, and McCulloch and Baulch, 2000, for extensions to the dynamic case).

In contrast, the measures arising from participatory studies of poverty are often internal since they are defined by the poor themselves. They are also predominantly (although not exclusively) outcome-based since they generally refer to being in an undesirable situation rather than not having sufficient income or inputs. Some measures are also relative: having to accept demeaning or low-status work, for example, is associated with how

Box 3.3 **The Foster–Greer–Thorbecke class of poverty measures**

Much quantitative poverty analysis uses a set of poverty measures known as the Foster–Greer–Thorbecke (FGT) class after their inventors, Foster, Greer and Thorbecke (1984). These measures provide an aggregate figure for poverty within a country or region based on measures of the welfare of individuals or households within that region. The welfare measure used is often consumption expenditure or income, but any other welfare measure can be used as long as an increase in its value always indicates a welfare improvement and the welfare measure can take any (positive) value. Thus, the number of years of schooling or the reciprocal of distance from the nearest clinic could be used instead of income or consumption.

The way in which the FGT poverty measure is calculated can best be seen by looking at a line of possible values for the welfare indicator (say income):

$0 \quad y_3 \quad\quad y_1 \quad\quad z \quad\quad y_2 \quad\quad\quad\quad$ value of the welfare indicator

z indicates the position of the poverty line. If the income of a household is y_1, then its income lies below the poverty line z and so it is classified as being poor. If the income of a second household is y_2, then this is above the poverty line and so it is not poor. A third household might have income y_3, which is again below the poverty line. Thus, the simplest aggregate measure of poverty can be obtained by calculating the proportion of households lying below the poverty line. This is known as the *poverty headcount* and is the first FGT measure of poverty.

continued

Box 3.3 continued

But if we know the actual incomes of the households, we can calculate other measures of poverty. For example, for each household below the poverty line, we can calculate how far their income is below the line: household 3 is clearly poorer than household 1 because it lies further below the poverty line. If we express the gap between a household's income and the poverty line as a proportion of the poverty line (for example, household 1 might lie 40% below the poverty line), add up these proportions for all poor households and divide by the total number of households, we obtain the *poverty gap* measure of poverty. This is an indication of the average shortfall from the poverty line and is the second FGT measure of poverty.

Finally, if the poorest households are of particular concern, then it would be useful to have a poverty measure that reflected this concern. This can be obtained by calculating the proportionate gap between each household's income and the poverty line as above and then squaring it. Thus, household 3 lies further below the poverty line than household 1 and this is reflected in the larger proportionate gap between its income and the poverty line. We can emphasize the shortfall of the poorest households by squaring the proportionate gap for each poor household. Adding up the squared proportionate gaps and dividing by the total number of households gives the *squared poverty gap* measure of poverty, which is the third FGT measure of poverty. This measure places a much stronger emphasis on households lying a long way below the poverty line.

the household is regarded within its community. And some of the measures are also dynamic in that they refer to risks that households face and their needs in the event of crisis.[11]

3.2.4 Poverty or inequality?

Discussions of poverty often tend to assume that poverty and inequality are the same thing: they are not. Poverty refers to the failure by the individual or household to rise above a given minimally acceptable standard of living (the poverty line). Inequality, however, refers to the distribution of well-being across households. Thus, it is perfectly possible to have a highly unequal society in which no one is poor (consider the case in which everyone except one person has an income just above the poverty line and one person has a huge income). Conversely, it is possible to have a very equal society in which a huge number of people are poor (as was the case in China prior to the economic reforms started in 1978).

Our concern in this Handbook is with poverty rather than inequality – that is, we are interested in the relationship between trade liberalization and the welfare of those whose standard of living is currently below a suitable poverty line. We will not therefore consider the relationship between trade liberalization and inequality directly.[12] But poverty and inequality are obviously linked. If the overall level of income stays constant, an increase in inequality will generally increase poverty and *vice versa*. Of course, the overall level of income in a country does not usually stay the same. Therefore, it is perfectly possible for growth to cause a fall in poverty while inequality increases; or for a recession to increase poverty significantly while improving the distribution of income.

Furthermore, inequality can affect poverty through its impact on growth. There is a long-standing debate about the impact of inequality on growth. Broadly speaking, there are two positions:

- *Inequality increases growth rates*: in which the argument is that the investment incentives for entrepreneurs, who are typically better off, will tend to improve growth.
- *Inequality reduces growth rates*: in which the argument is that a very unequal initial distribution of assets results in a poorer use of resources than might occur with a more equal distribution.

The latter point is key. There is considerable evidence that initial inequality in land, education and gender harms subsequent growth rates (see Birdsall and Londono, 1997; Ravallion, 1998; Thomas and Wang, 1998; Dollar and Gatti, 1999; Klasen, 1999; Banerjee et al., 2000; Deininger and Olinto, 2000). Thus, in addition to any other reasons for reducing initial inequality, there may be a case for redistributive policies on the grounds that they will foster faster growth and, as a consequence, greater poverty reduction.

3.3 The extent of poverty world-wide

Notwithstanding the preceding debate about the multidimensional nature of poverty, the only poverty measures for which there are data across countries and time are those based on income and consumption. Table 3.2 shows the number of people living on less than US$1 a day in each region of the developing world based on the latest available household survey data. Table 3.3 shows the proportion of the population in poverty for each region, the poverty headcount index.

As Tables 3.2 and 3.3 show, the evolution of poverty in the last decade has been very different in different regions. At a global level, the poverty headcount index fell between 1987–98 although the total number of poor people rose. Some regions have suffered stagnation and an increase in poverty: Latin America, for example, saw a slight increase in its poverty headcount over the period and a substantial increase in the number of people below the poverty line; sub-Saharan Africa saw a slight reduction in its poverty headcount but the number of poor people also increased; and Eastern Europe and Central Asia saw a substantial increase in poverty due to the transition to market economies. In contrast, East Asia and the Pacific have achieved great success in poverty reduction in the last two decades, reducing both the proportion and the absolute number of poor people, while South Asia has seen a reduction in the proportion of people below poverty, but a steady increase in the absolute number of the poor.

Table 3.2 Population living on less than US$1 per day in developing and transitional countries, 1987–98

Regions	Population covered by at least one survey (%)	Number of people living on less than US$1 a day (millions)				
		1987	*1990*	*1993*	*1996*	*1998 (est.)*
East Asia and the Pacific	90.8	417.5	452.4	431.9	265.1	278.3
(excluding China)	71.1	114.1	92.0	83.5	55.1	65.1
Eastern Europe and Central Asia	81.7	1.1	7.1	18.3	23.8	24.0
Latin America and the Caribbean	88.0	63.7	73.8	70.8	76.0	78.2
Middle East and North Africa	52.5	9.3	5.7	5.0	5.0	5.5
South Asia	97.9	474.4	495.1	505.1	531.7	522.0
Sub-Saharan Africa	72.9	217.2	242.3	273.3	289.0	290.9
Total	88.1	1,183.2	1,276.4	1,304.3	1,190.6	1,198.9
(excluding China)	84.2	879.8	915.9	955.9	980.5	985.7

Source: World Bank (1999c).

Table 3.3 Poverty headcount index for developing and transitional countries, 1987–98

Regions	Population covered by at least one survey (%)	Headcount index (%)				
		1987	*1990*	*1993*	*1996*	*1998 (est.)*
East Asia and the Pacific	90.8	26.6	27.6	25.2	14.9	15.3
(excluding China)	71.1	23.9	18.5	15.9	10.0	11.3
Eastern Europe and Central Asia	81.7	0.2	1.6	4.0	5.1	5.1
Latin America and the Caribbean	88.0	15.3	16.8	15.3	15.6	15.6
Middle East and North Africa	52.5	4.3	2.4	1.9	1.8	1.9
South Asia	97.9	44.9	44.0	42.4	42.3	40.0
Sub-Saharan Africa	72.9	46.6	47.7	49.7	48.5	46.3
Total	88.1	28.3	29.0	28.1	24.5	24.0
(excluding China)	84.2	28.5	28.1	27.7	27.0	26.2

Source: World Bank (1999c).

There have also been fluctuations in performance over time. The poverty headcount index increased in sub-Saharan Africa in the late 1980s and early 1990s, but then declined from the mid-1990s onwards (although the absolute number of the poor continued to rise). In contrast, East Asia and the Pacific saw a steady decline in poverty arrested by the Asian crisis of 1997–8. Sub-Saharan Africa now has the highest proportion of poor people of any region in the world, although in absolute numbers it had 290.9 million poor in 1998 compared with 522 million in South Asia and 278.3 million in East Asia and the Pacific including China. Thus, 43.5% of the world's poor live in South Asia, while a little less than a quarter live in sub-Saharan Africa and a further 23.2% live in East Asia and the Pacific.

Poverty continues to be mostly concentrated in the rural areas of developing countries with most of the countries in all regions having more rural than urban poverty (see IFAD, 2001). Unfortunately, accurate measures of rural and urban poverty that are comparable across countries are not available. But numerous country studies using national poverty lines shows that rural poverty is generally far more prevalent than urban poverty. For example, 77% of the rural population in Madagascar are below the national poverty line, whereas 47% of the urban population are below the same poverty line. Similarly, in Nicaragua, 76% of the rural population fall below the national poverty line while only 32% of the urban population fall below the same line.

But there are exceptions. In Honduras, for example, 56% of the urban population fall below the national poverty line compared with 46% of the rural population. Furthermore, Haddad et al. (1999) use survey data on poverty from 8 countries and child undernutrition from 14 countries to show that the absolute number of poor and undernourished individuals living in urban areas has increased, as has the share of poverty and undernourishment in urban areas. So although poverty is still predominantly rural, urban poverty is growing.

As discussed above, poverty is a multidimensional concept. Hence, it is also useful to look at alternative social indicators of poverty and deprivation. Table 3.4 shows an international comparison of social indicators between 1980–97.

Life expectancy has been rising in all regions of the world, although most slowly in sub-Saharan Africa, where it is lowest. Similarly, infant and under-five mortality has fallen significantly in all regions, but remains extremely high in sub-Saharan Africa and South Asia. Child malnutrition has fallen in all regions of the world except sub-Saharan Africa, where it has risen. Similarly, considerable progress has been made towards reaching 100% gross primary school enrolment in all regions except sub-Saharan Africa, where enrolment

Table 3.4 International comparison of social indicators, 1980–97

	East Asia & the Pacific		Latin America & Caribbean		Middle East & North Africa		South Asia		Sub-Saharan Africa	
	1980	1997	1980	1997	1980	1997	1980	1997	1980	1997
Life expectancy at birth (years)	65	69	65	70	59	67	54	62	48	51
Infant mortality (per 100 births)	56	37	60	32	95	49	119	77	115	91
Under-five mortality (per 1,000)	83	47	na	41	137	63	180	100	189	147
Child malnutrition (stunting)	52[c]	38[b,c]	25[d]	13[b,d]	31	22[b]	66	54[b]	37	39[b]
Primary school enrolment rate	111	118[a]	105	113[a]	87	96[a]	73	100[a]	78	77[a]
Youth illiteracy: male	5	2	11	7	27	14	36	25	34	20
Youth illiteracy: female	15	4	11	6	52	27	64	48	55	29

Notes: (a) 1996; (b) 1995; (c) South East Asia; (d) South America. Sources: for all except item 4, World Bank (1999d); item 4: WHO, (1997).

Source: White et al. (1999).

Box 3.4 'A better world for all': international development targets

1. Reduce the proportion of people living in extreme poverty by half between 1990–2015.
2. Enrol all children in primary school by 2015.
3. Make progress toward gender equality and empowering women by eliminating gender disparities in primary and secondary education by 2005.
4. Reduce infant and child mortality rates by two-thirds between 1990–2015.
5. Reduce maternal mortality ratios by three-quarters between 1990–2015.
6. Provide access for all who need reproductive health services by 2015.
7. Implement national strategies for sustainable development by 2005 so as to reverse the loss of environmental resources by 2015.

Source: Department for International Development (2000a).

on average has fallen. Nonetheless, youth illiteracy has fallen in Africa as in other regions and the disparity between female and male illiteracy, though large, is not as great as that in South Asia, the Middle East and North Africa.

Some attempts to monitor progress in poverty reduction have combined different social indicators into composite indices, most notably the Human Development Index and the Human Poverty Index of the UNDP (see UNDP, 1998). More recently, attention has focused on those indicators necessary to monitor progress towards the achievement of the International Development Targets resulting from the 1995 Social Summit in Copenhagen and the subsequent goals agreed by the Development Assistance Committee of the OECD in 1996 – see Box 3.4.

Progress towards meeting these goals has been uneven and, on average, the world has not been on track to meet them by the deadlines set.[13] Nevertheless, progress has been rapid in some countries and faster in some areas than others:

Primary school enrolment
Some regions – East Asia and the Pacific, and Eastern Europe and Central Asia – are close to meeting the target, while others, notably Latin America, have made good progress in the last decade. But for Africa and South Asia, it is unlikely that the target will be met. There are more than 110 million primary school age children in developing countries who do not attend school today (see UNESCO, 2000). Furthermore, there is a huge gap between the educational attainment of the rich and the poor both between countries and within countries.

The elimination of gender disparities
There are enormous gender disparities in educational outcomes and access. In South Asia, only a third of women are literate compared to two-thirds of men. In Nepal and Afghanistan, fewer than 15% of women are literate. Furthermore,

progress towards equal enrolments of girls and boys in primary and secondary school is slow. In 1995, girls made up only 43% of primary school enrolment and 40% of secondary enrolment and, although these figures are expected to increase, current progress suggests that the 2005 target will not be met.

Infant and child mortality
Infant and child mortality rates have declined around 10% over the last decade. But AIDS is having a devastating effect, particularly in some of the world's poorest countries in which life expectancy at birth is falling, and AIDS is making it difficult to meet the infant and child mortality targets.

There also remain large disparities between the rates in rich and poor countries, and between the rich and the poor within countries. Table 3.5 shows the under-five mortality rates for the poorest 20% and the richest 20% in Brazil, Ghana, Pakistan and South Africa. While under-five mortality in Pakistan and Ghana is highest, the mortality rate for the poorest 20% of the population in South Africa is more than twice as high as the mortality rate for the richest 20%; in Brazil the ratio is over 10:1. This suggests that dramatic improvements in under-five mortality could be achieved by ensuring that the poorest have access to the same basic care (and overall conditions) available to the rich. More controversially, it also suggests that a re-allocation of resources within existing budgets could substantially reduce under-five mortality rates overall, even if rates went up for the richest.

Maternal mortality
Currently, only around half of all births are attended by skilled health personnel. Furthermore, evidence from ten developing countries between 1992–7 shows that only 22% of births among the bottom 20% of the population were attended by trained staff, compared with 76% of those in the top 20% (see World Bank, 2000b). Data on maternal mortality rates are sporadic and subject to many types of error, making it difficult to make accurate comparisons either across countries or over time. But using the best available data, Hanmer and Naschold (1999) project that maternal mortality rates will fall well short of the target of a reduction by three-quarters by 2015.

Table 3.5 Under-five mortality rates (deaths per 1,000 live births) in four countries

Country	Period	Average rate	Poorest 20%	Richest 20%	Poor/rich
Brazil (NE and SE)	1987–92	63	116	11	10.4
Ghana	1978–89	142	155	130	1.2
Pakistan	1981–90	147	160	145	1.1
South Africa	1985–89	113	155	71	2.2

Source: World Bank (2000c).
Note: Rates use information from more than one LSMS survey, and so are averages across a period. Poverty is defined in terms of consumption per capita.

Access to reproductive health

Access to reproductive health has been improving in many countries. The contraceptive prevalence rate increased by around 10% between 1993–8 to over 60%. Also, encouragingly, data from demographic and health surveys in Africa show that the 'demographic transition' from high fertility and high mortality to low fertility and low mortality appears to have begun (see White et al., 1999).

National strategies for sustainable development

National strategies for sustainable development are in place in almost half of the world's countries. But given the extreme vulnerability of many poor people to their natural environment, it is essential that far more should be done to convert these national strategies into action at a local level.

3.4 Who are the Poor?

Global trends in the distribution of poverty across regions and countries provide useful information on the extent of poverty. But they tell us little about what will happen to poverty in any particular country as a result of trade liberalization. For this, it is necessary to have a more detailed understanding of the characteristics of the poor in the country in question. A large number of countries have undertaken 'poverty profiles' or 'poverty assessments' in the course of the last ten years.[14] Such profiles typically characterize poor groups according to a range of variables, including:

- *Location*: which includes not only geographical area and rural/urban distinctions, but also agroclimatic distinctions and measures of remoteness.
- *Demography*: which includes household size and composition, with particular attention to dependency ratios and age/sex profiles.
- *Education*: of both the household head and individual household members, disaggregated by gender.
- *Gender*: which not only disaggregates poverty by the gender of the household head, but also often looks at the intra-household distribution of assets, work and income.
- *Livelihoods*: poor households often have multiple income sources. Poverty profiles often provide details of the relative importance of different sources and activities.
- *Social capital*: some profiles also examine the extent to which households are connected to a variety of social networks, particularly those that may be able to provide mutual support in times of difficulty.

Table 3.6 features excerpts from poverty profiles for five selected countries. Several common characteristics of the poor emerge: the majority of poor people live in rural areas, often in areas with poor agroclimatic conditions and little access to utilities or services; poor households tend to be larger and have high dependency ratios (high ratios of children and elderly to able-

Table 3.6 Excerpts from poverty assessments for selected countries

Country	Who are the poor?
Indonesia	Mainly rural, but with large regional disparities. The poorest provinces are concentrated in the Outer Islands, but more than half the poor still live in Java.
	Pro-poor social spending has been responsible for major poverty reduction in the last 20 years; but the rich still benefit more than the poor from such services.
	Large-scale household surveys play a useful role in providing the necessary information for action against poverty.
Georgia	The poor are those who are unable to work (the inactive, elderly or disabled) or who do not have work (the unemployed).
	The employment status of the household head is the strongest correlate of long-term poverty.
	Urban poverty is more widespread, deeper and more severe than rural poverty.
	Poverty is very concentrated in some regions.
Peru	Poverty is particularly high among the indigenous population.
	The poor are found largely among two occupational groups: the self-employed and private sector workers.
	The typical poor person lives in a larger household than a typical non-poor person.
	Each worker in a poor household supports four family members while for the non-poor, the equivalent number is three.
	The informal sector is one of the main sources of income for the poor.
India	Poverty is mainly rural: 77% of India's poor live in rural areas, a total of 240 million people.
	Gender, literacy, land ownership, employment status, and caste are all closely associated with poverty.
	A 1994 survey showed that 68% of landless wage earners were poor; 51% of members of scheduled castes and scheduled tribes, and 45% of households where no one was literate.
	Where poverty is deepest, female literacy is exceptionally low.
	Poverty and the poor's access to social services vary considerably from state to state as well as within states.
	Tuberculosis alone kills 500,000 people a year. Half of all children under five are malnourished.
Zimbabwe	The overwhelming majority of Zimbabwe's poor live in semi-arid communal and resettlement areas.
	Poverty is more common in rural areas than in urban areas, with 88% of Zimbabwe's poor living in rural areas.
	Communal farming areas have 76% of the poor and 82% of the very poor in Zimbabwe.
	Poverty is most common and deepest in the low rainfall areas. Current communal farming practices in these areas are environmentally unsustainable. Drought and low assets make the poor particularly susceptible to food insecurity.
	The poor typically have limited access to good land and are heavily dependent on farming for their income as they receive little off-farm income and few remittances.
	The poor are typically less well educated, live in larger households and, in urban areas, are more likely to be unemployed.

Sources: Adapted from various 'Poverty Assessments Summaries', the World Bank , http://www.world
bank.org.

bodied adults); the members of poor households are often poorly educated; and poverty is strongly associated with unemployment and illness.

But there are also striking differences between the characteristics of the poor in different countries. For example, although poverty is predominantly rural, some countries have very high levels of urban poverty: Argentina's highly urbanized society makes urban poverty a particular concern, while urban poverty is more widespread, deeper and more severe than rural poverty in Georgia. Poverty is strongly associated with particular ethnic or caste groups in Bulgaria, India and Peru while in other countries, ethnic and caste distinctions are much less important. The household head being female is strongly associated with poverty in Bulgaria, Ghana, India, Russia and Uganda, but not in Nicaragua, the Philippines, Sri Lanka or Thailand, (see also Glewwe and Hall, 1998, and Quisumbing and Maluccio, 2000, on this controversial point). The elderly are particularly vulnerable in Algeria, rural Argentina, Bulgaria and Georgia, but not in the Philippines, Poland or Russia.

Also notable is the substantial difference in the sources of income of the poor. Smallholder agriculture remains the main income source for the poor in many African countries (although rural non-farm labour markets are also important – see Reardon, 1997). In contrast, agricultural labour markets are of critical importance in South Asia because of the large number of landless poor. In many countries in Eastern Europe and Central Asia, the most important income source is formal sector wage employment with the result that unemployment is the key proximate cause of poverty. But in other regions, self-employment, often in the informal sector, is a key income source for the poor in urban areas.

3.5 What causes poverty?

The previous section described the characteristics of the poor, highlighting the heterogeneity of these characteristics across different countries based on poverty profiles. But while understanding such characteristics is essential, poverty profiles suffer from the major limitation that they only describe the things that are associated with poverty rather than the causes of poverty. For example, poverty profiles typically find that rural households are poorer than urban ones, but this clearly does not mean that forced migration to urban areas will improve poverty.

The causes of poverty in any society lie not only with the characteristics of the poor, but with the social, economic and political processes and institutions that translate such characteristics into higher levels of poverty for different groups. There are myriad causes of poverty and numerous attempts have been made to provide a description of these causes.[15] But before moving on in the next chapter to outline a theoretical framework linking trade liberalization and poverty, it may be useful to illustrate some of the ways in which the different types of characteristics outlined above can interact with public policy and social institutions to cause poverty. Many of these processes have little or nothing to do with trade liberalization. But any

Figure 3.2 Income generation framework including vulnerability to shocks

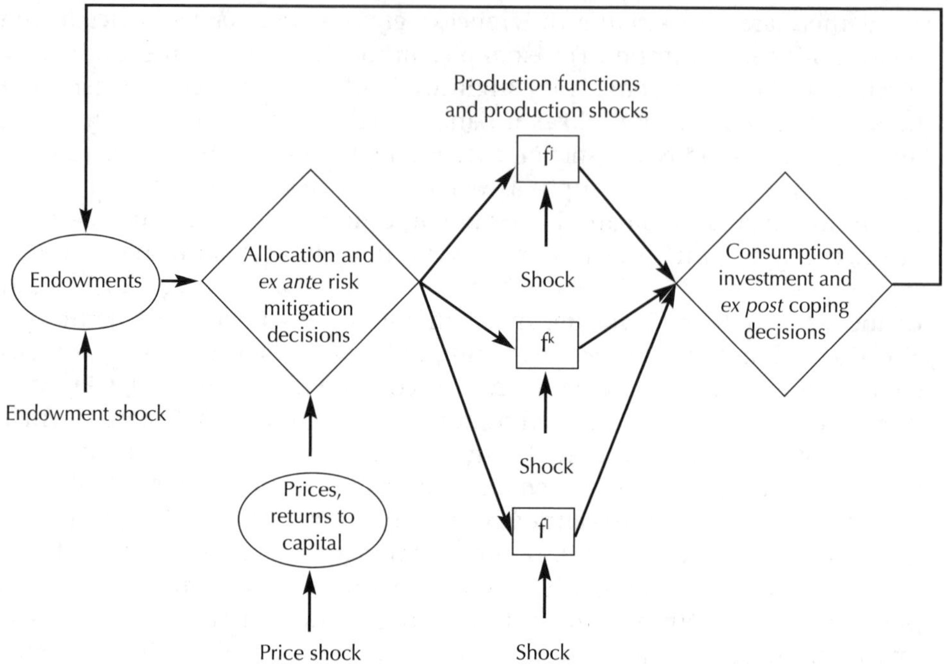

analysis of the impact of trade liberalization on poverty must take account of how the shocks induced by trade liberalization fit into a more general picture of the processes causing and perpetuating poverty in any country.

Figure 3.2 shows a framework for income generation that takes into account the variety of different characteristics and asset endowments households may have, as well as the range of positive and negative shocks they may experience. Households start with a set of endowments of different types of assets or capital (physical, natural, human, financial and social, as described above). In addition, the household will have a particular demographic structure (that is, the number of people of different ages and sexes) and each individual will have a given health status and a certain educational level. These characteristics may be considered as separate from the assets held by the household, or as part of its human capital in its broadest sense.

The framework explicitly recognizes the importance of shocks to endowments. These can take many forms, such as illness or death of household members, theft or loss of assets, etc. Similarly, households may be subject to price shocks that affect the returns they are likely to receive to their activities.

On the basis of these endowments and the activities open to them, households make decisions about how their endowments should be allocated among different income-earning opportunities. In doing so, they take into account both their knowledge about the prices of outputs and likely returns to their assets, as well as their knowledge of the sorts of shocks that may occur to wages or the prices of the products they sell. They may therefore invest some resources in *ex ante* risk mitigation; for example, planting robust but less high-yielding types of seed, fostering a child out to relatives in case their son or daughter fails to get a job in city, etc.

After making such decisions, they then undertake the chosen activities. Each of these activities is subject to potential production shocks – weather-related shocks to agriculture, the shock of unemployment, etc. After the activities have yielded their resulting income, households make decisions about consumption, saving and investment. These decisions are influenced both by the level of success in income generation, as well as by any shocks that may have occurred to the prices or availability of the goods they consume. If unanticipated shocks have occurred (both positive and negative), they decide how best to cope with the resulting situation through the coping mechanisms described above. This may result in a running down of their endowments in order to preserve current consumption in the face of negative shocks. Alternatively, there may be additional income remaining to invest in building up endowments, either through physical investment or investment in the human capital of the household. Thus, the household starts with a new (better or worse) set of endowments for the next cycle.

One element seemingly missing from the framework in Figure 3.2 is the role of policies and institutions. The reason this is not included is because the effect of policies and institutions pervades every aspect of the process. For example, the availability of good-quality health and educational services will have a direct bearing on the household's endowments; pricing policies will often determine the producer prices faced by households, while the availability of insurance mechanisms will influence households' decisions about risk mitigation. Government policies on technology, for example, through agricultural extension, will influence the technological options open to households, while financial policies and institutions will determine savings and investment decisions and the coping strategies adopted.

It should be remembered that the shocks illustrated in Figure 3.2 can take place at any time in the cycle; their position is only intended to illustrate their role conceptually. What is more, economists will typically think of the cycle length as that of a productive cycle (typically, but not necessarily, a year in the case of agriculture). But in reality, allocation, risk mitigation, consumption, investment and coping decisions are taken virtually on a daily basis. Thus, the different elements in the framework should be considered as occurring continuously in parallel rather than necessarily in a left-to-right sequence.

3.5.1 The interaction of endowments and shocks

Having outlined the framework, we can explore how the endowments and characteristics of households might interact with public policy to create or reduce poverty. Specifically, we consider six types of characteristics:

Location
Poverty profiles consistently reveal that remote households tend to be poorer than households near centres of economic activity. In one sense, this

is obvious: the costs of transport ensure that goods produced near economic centres will obtain higher prices than identical goods from further afield (and conversely, that goods purchased near centres of production are likely to be cheaper than those in remoter areas). Similarly, access to labour markets and flows of key economic information are likely to be richer near economic centres. Location therefore influences the ability of households to respond to shocks.

But remoteness may also insulate households from such shocks, while at the same time concentrating the shocks that do occur because of the lack of economic linkages with other areas. The transmission of shocks is critically determined by public policy. In particular, the provision of transport infrastructure will influence the extent to which external shocks are transmitted into remoter areas and the probability of local shocks, such as harvest failure, being transmitted to other areas.

Household demographic structure
The demographic structure of the household can have a key influence on the ability of households to respond to shocks. Households with high dependency ratios are consistently found to be poorer. One reason for this is that they are less able to take advantage of positive shocks. For example, able-bodied members of such households may not be able to take on better-paid work because of their commitments to care for children or elderly relatives.

Furthermore, demographic characteristics can interact with policy and market failures to generate poverty. For example, smallholder agriculture in many developing countries depends critically on family labour because of seasonality and failures in local labour markets. If households lack able-bodied labour at key times of the year, then they may be unable to increase output to benefit from a price increase. Public policy can play an important role here by ensuring that regulation of the labour market is appropriate and, for example, that the school year makes allowance for the need for family labour for key tasks during the year.

Similarly, demographic structure changes over the life cycle. Households are considerably more vulnerable at some points in this life cycle than at others. For example, poverty often increases after major structural shifts in a household such as the birth of a child, the departure of children to establish new households or the death of a key member of the household. Again, public policy may attempt to reduce such vulnerability, perhaps through special assistance for the elderly or free primary health care for pregnant mothers. The existence of appropriate policies in this area may boost the willingness of poor households to invest as a consequence of a positive shock (and may help to cushion the impact of a negative shock).

Gender
Gender discrimination is widespread throughout the world. Such discrimination acts as a constraint, preventing households from adopting strategies that might otherwise be to their benefit. For example, gender bias in schooling may deprive able girls from a higher subsequent standard of

living, with knock-on effects on the livelihoods of their families. Similarly, gender biases in labour markets, either through the assignment or prohibition of women from undertaking certain tasks, can prevent households from maximizing the opportunities resulting from changes in the demand for labour.

An understanding of the gender biases in any given society can therefore be essential for an accurate estimation of the impact of a trade liberalization on the poor. For example, if a trade liberalization increases the price of a crop produced by poor households, a generally positive outcome might be expected. But if social norms dictate that this crop is grown by women and that they are also responsible for all household maintenance tasks, then the supply response may be limited and at the cost of reducing the time available for child care.

Equally, if a liberalization benefits a 'male' crop, the increase in income may not be channelled towards goods likely to improve overall household welfare. Once again, policy can play an important role in determining the impact on poverty of an external shock. If policies reinforce existing norms, then the benefits of a potentially positive liberalization may be negated. Alternatively, public policy may seek to change norms and practices by enforcing laws against discrimination (including caste and ethnicity as well as gender), in which case the impact of the shock on poverty might be positive.

Health status
Poor health status is clearly a correlate of poverty, and again, it might be expected that households in which key productive members suffer from illness or disability are less able to respond to trade-induced shocks. But policies to reduce and mitigate risk are of critical importance here. The poor are extremely vulnerable to illness, both in the sense that their work environments make them more susceptible and also in the sense that illness has a greater impact on poor households. Consequently, the presence (or absence) of effective means of reducing the risk of illness can play an important role in household responses to policy shocks. Preventative health care can reduce the incidence of illness, while widely accessible and cheap primary health care can substantially reduce the risks faced by households. This can release resources formerly devoted to mitigating such risks and enable poor households to undertake potentially rewarding investments.

Note, however, that some forms of risk management, while useful and effective in some contexts, are explicitly biased against those with poor health status, notably food- and cash-for-work schemes. Thus, if a trade shock is known to have detrimental effects on a particular population, public policy must look further than purely work-based forms of social safety net.

Education
Low educational attainment is a key cause of poverty; at the same time, education is one of the most important routes out of poverty. Better education improves the likelihood of higher paid work and improves productivity and the absorption of new ideas. Furthermore, the provision of

accessible and reasonable-quality education is an essential component of ensuring that the poor can respond effectively to shocks.

One key issue here is the impact of a shock on the demand for child labour. If a trade shock gives rise to an increase in the demand for child labour (either because more labour is needed to exploit a new opportunity or because more is needed to compensate for a reduction in wages), then this may reduce long-term educational attainment and help to perpetuate poverty (de Janvry et al., 1992, describe precisely such a situation in Morocco – see Chapter 5). Thus, a trade liberalization may need to be complemented by incentives to ensure that children stay in school.

Assets

It is not surprising that poverty profiles show that the poor have few assets; indeed, a lack of assets is often a definition of poverty. But this fact has important knock-on effects on the poor's ability to respond to shocks. In particular, moral hazard typically means that poor households have difficulty in obtaining credit, since they are unable to put up substantial assets by way of collateral. This in turn reduces their ability to invest in response to new opportunities or to protect themselves from future vulnerability. Targeted micro-credit schemes may have a role here to ensure better access to financial services among the poor. In addition, redistribution of land can be effective at jump-starting a supply response and facilitating investment (see Putzel, 1998). Consequently, the long-term impact of trade liberalization on the poor may depend on the extent to which such reforms are complemented by public provision and (careful) redistribution of assets to the poor.

In conclusion, the precise causes of poverty depend not only on the characteristics of the poor in each country, but also on their interaction with many different elements of public policy. The shocks induced by trade liberalization are just one of the many shocks faced by households. So there is no 'direct' link between trade and poverty. Rather, trade liberalization affects prices, which in turn affect incomes. But the causes of poverty outlined above also influence the way in which trade liberalization affects poverty, because they affect the ability of households to respond to the price changes induced by trade liberalization. Therefore, the long-term impact of trade liberalization on poverty will depend on the success of measures to tackle the root causes of poverty, while the short-term impact will depend on the mechanisms available to protect the poor from any negative transitional shocks. To go further, we need a clearer conceptual framework specifically linking shocks from trade liberalization to poverty. This is developed in the next chapter.

Summary

- Traditionally, economists have defined poverty as having an income or level of consumption below a minimally acceptable level.
- But poverty is increasingly regarded as a broader concept relating to deprivation in such dimensions as assets, education, health, powerlessness, discrimination, vulnerability, as well as income and consumption.
- Household survey-based measures of income poverty can provide nationally representative estimates of poverty and, if surveys are repeated, enable comparisons of poverty over time.
- But the difficulties in capturing the non-income dimensions of poverty have lead to an expansion in the use of participatory methods of poverty assessment. These methods emphasize the active involvement of the poor themselves in defining the concepts of poverty that are relevant to them.
- Estimates of the proportion of the population living on less than US$1 per day (the poverty headcount index) show that poverty increased in sub-Saharan Africa in the late 1980s and early 1990s but fell thereafter. But poverty in East Asia and the Pacific saw a steady decline until the Asian crisis of 1997–8. Although the poverty headcount in South Asia has been falling, the absolute number of poor people has risen, with 43.5% of the world's poor living in South Asia.
- International comparisons of social indicators show wide variations. Considerable progress has been made towards the achievement of the International Development Targets, but some regions are still unlikely to achieve the goals set.
- Poverty profiles and poverty assessments characterize poor groups according to a range of variables including location, demography, education, gender, livelihoods and social capital. While there are many similarities, it is unwise to generalize about the characteristics of the poor across countries.
- Poverty has many causes including:

  - Poor endowments or access to physical, natural, human, financial and social capital, either chronically or arising from negative shocks such as illness or death of household members, theft or loss of assets and natural disasters.
  - Negative shocks to the productive activities of the poor, for example, harvest failure or redundancy.
  - Negative shocks to the prices faced by households, both for the goods and services purchased and for those produced.
  - An inability to insure against the risks faced or a lack of mechanisms to cope with the shocks when they do occur.

continued

Summary box continued

- A household's location and demographic structure and the gender, health status, education and assets of its members have a strong influence on the ability of the household to respond to shocks, both positive and negative.

Notes

1 See Brandolini and D'Alessio (2000) for an attempt to implement Sen's framework by doing precisely this.

2 Note that the term 'financial assets' in this context goes beyond its usual economic use to include issues of access to credit.

3 This section draws on World Bank (2001).

4 Of course, households may also take these actions in anticipation of a negative shock, in which case this is a form of insurance.

5 Again, households may undertake 'precautionary' saving in order to be able to have savings to run down during difficult times.

6 There is a large literature on insurance and consumption smoothing in developing countries – see Besley (1995), Morduch (1995) and Townsend (1995) for reviews.

7 This section draws heavily on Chapter 4, Assessing Poverty, in IDS et al (2000).

8 This said, the problems associated with collecting accurate measures of other dimensions of poverty, such as powerlessness, are also immense, which is one of the reasons why income and consumption measures are so common.

9 This issue is closely related to the debate described above over whether poverty should be understood in terms of an individual's *entitlements*, or their *capabilities* and *functionings* – see Sen (1981) and Sen and Dreze (1989) for a comprehensive discussion of these concepts and their relation to poverty.

10 This is distinct from the important topic of understanding why static measures of poverty change over time, that is, why some households or individuals are chronically poor while others are only transitorily poor. Baulch and Hoddinott (2000) review this issue; the policy implications are discussed in Chapter 7.

11 See Narayan et al. (2000) for an overview of poverty as experienced and described by the poor themselves.

12 Although there is a very large literature on this: Wood (1994) provides a comprehensive treatment; see Burtless (1995) for a review.

13 See Hanmer and Naschold (1999) for an evaluation of progress towards the targets.

14 The World Bank's Poverty Monitoring Database contains many of these. It can be accessed at: http://www.worldbank.org/

15 IDS et al (2000) provides an excellent introduction to the issues. The latest World Development Report (World Bank, 2001) provides a more comprehensive analysis. Also, see White et al. (1999) for the causes of poverty in sub-Saharan Africa.

4 Linking Trade Liberalization and Poverty: A Conceptual Framework

> ***This chapter*** provides an analytical framework for understanding the linkages between trade liberalization and poverty at the household level. In particular, it describes how trade liberalization can affect poverty through:
>
> - The transmission of prices from the border down to the household.
> - Its effects on profits, wages and employment.
> - Its effects on government revenue and pro-poor expenditure.
> - Its effects on the riskiness of households' livelihoods.

If trade liberalization and poverty were both easily measured, and if there were many historical instances in which liberalization could be identified as the main economic shock, it would be easy to understand the relationship between the two. Unfortunately, this is far from the case. For example, the fact that trade liberalization in East Asia was associated with great strides in alleviating poverty is not sufficient to show that it caused those strides; too much else was going on. Similarly, the mixed evidence that liberalization has accompanied increasing poverty in Latin America since 1980 is not sufficient to prove the opposite. This means that the only way to uncover the true impact of trade liberalization on poverty is to examine the fragments of evidence from a wide variety of different contexts.

One way of trying to discern the overall effect of trade liberalization on poverty is to analyse measures of openness and poverty over time for a broad cross-section of countries to see if increased openness reduces or increases poverty. This approach, which was described in Chapter 2, provides useful information about correlations between openness and poverty, but it also has serious problems because of the difficulty in designing good indicators of policy: the precise measures of 'openness' matter. Furthermore, the results of such analysis tend to be too general in their conclusions to guide practical policy-making.

In this chapter, we argue that the implications of liberalization for poverty are case-specific and that identifying the effects requires a detailed understanding of the pathways or channels through which such influence may occur. Hence, we devote most of this Handbook to an alternative approach, which develops a conceptual framework for identifying and understanding the channels through which trade liberalization might affect poverty. In other words, in the absence of clear empirical regularities, we have to appeal to theory about how trade shocks might translate into poverty.

This approach has a number of advantages. It allows us to:

- bring to bear our knowledge about the way economies work in order to assess how plausible the various theoretical links between trade liberalization and poverty are;
- identify places in which it would be sensible to seek empirical evidence about the connections between trade and poverty;
- start to fit the fragments of evidence into a single overall picture; and
- think through the policy issues involved in managing and responding to the poverty effects of liberalization.

It will be obvious from the discussion so far that tracing the links between trade liberalization and poverty is detailed and generally very case-specific work. There are no answers of the sort: 'liberalization of type A will have poverty effects of type B'. Instead, the answers will depend on such issues as why people are poor to start with, what the trade reform entails, whether the country is well-endowed with mineral wealth and what sort of infrastructure exists. The rest of this chapter puts together the conceptual framework to allow us to examine these factors. It is based substantially on Winters (2000b, c, e) from which further details can be obtained.

We explore the static effects of trade and trade liberalization on poverty via four broad groups of institutions, as shown in Figure 4.1.

The first section of this chapter looks at how to characterize individual and household welfare and the components of these that are likely to be influenced by trade liberalization. The next section explores how the

Figure 4.1 The analytical scheme

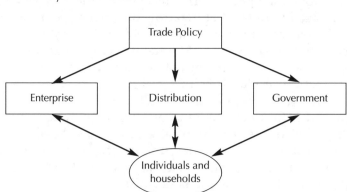

distribution system in a country affects the transmission of prices down to the household level. Then we examine how trade liberalization affects enterprises and hence households via profits, wages and employment. The following section focuses on the impact of trade liberalization on government revenues and expenditures and how these might affect households, while the penultimate section discusses how trade liberalization may affect households' vulnerability to shocks.

It should be noted that two key ways in which trade liberalization affects poverty are not addressed within our framework. These are:

- economic growth; and
- short-term adjustment costs.

Potentially the most important effect of trade liberalization on poverty is through its impact on growth, which was discussed at some length in Chapter 2 and to which we return briefly at the end of this chapter. Furthermore, the reason why trade liberalization generates so much public controversy is often due to the short- and medium-term adjustment costs, most notably job losses in formerly protected sectors. These are addressed in Chapter 7, which explores more practical issues of trade policy reform.

The reason why these issues are not described here is straightforward. Much of the public debate on the linkages between trade liberalization and poverty has become unclear precisely because of the confusion of dynamic issues of growth and adjustment with the important, but perhaps less dramatic, channels through which trade liberalization can affect the lives of the poor.

4.1 The individual and the household

4.1.1 A basic view of the household

Poverty is not an abstract concept – it affects real individuals and real households. Consequently, the most appropriate place to start our analysis is to describe the household. There are, of course, numerous different types of household and it would be quite impossible to analyse in detail the impact of a trade liberalization on each and every one. That is why we need a 'characterization' of the household, that is, a set of features and factors that are likely to determine how the household is affected by economic shocks of one kind or another.

One such characterization is provided by Singh et al. (1986), who describe what economists now refer to as the 'farm household'. This is not to be taken literally as referring only to people who work the land or the seas, but to any household that has to make decisions about how much to produce, as well as how much to consume and how many hours to work.

Note that many households, particularly in developed countries, are not 'farm households' in this sense. For example, government civil servants whose only activities are to work for their salaries do not need to make decisions about 'production': they simply receive their pay and then decide how to spend it. Farmers, in contrast, need to make decisions about what crops to plant, what inputs to use and when to sell; and these production decisions affect their incomes and hence their consumption. Similarly, informal sector workers selling goods by the side of the road have to make decisions about how many goods to purchase for sale, and how, when and where to sell them. These are also production decisions and will have a direct impact on the ability of those workers' households to consume the goods they desire.

By focusing on households, we are consciously setting aside gender and intergenerational issues, but we will return to these very shortly.

If we adopt this simple 'farm household' model, then we can think of household welfare as depending on income and the prices of all goods and services that the household faces. The former must be measured as what is known as 'full income', which comprises:

- the value of the household's full complement of time – the maximum amount of time that could be spent working, perhaps 12 hours per person per day – valued at the prevailing wage rate;
- transfers and other non-earned income, such as remittances from family members outside the household, official transfers, goods and services in kind, and benefits from common resources; and
- the profits from household production.

This view defines all the variables that need to be assessed in order to calculate the effects of a trade policy shock on income or consumption poverty.

How then will trade liberalization affect such a household? The direct effect of a trade liberalization will be to change prices. The effect of a single small price change on household welfare therefore depends on whether the household is a net supplier or net demander of the good or service in question. A price rise for something you sell makes you better off; a price rise for something you buy makes you worse off. More precisely, the effect of a small price change on household welfare is proportional to the ratio of its net supply position to its total expenditure.

Of course, the household's responses to the price change may also influence the size of the welfare effect. But unless their response changes them from being a net seller to a net buyer (or *vice versa*), their response will not change the sign of the welfare change. Thus, if the household has alternatives to purchasing a good whose price has risen, it can mitigate the cost of a price rise. Similarly, if it is able to switch to an activity that has become more profitable, it can increase its gains. Conversely, an adverse shock may entail large losses of welfare if no alternative goods or activities exist, or relatively small losses if they do.

Household responsiveness is particularly important when considering the vulnerability aspects of poverty. Policies that reduce households' ability to adjust to or cope with negative shocks could have major implications for the translation of trade shocks into actual poverty. Moreover, fear of the consequences of not being able to cope with negative shocks might induce households to rule out activities that would raise their average income significantly but run greater risks of very low income. Responsiveness is also important because it spreads shocks from the market in which the price change occurred, to other markets, whose prices might not have been affected by trade policy at all. All these factors are considered below.

4.1.2 Generalizing the basic view of the household

The simple view of the household described above is very useful for getting our thoughts in order, but it is not very realistic. Thus, we should consider a number of potential generalizations before seeking to apply it in practice:

- First, households can provide several forms of labour (for example, skilled and unskilled), so we need to consider their endowments of these and the different wages they command.
- Second, working on and off the 'farm' may not be perfect substitutes for household members (perhaps because off-farm working involves costly travel), and the 'farm' may prefer family to non-family labour (perhaps because non-family labour needs to be monitored). Thus, the (implicit) 'wage' paid to family members may be different from the wage paid to those outside the family even if they are doing the same task.
- Third, we need to incorporate some assumptions about how households allocate their time across the many different activities in which they are involved. Poor households typically earn income in a wide variety of different ways, and the mix of these may change significantly with changes in trade policy.
- Fourth, some activities – or sales or purchases – may be 'quantity-constrained'. Most obviously, some jobs (outside the 'farm') may only be available for a fixed number of hours per day. Thus, if trade policy creates employment or generates unemployment, it could have highly significant poverty effects if it involves dramatic changes in the amount of time that individuals work. For example, the amount of time might change from nothing to a full day's work or *vice versa*.
- Finally, the set of factors of production owned by a household, and their associated returns, needs to be generalized to include not only labour but also land and other assets. For example, trade liberalization might affect the rate of return to land as well as that to labour.

4.1.3 Distribution within the household

Another key extension of the approach above is to recognize the importance of intra-household distribution. It is frequently argued that the costs of poverty fall disproportionately on women, children and the elderly. Thus, although it may be useful to analyse the impact of trade liberalization on households, it is also important to consider the distribution of welfare within the household.

But the distribution of welfare among household members is not independent of the means by which welfare is generated. For example, many traditional societies make a distinction between 'male' and 'female' crops or activities. Thus, an increase or decrease in the price of, say, a female crop may have different effects on different members of the household. Whether this actually happens depends on whether there are transfers within the household to compensate individuals who bear the brunt of adverse shocks. Sometimes, such transfers may not occur, for example, if the subsistence needs of other household members make them unwilling to make transfers or if cultural factors make it difficult for transfers to occur.

Even if income is pooled in the household, economic shocks can have different effects on different members of the household if there are constraints on the types of activity that members are willing to undertake. For example, falling male wages and/or employment can reduce female welfare because women may be obliged to increase their work outside the home, but receive little compensatory help with their traditional in-home activities. The same effects could arise if the price of female labour rose, for example, because of improved export prospects for clothing. If pressure on female labour for cash crops reduces women's input to the family food crops, nutritional standards could also suffer: fieldwork described in Oxfam-IDS (1999) finds some evidence of these kinds of problems in Southern Province, Zambia; see Winters (2000b) for a brief account.[1]

Clearly, these sorts of effects will be very case-specific. But in the absence of general approaches to treating them, policy-makers should be conscious of the need to explore these issues where it is plausible that they will be significant.

4.1.4 Adjusting to trade shocks

As observed above, the size of the income change that a household experiences following a shock to the economy depends in part on its ability to adjust to the new set of prices (and incentives more generally).[2] And this in turn depends on a number of factors, some of which can be influenced by complementary policies by the government. (See Chapter 7 for more on complementary policies.) Among the factors influencing a household's flexibility in response to a trade liberalization may be:

Assets

- Are there *physical assets* available to enable the poor to take advantage of new opportunities from liberalization? For example, improvements in the transport and communications infrastructure can have a dramatic impact on the ability of the poor to gain from liberalization.
- Do the poor have access to the *natural assets* they need to exploit new opportunities? In particular, the distribution of land can be a key factor in determining the impact of liberalization on the poor.
- Are there means of *financial intermediation* available to the poor? In particular, is it possible for the poor to obtain credit for agricultural and non-agricultural productive enterprises?
- Do the poor have the *human capital* required for new tasks and can they acquire it? This refers not only to the availability of reasonable-quality

educational opportunities, but also to explicit improvements in knowledge generated, say, through better agricultural extension services.
- Do the poor have the *human resources* to switch to more profitable activities? The age, gender and health profile of the household may place important constraints on the nature of activities that can be undertaken, for example, if an able-bodied adult cannot undertake a new activity because of the need to care for an elderly or chronically sick relative.

Institutions

- Are there *social barriers* that will prevent the poor from realizing the benefits of liberalization? In particular, are there constraints on the activities that can be done based on gender, ethnicity or other criteria?
- Do *restrictions* on enterprise prevent the creation of new businesses or the contraction of declining ones?
- Are there *markets* for key goods and services? In particular, some reforms may remove institutions that provide a market function without ensuring that the role they played is replaced by others, for example, the market for fertilizer and credit after agricultural market reforms.
- Are there reliable sources of *information* about prices and market opportunities? Increasingly, informational failures are being recognized as a key constraint that the poor face. With little or no access to reliable information, poor households are likely to be extremely averse to taking actions to exploit opportunities when they cannot be sure that such opportunities are real. Ways of improving flows of information include facilitating the creation of local co-operative or business associations and supporting the development of the local media, particularly radio.
- The extent of *labour mobility* and the nature of labour market institutions may also influence the ability of households to take advantage of new opportunities. For example, policies that prevent individuals from moving to areas that are benefiting from trade liberalization can hamper the spread of these gains to poorer areas and households.

Processes

- Do key market institutions allow full *participation* of poor households? In some instances, institutions may provide little or no access to the poor or access may be conditional. For example, in rural Kenya, cash crop production generally improves a household's access to inputs distributed through the cash crop marketing firm.
- Are the poor involved in *discussion* about (and the formulation of) agricultural policy? Such involvement means that they can help to ensure that reforms are likely to achieve their aims and that the necessary complementary policies are put in place to enable them to do so.

4.2 Price transmission

We now consider how price changes induced by trade liberalization get transmitted down to households. This occurs directly through the distribution sector, but price changes may also be amplified or reduced due to the 'domain' of trade. We consider each in turn.

4.2.1 Direct effects through the distribution sector

We start by considering a change in the tariff facing a single good. Figure 4.2, adapted from Winters (2000a), summarizes the way in which such shocks might work through to the variables determining household welfare in a target country. The elements concerning distribution lie in the middle of the figure, where we trace the transmission of price shocks from world prices through to final consumers (in the rectangles), and briefly describe the factors influencing the extent to which shocks at one stage are passed through to the next.

Consider the transmission of price shocks in pure accounting terms. For an import, the world price of a good, the tariff it faces and the exchange rate combine to define the post-tariff border price. Once inside the country, the good faces domestic taxes, distribution from the port to major distribution centres, various regulations that may add costs or control its price, and the possibility of compulsory procurement by the authorities. We refer loosely to the resulting price as the wholesale price.

From the distribution centre, the good is sent out to more local distribution points, and potentially faces more taxes and regulations. Additionally at this point, co-operatives or other labour-managed enterprises may be involved. (It is useful to distinguish these because their behaviour in the face of shocks could be significantly different from that of commercial firms.) We term the resulting price the retail price, although of course, market institutions may well bear little resemblance to retail outlets in developed countries.

Finally, from the retail point, goods are distributed to households and individuals. Again, co-operatives may be involved, plus, of course, inputs from the household itself. More significantly, the translation of price signals into economic welfare depends on the household's characteristics – its endowments of time, skills, land, etc. – as well as technology and random shocks like the weather. The last two are important conceptually, because anything that increases the household's productive ability permits it to generate greater welfare at any given set of prices.

Exactly the same pathway applies (in reverse) for export goods, starting at the bottom of Figure 4.2. An export good is produced, put into local marketing channels, aggregated into national supply of the good and finally sold abroad. At each stage, the institutions involved incur costs and add mark-ups, all of which enter the final price. If the export price of the good is given by the prevailing price on world markets, all such additions come off the farm-gate price that determines household welfare.

Figure 4.2 Trade policy and poverty – causal connections

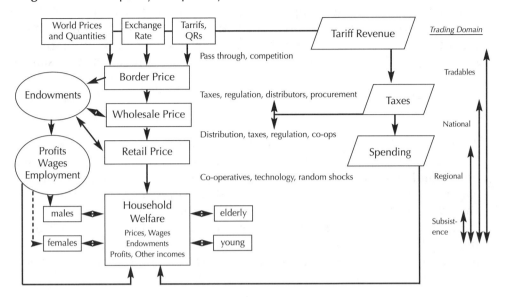

In determining the effects of world price or trade policy shocks on poor households, it is vital to have a clear picture of these transmission channels and the behaviour of the agents and institutions they comprise For example, sole buyers of export crops (that is, those to whom sellers have no alternative but to sell) will respond differently to price shocks than will producers' marketing co-operatives. Regulations that fix market prices by fiat or compensatory stockpiling can completely block the transmission of shocks to the household level.[3] Even more important, all these various links must actually exist. First, if infrastructure is so weak that it is prohibitively expensive to increase trade flows, price transmission will be attenuated or completely blocked. Second, if a trade liberalization itself – or, more likely, the changes in domestic marketing arrangements that accompany it – leads to the disappearance of market institutions, households can become completely isolated from the market and suffer substantial income losses. This is most obvious in the case of markets on which to sell cash crops, but can also afflict purchased inputs and credit. If official marketing boards provide credit for inputs against future outputs, whereas post-liberalization private agents do not, no increase in output prices will benefit farmers unless alternative borrowing arrangements can be made.

The importance of transmission mechanisms is well illustrated by the contrasting experience of markets in Zambia and Zimbabwe during the 1990s (see Oxfam-IDS, 1999). In Zambia, the government abolished the official purchasing monopsony for maize and the activity became dominated by two private firms, which possibly colluded to keep prices low and abandoned purchasing altogether in remote areas. Even if the latter was justified economically in the aggregate, it still left remote farmers with a huge problem. This was exacerbated by the difficulties of their re-entering subsistence agriculture, given that the necessary seed stocks and practical knowledge had declined strongly during the (subsidized) cash crop period.

In Zimbabwe, by contrast, when the cotton industry was privatized, three private buyers for cotton emerged, including one owned by the farmers. Here, the abolition of the government sole purchasing requirement resulted in increased competition and prices, and farm incomes rose appreciably.

This discussion provides two key lessons about the impact of liberalization:

The effects of liberalization depend on where you start
If an import ban plus government monopoly subsidizes remote farmers, the 'first-round' effects of liberalization will be to hurt those groups.[4] Similarly, Harrison and Hanson (1999b) suggest that Mexico's trade liberalization in the 1980s did not boost the wages of unskilled workers as many had expected precisely because its initial pattern of protection was designed to protect that group. In short, the analysis of the poverty effects of trade liberalization can be no more general than is the pattern of trade restrictions across countries.

If many goods are liberalized at once, the net effect can be quite complex
Usually many goods are liberalized at once, so that the effects on individual households will be the sums of many individual shocks. When some of the goods affected are inputs into the production of others, the net effect is quite complex and it is important to consider the balance of forces. For example, Zambian liberalization raised the selling price of maize in the 1990s, but even where purchasing arrangements continued, input prices rose by more as subsidized deliveries were abolished. As a result, maize farming generated lower returns and output fell (see Oxfam-IDS, 1999).

4.2.2 Indirect effects and the domain of trade

As discussed above, the overall welfare effect of a shock will depend on the household's ability to adjust, switching consumption away from and production towards goods whose price has risen. But the act of substituting one good or activity for another necessarily transmits the shock to other markets that may not have been directly affected by a trade reform. Thus, it sets off a whole series of 'second-round' effects, which may be an important part of the overall impact of the reform.

A critical consideration in assessing these second-round effects is the *domain* over which the second-round goods or services are traded. This is because the domain of trade defines the number of people and institutions whose behaviour will be altered as these markets adjust to the shock. The trading domains are illustrated on the far right of Figure 4.2. Let us consider the nature of these second-round effects at different levels between the border and the household level.

The border price of a good that is traded internationally will be largely, if not entirely, determined by the world price. Hence, putting aside any changes in the various margins identified above, the prices of such goods will not change further as the market responds to a shock. In other words, there will be no second-round price effects because, in effect, with a world market, all producers and consumers in the world will adjust their behaviour a tiny amount to absorb the changes in any given country.

At the other extreme, if things are traded only locally, the trading domain is small. With few market participants to absorb the second-round adjustments, prices will need to adjust significantly. But this will also mean that the impact will be narrowly focused geographically. For example, increases in farmers' incomes are often believed to have big 'spillovers' to employment-intensive local activities such as construction, personal servants and simple manufactures (see Timmer, 1997; Delgado at al., 1998; and Mellor and Gavian, 1999). These are precisely the activities in which the poor have a large stake. At levels in between the international and the local – for example, goods that are traded nationally or regionally – the price effects will be smaller but more spread out than they are for local goods.

There are two sets of goods for which explicit prices are not observed, but which nonetheless are important for assessing poverty effects:

Subsistence activities and goods
These, by definition, are not subject to direct trade shocks, but they will still be affected by spillovers from goods that are. It is easiest to think of these spillovers in terms of the ways in which inputs of labour and outputs of subsistence goods are affected by changes in the prices of tradable goods and services. One example of such a spillover would be the case mentioned above where changes in the prices of 'female' crops affect the time allocated to subsistence or traditional in-home activities.

Goods that are just not available
One effect of spillovers is that they may shift a good from being not available to available (or *vice versa*). Increasing the set of goods available may be important for the poor, as Booth et al. (1993) document for consumers in Tanzania, and Gisselquist and Harun-ar-Rashid (1998) show for agricultural inputs in Bangladesh.

4.3 Enterprises: profits, wages and employment

4.3.1 The elements of the enterprise sector

The ellipses on the left of Figure 4.2 describe the link from trade to poverty arising through its effects on enterprises. 'Enterprises' includes any unit that produces and sells output and employs labour from outside its own immediate household. The important distinction from the 'farm' household is that outputs are sold and inputs acquired through market transactions. Hence the link in Figure 4.2 to border, wholesale and retail prices.

Analysis of the enterprise sector requires three elements:

Demand
Demand for the output of home enterprises is determined by income, and export, import and domestic prices, which are affected by the issues considered above. Demand for a good must typically be matched by supply, which stems from the second element – firms.

Firms
Firms are the suppliers of both home and export markets. The total output of firms is determined by the relative prices on home and export markets and the costs that they face. Costs, in turn, depend on factor prices (wages for all sorts of labour, returns to capital, etc.), and on factor input-output coefficients (that is, the inputs necessary per unit of output), which, in turn, depend on technology and again on relative factor prices. In addition, costs may depend on the scale of operations. Given total output and the quantity of each type of factor needed to produce this output, the total demand for each factor can be calculated. This is confronted with total factor supply in the factor markets – the third element.

Factor markets
Factor markets allow the demand for factors to be matched with supply. This is typically done through movements in factor prices, with the result that employment and wages – the two variables of most relevance to poverty – are determined.

Implicit in the above analysis of the enterprise sector is the view that the distribution of assets and skills across households is given and that household welfare depends only on factor rewards and employment opportunities. Of course, in practice the distribution of assets and skills across households does change: asset stocks will increase as a result of economic growth, which may be induced by trade liberalization (see Chapter 2 for a discussion of this). In addition, public expenditure (particularly on education and health) may increase households' assets. Furthermore, governments may redistribute assets among households. While this may be beneficial for growth and poverty reduction (see Chapter 3; and World Bank, 2001, for a review of the evidence on this), it is a separate issue quite independent of trade policy.

Even if the distribution of assets and skills across households is fixed, the employment of factors across sectors is not. Indeed, the movement of factors between sectors plays a crucial role in the poverty effects of trade shocks. There are two diametrically opposite assumptions that can be made about the movement of factors:

- assume fixed total employment but variable wages – the 'trade' approach; and
- assume fixed wages but variable employment – the 'development' approach.

We consider each in turn.

4.3.2 The 'trade' approach

We start with traditional trade theory, in which total factor supplies are given, wages and returns are perfectly flexible and the domestic and foreign varieties of each good are identical. Price changes, including those emanating from trade policy changes, affect the incentives for enterprises to produce particular goods and the technologies they use. The simplest and most elegant analysis of these incentives, the Stolper–Samuelson theorem, generates very powerful results indeed. It proves that under particular conditions, an increase in the price of the good that is labour-intensive in production will increase the real wage and decrease the real returns to capital.[5]

Unfortunately, for all its elegance, Stolper–Samuelson is not sufficient to answer questions of trade and poverty in the real world, and it must be supplemented by more *ad hoc* approaches (see Winters, 2000a, c).

Nonetheless, the basic insight of the Stolper–Samuelson theorem applies very broadly. An increase in the price of any good will increase the incentive to produce it. This will raise the returns to factors of production specific to that good – for example, labour with a specific skill, specialist capital equipment, brand image, etc. – and assuming that some increase in output is feasible, it will also generally affect the returns to non-specific, or mobile, factors. Generally speaking (but not inevitably), if the prices of goods intensive in the use of unskilled labour increase, we would expect unskilled wages to increase. As these industries expand in response to their higher profitability, they absorb factors of production from other sectors. By definition, an unskilled-labour-intensive sector requires more unskilled labour per unit of other factors than do other sectors, and so this shift in the balance of production increases the net demand for unskilled labour and reduces it for other factors. If poor households depend largely on unskilled wage earners, poverty will be alleviated by the resulting wage increase (although, of course, poverty headcount indices[6] will vary only if the wage increase moves households from one side of the poverty line to the other).

It is important to note that the effect arises because the industry using relatively more unskilled labour increases its demand for *all* factors while other industries release all factors. It is the different compositions of these different sectors' preferred bundles of factors that matter, not any shifts within them.

A similar form of analysis concerns technical progress. Increases in the general level of efficiency in an industry will reduce the price of its output and/or increase its profitability. This will increase its level of output and thus generally increase demand for the factors that produce it. Factors specific to that sector will benefit, as will mobile factors that are used intensively in the sector.

Trade liberalization raises the prices of exportable goods (which are likely to use a country's abundant factors intensively) and reduces those of importable goods (which are likely to use scarce factors intensively).[7] Developing countries as a group are clearly abundant in labour, so that freer trade gravitates towards raising their wages in general.

Of course, this result cannot be simply generalized to all developing countries. For example, countries in Latin America have abundant natural resources and much less labour than Asian countries and so would probably not be considered abundant in labour. Similarly, within individual developing countries, the least-skilled workers may not be the most intensively used factor in the production of tradable goods (see Feenstra and Hanson, 1995). For example, the wages of workers with completed primary education may increase with trade liberalization, while those of illiterate workers may be left behind or even fall. One reason why agricultural liberalization is so important is that for this sector, we can be reasonably confident that low-skilled workers in rural areas will benefit.

4.3.3 The 'development' approach

The 'trade' approach is based on the idea that factors are in fixed supply. Consequently, an increase in the demand for a factor increases its wage (real return). The 'development' approach by contrast assumes that one factor – labour – is in perfectly elastic supply, that is, any amount of labour can be obtained at the prevailing wage. If this is the case then the wage will be fixed – for example, by what the factor can earn elsewhere – and the adjustment to a price shock will take place through changes in employment.

Suppose that the formal sector can draw effectively infinite amounts of labour out of subsistence agriculture and employ it at a 'subsistence' wage. If the formal wage is no more than the subsistence wage (as the model strictly implies), poverty will only be alleviated if the loss of labour in subsistence agriculture allows the workers remaining in that sector to increase their 'wage' (the case of successful development).

Alternatively, the formal sector may have a minimum wage, at which lots of people are willing to work. In this case, we can presume that as labour transfers to the formal sector, it earns a higher than subsistence wage and that, as a result, some poverty is alleviated. If trade liberalization raises the price of an exportable output, then employment is likely to increase and poverty will be alleviated. On the other hand, trade reform will reduce the prices obtained by firms producing importable goods. This is likely to reduce employment with adverse consequences for poverty.

In fact, neither of the two extremes given by the 'trade' and 'development' approaches – that is, wholly fixed or wholly flexible labour supply – is likely to be precisely true. An economy with a highly flexible and mobile labour force will conform more closely to the first extreme than to the second, making wage changes of particular importance. Conversely, an economy with many labour market rigidities and a large pool of unemployed workers may justify a focus on the employment effects of liberalization.

Furthermore, labour markets are often segmented, for example, by skill, gender or location, which makes it difficult to substitute one type of labour for another. This means that the 'trade' approach may be a close approximation for some labour markets while the development' approach is more suitable for others. For example, the market for labour with particular skills may be quite tight, with near full employment and easy mobility between sectors, suggesting that shifts in demand will translate into large wage changes. Conversely, the market for unskilled labour may conform more closely to the 'development' approach, with fluctuations in demand accommodated by changes in employment. Hence, in practical assessments of the effects of trade shocks on poverty, determining the elasticity of labour supply and knowing why it is non-zero, is an important task. Box 4.1 gives an example from a real liberalization.

Capital might also be available in infinite supply, for example, from multinational enterprises at the world rate of return. In this case, the inflow of capital into the liberalized sector is likely to boost wages and/or employment, which will increase the welfare benefits and, if they exist, the poverty alleviation benefits, of a trade liberalization. It is important to remember, however, that not all capital inflows are desirable: if they occur in response to market distortions, they may subtract value from the economy rather than add it , what is known as 'immiserizing' growth (see Winters, 1991).[8]

Box 4.1 **Employment and wages before and after liberalization in India**

A possible indicator of the relative importance of the effects described by the 'trade' and 'development' approaches comes from CUTS (1999). Using the years 1987/8–90/1 to reflect pre-liberalization performance and 1991/2–94/5 post-liberalization performance, CUTS finds formal manufacturing sector employment in India growing faster after liberalization, and wages more slowly. Employment grew at 3.8% before liberalization and 9.4% afterwards; wages, by contrast, grew at 8.1% before liberalization and 7.0% afterwards. This suggests that the 'development' approach is more applicable in this context since the expansion of employment would appear to be relatively insensitive to the level of wages.

A more perplexing aspect of the Indian reform of 1991 is that it appears to have been associated with a significant *decline* in employment in informal manufacturing, especially in labour-intensive sectors. This decline outweighs the increase in formal employment and seems to have been concentrated in the rural areas. Winters (2000b) speculates that – if the data are to be believed – the explanation is that the accompanying real depreciation (which will have raised the prices of traded relative to non-traded goods) switched output from non-tradable to tradable goods and that the former are disproportionate users of the informal sector. If true, this reminds us that analysis of poverty effects must consider the fate of the non-tradables sector as well as that of tradable goods.

From a poverty perspective, of course, the important question is what happened to those who lost their informal jobs. If they could move back into subsistence or other agriculture at approximately the same wage, then there will have been little effect on poverty and the observed increase in formal jobs seems to offer a net gain. If, on the other hand, the loss of an informal job signals a descent (deeper) into poverty, the net effect of these changes will be negative for poverty alleviation. Unfortunately, we just do not know.

Source: CUTS (1999).

4.3.4 **Feedback from the enterprise to the price transmission channel**

Of course, most developing countries do not face exogenously given prices for every good; the prices of some goods will be determined domestically. If this is the case, then developments in the enterprise sector will affect the prices faced by consumers and hence affect households through the price transmission channel described above.

An important element of the extent of price effects is the degree of substitutability between domestic and tradable varieties of each good. If this is less than perfect, the transmission of trade policy shocks to domestic prices is less direct than in the case where domestic and tradable goods are effectively the same. Where domestic and tradable goods are poor substitutes, then the transmission of trade policy shocks will affect fewer goods, but may have a stronger effect on those goods.

Conversely, where domestic and tradable goods are very similar, shocks will affect more goods, but the impact on the price of each good is likely to be less. This typically also attenuates the shock to factor prices because, as more goods are affected, the net shifts in the relative demands for different factors are less extreme. Thus, the degree of substitutability between the domestic and traded varieties that are affected by a trade reform can be a critical parameter: the higher it is, the more the shock is focused on the related domestic goods (see Falvey, 1999).

4.3.5 **Adjustment by enterprises**

Just as we needed to consider the ability of households to respond to trade related shocks, there are important factors determining how firms respond to such shocks. Crucial here is the relationship between trade policy and investment. Enterprises react (or fail to react) positively to improved production incentives created by trade policy reform according to whether they can mobilise the necessary resources to increase their production capacity and reorganise their business plans and buying/selling arrangements. Investment in fixed and working capital, and in know-how, is usually required. If funds for investment are not easily available locally, then this can seriously hamper the response to trade liberalisation even when firms are willing to undertake such investment. This also highlights the potential value of foreign direct investment (FDI) in helping developing countries to take full advantage of their trade policy reforms.

<u>4.4</u> **Taxes and spending**

The set of boxes on the right of Figure 4.2 – the trapezoids – illustrates the third of the major static links between trade and poverty: via taxes and government spending. The common presumption is that trade liberalization will cause falling revenues which can squeeze social expenditures and hurt the poor. In fact, this is far from inevitable.

For most countries, the early stages of trade liberalization in the 1980s and 1990s entailed converting quantitative restrictions and regulations into tariffs and reducing high tariff rates. When these measures were accompanied by a reduction in tariff exceptions and exemptions, it was as likely to increase tariff revenue, as to reduce it (see Pritchett and Sethi, 1994; and Hood, 1998). The effective *increase* in taxation implied by reducing exemptions could raise domestic prices, but given that exemptions are mainly granted to the rich and influential, it is unlikely that their loss has much impact on the poor.

Eventually, however, trade liberalization will reduce tariff rates so far that government revenue falls. This triggers the more common worry that the government will curtail expenditure on social and other poverty-alleviating policies and/or levy new taxes on staple and other goods consumed heavily by the poor. It is important, however, to put the possible declines in perspective. Table 4.1 lists all the countries for which the World Bank reports a share of total trade taxes exceeding 5% of current government revenue. Out of 96 countries for which data are available, 58 fall into this class. For these countries significant shares of revenue are at stake, although for the least developed countries in the set, trade taxes are substantially smaller as proportions of government expenditure than of their revenues.

Table 4.1 Trade taxes as a percentage of current revenues for countries where the figure exceeds 5% (average of 1994–6 as available)

	%		%		%
Belize	51.6	Papua New Guinea	23.7	Ecuador	11.3
Madagascar	51.0	Burundi	23.0	Panama	10.7
Seychelles	46.4	Guatemala	22.1	Mongolia	10.7
Sierra Leone	43.8	Fiji	21.9	Egypt, Arab Rep.	10.2
St. Vincent and		Nicaragua	21.3	Peru	9.8
the Grenadines	40.4	Malta	19.6	Chile	9.2
Lebanon	39.4	Zambia	18.7	Bahrain	9.2
Congo, Dem. Rep.	38.4	Sri Lanka	18.6	Croatia	9.1
Dominican Rep.	37.6	Grenada	18.6	China	9.0
St. Kitts and Nevis	37.0	Yemen, Rep.	18.3	Colombia	8.6
Mauritius	36.5	Thailand	16.1	Cyprus	8.3
Maldives	34.1	Botswana	16.0	Venezuela	7.8
Netherlands Antilles	32.8	Kenya	15.6	Poland	7.6
Nepal	28.5	El Salvador	15.2	Bulgaria	7.6
Jordan	27.3	Costa Rica	14.7	Trinidad and Tobago	6.6
Tunisia	26.9	Albania	14.0	Switzerland	6.6
Philippines	26.8	Syrian Arab Rep.	13.0	Bolivia	6.5
Cameroon	24.6	Myanmar	12.8	Argentina	6.3
Pakistan	24.2	Malaysia	12.3	Korea, Rep.	6.2
India	23.8	Russian Federation	12.1		

Source: World Development Indicators (1998)

Nonetheless, for the countries listed in Table 4.1, there is a potential problem to be addressed if liberalization reduces tariff and state-trading organization revenues.

The association between liberalization and loss of government revenue has some historical basis. Structural adjustment in the 1980s led to severe recessions in some countries primarily because of the contractionary policies associated with stabilization. This reduced government revenue and there were clearly cases where expenditure was severely cut back. This was particularly true for capital expenditure, harming subsequent growth (see White, 1997). Furthermore, in a significant number of cases, real expenditure and, even more so, real expenditure per head fell.

But it is important to recognize that the largest declines in expenditure arose because of economic crises preceding and during attempts at adjustment. For example, the reduction in government revenue due to trade liberalization in Zambia during the early 1990s was fully compensated by other forms of taxation. But overall revenue and expenditure fell markedly due to drought and a sharp stabilization designed to reduce high inflation (see McCulloch, Cherel-Robson and Baulch., 2000). Furthermore, even in the deepest of adjustments, most governments sought to protect social programmes relatively, with the proportionate declines in them being only about two-thirds of those in overall government expenditure – see Killick (1998) for a brief survey.

Experience during the Asian crisis of 1997–8 has been similar, but with greater consciousness of the need to protect social and anti-poverty programmes. Indeed, there are some cases of complete protection or even increases in expenditure, such as Thailand's freezing of education spending and increases in its student subsidy programme (see World Bank, 1999a).

So although it is essential to consider the likely impact of trade liberalization on revenue and expenditure, the relationship between reform and curtailing social expenditure is far from immutable. Over the last decade, the World Bank and IMF have focused considerable effort on protecting these programmes, including promoting the following guidelines (see IMF, 1999):

- choose stabilization policies that achieve their goals at the least cost to the poor;
- ensure that fiscal adjustment protects the items of spending most important for the poor and that services are provided by effective, inclusive institutions; critical to this is having honest and well-targeted programmes that deliver to the poor rather than to the influential or articulate middle classes;
- set up or reinforce safety nets capable of providing effective insurance before a crisis and assistance once a crisis hits;
- set up interventions that help preserve the social fabric of societies in crisis and build social capital.

The crises of the 1980s and 1990s were far deeper and more disruptive than any single trade liberalization would ever be. Thus, if it was realistic to protect social expenditures at those times, it certainly would be during a trade reform. If, as often happens, trade reform is part of a crisis package, then protecting pro-poor expenditures is harder, but it should still be feasible. Governments must display care and maintain a clear focus if they are to ensure that this indirect route does not cause trade liberalization to have adverse effects on poverty.

Some have argued that increased openness reduces governments' abilities to raise revenue because mobile factors can no longer be taxed so readily (see Rodrik, 1997). In its direct form, this argument applies only to factors that can move locations in response to taxation or other incentives. Thus, increasing capital mobility may make governments more inclined to tax labour. Furthermore, trade policy may encourage this development. For example, the general reduction in trade barriers since the mid-1980s has made it easier to 'cut up the value chain', which presumably fosters capital mobility. But if increased taxation of labour is done through an extension of payroll or income taxes, then this is likely to be pro-poor since the tax base of most developing countries is narrowly focused on the better off.

An example where a country's own import policy might matter would be if reducing tariffs on a good made it more difficult to tax local producers because they could more plausibly threaten to move offshore and supply the market from abroad. In this case, overall efficiency considerations would still mandate the tariff cut, but if, for some reason, consumption of the good could not be taxed instead of production, there is a danger of governments losing revenue.[9] Of course, as noted above, falling revenue does not inevitably lead to declining anti-poverty expenditure.

Increased mobility is not the only reason that trade liberalization may make certain forms of domestic taxation more difficult. Increasing world competition due to trade liberalization also makes it more difficult for an individual country to tax exports. This could result in the reduction of an important source of revenue for some countries. But export taxes impose costs of their own. In particular, they erode the tax base by preventing firms who would be able to compete at world prices from exporting. In addition, export taxes distort production patterns, discouraging exports relative to other forms of production.

Notwithstanding the above, governments often do attempt to substitute for the revenue lost from trade liberalization with increases in other taxes, most notably taxes on consumer goods, such as sales tax or VAT. The net effect on the poor of doing this depends on three factors:

- the extent of the trade liberalization;
- the size of the tax; and
- the nature of the goods on which it is imposed.

A further issue here is whether trade liberalization restricts a government's ability to manage spending and taxation in a way that affects poverty. On the one hand, binding a trade liberalization at the World Trade Organization (WTO) makes it less reversible. It constrains the government's (and its successors') ability to manipulate policy in arbitrary ways, and since such manipulation very often redistributes real income from the poor to the rich, and that uncertainty reduces the incentives to invest, the constraints are likely to be beneficial. Put more positively, the WTO may allow governments to tie their own, or their successors', hands in ways that would otherwise be politically impossible.

On the other hand, WTO rules are sometimes argued to constrain pro-poor policies. For example, it is argued that the ban on variable levies, which stabilize the domestic prices of internationally traded goods, could hurt the poor, or that the ban on production subsidies prevents pro-poor production activities. These are important issues that are taken up explicitly in Part 2 of this Handbook.

If WTO rules do actually constrain the ability of governments to implement pro-poor policies, then there is a clear conflict between multilateral trade liberalization and poverty alleviation. But whether banning variable levies or production subsidies actually hurts the poor is an empirical matter: they are trade interventions whose direct effects can be traced via the distribution and enterprise sectors outlined above.

Furthermore, even if some particular subsidies would be advantageous, there are important systemic effects to take into account. For example, there are substantial practical difficulties in identifying cases where specific subsidies or exceptions are likely to be advantageous and there are risks that any general exceptions are likely to be captured by interest groups. Consequently, a blanket ban through the WTO may be advantageous overall if it prevents far more undesirable subsidies than it prohibits beneficial ones.

Clearly, making such determinations in practice is going to be very complex. The key is that decisions about what policies to implement should be taken on the basis of evidence of success rather than the theoretical potential of such policies. We take up the general issue of whether the WTO agreements constrain pro-poor policy in Chapter 7. Overall, we believe that these effects are, at worst, slight.

4.5 Shocks, risks and vulnerability

The analysis presented so far compares two perfectly stable situations, one before a trade liberalization and the other after. In reality, the world is full of shocks of which trade liberalization is only one, and an important dimension of poverty is the inability to handle such shocks well. The impact of openness on terms-of-trade volatility and macroeconomic volatility has already been discussed in Chapter 2. Therefore, in keeping with the rest of this chapter, we focus here on how trade liberalization may affect vulnerability at the household level. In particular, we look at the impact of trade liberalization on the chances of falling into poverty (or of emerging from it). We also need to take account of the way in which people respond to the risky environment that they face, since this may affect their current poverty. Box 4.2 gives examples of the sort of shocks that must be considered.

The framework outlined above has shown how foreign shocks are

Box 4.2 **Shocks**

Economic shocks faced by households can be either positive or negative. Examples
include:

Positive: An increase in the price of a key export good

A new cost-saving technology

A particularly good harvest

Negative: The loss of a job

An increase in the price of a key consumption good

Drought or flooding

---

transmitted through a variety of different pathways. It is important to
reiterate that the extent to which foreign shocks are passed onto the poor
depends heavily on the institutions involved in each of the three pathways
described above: enterprises, distribution networks and government. For
example, if a sector makes heavy use of casual labour, then a negative shock
will have a large impact on the poor. Conversely, if price shocks are mostly
absorbed by an official purchaser of export crops, they may have very little
impact on the poor. Thus, sectors subject to apparently similar international
shocks can have very different implications for the shocks facing the poor
depending on the details of each sector's structure and the domestic
institutional context for passing on shocks.

Trade liberalization therefore affects the risks faced by households in two
ways.[10] Most obviously, it may increase (or reduce) the riskiness of existing
activities. Since liberalization increases the weight of foreign relative to
domestic shocks faced by the economy, the net effect on the household
depends on the relative riskiness of the foreign and domestic environments
and the nature of changes to the institutions responsible for the
transmission of shocks down to the household.

For example, world markets for most food crops are less volatile than
national or local markets. Thus, opening up should, in principle, reduce the
risks faced by individual food crop farmers in developing countries. But if
the government of a country operates a variable levy that insulates farmers
from movements in world prices, and this levy is removed concurrently
with the reduction in the overall level of protection, then it is perfectly
possible that farmers may face a more volatile environment than before.

In addition to changing the riskiness of individual activities, trade
liberalization may also lead poor households to change the emphasis among
the different activities in which they are engaged. For example, a trade
liberalization might encourage a poor farmer to switch more or less
completely from a subsistence food crop to a cash crop. Clearly, if they do
so, then the risk they face switches from that for the subsistence crop to that
for the cash crop, and could thus increase.

But if this switch is made with full knowledge of its implications (and does
not affect people other than the farmers who make the decision), it is not

obviously damaging for welfare. This is because even if risk increases, average returns from the activity might do so too; indeed, this may have been the reason for switching. Note that this means that farmers might prefer to accept higher risk in order to reap higher returns, even though observed poverty may increase if they periodically suffer bad luck.[11]

Of course, the switch from subsistence to cash crops may not be made with full information. For example, governments and markets do not always convey information on risk accurately, leading some farmers to make decisions that are not in their interests. Similarly, there may be important spillovers. For example, Oxfam-IDS (1999) report how in rural Zambia, switches to maize as a cash crop apparently eliminated the knowledge and seed supplies required for subsistence varieties, preventing farmers from reverting to traditional methods when the cash crop market disappeared.

In addition, switches between crops may have serious implications for intra-household income distributions. If, for example, adult males receive the returns from cash crops but females and children bear the risks of failure in terms of nutrition or schooling, the decision to switch could worsen female and child poverty, and may even be damaging to welfare for the household overall. The important point analytically, however, is that not every *ex post* descent into poverty is the result of an *ex ante* flawed trade liberalization.

Finally, it is important to recognize that an inability to bear the risks entailed in producing cash crops can explain the unwillingness to pursue higher average returns created by trade, and hence may explain some apparently disappointing supply responses to trade reforms. If households face catastrophe if things go badly, the poor may not be able to afford to be entrepreneurial (see Morduch, 1994). If so, they miss out on the opportunities that liberalization creates, while still bearing the costs through, say, increased prices. Policy-makers need to consider whether the inability to bear risk affects the distribution of gains and whether this can be addressed through complementary policies.

<u>4.6</u> Growth

The impact of trade liberalization, and openness more generally, on growth and poverty has been discussed at length in Chapter 2. The analytical scheme presented in this chapter has focused on the direct effects of trade liberalization on poverty and therefore growth does not appear explicitly in Figure 4.2. But it should not be forgotten on that account.

Growth will affect relative prices, as well as the incomes generated by the enterprise sector, both in terms of average wages and rates of return and the number of people working in that sector. By generating greater demand, growth will assist governments to raise revenue. Also if growth is based on technological improvements, this will further affect incomes from the enterprise sector, as well as increasing the output that farm households can generate at any given price level. Thus, although it is extremely important to understand the direct impact of trade liberalization on households, the long-term impact of trade liberalization on households, the long-term impact of trade liberalization on poverty will depend critically on the dynamic effects of openness discussed in Chapter 2.

Summary

The linkages between trade liberalization and poverty are complex and case-specific. It is therefore helpful to understand the detailed pathways through which trade liberalization in any given country can affect poverty. This chapter has outlined three pathways through which trade liberalization can have a direct effect on poverty (plus a fourth consideration of riskiness and household vulnerability to shocks):

Price transmission

The impact of trade liberalization depends on how changes in border prices get translated into changes in the prices actually faced by households. Price transmission depends on:

- the competitive structure of the distribution sector;
- the way in which government institutions such as marketing organizations operate; and
- the extent of the domain of trade.

Enterprises

Trade liberalization also affects households through its impact on profits, and thereby employment and wages. There are two opposite ways in which this may occur:

- If wages are flexible and labour is fully employed, then price changes caused by trade liberalization will be reflected in *wage* changes, with employment staying the same.
- Alternatively, if there is a large pool of workers who move in or out of jobs when circumstances change, then trade liberalization will cause changes in *employment*.

In reality, both effects will occur. The balance between them will depend on the relative flexibility of wages and employment.

Taxes and spending

Trade liberalization may affect poverty through changes in government revenue and expenditure. The key lessons here are that:

- liberalization often does not have to lead to revenue cuts if tariff peaks and exemptions are also tackled;
- it is important to look at the poverty effects of alternative forms of taxation introduced to cover any shortfall, particularly consumption taxes;

continued

Summary box continued

- it is generally possible to protect social and anti-poverty expenditures even if expenditures do decline;

- good macroeconomic management is far more important to maintaining social expenditure.

Shocks, risks and vulnerability
Households may become more vulnerable as a result of switching their activities in response to a trade liberalization. But if the new activities generate higher returns and the switch is voluntary, the change is not necessarily welfare-reducing.

Notes

1   Elson (1991) and Haddad et al., (1997) provide useful overviews of these kinds of situation and their consequences, while Fontana and Wood (2000) estimate the size of such effects numerically.
2   Even the sign can be affected if households can respond by switching from net consumption to net production of a good, or *vice versa*.
3   Lest blocking price transmission seems automatically a good thing, it should be remembered that many shocks are positive and that official bodies have a tendency to take a cut out of the price in return for providing the 'service' of insulation.
4   'Second-round' effects could, of course, be positive – see section 4.2.2.
5   The Stolper–Samuelson theorem is described in all international economics textbooks – see, for example, Winters (1991) or, in more detail, Bowen et al., (1998). A full account appears in Deardorff and Stern (1994).
6   See Chapter 3 for a definition of poverty headcount indices.
7   That is, goods that are cheap under restricted trade because they use abundant factors can now be sold abroad where those factors are relatively scarcer and hence their prices are higher. Similarly, importable goods are costly under restricted trade because the country is not well placed to produce them, but become cheaper when it trades with countries where they can be produced efficiently.
8   Furthermore, large speculative capital flows may have a destabilizing influence on the macroeconomy, with potentially severe knock-on effects on the poor, but this is a separate topic.
9   Remember that the tariff cut will have reduced consumer prices, so there will be 'political' space for consumption taxes.
10 Recall, however, that risks at the country level may have important systemic effects on the poor in a country – see Chapter 2 for a more detailed discussion of this issue.
11 Conversely, of course, observed poverty may sometimes be lower simply because of good luck.

5   Previous Approaches to Linking Trade and Poverty

> ***This chapter*** reviews the main approaches towards linking trade liberalization and poverty that have been taken in the past. In particular, it examines the advantages and disadvantages of:
>
> - Descriptive approaches.
> - Data-based approaches.
> - Modelling approaches.
>
> An annex to the chapter provides further details on household, community, national and global level models.

Many different approaches have been used by researchers to explore the linkages between trade and poverty. Most can be classified as one of three kinds:

Descriptive approaches
Descriptive approaches collect and analyse a large body of information about the nature of trade policy, the way in which reforms are implemented, and changes in the welfare of different groups within the country in question. From this information, such studies seek to construct a plausible account of the extent to which trade reforms have been responsible for the observed changes in welfare.

The advantage of descriptive approaches is that it is possible to obtain a rich understanding of the exact aims, nature and implementation of trade reforms, as well as a broad appreciation of changes in welfare experienced during the same period.

The disadvantage is that the linkages drawn between the reforms and the welfare changes are not designed to test a theoretical model of how such reforms might influence welfare. Consequently, it is not possible to know whether the conjectures offered by descriptive studies are true in general or simply specific to the particular group of people interviewed.

Data-based approaches

'Data-based' or empirical approaches attempt to remedy the weakness of descriptive studies by compiling the data necessary to test a specific theory about how trade liberalization and poverty might be linked. The data may be collected specifically for the purpose of analysing the links between trade liberalization and poverty or, more commonly, as part of a large, general-purpose survey. The data collection is done in a systematic way for a large number of units – typically individuals, households or firms – and the units are carefully chosen to ensure that the results of the analysis can be generalized to a particular level of interest – whether village, region or country.

The key strength of data-based approaches is that it is possible to test statistically specific hypotheses about the nature of the links between trade liberalization and poverty. Furthermore, if the data have been collected according to proper sampling conventions, the results can be generalized to the wider community.

The disadvantage of data-based approaches is that not everything of importance can be measured systematically (or sometimes even at all). If there are important unmeasured qualitative factors determining the link between trade liberalization and poverty, and it is not possible to take account of these in the technical analysis, then these may bias the results obtained.

Another 'disadvantage' is that data-based work, by definition, must be backward-looking, in the sense that it seeks to explain what actually happened rather than to predict what may happen. This can also be seen as an advantage, of course, in that such data-based results are grounded in empirical reality rather than in a theoretical construction of the world. But, obviously, policy-makers will need to supplement them with forward-looking analyses. Certainly, careful data-based work is a key tool in understanding the links that actually exist between trade liberalization and poverty in various contexts.

Modelling approaches

Modelling approaches construct a theoretical model of the linkages between trade liberalization and poverty and use this to predict what is likely to happen to poverty if certain trade reforms are implemented. A theoretical model is the creation of model-builders and is therefore based on their understanding and beliefs about the ways in which the key economic variables interact. Nevertheless, most modelling exercises do seek to base their models on empirical reality in the sense that the parameters of the models are often derived from empirical analysis of real data. Furthermore, models are typically set up to replicate the empirical data for at least one point in time (a process known as 'calibration').

The great advantage of modelling is that it provides policy-makers with an explicit view of the links between poverty and trade reform, so that the importance of different links can be assessed and different forms of reform and complementary policy explicitly explored. Furthermore, the model can be re-run many times making different assumptions about the economic relationships of most importance in order to test the robustness of the results to the assumptions made.

The disadvantage of modelling, of course, is that it is based on a theoretical construct that may, or may not, be an appropriate reflection of the real world. If the assumptions are significantly wrong, then the predictions of models may be seriously in error. But it should be noted that the fact that models rest on assumptions is not bad in itself. All models must rely on simplifying assumptions in the same way as a map uses contours and symbols as crude representations of the underlying physical reality. A completely accurate model of the economy would be as useful as a 1:1 map of the world. The issue therefore is not whether the model is 'right', but whether it is useful or 'good'. A model is 'good' if the assumptions it makes are appropriate for the purposes of exploring the problem at hand.

<u>5.1</u> The anti-monde and the role of theory

Before looking at each of the approaches in more detail, it is important to appreciate two of the key factors that determine the approach taken to analysis:

The anti-monde
The anti-monde or counterfactual refers to an assessment of what might have happened if an alternative set of policies (or none) had been applied instead of the one actually implemented. This is important because analyses of the impact of trade liberalization on poverty attempt to relate the observed changes in poverty to the reforms implemented. But the observed changes in poverty could, in principle, have nothing to do with the changes in policy. It is perfectly possible that such changes would have occurred anyway because of other factors, such as drought, technology changes, macroeconomic instability, etc.

Equally, no change in poverty might be observed over a certain period, but this could be because of two factors with equal but opposing effects on poverty. Therefore, no change in poverty is not a good indication that trade liberalization has had no effect. To have an accurate assessment of the role played by trade liberalization, it is necessary to have an anti-monde, that is, an indication of how poverty would have changed had everything else remained as it was, except for the changes in trade policy. The difference between the actual outcome and the anti-monde then shows the real effect of trade policy.

The role of theory
The need for an 'anti-monde' is closely related to the role of theory in determining the impact of trade liberalization. Descriptive studies often do not rely heavily on a theory of the linkages between liberalization and changes in poverty. In one sense, this is a strength, since it allows such studies

to focus on what actually happened regardless of whether this fits a theoretical framework. But the lack of theory also makes it difficult to construct a counterfactual since doing that requires a theory of how all the different factors at play might affect poverty. Only with some theoretical framework is it possible to say what might have happened in the absence of trade liberalization and therefore to assess the impact of liberalization appropriately.

Empirical or data-based analysis shares the concern of descriptive studies for a focus on what actually happened, but supplements this with a theoretical framework explaining how key economic variables, including trade policy variables, may affect poverty. This theory is then estimated and tested using the data to determine the economic and statistical significance of the different factors on changes in poverty. Data-based analysis therefore has the important advantage that it is possible to assess the strength of the impact of trade-related policy variables independently of the effect of other economic variables. But the availability of data limits the types of theories that it is possible to test. Consequently, data-based analyses often use relatively simple theories describing broad relationships between the variables. In particular, lack of data sometimes makes it difficult to test detailed microeconomic theories about the behaviour of individuals, households and firms.

In contrast, the aim of the modelling approach is precisely to be able to predict and simulate the behaviour of individuals, households and firms under certain policies. Consequently, theory plays an even stronger role in modelling exercises. Where possible and when data are available, the theories incorporated into models are based on empirical analysis. But sometimes this is difficult or impossible to achieve. In such situations, models make assumptions about the ways in which individuals, households or firms are likely to respond to different situations. Thus, for example, there may not be sufficient data to estimate how female hours vary with the male wage, but a plausible relationship for this can still be written into a household model. As mentioned above, making such assumptions is not necessarily a mistake; indeed, part of the purpose of modelling is to explore how robust the results are to the assumptions made. But it is important to recognize that the results that emerge from modelling exercises depend critically on the theoretical framework that is embedded in the model.

The following three sections provide a brief review of previous work adopting each of the three approaches. The annex to this chapter provides a more comprehensive review of the various approaches to modelling.

5.2 Descriptive and qualitative approaches

There is an immense literature describing the effects of policy reform in developing countries on poverty and inequality. Killick (1995) provides an excellent short review of the findings of such work; White (1997) provides a comprehensive review of the recent literature; while Squire (1991) and van der Hoeven (1996) provide reviews of the linkages between adjustment and poverty in the 1980s. This literature encompasses the impact of a wide variety of types of policy reform, of which trade reform is only one part.

The vast majority of work in this area applies a qualitative or descriptive approach. Typically, this entails a detailed description of the nature and timing of the economic reforms undertaken in a given country complemented by detailed qualitative and quantitative information on concurrent changes in a variety of indicators of welfare among different household groups. The best examples of such research also provide detailed information about the likely institutional pathways through which policy may have given rise to the observed changes in welfare.

The best known example of this approach is the series of studies incorporated within the 'Adjustment with a Human Face' volumes (Cornia et al., 1987). Although focused on adjustment programmes in general rather than trade liberalization *per se*, Cornia et al. provide a link between the structural adjustment policies pursued in many developing countries and the widespread economic decline and impoverishment that occurred at the same time.

Broadly, the same methodology has been applied in numerous studies over the last decade in an attempt to determine the impact of globalization (including trade reform) on poverty – see, for example, the series of Background Papers on 'Globalization with a Human Face' prepared for the Human Development Report 1999 (UNDP, 1999) and Cornia (1999). Handa and King (1997) provide an analysis of the impact of economic reforms (including trade liberalization) in Jamaica; and McCulloch, Baulch and Cherel-Robson provide similar analyses for Zambia and Mauritania (McCulloch, Baulch and Cherel-Robson, 2000; and McCulloch, Cherel-Robson and Baulch, 2000).

As mentioned above, descriptive approaches sometimes have difficulty in establishing a convincing causal link between the policy reforms adopted and the outcomes observed. To tackle this issue such studies have generally used one of three methodologies:[1]

Objectives achieved

This assesses policy reforms on the basis of whether the stated objectives of the reform were achieved. The obvious limitation with such an approach is that it is often not clear whether success is actually the result of implementing the policy reform – that is, a policy could have little or no impact on the stated objective, but the objective was achieved anyway for other reasons. Conversely, a policy may have had a direct impact on the stated objective but the objective was not achieved due to other factors. Finally, stated objectives might give a partial view of the true motivation of the reform.

Before/after

More commonly, the impact of policy is determined by looking at welfare outcomes before and after the application of the policy. Again, the difficulty arises that the change may or may not result from the policy implemented.

Policy on/policy off

Comparative studies often choose a group of countries implementing a policy reform and compare them with countries that are not implementing the reform. But there are clearly serious problems associated with such 'control' countries since their characteristics may be quite different from those of the countries implementing the reform.

Thus, although in-depth qualitative studies can be extremely valuable, there are serious methodological difficulties associated with them. As Cornia et al. (1987) argue 'as causation is not proven, ... results can only be used as evidence of the association between a given policy package and a given outcome.' In particular, the inability of descriptive studies to construct an 'anti-monde' has meant that researchers have tried to complement such studies with the data-based and modelling approaches to which we now turn.

5.3 Data-based approaches

As with descriptive studies, there is a vast range of data-based studies that attempt to explain the reasons for changes in poverty over time.[2] Such studies tend to be based on the large household surveys that are now available for many countries. The information from these surveys is typically used to construct measures of household income and consumption for the years in question. Income or consumption poverty measures are then calculated, sometimes along with other non-income poverty measures (see Chapter 3 for a discussion of poverty measures). Then econometric analysis is used to attempt to explain how changes in the characteristics of the location and the household (for example, education, assets owned, size and composition of the household, etc.) and changes in the returns to these characteristics have given rise to the observed change in income/consumption and therefore the observed change in poverty.

Many data-based analyses of changes in poverty restrict their attention to microeconomic determinants of changes in poverty, such as changes in household composition, education, assets or location. But from the perspective of understanding the poverty effects of trade liberalization, it is desirable to look at the impact of macroeconomic policies on poverty. This is difficult because of the many different pathways through which trade liberalization might influence the variables that are typically available at the household level (as outlined in Chapter 4). Furthermore, such analysis is complicated by the fact that most studies use household surveys, which interview different households in each of the years under study. While this has the benefit of ensuring that the poverty results are nationally representative in each of the years, it makes it very difficult to see to what extent the changes in returns to different activities are responsible for the changes in poverty observed. Since this is the key channel through which trade liberalization is likely to influence household poverty, this is an important limitation.[3]

Recently, there has been a rapid growth in the availability of 'panel data', that is, surveys that track the same set of households over a number of years.

Box 5.1 **The impact of economic reforms in Ethiopia**

Dercon uses data from six villages in rural Ethiopia collected between 1989–95. Because his data follow the same set of households over this period, he is able to show how changes in the consumption (and consumption poverty) of the households are related to changes in their assets and changes in the returns to those assets. He finds that:

- food market reform, different forms of taxation and currency devaluation contributed to producer crop price increases;
- farmers in one village gained substantial amounts of land due to the dissolution of the producer co-operative;
- fertilizer reform had relatively little impact;
- war had only a limited effect on the villages under study, though insecurity did contribute to the effects found;
- food consumption grew strongly in all but one village, primarily because of increased producer prices;
- but the gains primarily benefited a poor group with relatively good land and good access to roads and towns.

Source: Dercon (1998).

Such data do make it possible to explore whether a change in poverty results from a change in a household's endowments of labour or assets, or from a policy-induced change in the returns of these endowments. Dercon (1998) provides a good example of the application of this approach in Ethiopia, where he shows that food market reform, different forms of taxation and, to a lesser extent, currency devaluation contributed to much improved producer crop prices, and these in turn play a large part in explaining the growth in consumption (and fall in poverty) that was observed – see Box 5.1. Further work on panel data from many different countries may provide important empirical information on the impact of reforms on the poor.[4]

5.4 Modelling approaches

An immense amount of work has been undertaken modelling the impact of trade liberalization. Much of this work has been done at a very aggregate level, looking at the winners and losers from world-wide liberalization agreements such as the Uruguay Round. And much of it has focused on the consequences for developed countries of liberalization by developed countries. But there has still been a large amount of analysis of the impact of global (or nearly global) liberalization, particularly agricultural liberalization, on developing countries. Goldin and Knudsen (1989) provide a comprehensive survey of early work on agricultural liberalization prior to the completion of the Uruguay Round; and Martin and Winters (1996) include a quantitative analysis of the final Agreement.

Space does not allow us to summarize the huge literature on modelling in this chapter. Rather, we lay out the different dimensions that characterize the types of models built. Broadly, models tend to vary according to four different dimensions:

Geographical focus
Models of the impact of the Uruguay Round are typically global models since the focus is on identifying the winners and losers from global trade negotiations. Other models are multi-country regional models – for example, the models of the implications of free-trade agreements between the European Union (EU) and Southern Africa in Evans (1999) and Lewis et al. (1999). Alternatively, the focus may be on the trade policy of an individual country, treating the rest of the world as given.

While all of these models are useful for answering questions posed at each of these levels, the more aggregate the level, the less possible it is to examine the impact of policy on the poor. Thus, while global and regional models may give useful indications of the relative gains (or losses) experienced by different countries and groups of countries, they rarely provide information on the distribution of those gains between households within the country. Detailed national models, however, have been used to explore the impact of trade liberalization (by both the 'rest of the world' and the country in question) on the distribution of income within the country and the average poverty experienced by different household groups.

Sectoral focus
In additional to varying in their geographical focus, models also vary according to their sectoral focus. Some models attempt to incorporate a large number of different sectors of the economy or economies in question. Others focus on a single sector (such as agriculture), a single industry within that sector (such as tropical products) or even a single commodity (such as sugar).

As always, there are trade-offs between the different approaches. Multi-sectoral models make it possible to understand the way in which changes in one sector have knock-on effects on others, but the modelling of the technology and structure of each sector must of necessity be simple given the number of sectors. Single-sector models allow the exploration of interactions within the sector, and single-industry and single-commodity models provide even more detailed specification of the microeconomic basis for behaviour in each case. The appropriate choice of level therefore depends on the question being addressed and the degree of *a priori* knowledge of the relative importance of inter-industry and inter-sectoral linkages in the economy under study.

Dynamics
Many models are comparative static models, that is, they compare outcomes with and without some simulated policy intervention assuming that full

equilibrium is reached in each case. Such models may be extremely useful if the aim is only to understand the long-run impact of the policy. But the path by which a new equilibrium is achieved may also matter. Consequently, some models attempt to incorporate the short-run adjustment costs induced by liberalization by making assumptions about the speed and manner with which factors are redeployed after a policy shock.

Others allow a degree of 'hysteresis' or 'path-dependency', in which the same set of policy choices can result in different final outcomes depending on the sequencing of their implementation. Furthermore, some models attempt to integrate traditional equilibrium concepts with new concepts of 'endogenous growth' in which the learning that takes place during the development process feeds back to generate further growth. Dynamic models rely much more heavily on theory than data since the amount of empirical research on which to base them is severely limited.

Household disaggregation
Finally, models adopt different approaches to the analysis of welfare. Again, the distinction is between more and less aggregated approaches. Some models will treat the entire household sector as a single entity; others will disaggregate by position within the distribution of income, geographical location, skill/education of household head or sector of employment. Clearly, the greater the extent of disaggregation, the greater the ability to analyse the impact of trade liberalization on poverty.

5.4.1 Partial versus general equilibrium

Another key distinction in economic models is between partial and general equilibrium models. Partial equilibrium models assume that it is reasonable to analyse the behaviour of a particular sector of the economy separately, treating the impact of other sectors as fixed. In other words, partial equilibrium analysis ignores the mutual inter-relationships between the prices and outputs of goods and factors in different sectors, assuming that repercussions from one market to another will be slight enough to be disregarded. Such assumptions are reasonable in some circumstances: for example, in studying the effects of a change in the tariff on one particular commodity, it may be reasonable to assume that prices in other markets are unaffected.

But a comprehensive trade reform that changes many tariffs and removes many quantitative restrictions is likely to have more pervasive effects on the whole economy. In such circumstances, general equilibrium models are required that take account of the inter-relationships between the different sectors of the economy and the knock-on effects that changes in one sector may have on prices, output, employment and wages in other sectors.

5.4.2 Modelling versus empirical work

Although models can be extremely useful tools, policy-makers are sometimes rightly suspicious of them since the output can be sensitive to the behavioural assumptions they embody. Sometimes, these assumptions are based on detailed empirical work that has produced good estimates of the necessary behavioural parameters. But such empirical work can be extremely time-consuming and costly and hence many models rely at least in part on sensible 'guesstimates' of the value of such parameters. In either case, sensitivity analysis is essential to ensure that the model's predictions for the impact of policy are robust to a wide range of plausible choices.

Furthermore, some models are extremely complex and therefore not easily understood by non-technicians. This creates problems, not only in understanding the results they produce, but more importantly in explaining why a model has produced the outcome it has. If models are to be used as part of a policy-making process, it is essential that the reasoning behind the results is accessible to all stakeholders involved in the policy process.[5]

Models designed to predict the impact of trade liberalization (or any other policy reform) are forward-looking – that is, they start from an initial characterization of the country, sector or industry of interest and use this to predict how a new policy will change the outcome for households. This is, of course, the point of such models, but it does mean that models are not generally used to explain what has happened in the past.[6] This can create a tension between models that predict positive outcomes for the poor from a particular policy, and empirical research, which may show that similar policies in the past have been associated with worsening poverty.

Such tensions should be resolved through a constant process of interaction between modelling and empirical work to ensure that models used to predict the consequences of policy decisions are consistent with the outcomes actually observed by the empirical work. For example, if a model predicts large gains and few costs associated with a particular policy while empirical work shows that a similar policy resulted in major adjustment costs (such as increased unemployment), then it is important to examine the model's assumptions about adjustment costs. Some models *assume* immediate and costless adjustment to a shock and are therefore incapable of identifying such costs.

5.4.3 Examples of modelling

The annex to this chapter provides a fuller description of models linking trade reform and household welfare. In particular, it describes models at three different levels:

- *Household and community level modelling.* These models link changes in agricultural prices (which may be induced by trade reform) with changes in the marketed surplus, labour supply, nutrition and health of agricultural households.
- *National level modelling.* These models link trade reform at the national level with overall household welfare.
- *Global level modelling.* These models link changes in global trade policy with the aggregate welfare of developing countries.[7]

The aims of each type of modelling are described in the annex along with some examples and caveats associated with each type of modelling.

<u>5.5</u> Conclusions

In conclusion, there have been many attempts to analyse the links between trade reforms and changes in household welfare. Any attempt to understand the implications of a proposed reform on poverty should seek to learn from this rich literature. More recently, there has been a large amount of work on the analysis of poverty in developing countries using detailed household survey data. But most of this work has focused on the microeconomic determinants of changes in consumption and income, leaving linkages to national level policies like trade liberalization to more descriptive analyses.

In parallel with the development of more detailed microeconomic studies of poverty, a number of researchers have sought to extend national and global general equilibrium modelling approaches to the analysis of poverty. In some cases, this is done through the synthesis of a national general equilibrium model with detailed household survey data (see Robilliard and Robinson, 1999; Robilliard et al., 2001). In others, it is done through the connection of global Computable General Equilibrium (CGE) models with plausible assumptions about the distributional impact of reforms (see Hertel et al., 2000). But while these are welcome developments, such models still suffer from the problems of extreme complexity and strong dependence on theoretical assumptions discussed earlier.

The conceptual framework outlined in Chapter 4 seeks to provide a middle way between these two extremes. It describes precise theoretical linkages between national level trade liberalization and income and consumption changes at the household level. But it does not provide a detailed theoretical model. Rather, the intention is that the framework should be implemented in a strongly empirical fashion, by drawing on household survey data (both cross-sectional and panel) to test the relative strength of the different channels through which trade liberalization may influence poverty. The next chapter describes in more detail the practical aspects of implementing the conceptual framework.

Summary

- Three approaches have been used to analyse the linkages between trade liberalization and poverty.
- Descriptive approaches analyse information on the nature of trade policy, the way in which reforms were implemented and changes in the welfare of different groups within the country in question and attempt to infer the linkages from such information.
- The upside of descriptive approaches is that they provide a rich understanding of what actually happened. The downside is that it is difficult to construct a counterfactual in order to know what would have happened in the absence of reform.
- Data-based approaches attempt to test statistically specific hypotheses about the nature of the links between trade liberalization and poverty using detailed microeconomic data.
- The upside of data-based approaches is that results can be shown to be nationally representative and statistically significant. The downside is that the omission of unmeasured (or unmeasurable) qualitative factors may bias results.
- Modelling approaches impose a theoretical model of the linkages between trade liberalization and poverty and use this model to predict what is likely to happen to poverty if certain trade reforms are implemented.
- The upside of modelling approaches is that they provide policy-makers with a tool to explore the poverty implications of different reforms. The downside is that the results can be highly sensitive to the model's assumptions.
- All three approaches are useful and important. Descriptive approaches are essential to provide a detailed understanding of the context of reform. But assessing the impact of trade liberalization requires an 'anti-monde'; data-based and modelling approaches both provide this. The best results are likely to be obtained from continuous interaction between modelling and empirical work.

ANNEX: Examples of Approaches to Modelling

This annex explores in more detail some of the attempts at constructing models linking trade reform and household welfare. The first section describes models linking changes in agricultural prices (which may be induced by trade reform) with changes in the marketed surplus, labour supply, nutrition and health of agricultural households. The following section describes models in which trade reform at the national level is linked to overall household welfare, while the final section describes models that link changes in global trade policy with the aggregate welfare of developing countries.

5.A.1 Household and community level modelling

Starting at the level closest to the household, household and community level modelling can be used to explore the impact of changes in key prices on the behaviour of agricultural households.[8] Despite considerable growth in urban poverty in recent years, most of the poor in developing countries still live in rural agricultural households. These households differ from most households in developed countries because they are both producers and consumers of agricultural outputs. Consequently, policy-induced increases in output prices will have a positive impact on net producers but a negative impact on net consumers of that output.

Household models therefore link work estimating the sensitivity of consumer demand to changes in prices, with work that attempts to estimate the production effects of such price changes, in order to determine the overall effect on households involved in both production and consumption. Such models have been used to estimate the impact of price changes on:

- agricultural output;
- consumption of agricultural goods;
- consumption of non-agricultural goods;
- marketed surpluses;
- fertilizer demand;
- labour demand;
- labour supply.

Agricultural household models have also been extended to explore issues of direct relevance to poverty. Strauss (1986) shows how a household model can be extended to investigate the impact of pricing policy on the calorific intake of low-, middle- and high-income households. The different structures of production and consumption of poor households can mean that price effects have quite different effects on them than on better-off households. For example, Strauss shows that an increase in the price of rice would be likely to have a positive impact on the calorific intake of low-income households while having a negative impact on middle- and high-income households. Similarly, Pitt and Rosenzweig (1986) incorporate a linkage between nutrition, health and productivity into a household model, thereby providing a link between policy-induced price changes and the probability of household members falling ill.

Agricultural household models can also be used to investigate the impact of price changes on poverty in situations where markets fail. De Janvry et al. (1991) analyse the impact of a sharp rise in cereal prices in Morocco in a context in which animal production partly uses child labour for herding small flocks on common grazing lands. By taking account of this important structural feature of the economy, they show that the switch of the farm economy from livestock to crops resulting from the price change may also have resulted in a rise in forage prices, causing households to use more child labour and leading to greater use of common grazing lands for the remaining livestock production. Thus child labour and the market failure for access to commons may have increased the poverty impact of the policy-induced change in cereal prices.

Similarly, Alwang et al. (1996) model the impact of remoteness, lack of input supplies and health and nutrition problems on the effect of market liberalization on smallholders in Zambia. They show that although market liberalization is generally beneficial, the benefits to poor households subject to these constraints are dramatically reduced.

Moving above the household level, researchers at the International Food Policy Research Institute (IFPRI) have pioneered the use of farm/non-farm growth linkage models (see Delgado et al., 1998). These models show the extent to which increased rural incomes due to, for example, increased exports arising from a trade liberalization, have the potential to stimulate even further increases in rural incomes. Studies of the 'green revolution' in Asia during the 1970s suggest that an extra dollar of agricultural income was typically associated with an additional 80 cents of non-agricultural income from local enterprises. Further work suggests that these growth linkages may be even stronger in sub-Saharan Africa. For example, Hazell and Hojjati (1995) show that such linkages are driven primarily by household consumption demands for locally produced non-tradable foods.

It is important to recognize that growth linkage models do not explore the mechanism through which a trade liberalization gives rise to an injection of demand in local areas. But by modelling in detail the production technologies and demand linkages in poor rural areas, they give some insight into the extent to which growth resulting from liberalization trickles down to the poor. They also provide important information about the complementary policies that are needed to ensure that such benefits do accrue to the poor. For example, although jump-starting the production of agricultural tradable goods is shown to have much higher returns than previously thought, rising staple food prices have the potential to choke off growth unless the conditions for a high supply response are in place. This points to the need to tackle the constraints on agricultural supply response simultaneously with market liberalization to ensure that the gains from the resulting growth reach the poor.

Finally, it is important to note that there is a rich and growing literature looking *below* rather than above the household level. Models of intra-household behaviour are important because even when poor households do benefit from a policy reform, the members of the household often do not benefit equally. In particular, women and children may be relatively disadvantaged by the growth of some sources of income while they may gain from the growth of other forms of income, depending on the relative control that different groups within the household have over different income sources and the cultural norms regarding the sharing of resources within the household. Haddad et al. (1997) provide a comprehensive analysis of intra-household resource allocation issues in developing countries.

5.A.2 National level modelling

Household, community and regional level models are extremely useful in providing detailed analysis of how price and demand changes are likely to affect poor households. But in order to concentrate on the household and village responses, such models tend to take the price and demand changes as given. Yet such changes can result from shifts in policy. In particular, we are interested in price changes resulting from trade liberalization. National level models move the focus of analysis to the actions of national governments and explicitly aim to understand the implications of national level policy-making for the poor.

5.A.2.1 Partial equilibrium models

In order to model the impact of national policies on poor households, Sahn and Sarris (1991) construct an index of real income for rural smallholders in five African countries, which takes into account the shares of own-operated farm agricultural income derived from activities that produce exportable goods, tradable staple food and other non-tradable agricultural products. The index also incorporates the shares of household expenditures on tradable staple food, non-tradable food and non-agricultural products. Using time series data on the changes in the relative prices of exportable, tradable staple food and non-tradable agricultural products, Sahn and Sarris examine the trends in the real incomes of the smallholders. Their results show marked differences among countries and regions, illustrating the importance of understanding the structure of households' incomes and expenditures.

But the approach used by Sahn and Sarris suffers from a number of limitations (as the authors acknowledge). First, it is an aggregate model, that is, it models the effect of price changes on the household sector as a whole. It is therefore impossible to distinguish effects by household type. Poverty profiles show that the poor in most countries are not a homogenous group. In particular, different types of household have different budget shares and so price changes are likely to affect groups of households in different ways. Similarly, the model does not permit a role for differing household characteristics to influence household substitution between different productive activities. Thus, the real income index approach may give an indication of the long-term impact of a policy reform on the household sector, but the short- and medium-term impact for individual households will depend on the specific characteristics of the household.

Second, the model does not allow for substitution possibilities in consumption. Households faced with a price shock will substitute their consumption away from more expensive items towards less expensive ones. The existence of such substitution possibilities means that the results from Sahn and Sarris's approach probably overestimate the negative aspects of price shocks.

Nonetheless, the approach does provide an indication of the direction and order of magnitude of changes in smallholder welfare. It also provides an indication of the likely level at which analysis may need to be focused in order to construct models that can both account for price changes due to trade reform and provide useful disaggregated information on the likely impact on poverty at the household level.

A further step in this direction is provided by Bourguignon et al. (2000), who develop a 'microsimulation decomposition' methodology to analyse changes in the distribution of income in Taiwan. This methodology allows them to estimate the extent to which changes in both the income distribution and income poverty result from changes in prices, changes in participation in the labour force and changes in the demographic characteristics of households. By separating these effects, it is easier to identify the impact of policies designed to change prices (such as a trade liberalization). Similar work has been done by Grimm (2001) on Cote D'Ivoire.

A different approach that moves somewhat closer to general equilibrium modelling (see below) is to construct a 'spatial equilibrium model'. Minot and Goletti (1998) use such a model to estimate the impact of the removal of an export quota on rice in Vietnam on paddy and rice prices in seven regions of the country. The estimated price changes are then combined with household data on rice production and consumption patterns to study the distributional implications of liberalization. Their results show that the relationship between net purchase position and the poverty effects of policies that raise food prices is complex. This points to the need to take into account 'second-order' effects as Minot and Goletti do and, where possible, general equilibrium effects as discussed below.

5.A.2.2 General equilibrium models

The limitations of partial equilibrium models have led many researchers to use general equilibrium models to analyse the impact of government policy on different household groups. Adelman and Robinson's (1978) classic study of Korea contains 15 different occupational groups, including capitalists, self-employed people and wage labourers, and explicitly models the distribution of income within each of these groups. This approach allows for the estimation of the inequality effects of policy reforms. Similarly, Sahn et al (1997) estimate CGE models in the tradition of Dervis et al. (1982) for five African countries. They then consider the impact of different forms of adjustment to terms-of-trade shocks and show that both the urban and rural poor enjoy higher incomes from liberalized trade and exchange rate regimes. There are now a very large number of such country CGE models: for example, Tyler and Akinboade (1992) for Kenya; Karunaratne (1998) for Thailand; and Liu et al.(1996) for the Philippines.

Kanbur (1987) attempts a simpler approach, which exploits general equilibrium concepts to provide key sectoral divisions, but which also draws on literature on the quantitative measurement of poverty. His model examines the impact of switching policies (that is, exogenous relative price changes, which may be caused by devaluation or trade reform) on poverty, taking account of the fact that poor households in many countries have multiple sources of income. More recently, Thorbecke and Jung (1996) used a 'multiplier decomposition' method to measure the impact of different production activities on poverty alleviation. The total impact of a change in the output of a given sector on poverty alleviation depends on the resulting income gains accruing to various household groups and the sensitivity of the selected poverty measures to these income gains. Their technique is used to identify the pattern of sectoral growth most conducive to poverty alleviation.

Numerous studies have used the Stolper–Samuelson theorem to analyse the impact of relative price changes on income distribution (see Knight, 1976; and Addison and Demery 1985). These studies exploit the simple two-good/two-factor model in which, in the short run, both factors employed in the sector that gains from the price change should gain, while the factors employed in the other sector should lose. But in the long run, the factor that is used intensively in the gaining sector will benefit while the other will lose (see Winters, 2000e, for the limitations of simple applications of the Stolper–Samuelson theorem for poverty analysis).

Bourguignon et al. (1992) provide a more ambitious integration of distributional and poverty concerns into general equilibrium modelling. They construct a 'micro-macro' model that combines the explicit microeconomic optimizing behaviour of CGE models with the asset portfolio behaviour of macroeconomic models. The impact of policy changes on the distribution of income and wealth (and thereby on poverty) comes through four channels: changes in factor rewards affect household incomes; household real incomes are affected by changes in the cost of living; household real incomes are also affected by changes in real returns on financial assets; and the distribution of household wealth is affected by capital gains and losses. The authors provide estimates for the poverty effects of a number of adjustment policies when applied to a 'representative' developing country of the early 1980s.

Similarly, Bourguignon et al. (1991) use a similar model of two archetypal economies for Africa and Latin America to examine the impact of different adjustment policies on poverty and income distribution. The adjustments are made in response to terms-of-trade and interest rate shocks mirroring those that actually occurred during the early 1980s. Three adjustment packages are considered: a rationing adjustment package in which adjustment occurs through import rationing; a structural reform package, which applies the trade and tax reforms typically espoused by the World Bank and the IMF; and a redistribution package in which the structural reform package is augmented by food subsidies and a public works programme. The structural reform package provides the best poverty outcome, especially when complemented by the redistribution package. But the results are sensitive to the assumptions made about the structure of the archetypal economies. Furthermore, in a separate article, Bourguignon (1991) suggests that the scope for redistribution to alleviate poverty may be very limited following severe exogenous shocks.

Robilliard et al. (2001) take this one step further by linking a national level CGE model for Indonesia to a 'microsimulation' model based on household survey data. This allows them to look at the impact of economic crisis on the entire distribution of households rather than a set of supposedly representative households.

Finally, although most national level CGE models now incorporate several disaggregated household types, virtually none take account of the gender division of labour within households. One notable exception is Fontana and Wood (2000), who treat male and female labour as separate factors of production and include reproduction and leisure as separate sectors. Using data from Bangladesh, they show that the impact of trade liberalization on women can be quite different from the impact on men so that policies that 'non-gendered' analysis might regard as positive may have negative outcomes for poor women.

CGE models are an immensely useful tool for policy simulation and counterfactual analysis. They provide a comprehensive, powerful and consistent approach to the analysis of how policy affects sectors and households, moving beyond the potentially misleading results of partial equilibrium models (see Whalley, 1975). But CGEs have drawbacks: the results they give can be sensitive to the model assumptions. De Maio et al. (1999), for example, claim that Sahn et al.'s models of the impact of adjustment policies on the poor in Africa are highly sensitive to model assumptions. Furthermore, even simple CGEs are complex to most non-technicians and therefore difficult both to understand and to explain to others. And the greater the desire to model the world 'accurately', the greater the data requirements. The availability of microeconomic data at the firm and household level has improved enormously over the last 20 years for most developing countries, but the complexity of some CGE models has increased commensurately. It is still true that the construction of a useful CGE model requires considerable resources. Simple, non-CGE models generally require less data and are usually easier to understand. As always, therefore, the key is to choose the level of complexity necessary to answer the policy question being asked. Some policy questions can be satisfactorily answered with quite straightforward analysis. As Winters (1989a) says, 'We should not denigrate the passenger airliner just because it is possible to send a spacecraft to Neptune'.

5.A.3 Global level modelling

Trade liberalization is not merely a national phenomenon. Although substantial unilateral liberalization has occurred in recent years, particularly in developing countries under the auspices of structural adjustment programmes, much liberalization is still agreed in the context of plurilateral, regional or multilateral trade negotiations. The key difference between trade liberalization in this context and unilateral action is that multilateral action will tend to have an impact on world prices, which will then have welfare effects on individual countries. When modelling the impact of such global agreements involving several countries, it is generally not feasible to examine the impact on poor groups within each country. Consequently, both partial and general equilibrium models of the impact of changes in world prices tend to focus on their aggregate welfare effects on key developing countries.

5.A.3.1 Partial equilibrium models

Valdes and Zietz (1980) were the first to provide a comprehensive partial equilibrium analysis of the effects of developed country agricultural liberalization on developing countries. Their original model, which covered 99 commodities and 56 developing countries, calculated the changes in export revenues and import expenditures resulting from a reduction by 50% of agricultural protection by the OECD countries. Later versions of their model (Zietz and Valdes, 1989) explicitly incorporate commodity interdependence, the impact of productivity growth on supply and of income growth on demand.

Anderson and Tyers (1989) focus their attention on grains, livestock and sugar. They challenge the common assumption that price rises in these products due to agricultural liberalization in developed country markets would give rise to welfare losses for most developing countries. Their model suggests that introducing induced technical innovation (see Ruttan, 2001) means that many developing countries that might otherwise have lost, will gain from such price rises. Furthermore, they suggest that the gains to developing countries are likely to be larger if they also liberalize their agricultural markets. The distributional impact of such changes may not necessarily be harmful to the poor; it will predominantly benefit net producers of these products who may be poor rural farmers. But it is likely to have harmful effects on net consumers, who may include very poor households and the urban poor.

More recently, Ingco (1996) uses a partial equilibrium model to analyse the impact of agricultural price shocks resulting from the Uruguay Round for least-developed and food-importing countries. She finds that terms-of-trade losses resulting from the price changes are small relative to total GDP. But distortions due to domestic policies are large, so that the removal of policy distortions in least-developed net food-importing countries could reverse the losses resulting from the terms-of-trade shift in some countries.

5.A.3.2 **General equilibrium models**

Finally, there has been a tremendous growth in global CGE models that attempt to estimate the implications for individual countries of global trade liberalizations. For example, Harrison et al. (1996) provide one of the many detailed quantifications of the Uruguay Round.[9] Their model contains 22 productive sectors and 24 regions of the world, explicitly including South Korea, Indonesia, Malaysia, the Philippines, Singapore, Thailand, China, Hong Kong, Taiwan, Argentina, Brazil and Mexico while aggregating the remaining developing countries into regions (South Asia, rest of Latin America, Eastern Europe and former Soviet Union, Middle East and North Africa, and sub-Saharan Africa). In addition to providing estimates of the global welfare gains from the Uruguay Round, they model: tariff reductions in manufactured products; tariffication of non-tariff barriers in agriculture and binding commitments to reduce the level of agricultural protections; the reduction of export and production subsidies in agriculture; and the elimination of voluntary export restraints and the Multi-Fibre Agreement.

Similarly, Hertel et al. (1998) provide a detailed model of the implications of the Uruguay Round for Africa using a 10-region, 12-sector model of the global economy. They show that Africa is likely to be the only major region of the world to lose from implementation of the Uruguay Round, but that the induced costs would be far outweighed by the potential gains from catching up with other low-income countries in agricultural productivity and transport costs. Furthermore, implementing the Uruguay Round shifts Africa's comparative advantage further towards agriculture and trade with Asia rather than Europe.

Hertel and Martin (2000) also examined the potential gains associated with further tariff liberalization in a future round of multilateral trade negotiations using a model containing 19 commodities and 28 regions. They predict that a 33% cut in manufacturing tariffs world-wide would generate an increase in global trade volume of US$107.4 billion (about 2% of merchandise and non-factor service trade in 1995) and that nearly 95% of the welfare gains would accrue to developing countries (see Chapter 12 on manufactures for a more detailed discussion of their model).

Many global CGE models employ the Global Trade Analysis Project (GTAP) model of global trade (see Hertel, 1997) and use the GTAP database, which represents an internally consistent snapshot of global production, consumption and trade in the year 1995 (see Hertel and Martin, 1999).[10] This project provides a remarkable resource for researchers from around the world, enabling them to put together global CGE models for the welfare effects of trade and other policies of particular concern to them.

In the broadest sense, global CGE models are essential in determining the balance of benefits received by different countries by international trade agreements. But by their nature, they are not able to delve much 'below' the aggregate country results. They therefore provide a useful complement to other methodologies linking trade and poverty. But since global analyses using such models often conclude that the principal welfare gains for developing countries lie in their own liberalization and the removal of domestic distortions, it is likely that the most valuable approach to understanding the impact of trade liberalization on poverty at the household level will involve a combination of household-level and national-level models rather than a strong reliance on global CGE models.

Notes

1   See McKay (1999) for a detailed discussion of the methodological issues in assessing the impact of economic reform on poverty.
2   See Canagarajah, Mazumdar and Ye (1998) on Ghana; Appleton (1998) on Uganda; Coulombe and McKay (1996) on Mauritania; Dercon (1998) on Ethiopia; Grootaert and Kanbur (1995) on Cote D'Ivoire; Jalan and Ravallion (1998) on China; and McCulloch and Baulch (2000) on Pakistan.
3   It should be noted that it is possible to address this problem in part by looking at the impact on 'cohorts' of individuals of similar age, location and background – see Deaton (1997) for an application of this approach.
4   For a collection of articles on economic mobility and poverty dynamics using panel data from developing countries, see Baulch and Hoddinott (2000).
5   For example, Defourny and Thorbecke (1984) designed a method of 'structural path analysis' to help explain the outcomes from Computable General Equilibrium (CGE) models.
6   Bourguignon et al. (1991) is a notable exception to this; they simulate the impact of terms-of-trade and interest rate shocks on archetypal economies in Africa and Latin America and compare the outcomes with the *observed* changes in such economies.
7   Note that since global level models are generally only capable of indicating the effects on individual countries, they do not really analyse the impact of trade liberalization on poverty, but rather the impact on poor countries (although see Hertel et al, 2000, for an attempt to link multilateral liberalization to poverty).
8   Singh et al. (1986) provide the seminal survey. A detailed exposition of these (and other) models is provided in Sadoulet and de Janvry (1995).
9   See Safadi and Laird (1996) for a summary of models quantifying the Uruguay Round.
10 The Global Trade Analysis Project (GTAP) is designed to reduce significantly the cost of CGE modelling – further details can be found at: http://www.agecon.purdue.edu/gtap

6 Implementing the Conceptual Framework

> ***This chapter*** examines the practical aspects of implementing the conceptual framework outlined in Chapter 4. In particular, it lays out:
>
> - The questions that policy-makers may need to address in attempting to ascertain the effects of a trade reform on poverty.
> - The data needed to conduct the various types of analysis proposed and the sources from which they can be obtained.
> - Flowcharts for policy-makers to enable them to identify which pieces of analysis are likely to be critical in their particular context.

This chapter examines the practical aspects of implementing the conceptual framework linking trade liberalization and poverty that was outlined in Chapter 4. We look in turn at each of the components for analysis identified in the conceptual framework: trade policy reform itself; price and distribution mechanisms; production and employment; and government revenue and expenditure. In each case, we outline the key questions that a policy-maker may want to ask. For each set of questions, the data requirements are elaborated and possible sources described.

We have tried to be comprehensive about all the different kinds of analysis that might be needed to determine the poverty effects of various reforms. But we would stress that no individual country is going to need to undertake all of them. Clearly, performing detailed microeconomic analysis at a disaggregated level in each area is beyond the resources of the vast majority of countries. Fortunately, we believe it is not necessary. Indeed, in most cases we believe that the most important effects of trade reform on poverty can be identified from limited and relatively straightforward analysis. There will, of course, be cases where more detailed analysis is required and where 'second-round' effects are important. But for the most part, our framework should allow policy-makers to pick out the key pieces of analysis that will provide them with a reasonable indication of the orders of magnitude of the effects of different kinds of reform.

To aid policy-makers in identifying the elements of most importance to them, we feature three flowcharts containing the key questions that policy-makers need to ask and the steps they must take to answer them. By following these flowcharts, policy-makers should be able quickly to identify and initiate the most important pieces of analysis. The results of such analysis will then make it clear whether further work is needed in other areas. Often, of course, decisions will have to be taken in ignorance of the full set of behavioural parameters. But even then, the discussion of this chapter is useful in identifying where the critical uncertainties lie, what might have to be assumed in the absence of information and what might be the effects of incorrect assumptions.

6.1 Trade reform

The starting point in any analysis of the impact of trade liberalization on poverty is to look at the trade reforms themselves. The key questions are: what trade reforms have actually taken place or are proposed, and what are the implications of these reforms for the border price?

If the reform consists merely of a set of tariff changes, determining what has actually taken place or what is proposed, can be done by obtaining the current and reformed schedule of tariffs for the country in question. Even this, though, can be complicated by a number of factors. First, there is often an administrative delay in the production of accurate current schedules of tariffs, making it difficult to ascertain the starting point for trade reforms. This is a particular problem for information on exceptions, exemptions and derogations from the normal schedule. In addition, changes may have taken place since the production of the last set of published tariffs, with the result that official documentation may not reflect policy as currently implemented.

Furthermore, if the reforms are politically contentious, there may be an element of confidentiality about some reforms (particularly if they are incomplete), making access to information difficult (even for policy-makers within government). Even when it is clear what reforms are proposed, the political sensitivity of some reforms can lead to them being reversed or not fully implemented. Clearly, the impact of reforms on poverty will depend on the extent to which reforms are actually implemented.

In addition to identifying what trade reforms are proposed and their timetable for implementation, reforms often contain components with complex effects on the prices of the goods affected. For example, reforms sometimes include the removal of quantitative restrictions, changes to import licensing systems and the introduction of competition into marketing and distribution channels. Furthermore, there are often overlapping barriers to trade, for example, where a tariff and a quantitative restriction apply to the same good.

Thus, a further component of the analysis of trade reform is calculation of the price effects associated with such reforms. This requires information about the structure of supply and demand in the affected markets. For example, the removal of an import monopoly for a particular good should reduce its domestic price, but the extent of the fall will depend on the extent of competition following the reform. If substantial barriers to entry still remain after the reform, then the effect on the price may be quite limited.[1]

In some cases, it will be extremely difficult or impossible to determine the price consequences of a reform. For example, reforms to regulations (or to the institutional regulatory structures) may be extremely important, but there is no obvious way of calculating their price effects. Furthermore, some kinds of reform may give rise to qualitative changes in the market, for example, when a reform causes a good to switch from not being traded to being traded or *vice versa*.

The welfare implications of such switches may be dramatic. For example, if a reform enables a good that is a close substitute for a domestically produced good to be imported for the first time, then it is possible that consumers may switch in large numbers from the domestically produced good to the import. This may be good for the consumers, but bad (at least in the short run) for the employees involved in domestic production. Predicting such consequences is fraught with difficulties.

Finally, trade reforms typically involve simultaneous changes to several different products and regulations. Analysis of the price changes in any particular product may reasonably focus on the reforms relating only to that product, but it may also be desirable to calculate some measure of the aggregate change induced by a reform. There are several different measures of aggregate trade policy stance, each with different information requirements:

- *The nominal rate of protection (NRP)*, which requires only knowledge about the tariff schedule (and the calculation of tariff equivalents for quantitative restrictions).
- *The effective rate of protection (ERP)*, which requires an input-output matrix for the economy in order to calculate value added with and without the reforms.
- *The domestic resource cost (DRC)*, which requires information about domestic and international factor costs and factor intensities in production.

(See Greenaway and Milner, 1993, for a detailed practical exposition of these and other measures).[2]

Table 6.1 summarizes the data requirements for each type of analysis and identifies possible sources.

6.2 Enterprises

A key channel discussed in Chapter 4 through which trade liberalization affects poverty is via its impact on the activities of enterprises. The price changes induced by liberalization are likely to change production. This section examines how the type of good determines the effect of trade reform on production, followed by a discussion of how to identify the employment

Table 6.1 Data requirements for the analysis of trade-poverty linkages

Component for analysis	Analysis required	Data needed	Sources
Trade reform	Identification of change implemented	Current and reformed schedule of tariffs	Ministry of Trade/Commerce UNCTAD
		Estimates of supply and demand for the products in question	Industry associations
	Calculation of tariff equivalents	Knowledge of the competitive structure (see data needed under 'Distribution network')	Domestic central statistical offices
		Tariff schedule; input-output matrix; international and domestic factor prices	
	Calculation of aggregate measures of tariff protection (such as NRP)		Research organizations, such as GTAP
Distribution network	Analysis of whether and to what extent trade reforms have resulted in price changes at each level of the distribution chain	Price surveys of the goods of interest at the world, border, wholesale and retail levels	Ministries of Trade and Agriculture often conduct dedicated price surveys for particular goods
		Knowledge of the number of importers, wholesalers, retailers and their geographical distribution	LSMS surveys
		Information about barriers to entry in distribution, whether technical (such as economies of scale), administrative (such as licensing requirements) or anti-competitive (such as collusion)	WTO, IMF/World Bank for secondary data
			Major local businesses and business associations
			Competition authorities (if they exist)

Component for analysis	Analysis required	Data needed	Sources
Production	Analysis of the extent to which the reform has resulted in output changes in key sectors – this can include both detailed sectoral analysis and multi-sector models	The information required depends on whether the goods under consideration currently compete against imports and whether they are consumer or intermediate goods (see text). The information needed in each case includes: *Non-domestically produced consumer goods:* income elasticity of demand for different goods; cross-price elasticities *Non-domestically produced intermediate goods:* intensity of intermediate use in final good production; extent of technical substitution possible *Domestically produced consumer goods:* price elasticity of supply in the affected sector; income elasticity of aggregate supply *Domestically produced intermediate goods:* price elasticity of supply in the affected sector; intensity of intermediate use in final good production; extent of technical substitution possible	Ministries of Trade and Agriculture WTO, IMF/World Bank Major local businesses and business associations. Technical consultancies for individual industries Academic analyses of production and consumption
Employment and wages	Analysis of the extent to which the reform has resulted in employment and wage changes in key sectors	Intensity of use of different types of labour Skill endowments in the population Labour market regulations and rigidities; elasticity of labour supply Wage rates and employment levels for different types of labour (and their trend and seasonal fluctuation), preferably disaggregated by gender, age, location, sector, experience and skill	As for 'Production' *plus* Ministry of Employment, Labour Force Surveys Trade unions ILO Household surveys that include time use by activity

Component for analysis	Analysis required	Data needed	Sources
Government revenue and expenditure	Analysis of the revenue impact of trade reform and its consequent effect on aggregate demand and social expenditures	Importance of trade taxation in tax revenue Nominal and actual trade tax revenue and its distribution among different products Administrative capacity for tax reform Procedures for expenditure allocation Structure of expenditure and the existence of automatic stabiliser mechanisms	Ministry of Finance, Central Bank IMF World Bank Public Expenditure Reviews Ministry responsible for social services and safety nets, where applicable
Households	Analysis of changes in consumption, income and employment at the household level	Household surveys including, where possible: consumption expenditure by detailed item; income by source and sector; demographic and educational characteristics of the household members Regionally disaggregated price indices Panel data where available Geographical information at the village and regional level, for example, agroclimatic information, access to infrastructure and services, location of major employers, principal economic activities by region Participatory poverty assessments (PPAs)	National and regional household surveys Central statistical offices World Bank LSMS project Individual academic studies Donor-funded and independent participatory studies (see, for example, the World Bank website for details of its PPAs)
Domain of trade	Analysis of the extent of local, regional, national and international spillovers	Household surveys that disaggregate goods by the level of tradability Regionally disaggregated price indices	IFPRI Individual academic studies Central statistical offices

and wage effects of a trade reform. The section concludes with a flowchart for policy-makers to assist in identifying which pieces of analysis are likely to be of most value to them.

6.2.1 **Production**

Once information is available on the price changes that are likely to be induced by trade reform, it is possible to analyse the extent to which reform will result in output changes in key sectors. Such analysis can be done both at a detailed sectoral level and using multi-sector models (see Chapter 5 for a discussion of partial and general equilibrium approaches). But the impact of trade reform on production in the economy as a whole depends on the nature of the good(s) subject to liberalization. The key questions are whether the good subject to liberalization is a final consumer good or an intermediate good and whether or not it is produced domestically. We consider each of the four possible types of good:

Non-domestically produced consumer goods
For these goods, liberalization does not affect domestic production. Hence the impact on the production of other goods within the economy comes primarily from the 'income effect' on households resulting from the price change (see below for how to analyse the impact on households). Income effects arise when households' real incomes increase as the price of the liberalized good falls and they can therefore afford to buy more of all goods. But the fall in the price of the imported good will also tend to make households increase their consumption of the imported good and reduce their demand for substitutes that are domestically produced – a substitution effect. The net effect depends on the balance of the income and substitution effects. The key information needed to understand the impact of such a liberalization is:

- *The proportion of the household budget spent on the imported good for various different groups of households*: the higher the proportion of the household budget spent on the imported good, the greater the benefit of a reduction in its price, and the bigger the income effect.
- *The sensitivity of demand for the imported good to price changes*: demand for the imported good will almost always increase if the price falls. This effect could be very large.
- *The sensitivity of demand for other goods to changes in the price of the imported good*: as the imported good's price falls, demand for other goods is reduced by the substitution effect and boosted by the income effect. The net effect is uncertain, but overall we expect to observe a fall as expenditure is diverted to the imported good. For closely related goods, substitution effects are bound to dominate. But for dissimilar goods, the substitution effects may be negligible, and the net effect can be estimated just by knowing how sensitive is the demand for the other good to increases in income.
- *The sensitivity of demand for other goods to changes in income*: demand for

other goods increases as a result of the boost to income from a reduction in the price of the imported good. The extent to which this occurs depends on the sensitivity of demand to changes in income – the income elasticity of demand – and the size of the income effect.

All of this information can usually be obtained from economic analyses of household and consumer survey data.

Non-domestically produced intermediate goods
As above, liberalization does not affect domestic production since the good is not produced domestically. But a trade reform-induced change in the price of an intermediate good has a direct impact on the profitability of firms using the good. The impact on final production will depend on two factors:

* *The intensity with which the intermediate good is used in production*: some domestic production will use the intermediate good intensively and will therefore receive a strong benefit from a reduction in price. Others may use the intermediate less or not at all, in which case the benefit will be correspondingly smaller.
* *The opportunities for technical substitution*: if the price of an intermediate good falls, then there is an incentive for firms to switch from their current set of inputs to using more of the good whose price has fallen. If there are strong possibilities for doing this, then the benefit of the price fall to producer firms will be enhanced, although suppliers of the intermediate or primary factors of production that are displaced will lose sales. If, on the other hand, it is difficult for firms to switch from the current input mix, then the main benefit will be limited to those firms who currently use the intermediate good intensively. They may increase their demand for other inputs as they increase sales in response to lower costs.

Information on the intensity of input use and the ability to switch to other mixes of inputs can be found from input-output tables and detailed technical studies of different sectors, though often these must be found in studies in other countries.

So far, we have considered the effects of liberalizing goods that are not produced domestically. Liberalization is generally seen to be beneficial in such cases since it simply reduces prices for the relevant consumer or intermediate goods. The only potential negative impact comes from the possibility that reduced prices will make consumers or firms switch away from other domestically produced goods.[3] But since we are assuming that close substitutes are not produced domestically, this switching effect is likely to be quite limited. We now consider the impact on production of the liberalization of domestically produced goods.

Domestically produced consumer goods
A reduction in the price of an imported consumer good arising from a trade

liberalization has a mixed effect on overall production within an economy if the good is also domestically produced. Households will gain from higher real incomes as a result of the fall in the price, and again, they will substitute away from more expensive items towards greater purchases of the imported consumer good. As before, the combination of these income and substitution effects will determine overall demand in the economy and hence exactly the same information described under non-domestically produced consumer goods will be needed to analyse the overall effect.

But there is an important difference in this case: the good is assumed to have a reasonably close substitute that is domestically produced. If the price of the imported good falls, then the substitution effect of consumers switching away from the domestically produced good towards the imported good is likely to be strong unless the price of the domestic good also falls. If the price of the domestic good does fall, then this will affect the profitability of domestic production. It is highly likely that such a price reduction will result in reduced domestic production.

Thus, although the reduction in prices resulting from trade liberalization may increase production in other sectors of the economy through income effects, it is likely that production in the competing sector will fall. Whether this reduction is maintained over the long term will depend on the ability of domestic firms to cut margins or increase efficiency. Of course, it is the contraction of the import-competing sector that releases the resources required for other sectors to expand.

In order to analyse the potential impact of a trade liberalization on domestic production, it is therefore necessary to have additional information on:

- *The extent of competition in the liberalized sector*: if domestic production is perfectly competitive and as efficient as elsewhere in the world, then domestic prices will be the same as world prices. But if competition in the domestic market is imperfect, then this will raise prices above the world price towards the world price inclusive of the existing tariff, creating excess profits for domestic companies. Trade liberalization in this situation will cut these excess profits but overall production may be less affected.
- *The level of efficiency of the domestic industry*: if the domestic sector is competitive, but domestic prices exceed the world level, this must be because domestic production is less efficient than world production. In these circumstances, if trade liberalization brings the price of imports below the existing domestic price, it is likely to cause severe difficulties for such inefficient domestic firms. This will result in a loss of production unless such firms are able to improve their efficiency reasonably quickly.
- *The substitutability of the imported and domestically produced good*: the overall size of the impact from trade liberalization will be determined in part by the extent to which the imported and domestic goods are substitutes. If the goods are identical, then clearly they will be perfect

substitutes. But often there are important differences in quality, reliability, familiarity and so on, which mean that they are not perfect substitutes. To analyse the impact of liberalization, it is important to know how much consumers are likely to switch from the domestic good to the imported good when the price changes.

Information on the extent of competition within a sector can come from competition authorities (if there are any) or from detailed studies of the sector. Information on the efficiency of domestic industry is often harder to obtain. Again, detailed studies of the relevant sector are necessary. But if the sector is reasonably competitive, then it may be possible to infer the level of efficiency by the extent to which domestic prices rise above world prices. Unfortunately, sectors are often both inefficient and imperfectly competitive, so it is difficult to know whether higher prices result from inefficiency or lack of competition.

Information on the extent of substitution between imported and domestically produced goods can sometimes be obtained from economic analyses of household and consumer survey data. More usually, it relies on econometric studies of the markets for traded goods.

Domestically produced intermediate goods
The effect of a trade reform that reduces the price of an imported intermediate good that is also produced domestically will be a combination of the effects outlined above. The reduction in domestic production will depend on the extent of competition in the domestic market, the level of efficiency of production and the extent to which the imported good can be substituted for the domestic one. The benefits to users of the intermediate good will depend on the intensity with which the good is used in production and the opportunities for substitution towards the intermediate good as its price falls. The information needs are therefore a combination of the above.

Table 6.1 (see pages 113–5) summarizes the data requirements and sources in each of the above cases.

6.2.2 Employment and wages

Analysis of the wage and employment effects of trade reform follow naturally from analysis of its impact on production. Clearly, where liberalization has enhanced profitability or reduced costs, demand for labour is likely to expand. Conversely, import-competing sectors facing falling demand for their output may reduce their demand for labour. The net effect of these changes in demand must then be confronted by information on the supply of labour to see how it plays out in terms of changes in wages and/or employment. If wages are fixed, shocks will manifest themselves only in employment changes, which will in turn be driven only by changes in labour demand. We start therefore by considering labour demand but caution against immediately translating changes in labour demand into changes in employment.

Labour demand

Two key pieces of information are needed to analyse the impact of liberalization on labour demand within any given sector:

- *The output elasticity of demand for labour*: that is, how sensitive is the demand for labour to changes in output. Whether a 10% reduction in output gives rise to a 5% reduction in the demand for labour, a 10% reduction, or a 20% reduction will make a large difference to the overall employment effects. Note that if the industry is in equilibrium and there are constant returns to scale, we would expect demand for every factor to fall proportionately to output. Deviations from this situation will arise only where production conditions are quite complex in terms of scale effects or lumpiness of inputs. Thus, the more important consideration is:
- *The labour intensity of production*: clearly, if a sector is extremely labour-intensive, then even if the reduction in the demand for labour is proportionate to the change in output, the absolute number of people losing their jobs will be larger than in a less labour-intensive industry.

Highly capital- or resource-intensive industries employing only highly skilled labour are likely to cut back on their capital or resource inputs if output must be reduced – so the effect on the demand for labour will be small. Conversely, in garment manufacturing, for example, labour intensity is high and absolute employment numbers will be likely to vary strongly with changes in output. Consequently, the impact of trade liberalization on employment can be large.

Data on the labour intensity of production and the sensitivity of the demand for labour to changes in output can be obtained from input-output tables and detailed technical studies of specific sectors. The overall picture of the labour intensity of different sectors can be identified relatively easily from information about:

- the total value of production in each sector;
- total employment in each sector;
- the value of the capital stock; and
- the value of other fixed factors (such as land) in each sector.

Furthermore, if such information is available over a period of time, it is possible to identify how previous changes in output have affected employment within the sector.

An analysis of the labour demand effects of liberalization inevitably focuses on the scale and nature of job losses in import-competing sectors. But it is important that policy-makers take account of the effects on all sectors' demands. The positive income effects of liberalization and the extra exports that must eventually balance any increase in imports may create sufficient additional demand for domestically produced goods that the overall labour demand effect of liberalization will be positive. But the additional demand generated is likely to be diffuse since it may be spread over a large number of sectors and regions, whereas the negative employment effects are more likely to be focused in particular sectors or areas. Thus, a full evaluation of the impact of trade liberalization must monitor changes in labour demand across all sectors and regions not just the affected sector.

This is of particular relevance to the informal sector. In many countries, the poor find most of their employment from the informal sector. In particular, the informal sector is an important provider of locally traded basic goods and services. Employment in the sector can therefore be very sensitive to overall economic conditions. Thus, changes in paid employment in the informal sector – to the extent that they can be measured – can provide a useful barometer of the extent to which reforms have been successful in generating more widespread employment gains.

Furthermore, a full analysis of the potential employment effects of liberalization should consider the short- as well as the long-term impacts. In other words, it is necessary to consider the ease (or difficulty) with which people laid off from the sector are likely to find new jobs. This requires information about the flexibility of the labour market in addition to the customary data on the size of the labour force and rates of employment and unemployment over time. In particular, information on the length of time spent in unemployment by different groups from previous economic shocks can be useful in determining whether any negative effects of a liberalization are likely to be short- or long-lived for the individuals affected (Chapter 7 discusses this issue in more detail).

Different types of labour

The discussion above treats labour as a single homogenous group, but this is, of course, far from the case. In reality, labour is as diverse as the people who constitute the labour force. It is therefore useful to distinguish between different types of labour according to a wide variety of characteristics, including:

- *Skill*: the impact of liberalization may be completely different for skilled and unskilled workers. Furthermore, since the overall income levels of skilled workers are higher than those of unskilled workers and their prospects of re-employment often greater, the poverty effects of a liberalization that affects skilled workers are likely to be weaker than one that affects unskilled workers.
- *Sector*: some skills are highly sector-specific. Thus, if trade liberalization causes a negative shock to a sector containing a large number of people with highly sector-specific skills, then the welfare losses to these individuals may be high.
- *Gender*: labour markets are often highly segmented into male and female labour forces, which can change substantially the potential impact of liberalization. For example, it is possible that segmentation of the labour market means that a liberalization had a strongly negative effect on female labour but little impact on men or vice versa (see Chapter 4 for further discussion of gender).

- *Age*: different sectors and industries have different age profiles associated with their workforce. It is necessary to know this profile to appreciate the likely effects of a liberalization on different age groups. Such knowledge needs to be linked to an understanding of the demographic structure of society. For example, the young and the elderly may be particularly vulnerable in some societies and so a liberalization that affected them negatively might have important poverty consequences. In other societies, the young and the elderly may be primarily supported through family or state mechanisms, so that the impact of liberalization on the key income-earning age groups is of most importance to poverty.

- *Experience*: key to determining the poverty effects of an employment shock is knowing who within the workforce of any given sector is most likely to be affected. Sometimes (but not always), those with the most experience are able to retain their jobs while more recently employed workers are made redundant. If less experienced workers are more likely to be poor, then this heightens the poverty effects of a liberalization.

- *Location*: labour markets can be segmented by region or location, particularly where there are geographical or policy-induced restrictions to labour mobility. This can focus the effects of both positive and negative shocks. Similarly, very large shocks, for example, the closure of the main industry in a particular town, can have a dramatic and undesirable knock-on effect on otherwise unaffected activities.

It is clear that implementing the framework of Chapter 4 requires taking account of the highly differentiated nature of the labour force. Although understanding the impact of trade liberalization on aggregate employment is clearly important, from a poverty perspective, it is vital that a more disaggregated approach is taken. For example, while knowing the labour intensity of employment within a given sector may give a useful indication of the overall employment implications associated with a shock to that sector, the key factor for poverty analysis is the intensity with which the sector uses poor workers. Poverty profiles (see Chapter 3) may give a useful indication of the skills, sectors, age, gender, location and experience of poor workers. Combining this information with more general information on the labour market may enable a policy-maker to make a more appropriate judgement of the poverty effects of a liberalization.

Labour supply
The discussion in this section has so far focused only on labour demand, with the implication that this may translate directly into employment effects. From a poverty perspective, this may be intuitive in that the effects on any individual of losing or gaining a job are generally going to be much larger than the effects of any change in wages. But in fact, demand is only half the story and changes in real wages can have very important poverty effects in aggregate. Consequently, we now add labour supply to the picture and consider the impact of liberalization on wages, as well as employment.

As Chapter 4 described, the impact of a trade liberalization on wages depends critically on the wage elasticity of the supply of labour. To recap, there are two polar positions:

- *The 'trade' approach*, which assumes that factors, including labour, are fully employed and mobile across sectors. In this situation, the elasticity of labour supply is zero, that is, there is a fixed supply of labour at any point in time, regardless of the wage rate. Consequently, shifts in the demand for labour caused by trade liberalization will be reflected entirely in increases or decreases in wages; employment will be unchanged.
- *The 'development' approach*, which assumes that there is a 'reserve army' of unskilled labour willing and able to take any job that is offered. In this situation, the elasticity of labour supply is infinite, that is, the wage rate is fixed at a subsistence wage. Shifts in the demand for labour caused by trade liberalization will in this case be reflected entirely by increases or decreases in employment as wages are fixed.

Reality, of course, will be somewhere in between these extreme cases, and what matters is precisely where it lies. An economy with a highly flexible and mobile labour force will conform more closely to the first extreme than the second, making wage changes of particular importance. Conversely, an economy with many labour market rigidities and a large pool of unemployed workers may justify a focus on the employment effects of liberalization. Note also that labour markets are often segmented by type of labour, with some types having little substitutability for others. The market for such labour may conform more closely to the 'trade' approach above, while simultaneously, the market for other kinds of labour (for example, unskilled labourers) may conform more closely to the 'development' approach.

Implementing the framework and predicting the ultimate wage and employment effects, therefore, implies being conscious of the types of labour of most concern from a poverty perspective, and then analysing the available data on wage rates and employment by sector, skill, age, gender, location and experience from this perspective. Table 6.1 (see pages 113–5) summarizes the data requirements and sources of the information needed. Figure 6.1 provides a summary flowchart for policy-makers showing how trade liberalization may affect poverty through its impact on employment and wages in enterprises and identifying the critical pieces of analysis that need to be done.

6.3 The distribution network

Chapter 4 outlined a number of ways in which the distribution network may affect the transmission of prices and hence the impact of trade liberalization on poverty. The key question here is will the effects of changed border prices be passed through to the rest of the economy?

Trade policy and shocks operate primarily via prices. If price changes are

Figure 6.1 Flowchart for policy-makers: enterprises

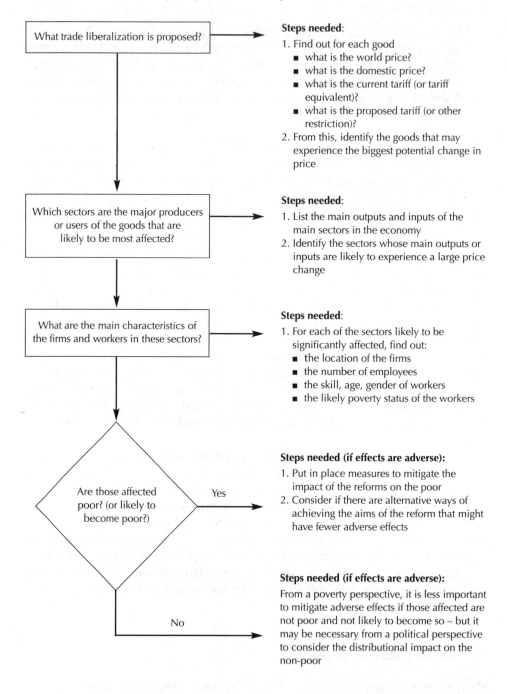

What trade liberalization is proposed?	**Steps needed:** 1. Find out for each good ■ what is the world price? ■ what is the domestic price? ■ what is the current tariff (or tariff equivalent)? ■ what is the proposed tariff (or other restriction)? 2. From this, identify the goods that may experience the biggest potential change in price
Which sectors are the major producers or users of the goods that are likely to be most affected?	**Steps needed:** 1. List the main outputs and inputs of the main sectors in the economy 2. Identify the sectors whose main outputs or inputs are likely to experience a large price change
What are the main characteristics of the firms and workers in these sectors?	**Steps needed:** 1. For each of the sectors likely to be significantly affected, find out: ■ the location of the firms ■ the number of employees ■ the skill, age, gender of workers ■ the likely poverty status of the workers
Are those affected poor? (or likely to become poor?) — Yes	**Steps needed (if effects are adverse):** 1. Put in place measures to mitigate the impact of the reforms on the poor 2. Consider if there are alternative ways of achieving the aims of the reform that might have fewer adverse effects
No	**Steps needed (if effects are adverse):** From a poverty perspective, it is less important to mitigate adverse effects if those affected are not poor and not likely to become so – but it may be necessary from a political perspective to consider the distributional impact on the non-poor

Note: Questions in rectangular boxes have multiple answers; the policy-maker proceeds to the next box when these questions have been addressed. Questions in diagonal boxes have yes/no answers; the policy-maker proceeds *either* to one set of steps/questions *or* to the other depending on the answer.

not transmitted, perhaps because the government continues to fix the internal prices of goods that it has ostensibly liberalized internationally, the most direct effects on poverty (positive or negative) will be nullified. To know whether the effects of changed border prices will be passed through to the rest of the economy requires a detailed analysis of the nature of the distribution network since this determines how changes in the post-border price are transmitted to the final consumer. For simplicity, formal analysis often assumes that the firms in the distribution network are either perfectly competitive or are monopolies. This may be a reasonable assumption for some distribution channels, but for others it may be entirely inappropriate. In such cases, it is necessary to collect and analyse information on the transmission of prices in order to estimate the effect this may have.

One approach to analysis of the transmission of prices within individual industries or sectors is known as 'value chain' analysis. Value chain analysis seeks to 'map' the production chain from the producer at one end of the chain, through the wholesalers and importer/exporters to the retailer and consumer at the other end.[4] At each stage, value chain analysis looks at:

- the number of firms[5] working at each level;
- the number of firms selling to and buying from them;
- the nature of the power relationships between the firms at different levels;
- the geographical spread of firms at each level;
- the market strategies employed by firms at each level; and
- the technical, administrative or anti-competitive barriers to entry (for example, economies of scale, licensing requirements and collusion).

Value chain analysis provides a rich picture of the operation of any given sector and the way in which market power is maintained at different points in the chain. But it has its limitations, particularly in its focus on the analysis of a single value chain, that is, a single sector of the economy. As a result, it is not well equipped to analyse the cross-sector effects of a trade liberalization, and in some cases, these may be important. For example, a price increase for a key good produced by the poor will raise incomes and therefore demand for locally produced services, which may be totally unrelated to the sector that has been liberalized.

Furthermore, the key strength of value chain analysis – that it provides a detailed picture of a given context – is also its principal weakness, for it is unlikely that the picture such analysis may paint will be applicable to other sectors or countries. It is not even clear that the structures it describes within a sector at a given time will be a good guide to the structures of that sector in the future. Nonetheless, an appreciation of the complexities of the value chain in a sector to be liberalized is more likely to give policy-makers an idea of how prices may be transmitted down through the chain.

It is useful to complement value chain analysis with simpler, less 'structural' forms of analysis. For example, many countries collect data on a wide variety of commodities in many places throughout the country, as well as on wholesale and import prices. From these, it is relatively easy to calculate the gap between the price faced by consumers and that paid at the border. More importantly, if such data are available over a long period of time, it is possible to see how this gap has changed in the past as a consequence of fluctuations of world prices and the level of protection. If price changes are historically reflected one-for-one with those at the border, then it is likely that future price changes arising from liberalization will be so too. If, on the other hand, the data show that government policy or the exercise of market power along the distribution network have restricted the movement of prices faced by consumers, then it is likely that future liberalizations will be similarly affected while such policies or structures remain in place.

Related to the question of whether changes in border prices will be transmitted vertically down to consumers, is whether price differences will be evened out horizontally between different areas of the country. In other words, the extent to which border price changes are passed through to the rest of the economy also depends on the degree of market integration. Market integration matters because, if integration is weak, then it is perfectly possible that a trade liberalization's effect will be felt quickly in urban areas with good transport links and larger markets, while the effect on more remote rural areas may be muted and slower to arrive. This is particularly important if the liberalization will be beneficial to the rural population but detrimental to the urban population, since then the urban population will experience a larger negative shock sooner than the long-term gain experienced by the rural population. Policy-makers are rightly concerned about such sequencing issues for both economic and political reasons (see Chapter 7 for a discussion of sequencing of trade reforms).

There are many approaches to calculating the extent of market integration. But all are based on the principle that if markets are functioning effectively, price differences between different regions should only reflect the transport and administrative costs of moving goods between those areas. Thus, in order to determine the degree of market integration, data are needed on both the prices for the goods in question in different parts of the country, as well as the costs of transporting those goods from different areas. Furthermore, to see how market integration has changed over time, it is important to have this information over a period of time.[6]

Market integration is an area in which government policy can have a major impact. This is because the extent of market integration is affected primarily by the provision of public goods such as transport and communications infrastructure, information on prices (for example, through newspapers, radio and TV) and storage facilities. So effective public expenditure in these areas can be essential to ensure that more remote populations are able to benefit from trade liberalization. Consequently, any effective implementation of the framework in Chapter 4 should also seek to analyse data on the extent and nature of expenditure on transport and communication infrastructure, information and (internal) trade facilitation services and storage facilities. Such information can help policy-makers to design effective complementary policies, which can be critical to the success of a trade liberalization.

Figure 6.2 Flowchart for policy-makers: distribution channels

For each good, ask:

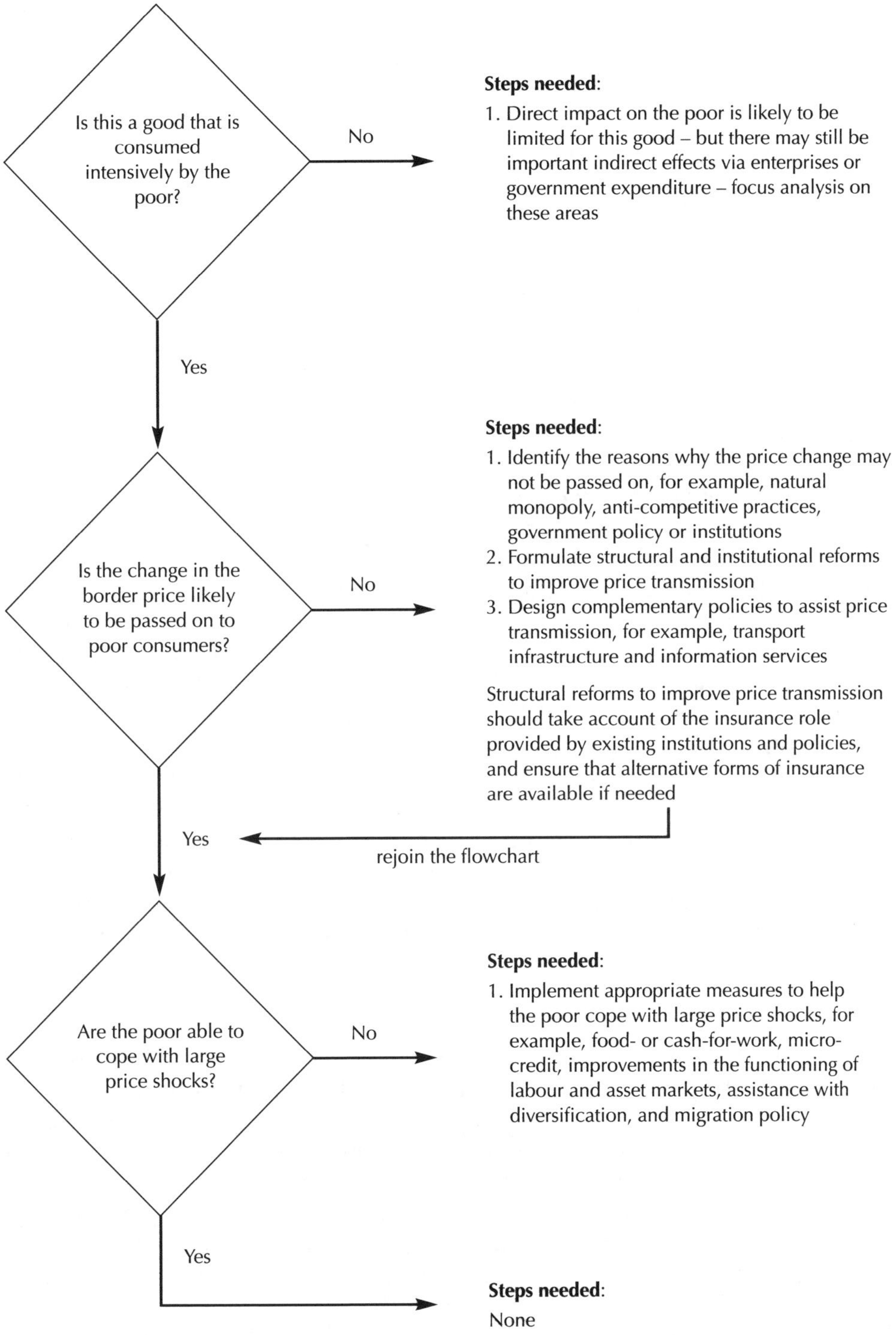

Is this a good that is consumed intensively by the poor? — No →

Steps needed:
1. Direct impact on the poor is likely to be limited for this good – but there may still be important indirect effects via enterprises or government expenditure – focus analysis on these areas

Yes ↓

Is the change in the border price likely to be passed on to poor consumers? — No →

Steps needed:
1. Identify the reasons why the price change may not be passed on, for example, natural monopoly, anti-competitive practices, government policy or institutions
2. Formulate structural and institutional reforms to improve price transmission
3. Design complementary policies to assist price transmission, for example, transport infrastructure and information services

Structural reforms to improve price transmission should take account of the insurance role provided by existing institutions and policies, and ensure that alternative forms of insurance are available if needed

Yes ← rejoin the flowchart

Are the poor able to cope with large price shocks? — No →

Steps needed:
1. Implement appropriate measures to help the poor cope with large price shocks, for example, food- or cash-for-work, micro-credit, improvements in the functioning of labour and asset markets, assistance with diversification, and migration policy

Yes ↓

Steps needed:
None

Table 6.1 (see pages 113–5) summarizes the data requirements and sources of the information needed for the types of analysis described in this section. Figure 6.2 provides a summary flowchart for policy-makers, showing the questions that policy-makers may need to ask in this area and the steps they might need to take to analyse the direct impact of trade liberalization on poverty through the price transmission network.

<u>6.4</u> Government revenue and expenditure

The third channel identified in Chapter 4 through which trade reform affects poverty is via its influence on government revenue and expenditure. On the revenue side, there is an immense literature on tax reform in both developed and developing countries (see Ahmad and Stern, 1991 and Thirsk, 1997, for theory and some applications; Boskin and McLure, 1990, and Ebrill et al., 1999, provide a large number of case studies). As always, the information required depends on the details of the analysis to be performed. But three broad aspects are common to most approaches:

The relative importance of trade taxation in tax revenue
It is essential to have a clear picture of the relative importance of trade taxation in tax revenue. Some countries are extremely dependent on duty from tariffs, licenses and export taxes and such dependence tends to be higher in poorer economies.[7] Others have different fiscal structures with a greater emphasis on corporate and capital taxation or they rely more heavily on indirect taxation such as sales tax and VAT. Clearly, trade reform is likely to have a larger impact if trade taxation constitutes a larger part of revenue.

In addition, it is necessary to obtain information about the extent to which revenue from trade taxation is sensitive to the trade reforms. Reforms to items that do not contribute greatly to overall revenue are likely to have few effects, though it is important to recognize that there may be second-round effects, for example, where a producer switches from a heavily taxed item to a substitute because the tax on the substitute has been reduced by the reform. Also, reforms to quantitative restrictions and exemptions may actually enhance rather than reduce revenues.

The administrative capacity of the tax authorities
Experience has shown that tax reform is most successful when it takes close account of the administrative capacity of the taxation authorities. In principle, most trade reforms should be revenue-enhancing in the medium term since they usually involve not only reductions in tariff rates, but also the removal of important exemptions. But reductions in tariff rates and simplification of tariff regimes can be implemented relatively easily even with limited administrative capacity; improvements in collection efficiency and the monitoring and punishment of evasion can take considerably longer.

Similarly, if new taxes (such as VAT) or improved systems are being introduced to compensate for lost tariff revenue, it may take some time for such systems to operate effectively (see Morrissey, 1995, for an interesting discussion of the sequencing of reform in such cases). Consequently, an assessment of administrative capacity is essential to provide an indication of the likely short-term impact of reform.

The structure of public expenditure
Information on the structure of public expenditure is essential. If trade reforms do result in lower revenue that cannot be compensated in the short run through borrowing, then it is necessary to have some indication of how expenditure cuts may be made. In part, this requires information about the government's procedures for expenditure allocation. It is also necessary to know the relative importance of social expenditures in government spending (Stewart, 1995, provides a taxonomy of the relative importance of priority social expenditures in government spending). If social expenditures constitute a small proportion of public expenditure, then the absolute impact on those who benefit from such services may be minimal.

Furthermore, it is useful to obtain information about the incidence of key elements of public expenditure in order to determine whether the beneficiaries are indeed poor. Studies in several countries have shown that key elements of government social expenditure, such as food subsidies, sometimes go to relatively well-off urban populations. Possibly of greatest importance is to protect those elements of public expenditure that assist poor households in risk management, for example, food- or cash-for-work schemes, and subsidies targeted at poor households. Such mechanisms can be critically important for poor households in adjusting to externally induced shocks (including, but certainly not restricted to, trade-induced shocks). The World Bank (2001) has an interesting example of an attempt by the Peruvian government to protect social expenditure in the face of expenditure cuts.

Table 6.1 (see pages 113–5) summarizes the information requirements on government revenues and expenditures and possible sources, and Figure 6.3 provides a summary flowchart for policy-makers.

6.5 Households

The ultimate aim of our analysis is to estimate the impact of trade reform on poverty at the household or individual level. Chapter 4 has detailed how households may be affected by changes in prices, employment and the provision of public services through three channels – the distribution network, enterprises, and government revenue and expenditure. But implementation of the conceptual framework should not rely only on the theoretical impact of trade liberalization through these different channels; it must also examine and monitor what actually happens to household welfare over time. This clearly requires information at the household and (where possible) the individual level. This clearly requires information at the

Figure 6.3 Flowchart for policy-makers: government revenue and expenditure

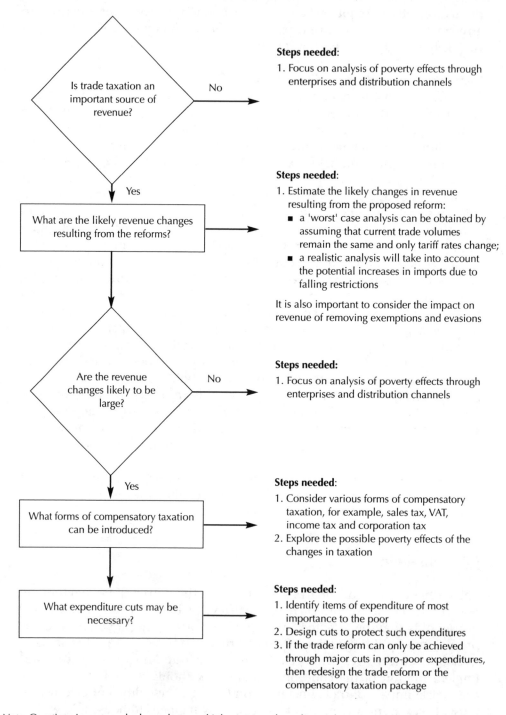

Is trade taxation an important source of revenue? → No

Steps needed:
1. Focus on analysis of poverty effects through enterprises and distribution channels

Yes ↓

What are the likely revenue changes resulting from the reforms? →

Steps needed:
1. Estimate the likely changes in revenue resulting from the proposed reform:
   - a 'worst' case analysis can be obtained by assuming that current trade volumes remain the same and only tariff rates change;
   - a realistic analysis will take into account the potential increases in imports due to falling restrictions

It is also important to consider the impact on revenue of removing exemptions and evasions

Are the revenue changes likely to be large? → No

Steps needed:
1. Focus on analysis of poverty effects through enterprises and distribution channels

Yes ↓

What forms of compensatory taxation can be introduced? →

Steps needed:
1. Consider various forms of compensatory taxation, for example, sales tax, VAT, income tax and corporation tax
2. Explore the possible poverty effects of the changes in taxation

What expenditure cuts may be necessary? →

Steps needed:
1. Identify items of expenditure of most importance to the poor
2. Design cuts to protect such expenditures
3. If the trade reform can only be achieved through major cuts in pro-poor expenditures, then redesign the trade reform or the compensatory taxation package

Note: Questions in rectangular boxes have multiple answers; the policy-maker proceeds to the next box when these questions have been addressed. Questions in diagonal boxes have yes/no answers; the policy-maker proceeds *either* to one set of steps/questions *or* to the other depending on the answer.

household and (where possible) the individual level as well as information on prices. Such information is typically obtained in three ways:

Household surveys
Household surveys provide a rich database of information essential in the analysis of the poverty effects of liberalization. Typically, household surveys include information on:

- the demographic structure of the household;
- the educational attainments of household members;
- the economic activities of the household including employment, agricultural activities and self-employment;
- household consumption (broken down by item of expenditure);
- household income (broken down by source[8]);
- the value of business assets;
- the possession of durable goods;
- health, nutrition and anthropometric data; and
- access to services such as health and education.

Such data are invaluable for monitoring progress in poverty reduction and the impact of government policies (including but certainly not limited to trade reforms). Note that household surveys usually collect information on many different dimensions of well-being. Thus, although our framework in Chapter 4 focuses on the direct economic effects of trade liberalization, household survey data may also be used to assess progress in reducing many different dimensions of poverty. In particular, one of the channels highlighted in Chapter 4 is the impact of trade liberalization on government revenue and expenditure, and the potential knock-on effects on the provision of public services to the poor. Household survey data, coupled with dedicated surveys looking at the use of public facilities such as clinics and schools (and information on actual changes in expenditure), can indicate the impact on both income and other dimensions of poverty of changes in expenditure on public services.

Household surveys are often repeated on a regular, sometimes even an annual basis. Clearly, from the perspective of monitoring the impact of policy on poverty reduction this is highly desirable. But nationally-representative household surveys can be costly and the administrative capacity for mounting such surveys and analysing the results may be limited. Nonetheless, it is highly desirable that reasonably regular surveys are carried out since this makes it likely that surveys will be available for analysis both before the initiation of major policy reforms, including trade reform, and after their completion. Only when information is available both before and after reforms is it possible to have a realistic prospect of determining the impact of any given reform.[9]

Household surveys typically take a different sample of households in each survey to ensure that the sample remains nationally representative and to avoid 'respondent fatigue'. But some surveys deliberately follow the same households or individuals over a period of time – thereby creating a 'panel' of data across time. Information from panel surveys can be extremely useful because, in principle, it allows analysts to find out how policies (and other shocks) actually affected individual households over time (as distinct from how policies affected poverty in the aggregate or the poverty of particular groups, which non-panel surveys can reveal). Furthermore, since the households remain the same for the years of the survey, panel data allow analysts to take account of the unobserved idiosyncrasies of households that may bias other forms of analysis. Consequently, if panel data are available during a period of trade liberalization, it is highly desirable to use them to understand how reforms have affected movements in and out of poverty.

Participatory assessments
Household surveys are typically nationally representative and are therefore invaluable as a means of generating aggregate statistics on poverty. But they are poor at gathering information on local understanding of the processes that give rise to the observed outcomes. Furthermore, they are difficult and costly to undertake and the quality of the data from long and complex household questionnaires is sometimes debatable.

Consequently, there has been considerable enthusiasm in recent years for participatory approaches to analysing the problems faced by households. Participatory poverty assessments tend to be community-based, with the content determined by the community (although usually facilitated externally). In addition, participatory approaches tend to focus on eliciting local understanding of the processes that give rise to a community's problems, rather than merely identifying the different dimensions of poverty. Since assessments are community-based, results tend to be reported for communities as a whole (although often disaggregated by gender) rather than at the household level. This also means that the process tends to internally 'cross-validate' the findings, since many of the responses given will have been discussed by several people.[10]

Participatory poverty assessments are therefore very different from household surveys (and often do not even share the central objective of data gathering with household surveys). Nonetheless, their very differences provide a useful way of cross-checking the information obtained from each (see McGee, 2000). If the analysis of household surveys provides similar results to the messages coming from participatory assessments, this suggests that the analysis is broadly correct. If on the other hand, very different results emerge, then it is necessary to understand the reasons for such differences (see Winters, 2000e, on differences in Africa and India). It is certainly desirable that household surveys and participatory assessments are designed with broad comparability in mind, so that each can be used by policy-makers as a check on the results of the other. Kanbur (2001) discusses some of the reasons for differences between the approaches.

Price surveys
Trade liberalization is, in essence, about changes in prices. It is therefore essential that good price data are available over time to monitor how

liberalization affects the prices faced by households.[11] Central statistical organizations in most countries collect such data on a routine basis for the purpose of compiling aggregate price indices. But from the point of view of analysing the poverty effects of reform, disaggregated data are particularly useful since the consumption basket of the poor may be markedly different from that of other households. Many statistical organizations take this into account by calculating a low-income price index using weights reflecting the pattern of expenditure of poor households. This is extremely valuable but more can be achieved: with disaggregated data, it is possible, in principle, to construct indices that reflect the price changes actually experienced by households, grouped by key characteristics that are known to be associated with poverty. For example, different price indices can be calculated for landed and landless households, or for households involved in food crop and cash crop farming, or for male- and female-headed households and so on (see Sahn and Sarris, 1991, for an example of this approach). Such disaggregated price indices can give a more accurate impression of how reforms have affected key poverty groups.

Many price surveys are based on data collected in the capital city or in a small set of towns or cities within the country. Although such measures may give a good indication of the plight of the urban poor, they may give a very poor indication of the prices faced by poor rural households.[12] This is unfortunate given the predominance of rural poverty. Thus, wherever possible, price surveys should include the collection of prices in rural areas, including more remote areas where prices are likely to differ substantially from those near urban areas, and which often have a high incidence of poverty. Even when this is not possible, there may be important differences in prices in different regions of a country. Therefore, it is highly desirable that analysis should use regionally disaggregated price indices to reflect this diversity; failure to do so may result in biased conclusions about the impact of reform on poverty. Table 6.1 (see pages 113–5) summarizes the data requirements and sources of the information needed.

6.6 The domain of trade

The final part of the framework is the 'domain of trade', that is, the extent to which goods are traded locally, regionally, nationally or internationally. The key question here is whether spillovers associated with trade liberalization are concentrated on areas or activities of relevance to the poor.

Sectors of an economy are interlinked and, if substitutability is high, a shock will be readily transmitted from one to another. Frequently, the diffusion will be so broad that it has little effect on any particular locality or sector, but sometimes – for example, where services are traded only very locally – the transmission is narrow but deep. Then it is necessary to ask whether the second-round effects have serious poverty implications. Again, it is important to note that such strong spillover effects can be positive as well as negative. For example, positive agricultural shocks can confer strong benefits on local economies where agricultural communities spend most of their income on non-traded goods and services produced locally (see Hazell and Hojjati, 1995).

Implementing the framework in this context means understanding the domain of trade. This can be done using detailed household surveys that classify goods in terms of how widely they are traded (not at all, locally, regionally, etc.) More generally, however, it is necessary to rely on less formal information describing how far afield buyers and sellers will roam and the structure of distribution chains. The domain of trade makes it possible to determine how people's expenditures might shift as a result of a trade liberalization and what the knock-on 'multiplier' effects on the local community are likely to be. For example, a positive shock that increases local demand can produce two responses: a 'quantity' response in the form of increased output and sales and a 'price' response in the form of increased prices. Both raise incomes and reduce poverty, although the latter might reduce real incomes for some groups if they are net purchasers of the good concerned but failed to benefit from the initial positive impetus. Whether the response takes the form of a quantity response or a price response depends a great deal on the ability of households and firms to respond through higher output. Thus, it is important to know the constraints that households and firms face in responding to new opportunities; this is information that may be gathered from household surveys, participatory studies and surveys of firms and employers.

There is an important role for complementary policies accompanying trade reform in order to facilitate a positive supply response. If the domain of trade is narrow and households and firms are severely constrained, it is likely that such positive shocks will lead to large increases in prices. It is important to be able to observe these and to respond with appropriate policies to remove the bottlenecks in a timely fashion. This emphasises the need for regionally disaggregated data on prices on a regular basis. Table 6.1 (see pages 113–5) summarizes the data requirements and sources of the information needed.

Summary

- Analysis of the impact of trade reforms on poverty is potentially complex. But in most cases, the most important effects can be identified from focused, but relatively straightforward analysis.
- It is essential to have a clear understanding of what trade reforms are actually proposed and which goods are therefore likely to experience the greatest price changes. Such analysis should include the impact of changes to non-tariff measures as well.

continued

Summary box continued

- It is necessary to identify the sectors that are major producers of the goods that will be subject to large price changes and to understand the characteristics of the firms in these sectors, for example, their location, number of employees, and the skill, age and gender of workers.
- The impact of a trade reform on employment and wages depends on the intensity with which production in the affected sectors uses different types of labour. If the labour market is highly flexible, trade-related shocks will be reflected mostly in changes in wages; if there is a 'reserve army' of unemployed, unskilled labour, then shocks will mostly be reflected in changes in employment.
- Assessing the direct impact of a trade reform on poverty through the distribution network involves identifying whether the good is consumed intensively by the poor and whether the change in the border price is likely to be passed on to households.
- If prices are not transmitted well, it is important to understand the reasons why this is the case, for example, because of natural monopoly, anti-competitive practices, government policy or institutions. This may require an analysis of the value chain within key sectors.
- It may be necessary to implement structural reforms to improve price transmission. Complementary policies to improve competition and market integration have an important role here.
- Assessing the impact on poverty resulting from changes in government revenue and expenditure requires an analysis of the relative importance of trade taxation and the likely revenue effects from any proposed liberalization.
- In general, trade reforms should be designed in conjunction with compensatory taxation measures to minimize any negative impact on revenues.
- There is a large quantity of detailed information on household welfare now available through households surveys and participatory assessments.
- Detailed information on prices disaggregated by product group and region is invaluable for determining the impact of reforms on the poor in remoter rural areas.
- There is an important role for complementary public policy in ensuring that households are able to respond to new opportunities presented by reforms and in widening the domain of trade through infrastructure development. If households are unable to increase output when a positive shock occurs, then the benefits of liberalization may be dissipated in increased inflation.

Notes

1   See Chapter 4 for more details on how the extent of competition and the domain of trading can determine the price effects associated with reform.
2   Note that our framework deliberately avoids looking at the linkages between such aggregate measures of trade policy stance and poverty reduction, preferring to focus instead on understanding the details of how each component of a trade reform may affect prices, wages, employment and incomes. For a discussion of how such aggregate trade policy measures may be related to growth and volatility, see Chapter 2.
3   And even in this situation, consumers gain more in aggregate than producers lose.
4   See Gereffi (1999) for an example of value chain analysis applied to the textile and clothing sector, and Humphrey (1999) for an analysis of the motor car value chain in Brazil. Kaplinsky (2000) describes how value chain analysis can be used in the study of globalization.
5   We are defining firm here in a broad sense. Thus, the most basic firm in an agricultural value chain might be a smallholder household selling their crop to a trader or wholesaler.
6   See Baulch (1997) for an example of the analysis of spatial market integration.
7   See Table 4.1 in Chapter 4 for a list of countries with a high dependence on trade taxation.
8   Income data are becoming less frequently available because of the difficulties associated with their collection (see Grosh and Glewwe, 2000). Even where income data are collected, the sector from which income is derived is often not recorded. This is a pity since this is a key piece of information for determining the poverty effects of trade liberalization.
9   Of course, having information both before and after does not necessarily tell us the impact of a reform since there may be many other things that have happened during the same period. But without such data, this kind of analysis is impossible.
10   See IDS (1996) for a description of common participatory methods. Narayan et al. (2000) provide an example of an extensive set of participatory poverty assessments.
11   This is in addition to the need for information on the prices faced by firms at different points in the value chain discussed above.
12   For example, Levinsohn et al. (1999) show that price rises in Indonesia during the economic crisis in 1997–8 were much higher for poor households in rural areas than for relatively well-off households in urban areas.

7 Trade Reform and Anti-Poverty Policy

This chapter discusses the ways in which trade policy reform and anti-poverty policy are linked, focusing particularly on:

- How an emphasis on poverty may change the timing, sequencing and speed of trade policy reform.
- How anti-poverty programmes may affect the success of trade reform.
- How trade reform affects anti-poverty expenditures.
- The nature and scale of short-term adjustment costs.
- The policy conflict arising from the different needs of the chronically poor, the transitorily poor and the productive poor.
- The arguments for and against compensating households for trade-related shocks.
- How trade reform can be integrated in the Poverty Reduction Strategy Paper process.
- The extent to which countries' anti-poverty policies are constrained by multilateral and regional trade agreements.
- Whether reform is optional.

Chapter 4 established the theoretical linkages between trade liberalization and poverty. In this chapter, we consider how they translate into practical linkages between policies of trade reform and policies designed to reduce poverty. The central issues are explored from a number of different perspectives.

First, we consider how a better appreciation of the linkages between trade and poverty might change the usual advice about how trade reform should be implemented. Numerous publications discuss the best way to implement trade policy reform; Nash and Takacs (1998), for example, provide a comprehensive review of the lessons of trade policy reforms supported by the World Bank. This chapter does not reiterate such arguments, but instead takes the current 'consensus' advice and asks how this might change when an explicit poverty perspective is added.

Second, we examine how anti-poverty programmes can directly affect the success of trade reform by removing the constraints faced by firms and households in responding to the new incentives that trade reform offers.

Third, the chapter explores the effects of trade reform on anti-poverty programmes and government responses to such effects. In particular, we look at how the revenue reductions that may result from trade liberalization can force a greater prioritization and targeting of expenditure on anti-poverty programmes.

Fourth, the chapter presents the evidence on the scale and nature of the short-term adjustment costs that may arise from trade liberalization. This impinges on anti-poverty policy because the different impact of trade reform on different groups can present dilemmas for the allocation of resources between chronically and transitorily poor households. The arguments for and against compensating households for trade-related shocks are presented, along with an assessment of the experience of such schemes in North America and Australia and the lessons for policy-makers in developing countries.

Next, we switch to look more practically at how trade reform can be integrated within the Poverty Reduction Strategy Paper process that currently governs donor assistance to national poverty reduction activities. The following section then examines the extent to which obligations under multilateral and regional trade agreements constrain developing-country governments in their pursuit of anti-poverty strategies. Finally, we briefly explore the question 'is reform optional?' and examine whether there are circumstances in which trade reform may not be economically sensible.

7.1 The impact of a poverty perspective on trade reform[1]

Three key questions are generally asked about the implementation of trade policy reform:

- should trade liberalization be implemented alongside or after economic stabilization?
- in what sequence should different accounts be liberalized?
- at what speed should liberalization take place?

The literature that attempts to answer these questions has often considered the welfare implications of different policy choices. But it has not generally considered the impact on the poor *per se*. We therefore concentrate on how a poverty focus changes the way in which trade reform might be implemented.

7.1.1 Initial timing

Many countries undertaking trade liberalization are doing so in the context of general macroeconomic problems that require stabilization programmes (often supported by the IMF). As a result, there has been a debate over whether to do stabilization first or to attempt trade reform at the same time. The general advice from the literature is that if the stabilization is competently managed, attempting both at the same time has some advantages.

In particular, exchange rate management has a very important role in trade liberalization. As Corden (1990) comments, 'the most important point about large-scale unilateral trade liberalization is that it must be associated with real devaluation if the current account is not to deteriorate and if the employment losses in protected import-substituting industries are to be compensated by employment gains elsewhere, especially in export industries.' And Ten Kate (1992) illustrates how systematic depreciation of the exchange rate cushioned the impact of trade liberalization on import-competing industries in Mexico during the 1980s, thereby enabling successful trade liberalization.

Four main arguments are made against simultaneous liberalization:

- *Administrative capacity*. It is vital that policy reforms are competently implemented. In countries with very limited administrative capacity, attempting simultaneous stabilization and sometimes complex trade liberalization can result in neither being achieved.
- *Political opposition*. Since stabilizations are often made necessary by balance of payments problems, they almost always involve reductions in aggregate demand and are therefore painful and unpopular. Combining trade liberalization with stabilization tends to result in the political opposition to stabilization also being attached to trade liberalization. See Morrissey (1995) for an analysis of the linkages between the administrative and political aspects of policy reform.
- *Currency appreciation*. Stabilization measures to counter inflation sometimes attempt to anchor the exchange rate against some external currency. In such cases, there is often a short-run real appreciation of the currency as domestic inflation runs ahead of inflation abroad. But successful trade reform requires a real depreciation (to encourage a shift of resources into tradable goods). So anti-inflationary stabilizations may run counter to the changes needed for successful trade reform.
- *Adjustment costs*. If the adjustment costs of reform are related to the speed and depth of the reforms, then the costs of combining stabilization and trade liberalization may be higher than the costs of implementing them sequentially (see Falvey and Kim, 1992).

How does a poverty perspective change these arguments? The administrative capacity argument for delaying trade liberalization until after stabilization applies equally to the administrative capacity for managing social safety nets and general anti-poverty programmes. Thus, simultaneous trade liberalization may affect a government's ability to respond effectively to the contractionary impact of stabilization, particularly if the contractionary impact is greater precisely because the two policy reforms have been combined.

Against this argument is the fact that simultaneous implementation allows a faster transition to the new equilibrium. Since it is often the poor, particularly those in rural areas and in agriculture, who bear the cost of the current distortions, delaying trade liberalization may not be in the best interests of the poor. Furthermore, simultaneous implementation may actually help some poor households (particularly the urban poor and the landless) by reducing price rises caused by a devaluation of the currency as part of the stabilization programme.

So introducing a poverty perspective does not suggest an unambiguous preference about the initial timing of trade reform; rather, it indicates the considerations that might lead to such a choice. A government that is in a strong position politically and which has a good administrative capability will probably wish to undertake reforms jointly. In contrast, a government with weak administrative abilities and which is susceptible to political pressure from the owners of import-substituting industries (or from organized labour in such industries) may wish to postpone trade liberalization until after successful stabilization.

7.1.2 Sequencing

Trade liberalization is rarely the only form of policy reform being undertaken by a government. There has therefore been considerable debate about the appropriate order for liberalization, particularly of the capital and the current account. This Handbook focuses explicitly on trade liberalization rather than wider issues associated with liberalization of the capital account. But the issue of the sequencing of reforms is inherent to the debate over successful trade liberalization. We, therefore, briefly review the arguments for and against simultaneous liberalization of the capital and current accounts, and note how a concern with poverty issues may change the emphasis of this debate.

The principal reason for simultaneous liberalization of the capital and current accounts is because of the economic welfare effects of the distortions caused by liberalizing one account but not the other. As Falvey and Kim (1992) argue, 'if the restrictions involve tariffs or taxes, it will not in general be optimal to fully liberalize one account while the other remains restricted'. The optimal strategy, according to this view, exploits the theory of the 'second best' to design a programme of reform that maintains interventions on both accounts until both are fully liberalized.

Against this, Edwards (1986) argues that early capital account liberalization encourages borrowing from abroad to maintain consumption. Some of this expenditure falls on traded goods, which is accommodated by a widening current account deficit; the remainder, however, falls on non-traded goods, causing a real appreciation of the exchange rate. Since successful trade liberalization requires the opposite – a real depreciation of the exchange rate to encourage a shift of resources into, rather than out of, the tradable goods sector – early capital account liberalization can make it more difficult.

Furthermore, the Asian crisis of 1997–8 has led to considerable scepticism about the advisability of full capital account liberalization because of concerns that the high speed and large volume of capital movements can cause increased volatility of investment, thereby lowering growth and increasing its volatility (see Razin and Rose, 1992). As a result, the 'consensus' advice typically offered is to liberalize the current account first and then, cautiously, the capital account.

A focus on poverty will, if anything, emphasize the importance of stability since poor households are typically less well insured against shocks than wealthier ones. Consequently, adding a poverty perspective probably lends further support to arguments for caution in liberalization of the capital account.

7.1.3 Gradualism versus 'big-bang' reform

One of the most heated debates in trade liberalization concerns the appropriate speed of reform. Some argue that trade liberalization should occur rapidly so as to remove distortions and send clear price signals to facilitate adjustment. Others argue that this is unrealistic and that gradual reforms are likely to be less costly and more successful.

The principal arguments for rapid reform are economic; Mussa (1986) provides several examples. Where welfare-reducing distortions exist, it is clearly better for these to be reduced and eliminated sooner rather than later. Of course, adjusting to the new equilibrium will be costly, but in itself this is not an argument for gradual reform since spreading the costs over a longer period of time does not necessarily reduce the overall cost.

If the social costs of adjustment are identical to the private costs, private agents, interested in minimizing the latter will also minimize the former and the optimal policy will be to reform completely at once and let nature take its course. The case for gradualism, therefore, relies on the assumption that society as a whole cares relatively more about the present (and less about the future) than individuals do.[2] If this is the case, then it could make sense to minimize the costs of adjustment experienced immediately and push more of them into the future by adopting a more gradual approach. But, in fact, individuals are generally thought to be more impatient than society as a whole, which would make it optimal to liberalize faster rather than slower.

In general, Falvey and Kim (1992) conclude that, 'the presence of distortions which may generate a difference between private and social costs and benefits of adjustment does suggest that an immediate shift to the long-run reformed level of trade barriers may not be optimal. There appears to be no necessary presumption that a gradual reform is to be preferred, however, overshooting may be the preferred response in many circumstances.' Thus, the general message from the literature is that long-term economic efficiency calls for rapid reform, with gradualism only desirable when short-term costs are high.[3]

But trade reforms are decided by politicians not economists and there are several practical and political reasons for gradualism. One of the most important is that many developing countries still rely on trade taxation for a substantial part of government revenue (see Chapter 4 for a discussion of this dependence; Greenaway and Milner, 1991, provide a more detailed description of the extent of such dependency). Trade reform does not necessarily reduce government revenue, particularly when the conversion of quantitative restrictions to tariffs and the removal of exemptions precede tariff reductions. But trade reform can be administratively complex and measures to improve revenue collection can take longer to implement than simple tariff reductions. Consequently, if rapid reductions in tariff rates are implemented before or even simultaneously with measures to increase revenue, it is likely that government revenue will be reduced, at least in the short term. For this reason, many governments are wary of rapid liberalization.

Furthermore, trade reform will only be successful if it is credible, that is, if economic agents believe that the changes will occur and alter their expectations and actions accordingly. Government may attempt to change these expectations by pre-announcing programmes of reform. But in many cases, the latest reforms come after a series of previous attempts at reform, which will have had varying degrees of success, suggesting that pre-announcement in itself is unlikely to generate commitment. Thus, governments face a complex 'chicken and egg' problem: credibility is necessary for reforms to succeed, but successful reform is necessary to achieve credibility.

Politicians often choose the reform path that they judge will give the reforms the greatest political chances of success. Whether economically optimal or not, rapid liberalization imposes a larger short-term shock than gradualism. This can arouse immediate and substantial political opposition. On the other hand, gradual liberalization (particularly with a pre-announced programme) allows time for coalitions opposed to the reforms to mobilize, although it also allows the government time to develop constituencies of winners from reform as well. Consequently, the actual speed of the reform process is often determined by the intricacies of an individual country's internal politics.

The only general advice that can be given with respect to credibility, therefore, is purely practical. The success of trade reform depends not only on politics but also on the government's capacity actually to implement the necessary changes. Governments are, therefore, advised to choose reforms tailored to their administrative capacity, even if this reduces the scope of the reforms. 'Narrow but deep' reforms are more likely to be implemented and, therefore, more likely to build credibility than poorly implemented sweeping reforms (see Rodrik, 1989). They must, however, be implemented in a manner that avoids serious distortions on the way to liberalization: for example, artificially stimulating production of inappropriate goods by reducing tariffs on inputs before those on outputs should be avoided.

Adding a poverty perspective

How does a focus on poverty change the arguments about the speed of trade liberalization? The most obvious point is that insofar as the poor are beneficiaries of public spending, measures that protect social expenditure are important.[4] This would suggest a preference for gradual reform to avoid the reductions in revenue and resulting expenditure cuts that can be associated with rapid reform. Furthermore, if urban poverty is a serious concern and labour markets are inflexible, then the large increase in urban unemployment that may result from rapid reform could increase urban poverty. Zambia may be useful case in point here: a combination of rapid trade liberalization and macroeconomic stabilization caused a large increase in urban poverty in the country during the 1990s (see McCulloch, Baulch and Cherel-Robson, 2000). Such large and sudden increases in poverty among relatively vocal urban groups can cause social and political instability and hence partial or complete reversal of reforms.

Nevertheless, in principle, the poor have much to gain from reform. Landless rural households who rely on employment for most of their income will benefit from the increased demand for rural employment that results from the removal of a bias against agricultural production. Along with the majority of smallholders who are net food consumers, they also stand to benefit if food prices are reduced because of liberalization. Delaying reform will not help these groups.

Against this is the common recognition that the poor are generally more vulnerable to economic shocks than other groups in society (see Glewwe and Hall, 1998) because of their poorer access to mechanisms for consumption smoothing and to the means that might enable a rapid and flexible response to the changing economic situation. If rapid trade liberalization leads to greater adverse price shocks, then gradual reform may be preferred in order both to reduce the stress on the uninsured and to allow suitable safety net mechanisms to be put in place.

Ultimately, a poverty perspective re-emphasizes the importance of successful liberalization and, as noted above, the appropriate speed that such reform should take often depends more on political exigencies than economic arguments. But it is worth noting in this regard that the poor in most developing countries constitute at least a large minority of the population. Since in many countries they are among the principal long-term beneficiaries of trade liberalization, trade reform may be achieved more quickly and more sustainably if greater efforts are made to increase the voice and ultimately the political mobilization of poor groups.

7.2 Anti-poverty programmes as complementary policies to trade reform

Many anti-poverty (as well as general development) projects are designed to enhance the productive opportunities of the poor, whether through education and training or improved access to land, irrigation or inputs. Since the poor, particularly in rural and agricultural areas, may be key beneficiaries of trade reform, it is important to ensure that they are able to respond to the new opportunities. Unfortunately, a poor supply response to the new incentives provided by trade liberalization is often a reason for the reversal of such reforms since the costs in terms of increased competition and unemployment are experienced prior to the benefits associated with the expansion of alternative activities (see Goldin and Knudsen, 1989). This is why trade reforms are often conducted simultaneously with programmes of structural adjustment designed to reduce the physical and institutional rigidities that inhibit economic flexibility (see Killick, 1993).

But structural adjustment programmes typically focus on adjustments in policies and institutions at the national and regional levels. Poverty studies, on the other hand, show that the difficulties faced by poor households in responding to new opportunities are often due to institutions and norms at the local level (see Box 7.1). For example, local trading or distribution monopolies may prevent price signals being perceived by small farmers or business people; similarly, deteriorating rural roads may prevent traders

Box 7.1 **Examples of anti-poverty and development programmes assisting trade reform**

Tanzania: the Economic Recovery Programme (ERP) of 1986–8 in Tanzania attempted to increase agricultural production by raising export crop prices. Prices for export crops rose by 10–80% each year of the programme, with similar rises in food crop prices. But the effects on production were mixed. In some years, price incentives were outweighed by the effect of drought. The ERP came increasingly to realize the critical importance of investment in fertilizer, seeds, technology, irrigation, replanting and extension. The failure of development programmes to address these areas resulted in a poor supply response to a substantial trade liberalization (see Killick, 1993).

Zambia: under ideal conditions, poor smallholders in Zambia should benefit from liberalization of the maize market. But Alwang et al. (1996) show that this will only be the case when markets are nearby, input delivery is timely, adequate cash exists to finance operations and good health prevails. In practice, poor households face many and sometimes all of these constraints. This research shows that the combination of all these constraints can reduce the gains from liberalization by half, with female-headed households particularly badly affected, as well as households without access to oxen. Again, this points to the critical role of complementary anti-poverty policies in ensuring poor households reap the gains from trade reforms.

Latin America: de Janvry and Sadoulet (1993) outline the key role that anti-poverty policy must play in enabling rural development in Latin America. These include:

- household-oriented strategies, which should promote a multiplicity of home-based activities, including animals and non-agricultural services, and should stress the key role of women and the importance of human capital formation;
- access to land and security of access (through redistributive land reform when possible, the titling of squatters and revival of the land rental market), which can be essential in enabling the poor to benefit from reforms;
- elimination of policy biases towards mechanization and extensive livestock operations, which will help poor households benefit from the employment creation resulting from reform.

from exploiting improved prices because of the higher costs of transport. Anti-poverty programmes can play an important role, therefore, in supporting trade reform through measures to enhance the flexibility with which poor households are able to respond to new economic opportunities. This suggests that there may be a trade-off between anti-poverty interventions that aim to protect consumption during reform and efforts to enhance investment and improve flexibility.

Of course, not all policies designed to improve the ability of individuals and firms to respond to the new incentives created by trade liberalization are necessarily intended to counter poverty directly. Nonetheless, complementary policies are very important to the success of trade reforms since the distortions and rigidities that they address apply to everyone and not just the poor. Although complementary policies such as transport infrastructure or improved communications may have relatively little direct anti-poverty effects, they may still be important for enabling firms to respond effectively.

The problem for policy-makers, therefore, is to identify the key constraints that inhibit a significant supply response and then to ask if the response that they frustrate would have a major effect on poverty. Thus, a major constraint on the growth of an industry or sector that predominantly employs poor people may be important, even if the direct benefits of removing it mostly reach the non-poor. Conversely, from a poverty reduction perspective, it may be a mistake to focus on removing constraints from sectors with few linkages to the poor. Indeed, one of the reasons why anti-poverty policy matters is that complementary policies addressing the constraints inhibiting adjustment will not necessarily enable the poor themselves to participate in the resulting benefits. In general, the best way of ensuring that the majority of the poor benefit from trade liberalization will be to enable them to benefit directly. Hence the importance of anti-poverty policy.

7.3 The impact of trade reform on anti-poverty programmes

The discussion above focused on how an emphasis on poverty changes the way in which trade reform might be implemented and how anti-poverty programmes can have a direct effect on the success of trade reform. But the linkages between anti-poverty policy and trade reform also operate in the reverse direction, that is, trade reform can also have an important effect on the size and effectiveness of anti-poverty programmes.

The primary mechanism through which trade reform affects anti-poverty programmes is via its effects on government revenue and expenditure. Trade liberalization is often conducted in conjunction with other economic reforms, some of which may have the effect of reducing government revenue, at least in the short run. If macroeconomic stability is to be maintained, this often results in a need for expenditure reduction. If social expenditures are to be maintained, it is necessary to evaluate systematically the effectiveness of existing expenditures in all areas of government spending and reallocate resources away from less productive expenditure into expenditures that are likely to benefit the poor.

In practice, this can be politically difficult since it involves some areas agreeing to accept additional hardship in order to relieve the burden on the social sectors. It is, therefore, crucially important that efforts are made to mobilize constituencies in support of such a reallocation of resources in order for the poor to be protected. Donors can play an important role here in 'softening' the budget constraint faced by governments attempting reforms through additional support for social sectors during the adjustment period.

But in addition to reallocating resources towards social sectors, it is vital that expenditures within these sectors are focused on the poor. Budget constraints, therefore, provide an opportunity for governments to examine critically what is being done with funds in the social sectors and to evaluate the 'value for money' of such programmes. The huge discrepancies among governments with similar social spending per capita in terms of social-sector performance (for example, in maternal, infant and under-five mortality, literacy and schooling enrolment) indicate that there are substantial opportunities for improvements in the efficiency of delivery of social services.

Furthermore, analyses of the incidence of public expenditure show that social-sector programmes are often very poorly targeted, with much of the expenditure falling on those most (rather than least) able to pay (see Castro-Leal et al., 1999). Of course, there are legitimate concerns about targeting: administrative costs can be high; targeting variables sometimes select the 'wrong' households; targeted households have an incentive to remain in the targeted group, inducing dependency; and targeting one group for assistance inevitably means excluding some other group, which has political costs (see Besley and Kanbur, 1993, for a review of targeting; and van de Walle, 1993, for the implications for research and policy).

Nonetheless, targeting resources on the poor can improve the incidence of public expenditure and the delivery of social services in a time of tight budgetary constraints (see Grosh, 1993). In addition to their social value, such actions can be critical to the success of trade (and other) reforms through forestalling opposition that might otherwise be caused by reductions in social services.

7.4 Trade reform and short-term adjustment

While trade liberalization typically has long-run benefits, there are almost always firms and households who lose in the short term. Trade reform, therefore, has an important indirect effect on anti-poverty policy by creating a conflict over the allocation of resources between the immediate losers from reform and the long-term poor. This section presents the evidence on the scale and nature of the short-term adjustment costs that may result from trade liberalization. The following section shows how concern for those who bear the brunt of these adjustment costs can affect the emphasis given to different groups who are poor.

Trade liberalization typically implies adjustment in the set of goods that a country produces if it is to capture the benefits of reform. If adjustment is costly, liberalization could lead to periods of decline and poverty before things get better. The key question for poverty analysis is whether individuals or households slip temporarily into poverty as an economy adjusts to open trade, and what can be done to prevent this and to help those who do.

The most significant adjustment problem lies in factor markets, especially employment, and so we concentrate on that.

7.4.1 How long does unemployment last?

The key to answering this question lies in the speed of labour turnover and the flexibility of the labour market. Unfortunately, there seems to be very little research directly on labour turnover in developing countries (see Matusz and Tarr, 1999).

There is no presumption that adjustment must be costly. For example, Mauritius has successfully combined a limited trade liberalization (in an export-processing zone) with poverty reduction – see, for example, Milner and Wright (1998), who identify increasing unskilled and female wages as exports boomed. Panama is another case of relatively costless adjustment: substantial liberalizations of trade in 1996–7 and of domestic regulations in previous years led to a decrease in unemployment (from 16.2% to 13.2% in one year) and to reduced poverty as informal-sector wages rose and poor workers entered formal employment (see World Bank, 1999b). And Harrison and Revenga (1998) find that manufacturing employment increased almost immediately after half the liberalizations they study; the other half are mostly transitional economies in which much more than trade liberalization was happening and in which the general retrenchment created a very unfavourable environment for workers displaced by changing trade patterns.

Life is not necessarily so rosy, however, even in non-transition liberalizations. Workers may suffer long-lived and deep losses of income if they have previously enjoyed very high levels of protection or if they had built up strong firm-specific human capital. For example, Rama and MacIsaac (1999) find that employees displaced from the Ecuadorian Central Bank in 1994 had regained on average only 55% of their pre-dismissal salaries after 15 months, despite generally low unemployment levels. And Mills and Sahn (1995) found that of Guinean public-sector workers laid off in 1985–8, half of those who found new jobs increased their earnings, but their average unemployment duration exceeded two years and 30% of them were still unemployed by 1992.

Overall, it is difficult to generalize about how deep and how durable transitional employment losses will be. It does seem likely, however, that the costs will be greater the more protected the sector originally was and the greater the shock. In particular, labour markets suffering very large shocks can become dysfunctional because even normal turnover ceases as incumbents dare not resign for fear of not finding a new job. Thus, major reforms, such as transition, or concentrated reforms, such as closing the only plant in a town, do seem more likely to generate transitional losses through unemployment than more diffuse reforms. On the other hand, it is precisely the sectors with highest protection or the economies with most widespread distortion that offer the greatest long-run returns to reform.

Transitional unemployment (or declining rewards for skills) is unfortunate for anyone who suffers it, but it does not necessarily lead to poverty. Individuals who have lived beyond the reach of poverty for some time will generally have assets, or access to credit, with which to smooth consumption. The poor, on the other hand, will have very few assets: even switching from one unskilled informal-sector job to another could cause hardship, especially if temporary stress led to permanent consequences, such as poor health or curtailed education. Thus, attention to transitional unemployment should focus on those who were initially poor or near-poor. This is not always the case in practice, however, for typically the middle class will be more articulate and more influential politically than the poor.

7.5 Transitory and chronic poverty

If the losers from trade reform are already poor or nearly poor, then the reforms will cause an increase in poverty. But if trade reforms are in keeping with the long-term comparative advantage of the country, such increases in poverty should be temporary. Anti-poverty policy, therefore, faces a difficult trade-off between programmes to assist the chronically poor and those to alleviate the increase in transitory poverty that may result from reform.

More precisely, anti-poverty policy needs to find a balance between devoting resources to three different groups:

- *The chronically poor*: these are households and individuals with diminished productive capability, for example, children, the elderly and the disabled. Such groups need consumption assistance to ensure their survival and well-being, particularly when they are not connected to supportive social networks that may provide for them.
- *The productive poor*: these are households with productive potential but few assets and opportunities. Such groups need investment assistance (whether in physical, natural or human capital) to enable them to improve their productivity and incomes. These are the households who are most likely to be able to benefit from trade liberalization with suitable interventions to improve their ability to respond to new incentives.
- *The transitory poor*: these are households who have lost as a consequence of the trade reforms and have therefore dropped below the poverty line. Given that these households are generally productive households, it is anticipated that they may be able to improve their incomes in the long term as they adjust to the new economic circumstances. Thus, their poverty is transitory (although no less real for that). Such households will benefit from interventions designed to smooth their incomes and

consumption over time, such as employment guarantee schemes, insurance and micro-credit programmes.

If reforms are likely to give rise to an increase in all types of poverty, then there is a case for increased resources for all of these groups. But reform typically affects some groups more than others. In particular, if reform increases transitory poverty, then there may be a case for devoting additional resources to interventions designed to reduce vulnerability and uncertainty in consumption. This is particularly the case where reforms threaten already poor households, with disastrous falls in their standard of living.

But policy-makers should recognize that this is a trade-off. Most transitorily poor households are substantially better off than chronically poor households. For example, McCulloch and Baulch (1999) found that their sample of transitorily poor households in rural Pakistan had twice the income of chronically poor households. Furthermore, the ability to insure consumption against shocks is related to income. Jalan and Ravallion (1999) show that while virtually no households in four provinces of rural China are completely insured against shocks, the better-off are far better insured than the poor. Thus, although devoting additional resources to transitorily poor households may be important to ensure the political sustainability of reforms, it may also involve diverting resources away from poorer households.

Finally, it is important to recognize that a balance should be struck between the need for economic adaptation and the desire to protect the poor. In reviewing general lessons about the impact of structural adjustment on poverty, Killick (1995) argues that 'as a general principle, however, overriding priority should be given to safeguarding investment, on the grounds that economic adaptation should not be impeded, with success in this task ultimately determining a country's ability to overcome absolute poverty.' Exactly the same lesson applies in the case of trade liberalization. The consequence is that governments wishing to ensure the political survival of reforms by supporting the transitorily poor and the long-term success of the reforms by supporting the productive poor, may end up reducing their support for the poorest and most vulnerable group, the chronically poor.

Is there any way to resolve this dilemma? One approach is to support interventions that assist more than one of the three groups at the same time. For example, improving and creating institutions designed to tackle uncertainty and manage risk will both help the transitorily poor and encourage investment (see Pindyck, 1991). In addition, long-term biases in the allocation of resources can be avoided by focusing on schemes where benefits automatically reduce as recipients become better off. For example, employment guarantee schemes tend to have this characteristic since wage rates are generally low, and hence individuals only participate when there are few alternative sources of income. Policy-makers should therefore consider carefully how to construct an appropriate portfolio of interventions in order to satisfy their political and poverty reduction objectives.

7.6 Should the losers from trade reform be compensated?

If trade reform is likely to give rise to both winners and losers, should not the losers be compensated? This section outlines the arguments for and against compensating the losers from reform, and describes the experience of three developed countries – the United States, Canada and Australia – in implementing such 'trade adjustment assistance'.

Lawrence and Litan (1986) provide four reasons for compensating losers from trade reform:

Welfare-based arguments

The fundamental idea at the heart of welfare analysis of trade reform is that liberalization should give rise to a Pareto improvement, that is, that nobody should lose from the reform and at least somebody should gain. If there are losers from a trade reform, then clearly it is not a Pareto improvement. But if society as a whole benefits from the reform, then it should in theory be possible for the winners to compensate the losers so that nobody loses and at least somebody gains (see Dixit and Norman, 1980, 1986).

Equity-based arguments

In principle, government assistance should be concentrated on the poor regardless of whether their poverty is the result of trade liberalization or anything else. But implementing redistributive policy can be both technically and politically difficult. Consequently, targeting assistance towards those affected by trade liberalization may be a second-best way of reaching the poor.

Efficiency-based arguments

Markets do not always adjust smoothly and instantaneously. Consequently, negative shocks resulting from trade liberalization can yield inefficient outcomes. For example, market failures can result in unemployment (over and above the transitional unemployment caused due to labour turnover) or in people being forced to take jobs less well matched with their skills because they cannot afford to be unemployed for too long. Furthermore, the existence of sunk costs in many sectors means that shifting resources to other uses can be costly. In such situations, compensation can help resources move to reflect comparative advantage. Thus, compensatory policies can promote training and relocation of workers, as well as the upgrading of existing facilities to enable them to compete in the new environment.

Political arguments

Unsurprisingly, those who are likely to lose from trade liberalization tend to lobby to prevent it from happening. Thus, a trade liberalization that is beneficial overall may be blocked by the political action of a minority of people who are negatively affected. By providing some recompense to those affected, compensation can both discourage lobbying and make a given trade liberalization more politically acceptable.

There are also several arguments against compensating the losers from trade liberalization. We outline five:

Incentive effects
A general problem with all forms of compensatory policy including trade adjustment assistance is that they can induce undesirable behaviour in actual and potential beneficiaries. In particular, if programme benefits are conditional on being in a disadvantaged state, then potential beneficiaries have an incentive to remain disadvantaged. For example, if workers displaced by a trade shock receive assistance only if they remain unemployed, then they have less incentive to find alternative employment (see Brander and Spencer, 1994).

Unfairness
People suffer negative consequences from many types of economic (and other) shocks; trade adjustment assistance only compensates them for costs resulting from one particular kind of shock. In theory, people should not mind if someone else benefits from assistance due to compensation for a trade shock when they do not benefit, say because their unemployment does not result from a trade shock. But in practice, many people would regard this as unfair. Furthermore, if we are concerned about poverty, the precise cause of a person's poverty should not determine whether they receive assistance; the key thing is appropriate action to enable them to leave poverty as soon as possible.

Creating precedents
A further argument against compensation for shocks resulting from changes in trade policy is that the creation of a programme of assistance creates a precedent that the government is prepared to compensate people who lose as a consequence of changes in government policy. Since governments are not likely to have the resources to be able to compensate all the possible losers from all possible changes in government policy, they may worry that the creation of compensatory programmes for trade adjustment may encourage others to lobby for compensation for a wide range of other shocks.

Institutional inertia
Similarly, compensatory programmes once started are politically extremely difficult to stop. Kapstein (1998), for example, describes how the Trade Adjustment Assistance (TAA) programme in the United State has become institutionalized. Consequently, governments are wise to think hard before creating a claim on their budgetary resources that will be hard to remove if experience shows that the compensation was ineffective or poorly targeted.

Efficiency of public expenditure and revenue
Finally, governments have a responsibility to ensure the most efficient use of public funds. If a government's objective is to reduce poverty, then it must be clear that the introduction of a trade compensation programme will be

more effective at poverty reduction than any alternative use of public funds. Experience suggests that this is highly unlikely since the workers affected by trade reform are often better off than other workers (although clearly this is very country-specific).

Furthermore, increased expenditure must be paid out of increased revenue, the collection of which through taxation creates further economic distortions. For example, estimates for the economic cost of raising an additional US$1 of government revenue in the United States range from US$1.17 to US$1.56. In other words, there is a net efficiency loss of 17–56% associated with raising additional revenue (see Ballard et al., 1985). While estimates of the cost of raising government revenue in most developing countries are not available, policy-makers must nonetheless take account of the efficiency cost of all forms of additional public expenditure, including trade adjustment assistance.

7.6.1 Experience with compensation schemes in developed countries

In practice, only a few developed countries have implemented explicit systems of compensation for individuals and firms negatively affected by trade reform. There are several possible explanations for this: trade unions in some developed countries are powerful and are, therefore, in a better position to lobby for compensation for lay-offs arising from trade liberalization than most of their developing country counterparts. More significantly, governments have been understandably reluctant to implement schemes of compensation when there is no clear mechanism for identifying the winners and losers from trade reform. Furthermore, if a government announces a compensatory policy, it is indirectly admitting the existence of costs from the reform, which can increase political opposition to the reform.

The best-known compensatory policy for trade reform is the TAA programme in the United States. This offers a composite of measures to support an industry damaged by liberalization with loans and assistance plus measures to compensate the displaced workers, including benefits to support income and training services.

The TAA was established by the Kennedy administration in 1962 as a *quid pro quo* for the wave of liberalization led by the Trade Expansion Act (TEA) in the United States and the Kennedy Round in the GATT. It provides trade-displaced workers with extended unemployment benefits, relocation expenses and (compulsory) training as a bridge to a new job with similar levels of income and benefits.[5] Several evaluations of the TAA programme have shown it provides additional income for temporarily displaced workers, many of whom obtain alternative employment relatively quickly anyway. But it fails to assist significantly those permanently displaced by trade-related closures. In addition, Decker and Corson (1995) suggest that training does not increase the future earnings of displaced workers.

Nonetheless, the TAA forms the basis of the North American Free Trade Agreement Transitional Adjustment Assistance (NAFTA-TAA) programme,

established in 1993. This assists workers who lose their jobs or whose hours
of work and wages are reduced as a result of trade with Canada or Mexico,
by providing them with the opportunity to engage in long-term training
while receiving income support.

Canada and Australia have operated similar schemes at various times in
the past – the General Adjustment Assistance Programme (GAAP) in Canada,
and the Special Adjustment Assistance (SAA) in Australia – and with
similarly unconvincing effects. Overall, experience with trade adjustment
assistance has not been particularly happy. Schemes are often bureaucratic,
providing limited benefits to a small category of workers who might well
have found alternative jobs anyway, while providing little long-term
assistance to the permanently displaced. Decisions on whether a worker is
displaced due to government trade policy or some other shock have
inevitably been rather arbitrary, leading to resentment among workers who
fail to qualify for the benefit. In some cases, such schemes have assisted
firms in moving to activities better reflecting comparative advantage, while
in others they have inhibited such a move.

For developing-country policy-makers, this presents a dilemma. On the
one hand, it is important, both from a welfare perspective and politically, to
identify as closely as possible those groups who will be affected by a trade
reform. In particular, it is necessary to understand how the reforms are likely
to change movements into and out of poverty and the depth of poverty
experienced. Policy should then be oriented towards minimizing the depth
and severity of poverty experienced as a result of the policy change.

In practice, given the extremely limited resources available to most
developing countries, this suggests targeting assistance towards those most
in need regardless of the reason for their poverty. In other words, although
identifying losers from a given trade reform is a key first step, public policy
in most developing countries is probably best concentrated on the provision
of social safety nets, targeted by the characteristics most likely to make
people vulnerable to poverty from a wide range of possible shocks. For
example, a general cash- or food-for-work scheme compensates people who
become unemployed as a consequence of job loss regardless of whether the
job loss resulted from trade liberalization. In most countries, this will be
preferable to compensation targeted at individuals suffering directly as a
consequence of trade reform.[6]

7.7 Trade reform and Poverty Reduction Strategy Papers

Trade policy reform in developing countries is often done in the context of a
donor-supported programme. It is, therefore, important to look at the linkages
between trade policy reform and the policy framework for donor support. At
the annual meeting of the World Bank and the IMF in 1999, a new approach
to donor engagement with the poorest countries was agreed. Countries are
invited to design their own poverty reduction strategies, which will be written
up into Poverty Reduction Strategy Papers (PRSPs). These will be the basis for

Box 7.2 **Underlying principles of the Poverty Reduction Strategy Papers**

Poverty Reduction Strategy Papers cover a three-year period initially. The intention is that they should be:

- **Country-driven**: with governments leading the process and broad-based participation in the adoption and monitoring of the resulting strategy.
- **Results-oriented**: identifying desired outcomes and planning the way towards them.
- **Comprehensive**: taking account of the multidimensional nature of poverty.
- **Long-term in approach**: recognizing the depth and complexity of some of the changes needed.
- **Based on partnership**: between governments and other actors in civil society, the private sector and the donor community.

Source: IDS (2000).

donor support. Box 7.2 describes the underlying principles of the PRSP.

At the time of writing, several countries have produced Interim PRSPs in order to become eligible for debt-relief under the enhanced Heavily Indebted Poor Countries (HIPC) initiative, and a few have produced full PRSPs. Consultations are underway with a number of other countries. In the long run, the intention is that all countries should have full PRSPs. Box 7.3 shows the elements of a full PRSP.

To date, PRSPs have understandably focused on the government's overall macroeconomic management and the ways in which public expenditure can facilitate pro-poor growth. But in the long run, it is desirable that trade reform should be integrated within the PRSP process. How can this be done?

Content
The PRSP should outline the key strategies for trade and anti-poverty policy drawn from an analysis of the poverty effects of trade reform conducted within the framework of Chapter 4. The detailed approach for conducting this analysis has already been outlined and the questions that policy-makers need to ask have been elaborated in Chapter 6. But the PRSP cannot (and should not) indicate all the policies and programmes that will form part of the country's trade policy reforms. Rather, it should outline broad strategies in three areas:

- the overall strategy for trade reform and the conclusions from any analysis of the likely impact on different groups of poor;
- the areas of complementary policy on which the government is going to focus in order to ensure that the poor benefit from the reforms; and
- the key social protection policies and safety nets that the government will use to mitigate the costs associated with the reform.

Box 7.3 **Elements of a full Poverty Reduction Strategy Paper**

A PRSP needs to include, in whatever format:

Analysis
- The nature of poverty.
- Obstacles to, and opportunities for, poverty reduction and faster growth: macroeconomic, structural, environmental, social and institutional.
- Trade-offs and 'win-wins' in policy choices: options.

Goals
- Long term for key anti-poverty targets.
- Linked to the International Development Targets.
- Indicators and monitoring system.

Policy actions – economic, structural, environmental, social and institutional

Medium-term budget framework

External assistance – requirements and coordination

Participatory process
- What has happened so far.
- Process for monitoring and review.

Source: Department for International Development (2000b).

Process

An important distinction between the PRSP process and previous frameworks for donor support is that the former is supposed to be country-driven and based on partnership between governments, civil society and donors. While much of the content outlined above would require detailed technical analysis, it is important that the process of examining these questions is open to all stakeholders. Of course, this presents a challenge to policy-makers: enabling public debate over the structure of trade protection and the winners and losers from such protection may, if handled skilfully, enable the formation of a constituency in favour of reform. But it may equally alert those who are likely to lose that such reforms are under consideration, encouraging political action to prevent them from being implemented.

Furthermore, the involvement in the process of worker and private-sector representatives, as well as representatives of poor groups themselves, is likely to lead to claims for compensation for the negative impact that trade reform may have on particular groups. As discussed above, governments may be unable or unwilling to meet such claims.

Does this mean that trade reform should adopt a less inclusive process? Probably not. The principal losses arising from existing trade policies are often borne by consumers, who are often unaware of the implicit subsidy that they are supplying to particular groups within society. An open discussion of the extent to which such protection is desirable and affordable can help to build consensus over trade reform. Furthermore, engagement of groups that will be negatively affected in the short term can provide a suitable platform for the development of social safety nets more generally in society, and the inclusion, if necessary, of targeted short-term assistance to those negatively affected can lessen resistance to reform.

7.8 Do international agreements constrain anti-poverty programmes?

It is sometimes claimed that international agreements on trade and other issues make it more difficult for governments to undertake anti-poverty programmes. This section explores this issue.

7.8.1 The WTO Agreements and anti-poverty policies

It is often claimed that some aspects of the WTO Agreements prevent countries from pursuing policies that other countries have used effectively in the past to counter poverty. For example, it has been claimed that the phasing out of certain trade-related investment measures (TRIMs) removes the ability of governments to control the actions of multinational companies operating within their country. Similarly, it is argued that the prohibition of production subsidies prevents governments from promoting labour-intensive growth in certain sectors or that the implementation of the agreement on trade-related intellectual property rights (TRIPs) will prevent governments from providing cheap access to essential drugs.

These are legitimate and important concerns. Clearly, if international trade (or any other) agreements prevent governments from implementing effective anti-poverty policies, then there is a case for re-examining such agreements. But the evidence to support such assertions is open to a number of interpretations and, as yet, there is insufficient research on the issue to come to a satisfactory resolution. The reason for this is two-fold. First, the merits of many of the policies are disputed (for example, it is not universally agreed that the East Asian countries benefited extensively from their interventions). Second, the precise limits of the WTO Agreements have not been fully tested. For example, policies only fall under WTO scrutiny when a partner complains and, in many cases, the agreements are so imprecise as to accept several interpretations.

In essence, the WTO Agreements constrain discrimination – either between different trading partners or in favour of domestic firms. The former case is covered by the 'most favoured nation' (MFN) principle, and it is difficult to see how violating this will assist anti-poverty policy. The only plausible way in which it might do so would be if a country felt that there were major advantages to the creation of a regional trading arrangement between some group of countries. But the creation of such regional groupings is explicitly allowed under GATT Article XXIV, as long as they cover 'substantially all the trade'. Thus, the MFN principle is not likely to be a major constraint on anti-poverty policy.

Most claims of constraints on anti-poverty policy, therefore, focus on the second case, where countries might seek to discriminate in favour of domestic firms by violating the principle of 'national treatment'. Although there are several specific areas in which it has been argued that the provision of national treatment to foreign goods and service providers could constrain the ability of national authorities to tackle poverty and promote pro-poor growth (such as the production subsidies, TRIMS and TRIPs examples given above), these specific suggestions for deviations from national treatment are typically derived from two general concerns:

- promoting learning and externalities; and
- controlling commercial power.

Some evidence from the success of the East Asian economies between the 1960s and the 1990s suggests that specific incentives to promote network formation, information flows and technological capacity-building were important in generating the dramatic growth rates seen in these countries. The way in which some of these objectives were achieved in some East Asian countries would no longer comply with WTO Agreements. But in general, the WTO Agreements do not prohibit the promotion of research and development or network or informational externalities. Neither do they restrict attempts to create demand externalities through regional development policies. The key prohibition is of subsidies that are likely to have a direct (rather than an indirect) effect on production. Given that wealthy countries have a far greater capacity than poor countries to use such subsidies and have, therefore, been responsible for dumping excess production onto world markets and hence depressing prices, their prohibition is likely to have a net benefit for developing countries rather than the reverse. These issues are discussed in more detail in Chapter 13.

The second area in which discrimination might be pro-poor is where it is intended to control commercial power. Large multinationals are likely to have more commercial power in any country's market than much smaller domestic companies. There is therefore a concern that if such foreign companies were provided with a level playing field they would be able to eliminate domestic competition and introduce monopoly pricing. This concern is not without justification: there are numerous examples of markets in which liberalization has given rise to the demise of local producers. But it is extremely difficult to determine whether this has been because the foreign provider is more efficient (a good thing) or whether the foreign provider has behaved in an anti-competitive manner (a bad thing).

Again, it could be argued that multinationals have an 'unfair' advantage over many local firms since they often have better access to international capital. But this suggests that the solution lies not with discriminatory trade policy, but with greater financial liberalization and more attention to the sequencing of reforms. Alternatively, if a foreign company's advantage results from anti-competitive practices, this suggests the need for both a strengthening of local competition authorities or, where this is not possible due to the lack of resources for effective regulation, increasing rather than reducing the 'contestability' of local markets. This implies greater openness rather than less, in order to ensure that competing multinationals are forced to provide competitively priced goods and services. Given that many of the most protected markets are themselves characterized by high concentrations of market power among a small number of local firms, it seems unlikely that the requirement to provide national treatment will, in general, result in a less competitive environment than the pre-liberalization situation.

Thus, while it is possible that a case might be made for a specific derogation from national treatment, theory does not suggest any general *a priori* case why deviations from national treatment (or MFN) might be advisable on anti-poverty grounds.

7.8.2 Inconsistent international commitments and anti-poverty policy

Many governments are signatories to several international agreements with a bearing on trade. For example, in addition to WTO membership, a country may be a member of one or more regional trade groupings. Botswana, for example, is a member of the WTO, the Southern African Customs Union and the Southern African Development Community, all of which have associated trade agreements. Such agreements are often overlapping in their coverage and commitments and are sometimes contradictory.

The extent to which agreements promote (or inhibit) poverty reduction clearly depends on the details of each agreement. Where agreements are contradictory, it is clearly impossible for governments to comply simultaneously with all their commitments. The impact of this on anti-poverty policy depends partly on the effects of the resulting uncertainty on economic activity and partly on which of three possible reasons lies behind agreeing to contradictory trade agreements:

Trade policy is contested
Like all government policy, trade policy is contested in most countries. While some governments have a clear and united policy on trade reform, others are divided, with some groups wishing to pursue one path while others prefer another. Thus, internal political dynamics may result in the government agreeing to one set of policies in one forum and a different set in a different forum.

Such contests can have both positive and negative effects on poverty reduction efforts. The process of debate over trade policy can lead to a much stronger sense of ownership of policy once the debate is resolved. Furthermore, if representatives of poor groups and poor communities are able to participate in this debate, it is likely that their concerns will feature more prominently in the trade policies finally agreed. But the political battle over trade policy may take a considerable amount of time. During this period, policy is likely to be subject to a series of reversals, which may undermine the effectiveness of the reforms undertaken.

Poor analytical capacity

Trade agreements are typically lengthy and complex. Countries therefore require considerable analytical capacity to be able to determine whether particular measures are in their best interests and are consistent with commitments made under other agreements. Many of the poorest countries simply do not possess the necessary level of economic and legal expertise and are, therefore, not in a position to participate fully in decision-making over international trade policy.

Thus, the proliferation of overlapping international agreements can effectively exclude some poor countries from international policy debates and result in their acceptance of agreements that do not necessarily reflect their best interests. In addition, the length and complexity of international trade negotiations can absorb scarce technical personnel who might be employed more effectively in the management and implementation of anti-poverty programmes.

Maximizing the benefits

In some cases, the assent to contradictory agreements on trade policy in different fora may result from an attempt to maximize the overall benefits obtained from the agreements. Governments enter into agreements (whether they be the WTO Agreements, regional trade agreements or loan conditions) because they feel that the benefits outweigh the costs. The benefits from such agreements usually depend on compliance with the terms of each agreement. But if it is possible to receive most of the benefits from any agreement without complying with every element, then there is scope for governments to agree to potentially contradictory policies in order to maximize the benefits that they receive (see Mosley et al., 1995). For example, countries may enter into agreements in part because of the credibility that subscribing to multilateral agreements may confer on their own reform commitments; the benefits of such credibility may outweigh the costs of the potential contradictions between different agreements.

Such benefit maximization is conducted by all governments, rich and poor, although clearly the parties to any particular agreement attempt to put in place conditions to ensure that each country will comply with the terms of that particular agreement. The impact of such behaviour on anti-poverty policy depends on how great the 'illicit' benefits are.

7.9 Is reform optional?

This chapter has looked at how a poverty focus might change the way in which trade reform is implemented and how anti-poverty policy can assist trade policy reform. But not implementing trade reform also has an impact on the poor. This section looks at the question 'is trade reform optional?' We interpret this question to mean 'is not reforming ever a good idea economically?'[7] The answer to this question depends on the extent to which the country is experiencing macroeconomic instability.

If an economy is facing major macroeconomic instability, then this is likely to be harmful to the poor. High inflation and the economic uncertainty that it promotes are particularly harmful to those members of society with the least ability to cope with shocks, although ironically, the very poorest households may be so disengaged from the market economy that they are less influenced by economic instability than slightly better-off households (see Killick, 1995; although Levinsohn et al., 1999, find the reverse in Indonesia).

Delaying adjustment in such circumstances can only result in a worse crisis in the long run. Indeed, many of the criticisms of stabilization and adjustment programmes do not consider the likely adjustment that would have eventually been necessary if stabilization and adjustment had not been attempted. Macroeconomic crises that result from unsustainable external accounts require real devaluation. But achieving real devaluation is difficult while maintaining a structure of protection that has an inherent tendency towards overvaluation of the exchange rate. Therefore, in conditions of macroeconomic instability, it is extremely difficult to achieve a sustainable stabilization without some kind of trade reform.

If, in contrast, a country is not experiencing macroeconomic instability, then in principle it is possible to avoid reform. Indeed, Rodrik (1999b) argues that trade liberalization is neither necessary nor sufficient for strong economic performance. He cites the experience of several East Asian countries that had highly distorted economies along with strong growth (see Amsden, 1989, and Wade, 1990, for similar arguments). Thus, trade reform in such circumstances *is* optional. But given that the structure of protection is generally strongly biased against rural areas and against agriculture, both of which are predominantly poor, failing to exploit the opportunities of a more efficient allocation of resources can hardly be regarded as pro-poor.

Summary
- Trade liberalization should be done simultaneously with stabilization if a government has good administrative capacity and is in a strong political position.
- A poverty focus reinforces the general presumption that current account liberalization should precede capital account liberalization.
- The economic arguments for gradual rather than 'big-bang' reform are weak, but the political arguments can be stronger.
- Anti-poverty programmes can enable poor households to take advantage of the potential gains from trade reform.
- Trade liberalization may reduce revenue – this emphasizes the need to protect social-sector expenditure and for appropriate targeting of the poor.

continued

Summary box continued

- The size of the adjustment costs created by trade reform varies greatly from country to country, but they are not always large. The same is true for the length of transitional unemployment.
- Trade reform forces governments to split their anti-poverty efforts between the chronically poor, the productive poor and those who are transitorily poor as a result of the trade reform.
- There are arguments both for and against compensating the losers from trade reform, but experience with trade adjustment assistance schemes in developed countries is not encouraging.
- The broad thrust of trade reform needs to be integrated in the Poverty Reduction Strategy Papers process.
- International trade agreements generally provide few real constraints on the nature of anti-poverty interventions that governments can implement.
- Trade reform is optional, but avoiding it is not wise unless a country is experiencing severe macroeconomic instability.

Notes

1   This section draws heavily on Falvey and Kim (1992).
2   In technical jargon, gradualism is economically preferable if social discount rates are higher than private discount rates. But it might also be so if discount rates are equal but other distortions make early social costs higher than the early private ones.
3   Bacchetta and Dellas (1997) offer the contrary view, arguing that if restructuring helps firms to learn about their true level of efficiency, a gradual approach may be better for the long run, though rapid reform will still be better if short-run adjustment costs are large.
4   Although it should be noted that the incidence of public spending on the poor is not always high (see Selden and Wasylenko, 1992; and Lanjouw and Ravallion, 1998).
5   See Kapstein (1998) for a history of the TAA.
6   It is worth noting that the European approach is to rely on pre-existing general welfare provisions as a means of cushioning trade liberalizations. These countries have not come under particular pressure to create trade-specific adjustment programmes (see Sapir, 2000).
7   There are, of course, other ways in which the question 'is reform optional?' might be interpreted. For example, it might mean, 'is it, in principle, possible not to undertake a trade reform?' The answer to this is, obviously, yes; in principle, a government can choose to maintain its current trading regime. Second, it might mean 'is it politically feasible not to undertake trade reform given the external pressures faced by the government?' The answer to this clearly depends on the circumstances of the country and the government in question. But trade reform is an integral part of many programmes of structural adjustment supported by both the IMF and the World Bank and so many developing-country governments feel that trade reform is not optional since they are dependent on the external financial support that such programmes provide. This is essentially a political issue, which we will not pursue here.

PART 2: The Effects of Specific Liberalizations

8 Introduction to Part 2

Part 2 of this Handbook puts flesh on the analytical skeleton of Part 1 with analysis of specific cases and examples. Each chapter looks at an aspect of trade liberalization defined by sector (such as agriculture or services) or by instrument (such as anti-dumping duties or competition policy) and explores the poverty effects of the reforms that might be implemented.

One of the main conclusions so far is that the poverty effects of trade liberalization are case-specific. This means that there is no substitute for policy-makers – or those seeking to influence them – working through their own particular cases in detail. Moreover, the differences between countries are more than simply differences in the weights attached to a set of standard cases. Rather, they are deeply embedded in the economic system and affect the way in which the system works to connect causes and effects. Policies that are pro-poor in one circumstance can be anti-poor in another. Thus, the following chapters do not provide a 'ready-reckoner' of effects that can just be added up to reach a final judgement about policy packages. Rather, they are templates for the sort of analysis that is required: they are about how to think through and answer concerns that trade liberalization causes poverty in developing countries.

There is sometimes a tendency to treat 'poverty' as the 'ace of trumps' in debates about trade liberalization. Once a concern for poverty has been expressed, the impression is given that decent people should just let the question of liberalization drop. This is wrong. For all its horror, poverty is like any other economic or social phenomenon. It is amenable to analysis and subject to the same trade-offs as other outcomes. By showing how specific issues might be worked through, we hope to equip policy-makers and commentators with better tools with which first, to take these important decisions, and second, to enter the public and increasingly acrimonious debates surrounding trade liberalization.

8.1 The WTO trade agenda and beyond

Since the matter is so case-specific, how do we choose the cases to describe in the rest of the Handbook? Our selection is guided by two broad principles. First, we have focused mainly on the effects of developing countries' own trade policies. In almost all circumstances, countries are more affected by their own trade policies than by those of their trading partners and, of course, it is the former over which they have most influence. Moreover, as well as being misleading economically, reducing the question of trade liberalization and poverty to a list of things that developed countries should do for developing countries would be unrealistic in political terms. Developed countries clearly have a responsibility to help with poverty alleviation, but the main policy responsibility lies in the developing countries themselves. Having said that, there are a number of cases in which developed countries' policies are so important that we have included them below; for example, in the analysis of agricultural and textiles and clothing protectionism and of trade-related aspects of intellectual property rights (TRIPs).

Second, we have selected – and organized our presentation around – issues that seem likely to come up in future rounds of WTO trade talks. There are several reasons for this. Policy-makers will inevitably have to start thinking about these issues soon. And they will have to come up with positions on many of them, not least in order to decide whether, and on what terms, they should be included on the WTO agenda. The prospective WTO talks have also become a major focus for civil society commentators on trade reform, and it is in this context that many of the questions surrounding poverty are being debated. One aspect of this emerging debate is whether or not *existing* WTO disciplines prevent developing countries from pursuing desirable development or poverty alleviation policies. So in addition to the generic discussion on this in Chapter 7, we comment on whether there are such constraints in the specific areas discussed in the following chapters. Finally, the cases in which we want to analyse the effects of changes in developed countries' trade policies make sense only in a multilateral context, for otherwise there is nothing developing country policy-makers can do about them.

It is important to realise, however, that useful though it is, the WTO agenda neither encompasses nor is encompassed by the role of trade policy in development. The WTO does not define the set of issues that a developing country trade minister should think about and, more importantly, neither does it necessarily define 'good' policy in what it does cover (see Finger and Winters, 1998). Sometimes, WTO requirements will be peripheral to development: for example, while customs is a crucial issue for effective international trade in developing countries, customs valuation (and the recent agreement in this area) is not (see Finger and Schuler, 2000). In other cases, the WTO permits policies that are harmful to development and poverty alleviation. For example, the rights to impose anti-dumping duties on fairly relaxed criteria or to define idiosyncratic national technical standards are not generally helpful. There are even cases in which commentators who are wholly committed to free trade find WTO requirements harmful to development, for example, Panagariya (1999b) and Srinivasan (2000) on TRIPs.

Most important, however, is that there are many trade policy issues that do not figure in the WTO. This is particularly true of services, where the scope of the WTO's General Agreement on Trade in Services (GATS) is currently rather limited. Thus, at present, there are no constraints on subsidies or government purchasing in services and no guidelines about how to use international trade and the desire of foreign companies to establish a commercial presence as a means of stimulating domestic competition. In goods, examples of the questions that lie outside effective WTO influence include:

- important issues of trade facilitation, for example, the organization of customs or of payments systems;
- the variability of tariff rates inside the maxima agreed at the WTO;
- infrastructure for international trade;
- issues of training personnel in carrying out foreign trade; and
- market research for exports.

Thus while, on the whole, the WTO offers developing countries a sound framework and guidelines for trade policy reform, it should not be seen as defining the extent of developing country interests in trade policy. That job belongs to ministers of trade and development, who should seek to use the WTO framework as an aid for achieving their own objectives through good policy. In particular, even though WTO procedures offer little encouragement for unilateral trade liberalization, governments should examine such possibilities carefully, for they will frequently offer considerable rewards. For this reason, we not only consider trade reforms that might occur in the context of a new trade round, but also those that are available unilaterally.

<u>8.2</u> Special and differential treatment

The WTO, and before it the GATT, has a long tradition of offering developing countries 'special and differential treatment' (S&D). Before the Uruguay Round, this basically entailed:

- preferential access to developed country markets in the form of the Generalized System of Preferences (GSP);
- a statement that developing countries need not offer reciprocal tariff reductions in tariff negotiations;
- allowing the developing countries to use forms of protection from which developed countries are disbarred (for example, protection ostensibly for balance of payments or 'infant industry' reasons); and
- allowing developing countries to exempt themselves from many of the agreements on rules.

By implying that trade liberalization was bad for developing countries, S&D legitimized the argument for avoiding it, and left developing countries almost wholly outside the liberalization dynamic of the world system. They undertook little liberalization of their own, and because they offered so little, they obtained very little liberalization by developed countries for the commodities in which they were interested (see, for example, Hindley, 1987, on the economics of S&D; and Finger, 1991).[1] Overall, most economists accept that 'old-style' S&D actually did very little for developing countries' development strategies.

By the late 1980s, developing country governments were more sympathetic to market solutions for development and disillusion with S&D was rife. As a result, the Uruguay Round made a deliberate effort to reduce its scope. Developing countries were expected, *de facto*, to join in the liberalization, although they were required to offer less in quantitative terms; everyone was, in principle, subject to the same rules (via the so-called 'single undertaking') though some rules admitted different treatment, and the balance of payments exceptions were tightened up. On the other hand, the GSP continued, developing countries were permitted longer adjustment periods for most Agreements, and there were a large number of non-binding and exhortatory pleas to take account of the special circumstances of developing countries.

Since 1994, the developing countries have faced great difficulty in implementing many of the rules-based Uruguay Round Agreements and have come to argue that the Final Act was unfairly asymmetrical, especially in the leniency with which it treated agricultural and textile and clothing protection by developed countries. This has led them publicly to regret the passing of S&D and to campaign vigorously for its revival in a more effective form. Where this entails recognizing that developing countries may genuinely face more difficulty in creating new trading institutions and may require different institutions anyway, S&D can be very constructive. S&D is also important where it points out that developing countries might need bilateral and multilateral technical assistance and funding support in order to implement particular rules and create institutions. In part, however, the calls for S&D have also been coded demands and political cover for an unwillingness to liberalize further. The use of S&D in this old-fashioned way would, if pursued very far, deter rather than enhance development.

The upsurge of interest in S&D was evident in developing countries' preparations for the Seattle Ministerial of the WTO in December 1999, as well as in general debate. It figures prominently in many of their positions on the various issues we discuss in the following chapters. It does not, however, figure prominently in our discussions. This is because our concern is with the poverty effects of a particular piece of trade liberalization, not with how that liberalization comes about. If developing country A fails to reduce protection on good X, our analysis of the poverty implications will generally be exactly the same whether that failure is due to X not figuring in the agenda, to A not offering a concession as part of its negotiating strategy or to A being expressly permitted not to liberalize it by S&D provisions.

S&D may matter where the determining variable for poverty effects is policy in developing countries *relative* to that in developed countries. In such cases, it may matter whether developing countries get a 'better' deal from the WTO than developed countries. But, in general, the key determinant of the poverty effects is the trade liberalization that the country actually undertakes, not whether S&D might permit it a lesser liberalization than some other country. Of course, the perceived 'fairness' of the outcome might matter politically (and might influence the feasibility of particular deals), but in terms of analysing a *given* outcome, S&D will generally not be important.

Similarly for rules-based issues: what matters in the treatment of intellectual property is, in the main, not whether developing countries have different institutions from developed countries, but simply the institutions that the developing countries actually have.

8.3 The chapter format of Part 2

In each of the following chapters we present the analysis in a fairly standard format. We start with a section describing the background, defining terms and explaining why the issue may matter for poverty. We then briefly discuss some of the economic analysis behind the issue, concentrating on those elements that are necessary to highlight the poverty effects. Next we consider where the issue is now in terms of the policy agenda. Where there are proposals within an international framework (usually the WTO), we present these and comment on them and, in other cases, we discuss issues that developing countries should consider for unilateral reform. While these sections may well inform developing country policy-makers' deliberations on their positions for upcoming talks, they make no pretence of being either comprehensive or a substitute for a handbook on negotiating positions or strategies. We view them first, as motivating our subsequent discussion on poverty by tying it to issues that are actually under consideration, and second, as illustrative of the sort of trade policy changes that will have to be thought through under any circumstances.

Each chapter concludes with a discussion of 'issue *X* and poverty'. This is the heart of the Handbook, not in terms of offering ready answers to anticipated questions, but in terms of showing how concrete proposals might be worked through. In some cases, these poverty sections constitute most of the chapter, but in others they are rather short. Moreover, they often conclude that under normal circumstances, the issue at hand has very little direct effect on poverty.

The reason for working through such cases is that in the public debate about trade liberalization, it is at least as important to be able to show why a measure has no direct impact (and hence why poverty concerns should not govern its introduction) as to be able to show where the poverty concerns are greatest and how to address them. Moreover, even when the normal case is of 'no poverty impact', setting out why this is the case will demonstrate how atypical conditions might affect the argument. Thus, even where our analysis suggests no effects, it sets the scene for a better and more informed debate about possible special cases. And if years of experience in trade policy-making have taught us anything, it is that there are always people who will claim to be special cases.

In the spirit of a handbook, we have made the chapters of this part fairly self-contained, so that readers can dip into them in almost any order. Where discussion of one issue draws on that of an earlier one, we have referenced the latter fully. So while up to this point, the reader should have read Part 1 fairly linearly, from now on, jumping around between chapters is fine.

Ideally, we would be able to draw on the analysis of a large number of experiences of trade liberalization to discuss its likely effects on poverty. In fact, as we have noted above, this turns out not to be the case: it is difficult to measure degrees of liberalization; liberalizations are often combined with other, larger shocks, such as structural adjustment or transition, and we cannot disentangle their effects; frequently, there are no poverty data covering the period of liberalization; and when there are, they are dominated by exogenous trends or extraneous shocks.

The result is that the analysis of trade and poverty must rely heavily on theory and on partial pieces of empirical evidence (see also, for example, Ben-David et al., 2000, and McKay et al., 2000). Thus, much of the evidence we report comes not from trade liberalizations *per se* but from domestic reforms and shocks that seem likely to have similar effects as trade liberalizations. We judge that such evidence is useful but clearly, in any actual liberalization, care must be taken to check that its effects on the variables of interest do parallel those of the incidents on which underlying justification is based.

Notes

1   Whalley (1999) and Michalopoulos (2000) update the story to the present.

9 Agricultural Trade Reform

This chapter argues that:

- Agriculture is the key sector for nearly all poverty analysis: the poor are predominantly rural and food accounts for a major share of all poor people's expenditure.
- Farm incomes have large spillovers to others within the rural economy and hence increases in farm incomes help to relieve poverty throughout the rural economy.
- Agriculture is the major source of national income for many developing countries, especially the least-developed ones.
- Agricultural markets are among the most distorted in the world, with both developed and developing countries maintaining high levels of intervention.
- The main costs of intervention are those imposed by countries' own policies, but in agriculture, developed countries' policies also impose high costs on developing countries.
- Developing countries should aim to remove anti-agricultural biases in their own trade policy, by reforming not only agricultural policies (such as export restrictions) but also policies that protect and promote other sectors of the economy.
- In the multilateral context, developing countries' main interest is in improved access to developed countries' markets, followed by the elimination of the latter's high levels of domestic and then export subsidies.
- Reforms in both developing and developed countries have the potential for considerable poverty alleviation, although particular groups of poor people may suffer from liberalization.
- To predict the effects of agricultural liberalization, governments need to know each poor group's net supply position in the goods to be liberalized and details of rural labour markets and demand patterns.

continued

Box continued

- To help reforms have pro-poor effects, governments need to ensure that increased agricultural incomes filter through to the poor by establishing domestic policies such as extension services, land redistribution and improved access to inputs and credit.

9.1 Background

Agriculture is a vitally important sector for developing countries. It constitutes 28% of GDP in the low-income developing countries compared with 2% in the developed (high-income) countries. More importantly, from a poverty perspective, agriculture employs the overwhelming majority of the workforce in most developing countries. (See Table 9.1, which shows the percentage shares of agriculture in GDP and employment for high-, middle- and low-income countries and for different regions of the world.) This means that agriculture is typically the most important source of income for poor households, and what is more, food is the dominant item of expenditure in their budgets.

At the level of the individual countries, agricultural trade policy is of particular importance to two groups of developing countries:

Table 9.1 Percentage shares of agriculture in GDP and employment

	1980			1990–7		
	Percentage shares of agriculture			*Percentage shares of agriculture*		
	GDP	*Male labour force*	*Female labour force*	*GDP*	*Male labour force*	*Female labour force*
Low-income countries	36	65	81	28	61	75
Middle-income countries	16	55	59	11	50	56
Lower middle-income	25	59	63	15	56	61
Upper middle-income	10	34	31	8	27	22
Low- and middle- income countries	18	59	67	13	54	62
East Asia and Pacific	28	69	75	18	66	72
Europe and Central Asia	..	26	27	12	24	22
Latin America and the Caribbean	10	39	21	8	29	12
Middle East and North Africa	10	37	53	14	27	55
South Asia	37	63	82	25	59	75
Sub-Saharan Africa	18	66	79	18	62	75
High-income countries	4	8	8	2	5	4

Source: World Bank (1999d).

- *Major exporters*: many developing countries have a comparative advantage in agriculture because of their relatively large endowments of land and unskilled labour. For these countries, access to the large markets of the developed countries and the prices they receive there are of central importance.
- *Major importers*: some other developing countries (and many developed countries) are extremely dependent on food imports for their food security. Changes to international and regional agricultural trade will affect world food prices and therby household welfare.

In terms of income distribution and poverty, agricultural policy is of great significance in nearly all developing countries. The many poor people who either draw most of their income from agriculture or spend most of it on food are highly exposed to changes in food prices.[1]

Agricultural trade policy matters to developing countries at two levels. First, at the global level, where it affects conditions on world markets. Here it is principally determined by the major developed countries, notably the United States, the European Union and Japan. These countries' extensive regimes of agricultural support and protection have a large impact on world agricultural markets and thus impinge directly on the welfare of the poor in developing countries. In this chapter, therefore, we consider the effects of trade liberalization at the international level, as well as the national level.

At the second level, that of the individual country itself, domestic agricultural products that compete with imports are highly protected in both developing and developed countries. Table 9.2 shows the levels of border protection on merchandise trade by commodity, source and destination. Border protection includes both tariffs and other restrictions on imports,

Table 9.2 Average tariffs and tariff equivalents on merchandise trade, by commodity, source and destination, 1995 (percentages)

Exporting region	Importing region		
	Developed countries	*Developing countries*	*World*
Agriculture			
Developed countries	15.9	21.5	17.5
Developing countries	15.1	18.3	16.4
World	15.6	20.1	17.1
Manufactures			
Developed countries	0.8	10.9	3.8
Developing countries	3.4	12.8	7.1
World	1.5	11.5	4.7
Minerals/energy			
Developed countries	0.1	1.3	0.4
Developing countries	0.4	5.2	2.4
World	0.2	3.0	1.1

Source: Hertel et al. (1999).

such as quantitative restrictions. Since converting specific tariffs ($x per unit) into *ad valorem* equivalents (percentages) and combining tariffs and other trade barriers into a single measure, is a pretty imprecise art, none of these protection numbers can be taken too literally. Nevertheless, the relative rankings are likely to be accurate. In addition to this border protection, developed country agriculture benefits from substantial export subsidies and domestic support measures.

Developing countries maintain higher levels of protection than developed countries for all classes of goods. But while their levels of protection are highest for agriculture (as in developed countries), the developing countries' higher tariffs on manufactures mean that their *relative* level of protection of agriculture is less. The difference in tariffs is about 14 percentage points for developed countries compared with about 9 percentage points for developing countries.

9.2 The economics of agricultural protection[2]

9.2.1 Developed countries

Since the Second World War, agricultural policy in developed countries has been driven by three main objectives:

- to ensure food security by promoting food surpluses;
- to increase agricultural productivity by promoting technical progress; and
- to maintain a fair standard of living for the agricultural community.

Since about 1970, agricultural policy has also been ostensibly concerned with preserving rural societies and the environment. Winters (1989) shows that while combinations of these objectives (and several lesser ones) are the proclaimed basis for agricultural policy in every OECD country, it is impossible to understand agricultural policy without recognizing the less laudable objective of transferring income from consumers and other sectors of the economy to farmers, especially the landowners.

The upshot of these objectives has been a complex and opaque assembly of instruments and regulations, including various trade controls, price support measures, income transfers, production subsidies and investment grants. Among the trade controls are ordinary tariffs, variable levies (whereby the tariff is varied daily in order to ensure that imports do not enter at a tariff-inclusive price below an officially determined minimum), quantitative restrictions on imports and export subsidies. In addition, agricultural imports face an array of health controls, such as sanitary and phyto-sanitary barriers, which, while ostensibly not restrictions on trade, can feel very much like that to exporters whose goods are excluded. These instruments are applied almost exclusively to temperate products or those tropical products that compete closely with them, such as cane sugar. Trade in most non-competing tropical products, such as beverages, is virtually undistorted.

The net effect of all these policies is to increase output and, by raising consumer prices, discourage demand. The resulting surpluses give rise to various production control measures (such as 'set-aside') but they eventually have to be sold on world markets, depressing world prices. In addition, the policies designed to stabilize internal agricultural prices in developed countries, such as variable levies, prevent farmers and consumers from responding to price information and thus throw a greater burden of adjustment to shocks onto other market participants. The result is that fluctuations in world prices are increased.

In summary, developed countries' agricultural policies tend to reduce world prices of temperate-zone products and their close substitutes and make those prices more volatile. The main losers are consumers in the developed countries, but significant costs also fall on developing country farmers and governments.

Increasingly over the post-war period, the rapid rate of technical progress in subsidized agriculture, coupled with the policy-driven incentives to expand land use and the input intensity of agriculture, have resulted in problems with agricultural surpluses on the one hand and budget deficits on the other. These problems have made it clear that price policies alone will never be able to solve the farming problem and that trying to use offsetting output restrictions is also doomed. As a result, since the mid-1980s, policy-makers have recognized the need to 'decouple' support payments from production. In other words, they have sought to support farmers (a policy that is perhaps a social responsibility and certainly a political expediency) and the environment rather than farming itself (which just produces expensive food that no one wants).

Decoupling is a sensitive issue and its implementation has proceeded slowly. But it is now accepted as a necessary evolutionary path for agricultural policy.[3] It featured in the Uruguay Round to some extent and it will doubtless become more prominent in future agricultural reforms.

9.2.2 Developing countries

Agricultural policy in most developing countries has followed quite a different path from that in the developed countries. Whereas most developed countries have instituted very high levels of protection for their agricultural sectors, between the 1950s and the 1970s most developing countries pursued policies of import-substitution that were heavily biased against agriculture. The economic thinking of that time argued that governments should cultivate a 'lead' sector, which would serve as an 'engine of growth' for the economy. For example, the work of Prebisch (1950) and Singer (1950) encouraged a widespread belief that the prices of agricultural products were in secular decline due to the low income elasticity of demand for such products.

In addition, agrarian society was regarded as socially and economically backward, impervious to market signals and devoid of links to other sectors that could bring the benefits of progress in agricultural production to the economy as a whole (see Schiff and Valdés, 1998). In parallel, the work of Rosenstein-Rodan (1943) and Nurkse (1953) encouraged an emphasis on industrialization and 'balanced growth' pursued through high import tariffs on manufactures.

Such theories dovetailed with the desire to protect the manufacturing sectors that had emerged in Latin America during its wartime isolation (see Winters, 2000d). They also chimed with the *realpolitik* that in agricultural countries, it is possible to increase significantly the incomes of the small urban and government elite by imposing 'bearable' taxes on the large rural sector (see Anderson, 1995b). The result was that while industry was strongly protected, tariffs on agricultural goods were relatively low (except sometimes for specific import-competing products) and export taxes were high. The economic effects of such policies are well known: they tend to shift production towards industry (where efficiency is low) and away from agriculture (where it is higher). The resulting income losses can be huge.

In addition to the indirect taxation of agriculture resulting from these relative price changes, agriculture was often subject to direct taxation. Moreover, overvaluation of the exchange rate often resulted in a further implicit tax on agriculture relative to non-agricultural activities. Schiff and Valdés (1992) find that the indirect tax on agriculture from industrial protection and macroeconomic policies averaged about 22% between 1960–85 for the 18 developing countries they studied. This was three times the direct tax from agricultural pricing policies, which was about 8%. But direct price policies did stabilize domestic agricultural prices relative to world prices, with an average reduction in their variability of a quarter.

Since the mid-1980s, many developing countries have started to address the worst distortions in agriculture. They have reduced the explicit and implicit taxes on the sector and often reformed marketing arrangements. In addition, exchange rate overvaluation and high industrial sector tariffs are less prevalent.[4] Thus, the situation is much improved although developing country farmers still suffer some discrimination.

9.3 The liberalization agenda in agriculture

This section discusses potential trade liberalization in agriculture from both a multilateral and a unilateral perspective. In the former, the agenda is defined by the aftermath of the Uruguay Round and primarily concerns the further reform of developed countries' policies – especially those of the EU and Japan – although developing countries will also have to contribute their own reforms.

In agriculture, developed country policies are unusually important for developing countries, so we consider them to a much greater extent in this chapter than elsewhere in the Handbook. In particular, we examine the need for further liberalization of domestic support, market access and export subsidies. But we also move beyond developed countries' policies to consider issues such as developing country participation in multilateral negotiations, the overall cost of agricultural restrictions, food security and the 'development box', the effect of sanitary and phyto-sanitary standards, the impact of other complementary policies on agricultural trade and the appropriate response to regional trading arrangements.

9.3.1 **The multilateral agenda**

The Uruguay Round almost came to grief several times over agriculture, with the United States and the Cairns Group (which comprised 14 agriculture-exporting countries devoted to freeing agricultural trade) pressing liberalization on a reluctant EU and Japan. But eventually the Round took a huge step forward with its Agreement on Agriculture (AoA), which codified several aspects of agricultural policy and brought their treatment under the GATT much closer to that of manufactures. The Round also took a much smaller step towards reducing agricultural trade barriers.

The AoA defines the current multilateral agenda for agriculture:

- first by leaving huge trade barriers in place;
- second, by making those barriers more transparent and hence more negotiable; and
- third, by committing WTO members to resume negotiations by the year 2000 in the so-called 'built-in' agenda – negotiations that are now underway.

It has done nothing, however, to reduce the sensitivity of agriculture in domestic politics, and so future negotiations look likely to be just as difficult as those in the past. And there is unfinished business in each of the three main areas the AoA covers:

Domestic support
The AoA agreed a 20% reduction in aggregate domestic support for agriculture over six years (13.3% for most developing countries but with no reduction required for the least-developed countries). But this commitment was weakened by the selection of a high-support period as the base from which to reduce and by the explicit exclusion of 'green box' and 'blue box' payments from reduction commitments. Green box payments are supposed to have no effects on production: examples include agricultural research and development, agricultural extension and land retirement, all of which may be of use to policy-makers in developing countries.

The 'blue box' included direct payments in the United States and the EU under their ostensibly production-limiting programmes. But since these effectively allowed the continuation of existing levels of producer compensation and tied it to continuing presence in farming if not to actual output levels, their actual effect was to increase production relative to the level that would have been the case had such measures been abolished (see Ingersent et al., 1995).

The continuing high level of domestic agricultural support in developed countries is highly distortionary. The increases in output that it induces depress world prices and undercut developing country producers. They also maintain the size of the sector in developed countries, making it more difficult to reform in future. There is a very strong case for drastically reducing support.

Market access

The AoA commitments to replace all non-tariff barriers by equivalent tariffs ('tariffication') and to bind all agricultural tariffs were probably the most important steps in facilitating future liberalization. No new non-tariff barriers can be created and (the new) tariffs must be reduced by 36% on average over six years, though developing countries have a lower reduction commitment spread over a longer period. Each individual tariff line must be reduced by at least 15%.

But there are many qualifications to this rosy picture. Certain exceptions were permitted (to Japan and Korea on rice, for example), and all countries can easily impose emergency protection to undo temporarily the effects of the Round. The base period for tariffication, 1986–8, was a period of particularly high barriers and, in many cases, governments declared base rates far exceeding their previous levels of protection.[5] The average cut of 36% was achieved by cutting small tariffs by very large percentages and high ones by the minimum 15%.

Very high tariffs (tariff peaks) remain. Tafiffs of over 50% exist for 60 tariff lines (1.2% of the country's total number of lines) in Canada, 71 (1.4%) in the EU, 14 (0.3%) in Japan and 8 (0.2%) in the United States .[6] These cover nearly US$5 billion of developing country exports (despite the trade-chilling effect of very high rates) and are almost exclusively focused on agriculture. The Appendix to this chapter gives the EU list of tariffs exceeding 50%. Only one lies outside agriculture.

Tariff escalation also remains a particular problem for agriculture. Escalation occurs when the tariff increases as a commodity becomes more highly processed. It essentially taxes developing countries for trying to process their products rather than exporting them raw, and so discourages processing (see Chapter 12 for more analytical details.)

Table 9.3 reports average tariff rates at three levels of food processing for a number of OECD countries. There is rapid tariff escalation, particularly for fully processed products. A further example is provided by tariffs in the sugar-processing and starch-production sectors in the United States – tariffs on the final products exceed tariffs on the inputs to these products by 63% and 33% respectively (see Lindland, 1997).

Finally, to ensure a minimum level of import penetration in the newly 'tariffied' commodities, the AoA commitments were to be implemented via tariff rate quotas (TRQs), whereby a minimum access amount was admitted at below 'most favoured nation' (MFN) tariff rates. This created a whole new

Table 9.3 Tariff escalation for food manufacturing

	Canada	EU	Japan
First stage of processing	3%	15%	35%
Semi-processed	8%	18%	36%
Fully processed	42%	24%	65%

Source: World Bank, based on WTO Trade Policy Reviews (several years).

set of quantitative restrictions, whose allocation across suppliers is arbitrary and biased, resulting in inefficiency (high-cost suppliers got the quotas), favouritism, political pressures and, sometimes, undershooting the minimum because the quotas go to countries that cannot supply the commodity. It is estimated that rents from TRQs on agricultural imports to OECD countries amount to US$25 billion per year based on 1996 international prices (see Elbehri et al., 1999).

Table 9.4 illustrates the remaining tariffs on agriculture and the degree of restriction involved in some of the TRQs. It also suggests that for most of the

Table 9.4 Tariffs and tariff rate quotas in selected markets

	Tariffs		Tariff rate quotas		
	In-quota ad valorem tariff(2)	*Out-of-quota ad valorem tariff (3)*	*Quota/total imports %*	*In-quota imports/quota (quota fill rate) (1) %*	*Importer's share of quota rents (4) %*
United States					
Sugar	3	129	76	97	25
Dairy	11	70	95	77	75
Meats	5	26	102	67	50
European Union					
Wheat	0	87	2	21	75
Grains	35	162	26	74	75
Sugar	0	147	87	100	100
Dairy	24	91	80	99	55
Meats	19	128	73	100	50
Japan					
Wheat	0	234	95	109	100
Grains	0	491	84	109	100
Dairy	29	344	91	93	75
Canada					
Wheat	1	49	218	27	75
Grains	1	58	2397	5	75
Dairy	7	262	75	100	52
Meat	2	27	72	124	50

Notes: (1) Quota fill rate may exceed 1 if imports subject to in-quota tariffs exceed the declared minimum access commitments.

(2) Uruguay Round tariff schedules reported as in-quota tariff rates. For aggregate commodities, values are trade-weighted *ad valorem* rates.

(3) For OECD countries, these are OECD calculations of *ad valorem* equivalents based on comparing specific tariff rates with world market prices for 1996. These specific tariffs were derived based on import values and volume per tariff lines. For Korea and Philippines, these are MFN rates from the TRAINS database.

(4) These quota allocation shares are based on a simple rule that assigns a share of 1 in the case of a required import license; 0 if only an export licence is required; 0.5 if both import and export licences are required; and finally 0.5 if the product is imported on a first-come-first-served basis.

Source: Elbehri et al. (1999).

latter, the bulk of the rents created by permitting some imports at lower tariff rates accrue to residents of developed countries.

The need to address these huge distortions is self-evident. They cost the developed countries dearly in terms of forgone income. But they also penalize those developing countries that have a genuine comparative advantage in temperate agricultural products and their substitutes.

Export subsidies

Contrary to the general prohibition of export subsidies arising from the Uruguay Round, they are still permitted in agriculture at levels defined by those existing in the base period (1986–90). Subsidized export expenditure is to be reduced by 36% over six years (24% over ten years for most developing countries but with no reduction required for the least-developed countries). In addition, the volume of subsidized exports is to be reduced by 21% over six years in each of 22 product categories (14% over ten years for most developing countries and again with no reduction required for the least-developed countries). Given that they had few subsidies in the 1980s, these provisions very nearly amount to a prohibition on export subsidies for developing countries.

For the developed countries, while these commitments look impressive, they are not so very radical in practice. The choice of 1986–90 as the base line – a period of low world prices and very high subsidies – ensured that neither the United States nor the EU had to cut actual subsidies by very much. What is more, food aid is exempt from the commitments, as are export credits. Unlike tariffs, there are no restrictions on the size of the per unit export subsidy, only on the aggregate expenditures and volumes. Also the product categories over which these are measured are very broad, allowing scope for very high subsidies in particular cases. The cumulative effect of these exemptions is to allow considerable leeway for continued intervention in export markets.

Subsidies remain a major factor in world food markets. For example, the total value of OECD agricultural export subsidies exceeds the GDP of sub-Saharan Africa (see World Bank, 2000a). Given the huge adverse effects of export subsidies on developing country agriculture, which is trying to compete with the subsidized exports, Wang and Winters (2000) argue that nothing short of their complete abolition should satisfy developing countries in future negotiations.

9.3.2 Developing countries

Developing countries were mostly spectators in the agricultural negotiations of the Uruguay Round. They were required to undertake smaller reductions than the developed countries under the AoA and, in many cases, they were not major users of the various instruments whose use was curtailed. The standstill on export subsidies would constrain their future use of these policies, though few would think of doing so anyway. But they are almost unconstrained in most tariffs since they were allowed to use so-called

Table 9.5 Border protection in selected products, pre- and post-Uruguay Round

	Wheat			Sugar			Dairy		
	Actual protection	*As bound in the Uruguay Round*		*Actual protection*	*As bound in the Uruguay Round*		*Actual protection*	*As bound in the Uruguay Round*	
	1986–8	*1995*	*2000*	*1986–8*	*1995*	*2000*	*1986–8*	*1995*	*2000*
European Union	106	170	82	234	297	152	177	289	178
United States	20	6	4	131	197	91	132	144	93
Japan	651	240	152	184	126	58	501	489	326
Brazil	98	45	45	na	55	35	–21	53	46
Mexico	–1	74	67	–58	173	156	–3	66	54
Other Latin America	–17	34	34	41	85	80	na	75	69
Sub-Saharan Africa	10	na	133	44	na	100	na	na	100
Maghreb[a]	36	196	151	64	220	165	50	113	87
Mediterranean[b]	25	169	152	–13	107	93	na	166	150

Notes: a Includes Algeria, Morocco and Tunisia.

b Includes Cyprus, Egypt, Israel, Jordan, Lebanon, Libya, Malta, Syria and Turkey.

These data are based on comparisons between internal and world prices. Negative numbers reflect policies such as price controls that bring internal prices below international levels.

Source: Hathaway and Ingco (1996).

'ceiling bindings' – rates unrelated to existing applied tariffs – when they bound their rates. This 'think of a number' approach led to bound rates far in excess of actual tariff rates – see Table 9.5. Such 'water in the tariff' leaves room for future large increases in tariffs should governments so wish, greatly reducing the efficiency benefits of the lower applied rates. There is clearly an important piece of liberalization to be implemented here, either multilaterally or unilaterally.

9.3.3 The cost of agricultural trade restrictions

The portfolio of trade restrictions in agriculture that remains after the Uruguay Round is broad and deep. It is impossible to quantify the costs of these restrictions at all precisely: first, because many of the necessary data are missing, and second, because the cost of a policy so often depends on very precise details of its implementation. But broad modelling studies suggest that there are large benefits to liberalization. For example, Binswanger and Lutz (2000) cite gains of approximately US$20 billion a year for developing countries from a full agricultural liberalization, and Anderson et al. (1999) estimate gains of US$15 billion per year from a 40% liberalization. These numbers should not be taken literally, but they certainly suggest big returns to improving agricultural trade policy.

9.3.4 **The development box and food security**

Developing countries' frustrations with the asymmetries of agricultural policy have partly been crystallized into demands for a so-called 'development box', which would insulate some of their agricultural policies from the WTO agreements. The principal argument is that their food security could be undermined by both the costs of adjusting to liberalization and the AoA, which, they fear, could limit the policy options available to their governments.

There are several variants of the development box proposal, but the general idea is that for developing countries, agricultural policies that target the viability of small-scale subsistence farmers, rural poverty alleviation and product diversification should be insulated from WTO agreements and disciplines.[7]

In fact, however, Stevens et al. (1999) show that the AoA does not constrain developing countries' ability to pursue food security and rural development policies. Their concerns can be addressed under current WTO rules, using the green box, *de minimis* provisions, the domestic support rules, and the special safeguards provision of the AoA, as well as other specific articles in the AoA.[8] Nevertheless, it is possible that future agriculture agreements could be limiting, so care may be required.

But it is important to be specific about the policies that need to be altered or maintained and not let the development box mask a general reluctance to rationalize agricultural policy. The objectives of the box are very similar to those expressed by the EU and Japan in their defence of agricultural policy. This shows, first, that such laudable aims can easily get out of hand, and second, that a development box could encourage these developed countries to seek similar exclusions as a *quid pro quo* for the development box. An example of a concrete proposal to avoid this is to allow developing countries to offset negative support – that is, production-reducing policies – against positive support to maintain a zero balance of agricultural support overall (see Stevens et al., 1999). At present, negative support is ignored.

Furthermore, two of the three major worries expressed about food security by Stevens et al. (1999) do not concern developing country agricultural policy. They are that government revenues will be eroded by tariff liberalization and that reductions in developed country export subsidies will not be accompanied by transfers to allow food-vulnerable countries to maintain safety nets until they develop alternative food sources. Neither of these concerns can be addressed by a development box.

An entirely different dimension of food security for developing countries was the concern that agricultural liberalization under the Uruguay Round would increase world food prices. In fact, the impact was always going to be small relative to other shocks to these markets, and in the event, the anaemic level of liberalization achieved for agricultural products meant that it has been undetectable. Nonetheless, the possibility remains for the future. Overall, while concerns over food security are clearly important, the development box does not seem likely to contribute much to poverty alleviation.

9.3.5 Sanitary and phyto-sanitary standards

A separate agreement under the Uruguay Round concerns sanitary and phyto-sanitary standards (SPS) for agricultural goods. There are two aspects of this agreement that concern developing countries. First, many developing countries have only a limited ability to manage their own standards, to create the institutions and undertake the processes called for in the SPS Agreement. Thus, the agreement imposes an administrative burden on them – see Finger and Schuler (2000) for an estimate of the costs involved. It may also prevent them from restricting imports in order to achieve legitimate public policy objectives because they fear international challenge under the agreement. Such challenges are not likely to be a widespread problem, however, and the discipline that SPS offers against the covert use of standards as instruments of protection will be useful.

The second aspect is more important: the possibility that the SPS Agreement will be used to exclude developing countries' exports from developed country markets. The SPS Agreement permits governments to impose a variety of standards on imports, which could be seriously restrictive. It sets out procedures for imposing such standards, which should either be internationally agreed or allow for challenge and negotiation by trading partners. But if developing countries lack the expertise or resources to contribute to international standards-setting, they may find the chosen outcomes put them at a disadvantage. Similarly, if they lack the ability to challenge partners' standards, they could find that they have very little defence against covert protectionism.

Possibly more importantly, once (legitimate) standards have been imposed, developing countries may have great difficulties proving that their exports meet them. Testing procedures can be very expensive and are clearly a discouragement to new and small exporters. Moreover, achieving the standards may be expensive, and relatively more so for smaller exporters. Overall, the SPS Agreement raises serious doubts about market access for many developing country exporters, increases their costs of exporting, and probably discriminates against poor and small farmers. As such, its effects on poverty are essentially the same as tariffs or non-tariff barriers.

Of course, sanitary and phyto-sanitary standards are important and no one would suggest that they should be dispensed with. For that reason, it is desirable that there are multilateral rules for their implementation to prevent wanton protectionism. But it is not clear that the current rules recognize the real difficulties that developing countries have, either in imposing the standards or having them imposed on them. For example, Otsuki et al. (2001) argue that compared to international standards, new EU standards on aflatoxin will save 1.4 deaths per billion of population while costing African exporters around US$670 million in lost sales per year.

Technical assistance with managing the various aspects of the system, plus some sort of agreement by importers to make the system as light as possible for developing countries and/or small exporters would be useful. An example of the latter would be to permit imports from parts of a developing country

Box 9.1 **Sanitary and phyto-sanitary adaptation to regional conditions: problems and achievements**

There has been a mixture of frustration and progress in the adaptation to sanitary and phyto-sanitary regional conditions. Zarrilli (1999) identifies positive and negative experiences in this issue:

- '..Brazil and the United States have held talks to liberalize imports of fresh bovine meat from certain southern states in Brazil which are aftosa-free. However, until now, the talks have been inconclusive. The same is happening in the case of Brazilian exports to Japan and Canada. Both countries are banning imports of fresh bovine meat from Brazil, including from the states of Rio Grande do Sul and Santa Catarina where no cases of aftosa fever have been reported since 1994...'

- '..More optimistically, however, the EC has recognized that some Brazilian states are aftosa-free and is, therefore, authorizing imports of bovine meat without bones from these states. Similarly, the United States now allows imports of uncooked beef from regions in Argentina which have been recognized aftosa-free after a 80-year ban. It has also recently replaced a 83-year ban on imports of Mexican avocados with a process standard which allows avocados from a specified region in Mexico to be exported to the north-eastern United States during winter months...'

Source: Zarrilli (1999).

certified to be free of a disease, rather than banning all imports on the basis of problems just in certain localities – see Box 9.1. For their part, developing countries need to be willing to adjust their institutions to make the best of the SPS Agreement, including making compliance as easy as possible for their exporters.[9] That may well entail finding ways of enabling small traders and farmers to prove compatibility at low cost – perhaps through co-operatives – although it is not clear that small-scale export agriculture is preferable to commercial farming in terms of its poverty-reducing potential.

9.3.6 Agricultural liberalization by other means

Agriculture is substantially affected by policies aimed at and operated in other sectors. Thus, agricultural liberalization concerns much more than just the AoA. There are both broad 'general equilibrium' effects – for example, the protection of industry disadvantaging agriculture – and more specific spillovers. For example, in India the expansion of commercial bank networks and the availability of financial services has had a very substantial positive effect on private agricultural investment (see Hoekman and Anderson, 1999). Similarly, Chile's liberalization of shipping services in the 1970s resulted in a substantial reduction in shipping costs for local exporters. This, and the associated improvement in reliability, were important drivers of Chile's expansion into high value-added agricultural markets such as fruits and vegetables.

9.3.7 Regional trading arrangements

Most of the action in agriculture is (potentially) in the multilateral arena, not least because the principal progenitor of regional arrangements, the EU, seeks to exclude much of agriculture from the majority of its bilateral trade agreements. But there have been important agricultural dimensions to some regional agreements, and there could be more in future.

The North American Free Trade Agreement (NAFTA) will eventually free from tariffs all agricultural trade between its members, which will have benefits for Mexican citrus and tomato producers and costs for small maize farmers. Similarly, the EU Agreements with Mediterranean countries have reduced protection on the latter's temperate agriculture sector, which again could exacerbate poverty among small farmers. The Euro–Med agreements have another side, however: favoured access to protected EU markets. Partners have every interest in the short run in maximizing this access and reaping the maximum possible rents. This applies not only to the Euro–Med agreements, but also to any preferences, reciprocal or not. For the poorest and smallest countries, they apply particularly to the negotiation of the Regional Economic Partnership Agreements, which are to replace the Lomé Convention.

In the long run, however, relying on the rents from preferences is unlikely to be sustainable and the development that such incentives provide is not necessarily pro-poor. Preferential access is insecure and can disappear very suddenly, with very high, poverty-creating adjustment costs. The EU's former banana regime is an extreme example, but there are plenty of lesser examples of preferences being eroded by multilateral and/or domestic liberalization. If countries earn rents from such access, they should treat them as temporary, instituting policies such as compulsory savings and reserve accumulation to manage the expansion of the favoured sectors and provide a cushion for future adjustments. In the long run, relying on the rents from preferences is unlikely to provide a sustainable basis for long-term poverty-reducing development.

9.4 Agricultural liberalization and poverty

Given the importance of the agricultural sector to the poor, the liberalization of agriculture seems likely to have a larger impact on poverty than liberalization in any other area. The remainder of this chapter, therefore, considers how agricultural liberalization affects the poor. This section looks at internal agricultural liberalization (as opposed to trade liberalization); the following two sections examine how specific changes in agricultural trade policy, first in developing and then in developed countries, would affect the poor.

Figure 9.1 Pathways between agricultural policy and poverty

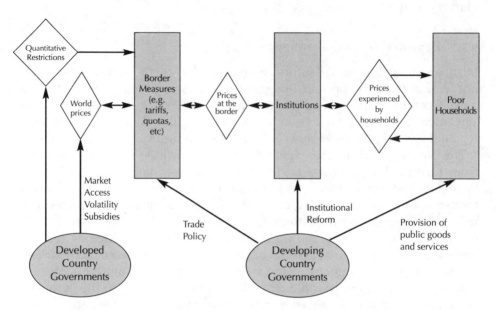

This section on internal liberalization is useful partly as a scene-setting and information-gathering exercise for the trade policy sections. It identifies key features of the agricultural economy and/or the conditions of the poor that determine the likely effects of reforms and it explores many actual experiences of liberalization that involve the same sort of effects as a trade liberalization – for example, changes in key prices. It is also useful in its own right, however, because trade policy reforms very frequently require associated internal reforms in areas such as marketing and distribution.

Figure 9.1 shows the pathways through which agricultural policy can affect the poor. It suggests three major sets of considerations in developing countries – trade policies, institutional structures and complementary policies – and two in developed countries – trade policies and other production-raising policies, such as high levels of domestic support.

9.4.1 The pattern of net consumption

The framework developed in Chapter 4 showed that the effect of a liberalization on a poor household depends fundamentally on its net consumption of the good(s) affected. And in agriculture above all other goods, there are likely to be both net consumers and net producers. The 'second-round', general equilibrium effects working through production, employment and demand linkages should not be ignored. Nevertheless, as most poor households live in rural areas, are highly dependent on agriculture and spend a large proportion of their income on food, the direct price effects will rarely be overturned by such 'second-round' effects. Thus, the most important observation about this issue is that if a poor household is a net consumer of a good, it will lose from a price rise, and if it is a net producer, it will gain.

Practical examples of the importance of this observation are many, including Ravallion and Van de Walle's (1991) analysis of the Indonesian rice reform of the early 1980s. They find that the effect of a 10% increase in rice prices (approximately the increase induced by the reform) on poverty depended critically on which poverty line was chosen. At relatively high poverty lines, the poverty count decreased because Indonesia's 'less poor' farmers were net producers of rice. At low poverty lines, however, the rice price increase worsened poverty because the most poor farmers, who were mainly net consumers of rice, were pushed further into poverty. The latter effect also meant that poverty measures that were sensitive to the depth of poverty (the poverty gap measures described in Chapter 3) worsened with the price increase regardless of the poverty line used.

9.4.2 The impact of comparative advantage, social structures and policy

The comparative advantage of a country is likely to have a strong bearing on the principal income sources of the poor. For example, a larger number of poor households are likely to gain their income from agriculture in countries that have a comparative advantage in agricultural production than in ones that do not. And in the case of agriculture, comparative advantage seems likely to depend primarily on relative factor endowments. Countries that are abundant in land and labour relative to capital are likely to have a comparative advantage in agricultural production, while others that are scarce in land but still abundant in labour are more likely to focus on labour-intensive manufactures. Yet other countries will have substantial endowments of natural resources but little labour, and may therefore have a comparative advantage in capital-intensive extraction of natural resources.[10]

But there is another consideration as well. The extent to which the national pattern of comparative advantage is translated into the income sources of the poor depends heavily on the structure of asset ownership within society. If a land-abundant country has a highly skewed distribution of land, then the majority of the poor may earn their income from agricultural wage labour rather than from their own agricultural production. This initial inequality in the distribution of assets can have an important effect on the way in which shocks associated with trade liberalization are transmitted to poor households, as well as harming subsequent growth (see Birdsall and Londono, 1997; Ravallion, 1998; Banerjee et al., 2000 and Deininger and Olinto, 2000).

On top of comparative advantage, national governments can have a significant influence on the net consumption patterns of the poor. Traditional anti-poverty policy has rightly focused on building up the assets of the poor. But the way in which this is done will influence the activities that the poor undertake. While programmes in the health and education sectors are likely to be of benefit to all types of economic activity, government directly influences the choice of economic activity through the provision of infrastructure (especially rural roads), land reform, market information, incentives for small business, access to credit and taxation policies. The combined effect of comparative advantage, the social structures that determine the distribution of assets, and government policy, gives rise to the pattern of net production or consumption observed.

9.4.3 Institutional reform: marketing arrangements

In addition to intervention in asset markets, governments can influence the way in which agricultural liberalization affects the poor by changing agricultural institutions. In the 1950s and 1960s, many developing countries set up centralized agricultural marketing organizations. These organizations were often responsible for the provision of inputs and credit to farmers, often at subsidized prices, and the purchase, storage and processing of outputs. But the protection offered to state marketing bodies, compounded by their monopsony and monopoly powers, led many of them to become extremely inefficient. In addition, political pressure to supply subsidized food for urban areas, combined with their high costs of operation, caused large budgetary losses. Thus, these institutions both imposed their own costs on the poor and prevented the transmission to them of favourable external shocks.

In the 1980s and 1990s, faced with strong pressures to make structural adjustments to their economies, as well as a general disillusionment with the effectiveness of state-led development strategies, many developing countries adopted sweeping reforms to their agricultural marketing systems. In many countries, such reforms included the outright privatization of state marketing bodies or simply their abolition. Experience suggests that such reforms have had a mixed impact on the poor. Governments need to ensure that the institutions are replaced by satisfactory arrangements: substituting private monopoly for public monopoly will not generally be pro-poor.

In situations where competitive private traders have replaced the public bodies, poor producers are likely to have benefited from the higher purchase prices arising from the end of state monopsony power. Furthermore, the introduction of competition in the provision of inputs and services can result in substantial cost reductions. For example, the removal of the state monopoly of milling services in Zambia during the early 1990s was accompanied by the emergence of large numbers of hammer mills providing milling services at much lower cost than the state-run mills. At least in part, this emergence was the consequence of deliberate policy interventions (see Oxfam-IDS, 1999 and Winters, 2000c). Similarly, in Zimbabwe's cotton market, prior to liberalization, the monopsony buyer (the Cotton Marketing Board) held producer prices low to subsidize inputs into the textile industry. While large producers were able to diversify out of cotton into other, unregulated products such as tobacco, small farmers could not do so and suffered from the low prices. After deregulation and privatization, three buyers have emerged, producing price competition and better prices for producers, and competing to offer extension and input services (see Oxfam-IDS, 1999 and Winters, 2000c).

Similarly, a study of food market reforms in Kenya, Mozambique, Zambia and Zimbabwe (Tschirley et al., 1999) suggests that the availability of grain improved in deficit areas after marketing reform because of increases in private grain trade between rural areas. This illustrates the fact that provided that trade is possible, consumers are not necessarily vulnerable to price instability when liberalization removes public stabilization measures. Private investment in grain distribution and cross-border trade is a perfectly feasible alternative.

China provides a further example of success. Here, the grain bureau is responsible for the purchase of grain, and used to be responsible for its distribution through ration shops until the early 1990s. Farmers are required to supply a minimum quota of grain to the bureau at an official price, while ration shops at that time capped the amount of grain that consumers could purchase at another (lower) official price. In the early 1990s, China commercialized the grain market by permitting the private marketing and sale of grain after fulfilling quotas for the grain bureau. Simultaneously, the subsidy to urban consumers was removed by allowing ration shops to sell at market prices. The result, ironically, was *improved* fulfilment of sales quotas, as farmers expanded production to benefit from higher above-quota prices obtainable on the free market. Urban consumers, on the other hand, saw substantial increases in prices (see Sicular, 1995).

In other cases, however, the dismantling of state marketing organizations has been damaging to the poor in some areas. For example, in contrast to the success story of Zimbabwean cotton above, some rural poor in Zambia have had a bad experience with the liberalization of maize markets – see Figure 9.2.

Figure 9.2 Changes to markets: maize in Zambia

Before:
- government subsidized inputs;
- government/co-operative crop purchasing;
- pan-territorial, pan-seasonal pricing;

⇩

- and growth of (imported) input-dependent production across the country.

Now:
- input prices have risen;
- markets for crops have shrunk (especially away from rail lines and major roads);
- limited availability of sustainable seeds;

⇩

- fall in area planted to maize and production;
- only partly offset by growth in more sustainable coarse grains because of consumer preference for maize;

⇩

- and shift to cotton, which is less profitable, but in which 'better' markets exist.

Source: Oxfam-IDS (1999).

Prior to liberalization, pan-territorial and pan-seasonal pricing meant that remote farmers were subsidized by those living close to rail lines, small farmers were subsidized by those with storage facilities (and the whole sector was subsidized by mining). Consequently, maize sellers and consumers near the rail lines benefited from the reforms, but remote producers lost: very high physical transaction costs arising from remoteness, compounded by a severe deterioration of transport infrastructure, made it difficult for traders to reach producers far from main roads. This forced many poor households into a greater reliance on subsistence farming and worsened the transmission of market information to remote areas (see Oxfam-IDS, 1999 and Winters, 2000c).

This last case was essentially one where the marketing reform eliminated the implicit subsidies that pan-seasonal and pan-regional pricing were making to poor and remote farmers. It illustrates the importance of understanding the impact of existing policies before reform is implemented. It also illustrates the point made in Chapter 4: i.e. the most dramatic gains and benefits from reform tend to be associated not with changes in the prices of goods that are traded both before and after a policy change, but with the creation or destruction of markets – that is, where goods start or cease to be traded.

9.4.4 Markets for inputs

Even when markets for outputs continue to exist, it is important that those for inputs, including capital, also function adequately. For example, if input prices rise by more than output prices, supply responses will be negative despite product market liberalization. This appears to have been the case with maize in Zambia in the 1990s (see Oxfam-IDS, 1999).

At a more sophisticated level, if some input markets are missing, the liberalization of other markets will not necessarily be welfare-improving even in aggregate, let alone for a subset of consumers (the poor).[11] Thus in Malawi, although market liberalization provided new opportunities for traditional large-scale commercial farmers (through tobacco and maize sales), the poorest 25% of farmers apparently experienced a relative worsening in income and food security (see Peters, 1996).

Similarly, in Tanzania, the gains to the poor from the liberalization of the cotton market in 1994 were reduced by the 'monetization' of input supply, which resulted in their using fewer material inputs than previously. Coupled with the persistence of local marketing monopolies and a slow production response due to the 'embeddedness' of certain farming systems, it seems that poor households have not reaped any benefit from liberalization (see Gibbon, 1998). The same is true in the cashew nut sector, where the gains of liberalization have been appropriated primarily by traders owing to the very poor flows of price information available to remote rural households (see Poulton, 1998).

9.4.5 Markets for credit and risk

Lopez et al. (1995) find similar evidence from Mexico, where poorer farmers seemed less able to respond to trade liberalization than richer ones. The critical determinant of responsiveness appears to be lack of access to physical assets, and Lopez et al. speculate that this is ultimately due to credit constraints. Interestingly, they find that despite their weaker responses to liberalization, poorer farmers experienced a greater rate of improvement in their use of inputs, arguably because of complementary policies to support them.

One way of smoothing risk is for the public sector to complement private insurance. For example, in Gujarat, India, an insurance scheme partially funded by government contributions has allowed around 20,000 landless agricultural labourers to receive life and accident insurance coverage (see World Bank, 2001).

9.4.6 Can the poor respond?

As we argued in Chapter 4, the initial endowments and income sources of a poor household are likely to determine whether a trade reform has a positive or negative effect. But the size of that effect depends at least as much – and the long-run dynamic effects depend even more – on the ability of the household to respond to the changes made. Specifically, we need to ask whether the poor are well placed to take up the opportunities offered by trade liberalization and/or to cope with the stresses that it creates. Chapter 4 described how access to assets, the nature of institutions and the extent of involvement of the poor in the institutions and processes that shape policy, can determine how the poor respond to trade liberalization. These arguments are particularly pertinent in the agricultural sector. In particular, the access of the poor to land can often determine their ability to capture the direct benefits from agricultural reforms. Box 9.2 explores some of the restrictions on women's access to land, at least some of which cause poverty among women.

9.4.7 Agriculture's strong positive spillovers

Agricultural policy is undoubtedly important to farmers who are poor, but it is also critical to other poor households in rural, and arguably even in urban, areas. A number of commentators have argued that for agriculture, spillovers to non-farmers are particularly beneficial because they focus income and price increases on precisely those sectors and regions in which the poor are strongly represented. Because most rural economies are relatively isolated and self-sufficient, much of any extra spending that is generated by a positive shock remains within the local economy, boosting the incomes of other (usually poor) households within it. In other words, beneficial agricultural reform has the capacity to advance the whole of the rural economy, not just farmers.

A considerable body of research now shows that in Asia, the increases in agricultural productivity brought about by the green revolution in the 1970s were very effective in reducing poverty because, in addition to their direct effects, they had large multiplier effects on rural economies. An extra dollar of agricultural income was typically associated with an additional 80 cents of non-agricultural income for local enterprises (see Delgado et al., 1998).

Box 9.2 **Obstacles to the purchase of land by women**

Institutions, both formal and traditional, govern the access of females to land and land use. In exploring likely poverty effects, it is important to consider whether female-headed households will be left in poverty following a trade liberalization because they cannot access the land necessary to take advantage of the new opportunities. IFAD (2001) documents some of the differences around the world:

- **India**: daughters rarely inherit land, even though they are legally eligible to do so. Some areas do, however, traditionally give unmarried daughters usufruct rights,[1] and in Bihar, some Ho women remain unmarried in order to keep this access. In Rajasthan, a survey of three villages found that of the 36 women with land in their names, 34 were widows; for 27, the land was registered with their sons. Most areas of matrilineal inheritance (such as much of Kerala, and many tribal land systems) show less gender-biased land control than areas of patrilineal inheritance.

- **East and Southern Africa**: poverty is explained much less by gender bias than by policy and institutional bias against all smallholders (men and women). In Ethiopia, there is no legal discrimination by gender. In Southern Africa, women can usually inherit land, and male migration has left many rural women as heads of household; hence, female land control is common.

- **West and Central Africa**: poverty alleviation is closely linked to intra-household distribution of, and control over, resources and incomes. In Imo and Abia States, Nigeria, the average household farms 9.8 hectares, but only 2.4 hectares are allocated to women and then not as a claim on land but through lease, from their husbands, for a farming season. Even widows do not have land as it is kept in trust by their husbands' families for the children.

---

1   An usufruct right is the right to use the land; but unlike ownership, the right is lost if the land is not used.

Source: IFAD (2001) based on the following sources in order of region: Agarwal (1994); IFAD (1999b) and UN (1991); and IFAD (1999a) and Odii (1997).

Bautista (2000) argues that such high multipliers on agricultural incomes make agriculture-led growth the optimum strategy for Vietnam in the twenty-first century.

Until recently, it was thought that such linkages were of less importance in Africa. But extensive research in Burkina Faso, Niger, Senegal, Zambia and Zimbabwe by the International Food Policy Research Institute suggests that household spending out of the extra income generated by increased exports could stimulate further rural income increases on a scale that even surpasses the experiences of Asia (see Delgado et al., 1998).

The high costs of trade in rural areas of many developing countries mean than most business is done at an extremely local level. For example, Hazell and Hojjati (1995) find that growth multipliers in the Eastern Province of Zambia are driven primarily by household consumption demands and that they arise largely within the agricultural sector itself because a large proportion of each additional kwacha is spent on local non-tradable foods. In addition, the smallest farms tend to use inputs and milling most intensively, so agricultural growth among small farms will lead to the strongest production linkages within the regional economy, although whether these translate into strong poverty alleviation is not clear.[12]

Income multipliers depend on output, and hence income, being able to expand without inducing price increases. If institutional or other rigidities prevent this, however, all is not lost because the price increases will raise the incomes of net suppliers of those goods or services and these could be the poor. This effect could be enhanced if they are able to adjust their economic activity to increase the advantage reaped from the price increases.

One instructive study of induced price increases is that of Ravallion (1990) on Bangladesh. This shows that while increases in food-grain prices hurt the rural poor, who are net grain consumers, in the short term, in the longer term, they translate into increased rural wages. For the very poor, who earn the highest proportions of their incomes from wage labour, the wage increases more than compensate for the cost of food, so that eventually the very poor benefit from food-grain price increases. The 'less poor', however, only break even.

Finally, at a macro-level, Datt and Ravallion (1996) demonstrate for India that rural growth not only directly alleviates rural poverty, but spills over into urban growth and poverty alleviation. Urban growth, on the other hand, has only mild effects on urban poverty and none on the much higher levels of rural poverty.

<u>9.5</u> The effects of liberalizing developing countries' trade policies on poverty

This section moves from the effects of agricultural liberalization in general to the specific issues that might figure in developing countries' future trade policy packages. Some of it concerns developing countries' positions in the WTO negotiations, but most could equally well be pursued unilaterally.

9.5.1 Tariff liberalization

Many developing countries have quite high tariffs on sensitive agricultural imports that compete with domestic products – just like the developed countries. And just like the developed countries, they will almost certainly benefit overall from reducing them. Reducing tariffs will lower domestic prices (often by the full amount of the tariff cut) and its effect on the poor will principally be related to whether they are net suppliers or net consumers of the good in question.

Since for most countries, the number of products involved is small, there are unlikely to be strong overall effects on agricultural, rural activity or on government revenue. So these price effects are likely to be the most important of the poverty effects. The main exception will be if production of the crop is strongly localized, in which case large local shocks may occur. Thus, the main information requirement for predicting poverty effects here is simply consumption and production data by households.

As an example, research on Morocco suggests that reductions in agricultural protection mandated by the Euro–Med Agreement with the EU would generate significant welfare gains in aggregate, but disadvantage a significant part of the rural population. This is because agriculture, and especially livestock farming, was originally the more protected sector, so that liberalization reduces its prices and incomes. But compensatory policies would offset the problems via such measures as transfers to the owners of rain-fed agricultural resources, and improvements in rural skill levels and non-agricultural productivity (see Löfgren, 1999). Box 9.3 discusses similar problems for corn farmers in Mexico following establishment of the NAFTA.

9.5.2 National food security

As discussed above, one argument for protection – as well as for export restrictions – is to improve food security. In general, a reduction in protection should not compromise food security at a national level, though ensuring that it does not may require some conscious policy decisions. Domestic production of most agricultural products will be far more variable than world

---

Box 9.3 **Liberalization of the corn sector in Mexico**

Nadal (2000) analyses the impact of trade liberalization in the corn (maize) sector in Mexico following the establishment of the NAFTA. His evidence suggests that the NAFTA had an overall negative impact on small farmers, although it appears to us that this was more due to the macroeconomic crisis and the consequent failure of complementary policies than to tariff reductions *per se*. Concretely:

- In spite of a sharp drop in corn prices and an increase in imports, Mexico's corn production has remained stable, with a greater cultivated area not fully offset by lower yields.
- There has been little incentive and opportunity for farmers to re-allocate productive resources to other crops, as their prices have dropped too.
- Due to market imperfections and segmentation in the processing sector, the expected benefits in terms of lower consumer prices for maize products have failed to materialize; tortilla prices have actually risen.
- The government had originally planned a long adjustment period over which tariffs would fall gradually and other support policies would have been implemented for the poorest corn farmers. In fact, however, the crisis of December 1994 led to the immediate removal of tariffs and abandonment of the complementary policies.

Source: Nadal (2000).

production, and so in physical terms security should be improved by opening up. World markets may, however, have greater price fluctuations, so that governments may need to take steps to ensure that they have sufficient reserves to continue to import necessary foodstuffs under all circumstances.

Since trade liberalization will almost always increase aggregate incomes, it would seem plausible that governments should be able to make arrangements to ensure food security if they wish to. But if governments have difficulty in taxing the gains from trade and/or keeping reserves, food security problems may sometimes arise and policy responses may be necessary. Maintaining tariff levels may help, but because tariffs raise prices and encourage inefficient production while doing nothing to tackle the critical requirements of taxation or reserve holding, they are unlikely to be the best policies available. Similarly, production subsidies for agriculture are unlikely to figure in any optimal policy package, save perhaps as temporary measures to ease one-off adjustment pains from a major liberalization. Subsidizing sectors that cannot survive at world prices is not an efficient use of resources and there is no reason to believe that developing countries will prove better than developed countries have been at managing the political economy of agricultural protection.

One issue of timing might arise: if developing countries liberalize their imports before developed countries cut back their agricultural subsidies, developing county agricultural production may fall excessively. If changing the scale of production is complex and costly, this could entail excess costs if agricultural production needs to rise again when the subsidies are removed.

9.5.3 Household food security

Turning to individual households, the nature of the shocks facing the rural poor may change with greater openness. Provided that it has reasonably stable macroeconomic conditions, the main shocks to a closed economy's food markets will be supply shocks. Hence prices and quantities will be negatively correlated (lower output will lead directly to higher prices) and fluctuations in farmers' revenues will be proportionately smaller than those in output.[13] For a perfectly open price-taking economy, on the other hand, quantities and prices will fluctuate independently so there will be no offsetting effects and the variance of income will be higher. Thus, a liberalization that shifted an economy from purely local price-determination to one following world prices could increase the variability faced by farm households.

Excess variability could impinge very heavily on the poor, for they are least able to cope with it. Box 9.4 reports on Madagascar, where a reform raised the average real incomes of the poor but still appeared to reduce their welfare. Coping with the extra uncertainty that the reform created hurt more than the extra average income helped.

Of course, if a reform of any kind reduces a poor household's income, it will almost invariably worsen its food security as well. But this is just another aspect of the general question of reducing the incomes of the poor, and requires no independent consideration here.

Box 9.4 **Food insecurity and price variability**

Food insecurity is an important aspect of poverty and can significantly influence the behaviour of the poor. An agricultural liberalization that simultaneously increased average food prices and the extent to which they varied through time could both increase farm incomes and food output, and reduce welfare by increasing variability.

Barrett (1998) argues that this situation arose in Madagascar as a result of its rice reforms in the 1980s. The mean price of rice rose by 42%, and price variance by 53%, and rice output growth accelerated. Interestingly, however, the increase in output was concentrated among small farmers, who were actually net purchasers of rice and whose nutritional, educational and overall expenditure data indicated a decline in welfare. If these households were risk-averse – as the very poor have to be – their losses from the increased variance and higher consumption price outweighed any benefits from increased sales. In fact, Barrett argues, the increased output was an attempt to compensate for the higher variability – by raising the mean level of income around which variance occurred. For richer, net rice-producing farmers, who could afford to be less risk-averse, the response was the opposite, with the higher variability leading to declines in output growth, or even absolute output.

This analysis indicates that the effects of reform must be considered not only on the mean levels of prices and incomes but also on their variances. Price variance is of particular consequence for the poor.

Source: Barrett (1998).

9.5.4 Reducing the anti-agriculture bias in developing countries

Despite dramatic reforms in the last two decades in some developing countries, many still retain a strong policy bias against agriculture. Krueger et al. (1992) and Tyers and Anderson (1992) find that policies often tend to discourage farm production and that this anti-agriculture bias arises principally from non-agricultural policies (notably, manufacturing protectionism and overvalued exchange rates) rather than from agricultural policies. And there are still some cases of export restrictions, which are the ultimate anti-agriculture policy where countries have comparative advantage in that sector.

The effect of high tariffs for manufacturing is to raise the domestic price of manufactures relative to agricultural goods. This tends to draw resources away from the agricultural sector towards the manufacturing sector, diverting the allocation of resources away from the sector that enjoys comparative advantage. Similarly, an overvalued exchange rate reduces the price of tradable goods (both imports and exports) relative to non-tradable goods. It thus discourages agricultural exports where they might have been profitable (though it also protects the production of non-tradable services, which may be important for some categories of poor household). Thus, in considering the effects of agricultural liberalization on poverty, it is important to recall that the major effects may well come from policies outside the sector.

Box 9.5 **Export restrictions and poverty: rice in Vietnam**

Using both real data on household consumption and production and a computable model of trade policy, Minot and Goletti (1998) study the aggregate and distributional effects that would have accompanied the liberalization of Vietnam's rice exports in the mid-1990s. In aggregate, the effect would be to increase real incomes by an average of 2.9%. Eliminating the rice export quotas would raise rice prices, at the expense of the many (heavy) net rice-consuming households, especially those in urban areas. But it would also reduce the incidence and depth of poverty because net sellers of rice are mainly among the poor, and even those who were originally small-scale net purchasers would gain because producer prices would increase by more than consumer prices. The poor would do better than the non-poor in all regions, and the aggregate effects would be beneficial in all regions except one. Within these groups, however, there would be poor who loose, even in the countryside. Hence, even a reform that generally strongly benefits the poor will need complementary and/or compensatory policies if everyone is to benefit.

Source: Minot and Goletti (1998)

Correspondingly, of course, the poverty effects of manufacturing trade reform must be informed not only by the results in the manufacturing sector, but also by its general equilibrium effects, including those on agriculture.

The consequences of export restrictions for poverty will vary according to the poor's net consumption positions, but they can certainly be negative – see Box 9.5.

9.5.5 State trading: making developing country agricultural markets contestable

In addition to removing the anti-agriculture bias of policy, there are also large long-term gains to be made from improving competition in agricultural (and other) markets. Notwithstanding the reforms of the last decade, many developing countries still support state-run import, export and marketing monopolies for many agricultural commodities. In practice, these organizations have often been extremely inefficient, resulting in lower prices paid to producers, higher prices for consumers and poor-quality marketing services. Substantial gains are therefore attainable through the careful introduction of foreign competition into the domestic markets for marketing, distribution and import/export services. Pressure to address the activities of state trading companies will probably feature quite prominently in any future trade negotiations.

Developing countries are understandably concerned about the possible increase in dependency associated with a rapid move towards foreign provision of trading services. But experience suggests that improving the 'contestability' of domestic agricultural markets (that is, increasing the ease with which new firms can move into the markets if margins become unusually high) frequently offers large gains, because it forces domestic firms to upgrade to world standards.

In the short run, there can be large adjustment costs associated with improving the competitiveness of domestic firms in this way. Often governments are forced to liquidate or severely scale back employment in 'parastatal' enterprises, while private monopolies can experience substantial job losses. If poor urban households depend on incomes from such formal-sector jobs, then such reforms can have negative short-term effects on poverty.

But in the long run, improved contestability encourages faster growth of the sector than would have occurred otherwise and releases public resources for investment in more direct anti-poverty actions. Nonetheless, where reforms are likely to have immediate negative effects, choosing an appropriate sequencing and speed of reforms may mitigate the impact on the poor and allow time to design compensatory policies to safeguard the livelihoods of the poor during the transition period.

9.6 Developed country trade policies and poverty

We have argued that in general the effect of international trade policy is primarily a matter of what countries do to themselves rather than what other countries do to them. And it is true, as we have seen above, that developing countries' own trade polices do have serious implications for their overall performance and success in poverty alleviation. But in the case of agriculture, other countries' policies – specifically those of the developed countries – do have a major impact and so in this section, we turn to what developing countries might seek from developed countries in the context of multilateral negotiations on agriculture. Quite simply, improved market access to developed country markets and the rolling-back of high agricultural subsidies must be one of the developing countries' main goals in any future world trade talks.

9.6.1 Market access for temperate products

There are potentially huge gains for some developing countries from improved market access to developed country markets. Table 9.4 (see page 179) showed the absurd levels of some of the developed countries' trade barriers, for example, 129% for sugar in the United States and 162% for grains in the EU. For developing countries that can supply these temperate products, improved market access offers the potential for huge increases in income and also for reductions in poverty where production is highly labour-intensive.

Improved access will generate higher returns to agriculture by raising the prices of exports to developed countries. Some of the tariff reductions will probably accrue to exporters rather than consumers, although given the competitiveness of many of these markets, the direct effect may not be large. More importantly, lower internal prices will stimulate net consumption of agricultural goods in the developed countries and so help to raise the world prices of these products (see below).

Relaxing TRQs would also stimulate exporter incomes by allowing more to be sold at below the 'standard' tariff. In effect, extending the quantity that can be sold at below standard tariffs creates a rent at least part of which can be appropriated by developing country exporters. But, TRQs and other forms of preferential access, such as that proposed in the Cotonou Agreement or the Generalized System of Preferences, complicate the welfare analysis of liberalization for developing country exporters and can lead to 'perverse' outcomes in which liberalization is actually deleterious rather than beneficial for them. For example, if out-of-quota tariffs fall, developed country internal prices will fall. This will cut the rents associated with preferential (in-quota) access and if these previously accrued to exporters, it could cut export returns. Ideally, developing country negotiators should investigate the structure of each of the markets facing liberalization to see how much rent they are getting, and seek policy relaxation accordingly. In fact, however, this is extremely complex to do and the most appropriate rule of thumb appears to be that unless an exporter currently has a large share of the preferential market and has little comparative advantage, liberalization is likely to bring benefits in the long run.

An important qualification to all this is that agriculture is a land-intensive, rather than a labour-intensive activity. Thus, the ability to translate improved market access for agricultural products into significant poverty reduction depends significantly on having a structure of land ownership that encourages labour-intensive use of the land, either through smallholder grower schemes or large-scale wage employment. IFAD (2001) shows that the former may have advantages in terms of aggregate output as well as distribution, for in many countries, by virtue of their more intensive and careful farming techniques, smallholders generate greater output per hectare than larger farms.

In addition, for long-run benefits to accrue, reasonable supply responses are essential. These will be aided by domestic policies to assist:

*   investment in complementary infrastructure (irrigation and rural roads) to ensure that agricultural production can be connected to world markets;
*   property rights to encourage investment in the land;
*   appropriate agricultural extension and mechanisms for the dissemination of market and technical information;
*   the development of complementary markets for credit, agricultural inputs and services.

Overall, improvements in access to developed country markets, combined with domestic policies in developing countries designed to maximize the potential of such increased access, seem likely to provide a strong stimulus to growth that will alleviate poverty in beneficiary countries. The major beneficiaries of such growth are likely to be the rural poor and the same sort of positive spillovers that were discussed above are also likely to arise to wages, input providers, local service markets and so on.

9.6.2 Market access for tropical products

Developed countries tend to be open to most tropical products at low tariff rates because they offer no competition to local producers. Thus, there is little direct liberalization to seek. But there are exceptions, most notably in the EU where tariffs and other barriers are maintained in order to protect output and margins in those parts of the EU capable of growing tropical products and in favoured developing countries, especially the ACP countries. The most notorious case is bananas, but EU tariffs are also high on tobacco, manioc and sugar. In these cases, non-favoured exporters have a strong interest in improved market access, although in some cases the opening would need to be very large to allow them to compete on a level playing field with the preferred ones. Of course, MFN liberalization would reduce margins of preference for existing exporters and thus could have negative poverty effects in those countries, particularly where preferential access has encouraged strong dependence on a particular crop.

Tariff escalation is also a problem in tropical products, although less so than for temperate import-competing products. Thus, for example, cocoa and coffee processing both face higher tariffs than do the equivalent raw and unprocessed goods.

Reducing escalation should be a major objective for developing countries during any trade talks (not only for tropical products but for temperate and industrial products as well). If developing countries can enter (higher value added) processing industries, the impact on poverty is likely to be beneficial via the creation of better-paying jobs. In addition if, as is often suggested, processing local raw products offers the easiest way into manufacturing, there may be positive spillovers for other industries as entrepreneurs and workers become more adept in that field. Again, while the direct effect on the poor is unlikely to be strong, the general increases in productivity will be a major force for good in the long run.

9.6.3 Fish

If agricultural policy in developed countries seems perverse, fishing policy is even worse. It is driven partly by concern for fish stocks, which naturally leads to restrictions on fishing and fish sales both within and between countries. Policy is primarily driven, however, by concern for fishing communities with the result that despite the obvious diminishing marginal returns, governments have poured huge subsidies into this declining sector (see Milazzo, 1998). Tariffs are high in the EU, averaging approximately 12% in 1996, and non-tariff barriers widespread. In addition, health and, sometimes, environmental regulations significantly discourage trade.

The Uruguay Round excluded discussion of fishing subsidies, and tariffs were subject only to small reductions. Finger et al. (1996) put developed countries' post-Uruguay Round average tariff at 6.4% (third only to agriculture and textiles), and the reduction at 2.8 percentage points (measured in terms of the change in landed price induced by tariff reductions).

The liberalization of trade in fish – especially for coastal and inland fisheries – could have significant positive effects on the poor in developing countries, since many fishing families are poor. Induced increases in prices may, however, have adverse effects on the many that survive on fish but earn their living in other ways. Liberalizing deep-sea fishing is less directly beneficial to the poor, but if the developed countries withdrew their subsidies and allowed developing countries to staff the world-wide industry, there could be important income and government revenue effects. Moreover, if doing so led to less voracious exploitation, there would probably be long-run benefits in terms of sustainability.

A particularly sensitive practice is the way in which developed countries sometimes 'purchase' the right to fish in developing countries' exclusion zones by promises of market access (in fish and other products) and other incentives, including straight transfers, and then exploit them very heavily over the short term. Milazzo (1998) describes such practices in, for example, the 1996 EU agreements with Mauritania. He reports that the EU authorities (not the EU fishing industry) pay about US$350 million per year for access to fishing grounds. Of course, for the developing countries, collecting rents for access to resources that they cannot exploit effectively themselves makes good sense. But governments need to be very sure that they are receiving the right price, that sustainability is assured and that inviting in industrial fishermen does not undermine the local industries that employ much less well-off workers.

9.6.4 **Reductions in export subsidies and domestic support**

Further reductions in developed countries' export subsidies and domestic agricultural support, coupled with cuts in import barriers, should reduce the global supply of many commodities, causing prices to rise. Table 9.6 presents some of the predictions for liberalization-induced price increases made for the Uruguay Round. As shown above, these increases did not come about because so little liberalization has actually been achieved. Moreover, given that most predictive models tend to underestimate the flexibility of the world economy, they are probably over-estimates. Serious liberalization in future seems likely to have some price-raising effects, although not to the extent often forecast and against a trend of secular declines in agricultural prices. Thus, while this is an issue on which policy-makers should maintain a careful watch, it is probably not one of the major considerations in agricultural liberalization for most countries.

Such price increases are likely to have important effects on the poverty of different groups within developing countries. First, the budgetary cost of food aid will rise. If donor-government budgets for the provision of food aid remain the same, then this is likely to lead to a reduction in the supply of food aid. More generally, developing countries that are very reliant on food imports (including food aid) will suffer adverse terms-of-trade effects, tending to reduce their aggregate incomes.[14] Even more generally, increasing world prices will raise agricultural prices in any country open to world price signals. This will affect the poor according to their net consumption.

Table 9.6 Predictions of the impact of Uruguay Round liberalization on world agricultural prices (percentage change from benchmark levels at the end of implementation period)

Commodities	Brandao and Martin (1993) Dunkel Scenario	Goldin, Knudsen & van der Mensbrugghe (1993)	Goldin & van der Mensbrugghe (1995) Scenario I 79–93 base	Goldin & van der Mensbrugghe (1995) Scenario II 89–93 base	Goldin & van der Mensbrugghe (1995) Scenario IV (with no slippage)	FAO (1995)
Wheat	6.2	5.9	1.2	3.8	10.3	7.0
Rice	4.0	−1.9	−1.5	−0.9	3.6	7.0
Coarse grains	3.3	3.6	0.1	2.3	5.4	4.0
Sugar	9.9	10.2	−1.0	1.8	11.4	na
Beef and veal	7.2	4.7	0.2	0.6	6.0	8.0
Other meats	4.0	1.0	−0.9	−0.6	2.3	na
Coffee	1.3	−6.1	−1.7	−1.5	−0.7	na
Cocoa	0.9	−4.0	−1.3	−0.7	0.3	na
Tea	2.7	3.0	−1.6	−1.4	0.9	na
Vegetable oils	3.8	4.1	−0.6	−0.3	5.4	4.0
Dairy	12.2	7.2	−1.3	1.2	12.1	7.0
Other foods	1.3	−1.7	−1.3	−1.4	−0.7	na
Cotton	1.8	3.7	−1.1	−1.2	1.2	na
Other agriculture	2.6	5.9	0.5	0.8	2.9	na

Source: Ingco (1996).

Yet again, however, it is important to recognize that poor households vary greatly and that particularly in agriculture, second-round spillovers can be expected to have beneficial effects. Thus, the principal divide between winners and losers from reductions in developed countries' export subsidies or domestic support is likely to be between rural and urban households. If the rural economy is primarily agricultural, rural households may gain even if they are not themselves agricultural producers. Poor urban households, however, are likely to lose as they are generally neither employed in, nor closely linked to, food production. In addition, the poorest households, which are often economically inactive because of old age, youth, disability or illness, will be hit by food price rises.

9.6.5 Letting price signals work

The hope of the Uruguay Round was that by tariffying quantitative restrictions and variable levies, the transmission of world price signals to farmers in developed countries would be dramatically improved, and that this in turn would increase the price sensitivity of output and consumption and so reduce the variability of world prices. The same hope applied to the replacement of domestic price support policies, in which governments boost farm incomes by increasing the prices farmers receive, by income support policies, whereby they merely top up the income of farmers facing hardship. While the former encourage farmers to produce regardless of demand, the latter allow them to respond to price signals and offer support if the consequences are deemed to be unacceptable. These transformations may have happened to some extent, but farmers in many countries still receive fixed domestic prices and in some cases are encouraged to remain in farming as a condition for drawing their compensation payments for lower prices.

Thus, in a future round of trade negotiations, there is still scope for improving transmission and hence reducing volatility. This reduction in risk will benefit both food-importing and food-exporting nations alike. But it will be particularly beneficial to the poor, since there is now a considerable body of evidence to suggest that the poor are less well equipped than the better off to insure themselves against such risks (see Jalan and Ravallion, 1999). In addition, if world prices become less volatile, one of the main political pressures (or perhaps, needs) for market intervention is reduced, and with it the chances of distorting market behaviour.

9.7 Conclusion

Agriculture lies at the very heart of the trade and poverty issue. Much agricultural trade is highly restricted – often in very inefficient ways – and agriculture and food are the key activities and consumption goods of most of the poor. Agriculture also has very desirable spillover characteristics so that it delivers more anti-poverty bang per reform buck than other sectors.

But having said all this, it must be remembered that the links are very idiosyncratic. While in the large majority of cases, liberalization is benign, there are still plenty of specific cases where trade and other reforms have adverse effects on the poor, and there is no substitute for responsible policy-makers knowing the structure of their economies and understanding the lives of the poor. In general, there is little case for eschewing reform on poverty grounds, but there may be cases where timing is important, and there is an overwhelming case for ensuring that complementary and compensatory policies are used to shield the poor from adverse effects.

In terms of trade policy, whether multilateral or unilateral, the most important considerations are:

- reversing the anti-agricultural bias in developing countries, particularly by reducing manufacturing protection and exchange rate overvaluation;
- implementing institutional reforms to ensure that the poor have access to fair markets, including marketing arrangements, infrastructure and credit markets;
- improving access for developing countries' agricultural products to developed country markets, including the removal and reduction of tariffs and non-tariff barriers;
- abolishing export subsidies and dramatically reducing domestic support in developed countries.

In assessing the likely poverty effects of trade liberalization in agriculture (including those emanating from reforms in other sectors), policy-makers should bear in mind the questions posed in Box 9.6, the agricultural liberalization checklist.

Box 9.6 **Checklist on agricultural liberalization**

- What are the net food supply positions of the poor? Are net consumers of food nevertheless part of the rural economy and thus potential beneficiaries from agricultural liberalization even if prices rise?
- Would boosting agricultural incomes lead to strong multiplier and/or rural price/wage effects in your economy?
- Does your economy suffer a significant anti-agriculture bias via either direct or indirect means?
- Is the distribution of assets – physical, land and human – such that the benefits of agricultural expansion would impinge directly on the poor? Could policies be designed to ensure that they did?
- Do agricultural markets – for both outputs and inputs, including rural credit – and institutions allow the poor to exploit the advantages of openness?
- Is food security a serious concern at either national or household level? If the former, can you address it via savings and reserves rather than output-distorting measures? If the latter, can you address it via safety nets and other insurance-type policies rather than by market intervention and allowing the poor to retreat into low-productivity self-sufficiency?
- Are major export commodities constrained by market access restrictions in developed countries? Are your own markets disrupted by developed countries' output-raising policies? Who are your natural allies and what can you offer to try to improve access and reduce subsidies?
- Are your exporters beneficiaries of preferences in those markets? If so, what can be done in the long run to put them on a sounder commercial footing?

Annex to Chapter 9

Table 9.A.1 High tariff lines for the EU at the six-digit level (>50%)

HS6	Description	MFN tariff (%)	Total imports (thousand US $)	Share of developing countries	Share of developing countries' exports going to the EU
020610	Fresh or chilled edible bovine offal	252	137,218	0.001	0.128
020220	Frozen unboned bovine meat (excl. carcasses)	195	79,945	0.010	0.010
020230	Frozen boneless bovine meat	193	732,472	0.404	0.429
040590	Fats and oils derived from milk (excl. butter and dairy spreads)	161	422,215	0.000	0.004
020443	Frozen boned meat of sheep	157	217,127	0.047	0.760
020210	Frozen bovine carcasses and half carcasses	153	31,853	0.000	0.000
020120	Fresh or chilled unboned bovine meat (excl. carcasses)	132	2,145,310	0.008	0.145
020430	Frozen lamb carcasses and half carcasses	125	79,411	0.079	1.000
020450	Fresh, chilled or frozen goat meat	124	1,8601	0.028	0.090
100110	Durum wheat	123	532,654	0.118	0.528
020110	Fresh or chilled bovine carcasses and half carcasses	119	967,181	0.002	0.105
020441	Frozen sheep carcasses and half carcasses (excl. lamb)	118	3,118	0.032	0.007
100590	Maize (excl. seed)	115	1,572,481	0.145	0.102
152200	Degras; residues of fatty substances or animal or vegetable waxes	114	10,590	0.144	0.150
040610	Fresh (unripened or uncured) cheese, including whey cheese and curd	108	741,117	0.001	0.014
040510	Butter	107	1,895,873	0.016	0.430
100400	Oats	105	43,637	0.001	0.007
230310	Residues from manufacture of starch and similar residues	105	188,625	0.031	0.591
100200	Rye	104	40,260	0.018	0.502
240310	Smoking tobacco with or without tobacco substitutes	103	502,793	0.003	0.011
010290	Live bovine animals, other than pure-bred breeding	103	1,917,731	0.055	0.199
230230	Brans, sharps and other residues of wheat	101	84,518	0.036	0.060
071410	Manioc, fresh or dried, chilled or frozen	99	272,681	0.854	1.000
020442	Frozen unboned meat of sheep	99	380,688	0.012	0.321
100620	Husked (brown) rice	98	474,460	0.505	1.000
100630	Semi-milled or wholly milled rice	97	555,159	0.142	0.061
020423	Fresh or chilled boneless meat of sheep	96	42,528	0.088	1.000
040520	Dairy spreads	94	19,012	0.000	0.002
020130	Fresh or chilled boneless bovine meat	91	1,679,149	0.249	0.783
020421	Fresh or chilled sheep carcasses and half carcasses (excl. lamb)	90	36,785	0.007	0.056
040221	Milk and cream in solid forms of >1.5% fat, unsweetened	90	611,660	0.031	0.059
230910	Dog or cat food, put up for retail sale	87	1,955,219	0.025	0.423
040299	Sweetened milk and cream (excl. in solid form)	86	146,804	0.001	0.002
170199	Cane or beet sugar, in solid form, nes	83	1,611,361	0.037	0.033
170111	Raw cane sugar, in solid form	82	1,077,375	0.939	0.404
150910	Virgin olive oil	81	1,281,012	0.324	1.139

HS6	Description	MFN tariff	Total imports (thousand US $)	Share of developing countries	Share of developing countries' exports going to the EU
020629	Frozen edible bovine offal (excl. tongues and livers)	80	44,514	0.121	0.136
151000	Other oils and their fractions, obtained solely from olives, nes	79	41,552	0.589	0.844
240290	Cigars, cigarillos, cigarettes, etc., not containing tobacco	79	2,220	0.024	0.001
100610	Rice in the husk (paddy or rough)	79	55,057	0.341	0.206
020410	Fresh or chilled lamb carcasses and half carcasses	78	532,175	0.006	0.259
020422	Fresh or chilled unboned meat of sheep	77	136,764	0.003	2.107
121291	Sugar beet, fresh, dried, chilled or frozen	74	30,737	0.000	0.002
240130	Tobacco refuse	74	92,573	0.660	0.796
110814	Manioc (cassava) starch	74	4,351	0.782	0.127
040210	Milk and cream in solid forms of =<1.5% fat	72	1,014,570	0.037	0.166
240220	Cigarettes containing tobacco	71	4,119,217	0.001	0.002
190490	Prepared cereals in grain form (excl. maize)	71	121,343	0.032	0.107
150990	Olive oil and fractions (excl. virgin)	70	158,875	0.254	0.501
040120	Milk and cream of >1% but =<6% fat, not concentrated or sweetened	69	1,694,888	0.035	0.386
100640	Broken rice	68	97,368	0.359	0.794
040690	Cheese, nes	68	5,411,532	0.015	0.279
040630	Processed cheese, not grated or powdered	67	580,459	0.005	0.097
110311	Groats and meal of wheat	66	69,023	0.008	0.030
110329	Pellets of other cereals (excl. wheat)	66	8,225	0.005	0.062
110900	Wheat gluten	66	106,798	0.006	0.083
100190	Spelt, common wheat and meslin	65	3,159,295	0.017	0.033
110813	Potato starch	65	114,840	0.001	0.060
200960	Grape juice (incl. must), unfermented, not containing added spirit	65	133,075	0.060	0.083
100700	Grain sorghum	64	71,658	0.089	0.052
220710	Undenatured ethyl alcohol, of alcoholic strength >=80%	64	317,943	0.066	0.112
040291	Concentrated milk and cream, unsweetened (excl. in solid form)	61	469,049	0.002	0.032
110100	Wheat or meslin flour	61	244,382	0.019	0.012
382460	Sorbitol (excl. that of 2905.44)	61	36,029	0.001	0.165
220430	Other grape must, nes	60	55,5789	0.063	0.168
200919	Unfrozen orange juice, unfermented, not containing added spirit	57	525,740	0.174	0.962
100300	Barley	57	667,674	0.005	0.023
220890	Other spirituous beverages, nes	56	338,776	0.175	0.172
110422	Other worked grains of oats, nes	54	2,986	0.024	0.010
040640	Blue-veined cheese	53	234,565	0.001	0.118
110710	Malt not roasted	50	304,574	0.002	0.005

Notes: Peaks defined at six-digit level – see this chapter endnote 6
  Shaded row is non-agricultural.

Source: World Bank, based on OECD, Tariffs and Trade: OECD Query and Reporting System, 2000 edition, CD-ROM.

Notes

1 Where they both draw their income *and* spend it mostly on food, they are, of course, less exposed to prices. But given that in the course of development, such self-sufficiency becomes much less common, changing food prices become increasingly important.

2 There are many expositions of the economics of agricultural protection that contain far more detail than can be included here; for example, Tyers and Anderson (1992) and Colman and Roberts (1994).

3 Baffes and Meerman (1998) suggest that although decoupled income support has smaller distortionary effects than price support, problems still arise from these schemes. The main problems are the risk of variability of agricultural prices and the difficulties of targeting the groups of farmers that need the subsidy.

4 Indeed, it is often tracing these reforms that has provided the evidence of the effects of trade reforms on poverty referred to below.

5 For example, 207% for rice in the EU, 66% for sugar in the United States, 75% for wheat in Mexico and 159% for dairy in South Africa (see Hathaway and Ingco, 1996 and Ingco, 1996).

6 In fact, these statistics refer to peaks defined at the six-digit level of the HS (Harmonized System) trade classification. They are averages of tariffs at the finer levels of disaggregation used by individual countries, at which some individual tariffs are even higher.

7 These policies include investment subsidies, input subsidies, subsidies to encourage product diversification, government development of industries and employment promotion in rural areas, and support to farmers who lose preferential access as a result of trade reform.

8 See Lal Das (1999) for a detailed description of these provisions.

9 Henson et al. (1999) offer a useful insight into the requirements for developing countries.

10 See Chapter 2 for a discussion of how countries' trading patterns are related to their factor endowments, and Chapter 4 for a discussion of how this affects poverty.

11 This observation – what economists refer to as the theory of 'second best' – does not say that in the absence of one market, liberalizing another *will be* harmful, nor that it is impossible for us to tell whether it will or will not be. It merely says that we can no longer rely on the proposition that liberalization will be unambiguously beneficial.

12 See Haggblade et al. (1989) for a survey of farm/non-farm linkages in rural sub-Saharan Africa.

13 This will not be true if supply and demand are very inelastic, because then prices will rise so far that farm incomes will be higher when output is lower.

14 There is, however, one important caveat to this. If countries are net importers of food because of their own policy distortions – various anti-agriculture biases and/or import/consumption subsidies – increasing world food prices can actually benefit them. Essentially, they are losing welfare by constraining agricultural output below optimal levels and a price rise tends to correct this distortion (see Tyers and Falvey, 1989).

10 Trade Related Intellectual Property Rights (TRIPs)

This chapter argues that:

- The protection of intellectual property rights (IPRs) was introduced into the WTO agenda by developed countries. The resulting TRIPs Agreement protects innovation by giving temporary monopolistic rents to innovative companies, which are mainly located in developed countries.
- The implications of the TRIPs Agreement for developing countries depend on their market size and capacity for innovation. Countries with small markets and low innovative capacity gain little because they have little to protect.
- Whether the TRIPs Agreement will increase the flow of innovation from developed to developing countries remains an open question.
- Some evidence suggests that in some sectors, like pharmaceuticals, the increase in prices from IPR protection is a serious danger. The extent to which this impinges on the poor rather than the middle classes is uncertain, however, for the poor would get very few patented medicines, even at low prices.
- Developing countries should exploit the exceptions in the current TRIPs Agreement to ease the restrictions that it imposes. They should try to ensure that any renegotiation includes areas in which they could be gainers.
- But they must also ensure that any such gains (or losses avoided) actually get transferred to the poor rather than being absorbed by local monopolists.

10.1 Background

Some goods and services have high fixed costs of production.[1] This is particularly true of goods that require considerable effort in advance of the creation of a new invention or design. But once this invention or design exists, it may be relatively straightforward to copy the product based on it. And if everyone has access to the invention or design, then the benefits associated with the manufacture of the product will not accrue to the inventor or designer. This fact can be a strong disincentive to innovation. Intellectual property rights (IPRs) are therefore designed to enable inventors and designers to appropriate the returns from their efforts. In other words, IPRs attempt to prevent 'free-rider' behaviour by ensuring that the benefits created by an innovation are internalized by the company responsible for it.

Of course, restricting access to intellectual property (IP) has its costs. Once created, IP can be used by any number of people without imposing costs on each other (it is, in economists' jargon, a public good) and so it should, in principle, be exploited for as long as it generates any positive returns. Thus, the ultimate policy trade-off in IPRs is to balance the short-term costs to users of having to pay for IP (which restricts the exploitation of any given piece of IP) against the long-term (dynamic) benefits of an increased flow of IP (and hence a greater rate of knowledge creation).

If we take the stock of IP as given, however, the immediate trade-off is frequently conceptualized as being to balance the interests of the creators of IP with those of its users. Within a country, the government has to consider both creators' and users' interests and thus faces opposing forces in trying to determine a reasonable balance. But once we recognize the international dimensions of IP, national interest might be dominated entirely by one side or the other, with the result that attitudes towards international policy become polarized. In the current debate, developing countries are usually seen as the users – and hence immediate losers from IPRs – and developed countries – especially the United States – as the creators and gainers.

Some developed countries have had intellectual property legislation protecting the interests of domestic inventors for a long time, but in most countries this has not been a high domestic policy priority.[2] But technological progress and the enormous increase in world trade over the last few decades have encouraged many developing countries to undertake large-scale copying of research-intensive products and creative works, and such activities have been accommodated by their low levels of protection of IPRs. And the growing importance of developing country production and markets has encouraged companies in developed countries (and the United States in particular) to try to enforce IPRs outside their domestic economies.

IPR protection was traditionally coordinated via the World Intellectual Property Organization (WIPO), through the 1967 Paris Convention on patents and the 1971 Berne Convention on copyright. The WIPO adopted the principle of national treatment, whereby foreigners received identical treatment to nationals, but allowed countries to determine the level of protection that they deemed most appropriate. The result was that most developing countries, which perceived themselves as having little IP to defend, maintained low levels of protection, while the developed countries opted for higher levels. But as well as seeking to get more IP protection in developing countries, the developed countries also felt the need to ensure that the tighter laws would be enforced and, in this respect, they saw the WIPO's lack of enforcement power and dispute settlement procedures as a serious weakness. Consequently, they pressed for the inclusion of IPRs in the Uruguay Round, resulting in the TRIPs Agreement of the WTO.[3] This both extended minimum standards of protection to a wide range of countries (the TRIPs Agreement was part of the single undertaking whereby every WTO member adheres to the same rules) and endowed them with much more formidable enforcement procedures.

10.2 The economics of TRIPs

The protection of IPRs provides an inventor with temporary monopoly rents[4] from the innovation. This has two effects, which have opposite welfare implications.

10.2.1 The costs of protecting IPRs

Monopolizing the use of an innovation reduces the welfare of consumers since they have to pay higher prices for the goods based on the innovation. Although the holder of the IPR obtains rents, this does not fully offset the loss of consumer surplus because of the loss in economic efficiency associated with monopoly. This efficiency loss occurs because there are some consumers who would be prepared to purchase the good were it marketed at its marginal cost, but who will not do so at the higher monopoly price.

An important extension of this analysis is that for an individual country in the international economy, losses occur not only via consumption inefficiency, but also because any rent or royalty paid abroad is a straight loss of national welfare. Thus, in the short term (that is, when the stock of knowledge is held constant), IP rents redistribute income from the user to the creator of IP – typically from the poor to the rich.

While consumers are the ultimate users of IP, the direct users are usually firms and it is important to consider how their access to IP is translated into demand for factors of production, and especially in the context of poverty, labour. Stronger protection of the intellectual property of foreign companies is likely to reduce employment in domestic industries that have been copying technology and designs from abroad. Of course, some of the labour may be re-absorbed into legitimate copying activity once the IP is purchased. But the net effect on jobs in poor countries is likely to be negative – see, for example, Maskus (2000a), who estimates that the TRIPs Agreement will cause up to 5,000 job losses in the Lebanon.

IP protection might also give rise to costly duplication of research and development (R&D) as rivals seek to work their way around each others' patents, and to wasteful efforts to assert ownership rights and extend them beyond the intention of the original grant (see Maskus and Eby, 1990). On the other hand, a benefit sometimes claimed for the patent system is that it reduces duplication by requiring applicants for patents to publish their innovations and by making the market for their use more orderly. An important element of this argument is that patent systems should have strong provisions to prevent the abuse of patent monopolies. If these are not in place, there may be a strong diminution in effective competition, which is likely to be costly. Some of the results in the classic analysis of technology by Grossman and Helpman (1991), for example, suggest that *reducing* the rents from IPR protection can encourage innovation since companies are then forced to work harder to keep ahead of their competitors.

A final consideration is the bureaucratic cost of establishing and operating an IP regime. Finger and Schuler (2000) show that this is quite considerable for the least-developed countries seeking to implement the TRIPs Agreement, often exceeding a whole year's development budget. UNCTAD (1999a) suggests over half a million dollars per year in Bangladesh, and Maskus (2000b) cites higher figures for Chile and other middle-income countries. The use of public revenue and skilled labour for this purpose necessarily excludes some other purpose – that is, it has opportunity costs – and this needs to be factored into the balance.

10.2.2 The benefits of protecting IPRs

The main benefit of protecting IPRs is the impact such protection may have on innovative activity and technology transfer. Innovators will be reluctant to invest in new research, technological development or designs if they will be unable to reap the benefits from their work. The protection of IPRs can therefore act as a spur to further innovation. Consumers value such innovations (because of a preference for improved quality and diversity) and it can therefore be in their long-term interest to support limited protection of IPRs in order to stimulate IP production.

But it is not clear to what extent improved IPRs in developing countries will lead to a greater degree of innovation by companies in developed countries. It is possible that improvements in IPRs may make companies in developed countries invest more in providing goods and services tailored to the needs of developing countries (drugs to fight AIDS or malaria, for example) since they will be assured a better return on such investments. On the other hand, the amount that developing countries can pay may be too small to have any material influence on the rate of innovation in developed countries.

An alternative source of benefit of IPRs could be from speeding up the transfer of existing IP to developing countries. If multinational companies are discouraged from transferring current technologies to developing countries because the latter permit free copying, stronger IPRs may encourage transfer and boost productivity and competitiveness. In particular, stronger IPRs may encourage inflows of foreign direct investment (FDI).

10.2.3 **How much protection should be given to intellectual property?**

The optimal extent of protection for intellectual property depends on the schedule of marginal costs and benefits associated with increasing protection. Figure 10.1 shows a stylized graph of the marginal cost and marginal benefit of increased protection of IPRs for a single closed economy, perhaps the world economy as a whole. The marginal cost curve is increasing since, as protection is tightened either through stronger legislation or more effective enforcement, more and more opportunities for using IP are forgone. On the other hand, if stronger enforcement and the resulting higher rents encourage greater investment in R&D and design, then higher protection will be associated with a greater diversity and higher quality of products and services. Assuming that there are diminishing returns to protection in terms of quality generated or of the value placed on 'quality', the marginal benefit accruing to consumers from further IP protection will fall as IP protection increases.

The optimal level of protection is where the marginal benefit of increased protection equals its marginal cost. If we were a little to the right of that point in Figure 10.1, the costs of protection would exceed the benefits and we should protect less, whereas if we were a little to the left of the optimum the opposite would apply.[5]

When we consider a single country within the world economy, we need to modify Figure 10.1 to reflect the share of the different costs and benefits that it can capture. For many developing countries, the extent of their IPR protection will have little or no influence on the level of innovation in developed countries because of the very small size of their markets.[6]

Figure 10.1 Marginal cost and marginal benefit of increased IPR protection

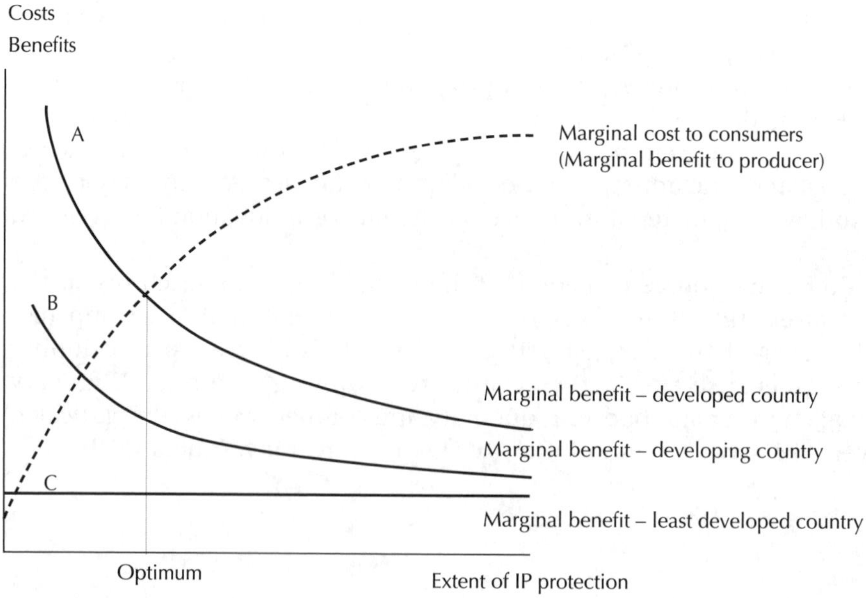

Consequently, although their marginal cost schedule remains unchanged, the marginal benefit they obtain from additional protection is lower (curve B in Figure 10.1). In the case of the least-developed countries, which may well have no influence at all over the flow of IP, their marginal benefit is very low and does not change with the level of IP protection (curve C in Figure 10.1).

Clearly, the optimum level of protection is likely to vary by country, as Subramanian (1990) suggests. If activities infringing IPRs (such as commercial copying) in small developing countries do not affect world prices, then the only effect of their IPR regulation is to transfer benefits from such countries to inventor companies. In such cases, it would be optimal for countries to have very lax or non-existent protection of IPRs.

But there is an important caveat to this conclusion. In plotting the marginal benefit curve for a particular country, we implicitly held IP protection in all others constant. A country received virtually no benefit from restricting its own IP use on the assumption that others continued to offer sufficient protection to maintain the flow of IP. In other words, we assumed that it could free-ride on others' incentives to innovate. But if every country behaved like this, there might be no IP flow to copy.

Thus, we also need to ask what would the marginal benefit curves look like if whole classes of country varied their IP protection together. Least-developed countries may still have curve C: they may, collectively, still be so small as to generate no new IP by offering higher protection. But if we considered, say, all middle-income countries together, the 'collective' marginal benefit curve would be significantly higher and steeper than the individual one: increased protection would increase the flow of IP. Thus, if a country were choosing the optimal level of protection not only for itself, but also for all its fellows, it would opt for a higher level than if it could choose individually, knowing that no others would emulate it.

This discussion makes clear that developing countries do not necessarily all have identical interests in the TRIPs debate. The introduction of minimum standards of IPR protection may have a negative welfare impact on developing countries with low levels of technological diffusion, but it could benefit newly industrialized countries with greater technological capacity (see UNCTAD, 1996).[7]

Table 10.1 Summary of the advantages and disadvantages of protecting IPRs

Advantages of IPR protection	Disadvantages of IPR protection
• Encouragement of innovation via monopolistic rents • Increased supply and diffusion of technology in developing countries • Potential expansion of FDI	• Price increases on protected goods (and therefore potentially worse access to technology for the poorest countries) • Possible discouragement of innovation through stifling competition • Net losses of employment and profit in industries benefiting from lax protection • Bureaucratic opportunity costs

10.2.4 Quantifying the costs and benefits of stronger IPRs

Theory is ambiguous; so an assessment of IPRs must ultimately be empirical. Unfortunately, however, while there is plenty to say about the issue, hard evidence is scarce. Maskus (2000a) summarizes the possible effects of implementing the TRIPs Agreement. First, he estimates the rent transfers entailed in strengthening IPRs, based on work by McCalman (1999). These transfers are large and negative for many developed countries, as well as for all developing countries.[8]

Offsetting these, at least in principle, are increases in technology inflow. These might be approximated by increases in manufacturing and high-tech manufacturing imports, by increases in FDI flows and by increased royalty inflows. The current levels of these are summarized for developing countries in Table 10.2.

Table 10.2 suggests that for middle-income and large low-income developing countries, the current flows of economic activity are quite large, so that it is not inconceivable that changes in them could offset higher IP costs. In fact, Maskus argues that on balance, middle-income countries could be net gainers from the stronger IPRs induced by the TRIPs Agreement (although he argues that the Agreement is not certain to increase effective IPRs in these or any developing countries). For the poorest countries, however, the current regime seems likely to impose net costs compared to more or less unrestrained IP copying and exploitation.

Table 10.2 Current levels of technology inflows and net patent rents for selected countries (millions of 1995 US dollars)

Country	Manufacturing imports[b]	High-tech manufacturing imports	FDI assets[c]	Unaffiliated royalties and license fees[d]	Net patent rents[a]
United States	233	–3	na	na	**5760**
Germany	2304	–18	–1084	92	**997**
Japan	918	–21	–2326	719	**–555**
Mexico	5749	1519	3182	136	**–562**
Brazil	3125	627	3219	114	**–1172**
Panama	16	na	284	na	**0.4**
Colombia	2927	479	1093	na	**–97**
South Africa	154	21	23	10	**–143**
China	15379	2585	631	na	**na**
Indonesia	6628	667	1805	166	**na**
India	1465	146	128	58	**–665**

Sources: Maskus (2000a); a McCalman (1999); b Maskus and Penubarti (1995); c Maskus (1998); d Yang and Maskus (1999)

10.2.5 **Public versus private knowledge**

The discussion above presupposed that IP was privately owned and asked how the private market could be managed to produce an acceptable compromise between the use and the production of IP.[9] But there is an alternative: that knowledge is generated and owned publicly and then distributed freely to those who can use it productively. In an ideal world, this would entirely overcome the problems identified above. The public sector would determine what needed to be researched and provide funding independent of users' potential ability to pay; users would merely draw on the public stock of knowledge. There would be fewer lawyers too.

In fact, much knowledge was generated publicly in the past – as, for example, with space technology, medical research and, most notably for development, the green revolution. But the recent past has seen a strong trend away from this towards the privatization of knowledge, driven by faith in the greater ability of markets to identify issues for which demand is high and to achieve greater technical efficiency and lower costs in meeting that demand.

This clearly has implications for developing countries and the poor in general, who will figure less heavily in dollar-based demand than in public-sector, needs-based, assessments of priorities. Putting aside any questions about the ultimate efficiency of private versus public management of research, the current trend, arguably, amounts to a stark reduction in the subsidy paid for pro-poor research activity, and will very probably have adverse poverty consequences. The widely acknowledged underfunding of public agricultural research for developing regions (despite the high returns to such activities) represents one of the most obvious aspects of this (see IFAD, 2001).

10.3 **The current debate on IPRs**

The Uruguay Round Agreement on TRIPs is central to the current debate on IPRs. It represented a major change of regime for developing countries and one that most of them did not welcome. Developing countries continue to have difficulties (technical and political) with implementing the Agreement and a broad-based and passionate debate continues about whether or not it is beneficial to their development efforts. The Agreement was accepted, at least to some extent, on faith, but subsequent research has not yet provided the strong evidence that many expected that better IPRs would stimulate innovative activity of interest to developing countries. Few developing countries would wish unilaterally to adopt stronger enforcement of IPRs than the TRIPs Agreement requires, so their interest focuses mainly on whether the Agreement can be relaxed. An alternative (and partly complementary) strategy is emerging, however, in which developing countries seek to extend or clarify TRIPs Agreement protections to include IPRs in which they have an export interest, for example, traditional knowledge. Box 10.1 reports a graphic example of this idea.

Box 10.1 **'Have you tried our** *NEW* **curry and rice?'**

Both rice and curry have been the subject of patents by foreign companies since India implemented the TRIPs Agreement in March 1999. Basmati rice, a long-standing Indian traditional foodstuff, has been patented by RiceTec Inc., a United States-based company. A Japanese firm applied for a patent on curry, described as a process of 'adding extracted spices to ingredients like cut and processed onions, heating the mixture, and adding curry powder, and heating until the mixture becomes viscous'.

The lack of novelty and the absence of payment to traditional users of these foods in these applications are respectively causes for surprise and concern.

Source: Christian Aid (1999).

10.3.1 The TRIPs Agreement

The TRIPs Agreement covers seven types of intellectual property: patents, copyright, trademarks, geographical indications, industrial designs, layout designs of integrated circuits and undisclosed information. The Agreement provides for the extension of IPR protection and its enforcement through WTO disciplines. The main measures agreed were:

- the introduction of national treatment and 'most favoured nation' (MFN) treatment;
- the introduction of minimum standards of protection in each area; and
- provisions for dispute prevention and settlement.

Table 10.3 shows the main provisions in each of the seven areas (for more detailed expositions, see Lal Das, 1999 and UNCTAD, 1999a).

Developed countries were required to implement the agreement within one year. But in recognition of the difficulties they may encounter in implementing the TRIPs Agreement, developing countries and transition economies were allowed five years to implement the measures, and least-developed countries 11 years (with the possibility of extending this further). In addition, protection for high-tech sectors, which had previously received no protection, could be postponed by developing countries until 2005. This means, for example, that few developing countries yet have IPRs for pharmaceuticals.

10.3.2 Plant varieties

Of particular importance to developing countries are the TRIPs Agreement provisions for the protection of plant varieties. The subject of a patent must be an invention and not merely the discovery of something already existing in nature, even if it was not previously known. So it is possible to exclude plants and animals (including genetically modified ones) from 'patentability', along with biological processes for their production. But micro-organisms and non-biological and microbiological processes for the

Table 10.3 Main provisions of the TRIPs Agreement

Type of intellectual property	Main provisions	Qualifications
Patents	• Must be new, non-obvious and useful • Must allow patents on processes to produce plants or animals • Minimum term of patent is 20 years • Plant varieties must be protected by patents and/or a *sui generis* system • Restrictions over compulsory licensing • Must comply with the Paris Convention (1967)	• Do not have to allow patents on animals or plants • Can avoid patents to protect public order, human, animal or plant life or health or to avoid serious prejudice to the environment • Compulsory licensing in some circumstances
Copyright	• Must comply with the Berne Convention (1971) (except 'moral rights') • Typically 50 years duration • Includes computer programs	• Protection only extends to the 'expressions', not to the ideas behind the expressions
Trademarks	• Covers any sign that distinguishes the goods or services of one undertaking from another • Minimum period of seven years • No limit to the number of renewals	• Registration is liable to cancellation after non-use for three years
Geographical indications	• Covers indications of origin • Special disciplines for wine and spirits	• Not required to prevent the use of a geographical indication if it has been used for 15 years prior to 1994
Industrial designs	• Covers features concerning the look of an article • Special provisions for the textiles sector	• Utility models are not covered
Layout designs of integrated circuits	• Incorporates the Treaty on Intellectual Property in Respect of Integrated Circuits (1989) (IPIC) • Term of at least ten years	• Can reject if application is more than two years after its first commercial exploitation
Undisclosed information (trade secrets)	• Covers both trade secrets and information lodged with governments for approval of the marketing of pharmaceutical or agricultural chemical products	• The information must be secret, have a commercial value and reasonable steps must have been taken to conceal it

Source: Lal Das (1999).

production of plants and animals *must* be patentable, as must new varieties of plant. The TRIPs Agreement does not define the levels of inventiveness required, however, with the result that in some countries very small developments of natural products are held to create new varieties that must be protected in some way.

These asymmetries are potentially quite harmful to developing countries' interests. While companies can claim patents for small changes or processes based on traditional crops or knowledge, crops developed over generations through cross-breeding by farmers are not patentable. Thus, for example, the extraction and patenting of the protein brazzein found in a West African berry and the patenting of a minor development of Basmati rice from South Asia are clear examples where companies have benefited from work or knowledge from developing countries without making any payment in recompense (see Consumers International, 1999). Such patenting should not prevent developing countries from accessing the original (traditional) products freely, but it could clearly undermine their potential for future commercial exploitation.

The TRIPs Agreement requires that plant varieties be covered by some effective form of protection. This could be patents or a *sui generis* (which literally means 'of its own type', that is, specific) system (or both). One such *sui generis* system is included in the International Convention for the Protection of New Varieties of Plants (UPOV), which seeks to balance the rights of plant breeders with those of users, the farmers.

In the 1978 version of the UPOV convention, breeders have exclusive rights over the marketing, selling and production for commercial marketing of the propagating material (seeds, cuttings, etc.). But this right does not extend to the harvest from these plants or to the production of seed by farmers for use on their own farms (known as 'farmers' privilege'). But the 1991 revision of the UPOV convention substantially extends breeders' rights: it allows authorities to extend breeders' rights to the harvest in some circumstances; it gives breeders control over varieties derived from their protected variety; and it reduces the status of farmers' privilege from a right to an option that authorities can grant.

While there is no requirement within the TRIPs Agreement that countries adopt the UPOV system, they must be able to argue that the system they employ is effective in protecting rights over plant varieties. Developing countries have argued that UPOV is not particularly suitable for their needs, and there have been some efforts to develop other *sui generis* systems. Nonetheless, there is a tendency for UPOV to be seen as a *de facto* standard.

10.3.3 To renegotiate or not?

Despite the transition periods built into the Agreement, several developing countries had failed to implement the necessary TRIP measures by 31 December 1999, when the transition period ended (although the least-developed countries do not have to comply until 1 January 2006). Many developing countries would like to see the disciplines in the TRIPs

Agreement relaxed, or at least sympathetically clarified, in a future negotiation. But two arguments might caution them against raising the issue:

- First, the novelty and complexity of the current agreement may make the clear implementation of existing commitments more important than entering into further uncertain ones.
- Second, the United States (and possibly Japan) might press to extend TRIPs Agreement obligations further – for example, to permit the patenting of plants and animals – if negotiation commenced.

Thus, it is important to consider the possibility of movement in both directions in assessing potential negotiating outcomes.

One area in which progress looks possible is in the compulsory licensing of drugs. The TRIPs Agreement is vague about the exact conditions under which this should be permitted, but a consensus is growing that it is certainly justified in response to public health crises such as AIDS and malaria in Africa and elsewhere. There is also a serious debate about extending compulsory licensing to trade flows. The Agreement currently requires that licences be 'predominantly for the domestic market', but this is not useful for countries too small or too poor to have a domestic industry. The EU has displayed flexibility in this matter, suggesting that it would consider a situation in which trade occurred between countries where both importing and exporting governments had compulsorily licensed a product. This extension could be important to small and poor countries, especially if the public health clause is interpreted liberally and if the compensation required for compulsory licences is not excessive.

One important factor that developing countries should consider before embarking on negotiation is whether the existing Agreement gives them sufficient flexibility to achieve roughly optimal degrees of IP protection. Maskus (2000c), in particular, argues that by exploiting the various permissible exceptions, developing countries can actually tailor the Agreement to their needs reasonably well, especially if they use IP law to foster dynamic competition and technology transfer. For example, patents may be ignored for research purposes, teaching, approving generic drugs, making up medicines by individual pharmacies, and to overcome anti-competitive behaviour by holders. And farmers may be permitted to use seeds from their own harvests. Arguably, reverse engineering is a perfectly legitimate process of discovery. The Appendix of Correa (1999) also suggests that by selecting judiciously from the current IP laws of developed countries, developing countries can achieve a fair degree of latitude.

10.3.4 Extending protection to developing country interests

The Uruguay Round Agreements required members to review Article 27.3b of the TRIPs Agreement (which exempts plants and animals from patent protection) in 1999, and at the beginning of 2000, when the first general review of the implementation of the TRIPs Agreement became due. Neither review is anything like complete. Among the issues that might conceivably arise in the reviews or in future talks are the following.

Article 27.3b has become a contentious issue, with most developing countries strongly resisting the extension of patent protection. In addition, the developed countries may push for plant variety protection to be increased in accordance with the UPOV convention as revised in 1991. A possible compromise may be to accept patents over plants and animals and/or increased protection of plant varieties in return for similar protection of indigenous knowledge in developing countries. The latter would require a good deal of imaginative preparatory work since there is no existing mechanism for such protection. But if such a compromise were achievable, it would essentially increase the set of IP in which developing countries had a beneficial interest. A related proposal would be to clarify the TRIPs Agreement to ensure protection for geographical indications for food and handicraft products of interest to developing countries.

The TRIPs Agreement also interacts with environmental concerns, most prominently in its questionable compatibility with the intent of the 1992 Convention on Biological Diversity. While probably legally compatible, there is a widespread feeling that the TRIPs Agreement and the Convention conflict in spirit, with the latter offering a far more sympathetic hearing to developing countries' desires to exploit and benefit from their own bio-resources.[10] In particular, the Convention calls for access to genetic resources to have received prior informed consent from the country of origin; some developing countries wish to see this become an explicit condition for granting patents and for all germplasm patents to be accompanied by explicit information on countries of origin. Again, this is essentially about developing countries seeking to extend the TRIPs Agreement to reinforce IPRs in their own endowments.

10.3.5 Weakening the scope of IPR protection

A different approach to increasing developing countries' interests in the TRIPs Agreement is to try to weaken its scope by narrowing the range of patentable goods. Thus, for example, it might explicitly rule out patents on naturally occurring substances (including genes), or minor developments of processes that were publicly known prior to application (including within traditional societies), or products previously deposited in public institutions for public use (such as germplasm banks). These issues hinge around the definitions of invention, novelty and use in application, all of which are fiercely legal, but which have different interpretations (or terminology) in the existing laws of developed countries. Pressing to get clarification that tight and demanding interpretations of these terms were 'WTO-legal' would essentially be to seek to reduce the costs of IPRs by reducing their scope.

A major issue both economically and politically is the fear that the TRIPs Agreement is taking important medicines beyond the reach of people in poor countries, by allowing the drug companies to prevent local production and/or charge high royalties. There is some evidence of this danger – see

Maskus (2000a) for a summary and consider the court case over HIV/AIDS cocktails in South Africa in 2001. Moreover, given that most developing countries have not yet implemented pharmaceutical IPRs, there is clearly an issue to be faced in the future.

On the other hand, there is debate about exactly how much money is at stake. Watal (2000), at the low end of the range of estimates, suggests that in India, welfare losses might amount to between 3–8% of total expenditure on drugs. A key difference between studies is the assumption that authors make about the competitiveness of the market in the absence of the TRIPs Agreement. If competition is weak before the introduction of IPRs, the rents exist already, and while the TRIPs Agreement might affect their distribution (transferring them abroad), it creates no new inefficiencies. Oxfam (2000), on the other hand, argues passionately that IPR protection increases drug prices – see Box 10.2.

Whether stronger IP protection generates increased flows of drugs for developing countries is not established. Maskus argues that there is little evidence of such benefits and commends the suggestion by Sachs (1999) that public funds should be used to encourage research specifically geared for developing countries' medical needs. Sachs refers explicitly to bilateral and multilateral aid, such as the United Nations' global fund for AIDS, and also to private funding as provided by Bill Gates and the founders of the International Aids Vaccine Initiative (see *The Economist*, 29 April 2000) financing the search for vaccines.

This is quite different from the recent Exim Bank proposal to provide US$1 billion to finance sub-Saharan Africa's purchases of HIV/AIDS medicines from US pharmaceutical firms.[11] While this proposal aims to lower the cost and increase the availability of HIV/AIDS-related medications to the region, it runs the risk of doing so by increasing its already substantial debt burden. This would implicitly redirect donor resources away from locally-owned prevention schemes towards payments to US firms for high-cost curative care. But even donor-driven initiatives should recognize that to be successful, they should not just be about publicly paying for commercial IP, but also about increasing the resources (and the security of the resources) devoted to solving developing countries' problems. And it is worth noting that the attractions of such schemes will be greater (and their cost correspondingly smaller) if the firms involved also receive commercial IPRs for their efforts.

An area of uncertainty both in the legal texts and in the economic analysis of TRIPs is what protection should be given against 'parallel imports' – when a genuine brand product (which is not a copy or a generic) is imported from another country where it has been marketed at a lower price. Parallel imports can undermine differential pricing regimes for pharmaceuticals, which can be good for competition by reducing market power, but can also interfere with public policy interventions such as price regulation for drugs. At present, there does not seem to be a case for raising the issue, but a number of developed countries, moved by domestic commercial interests, are keen to see regulations tightened up. If plans are developed for the tiered

Box 10.2 Drugs in developing countries

- Price comparisons between Pakistan, which has traditionally provided strong product patent protection, and India, which has one of the world's strongest generic-drugs industries, are instructive. They show that prices for ciprofloxacin, a safe anti-infective medicine used in the treatment of illnesses such as resistant bloody diarrhoea in children, are up to eight times higher in Pakistan.

- In Thailand, the introduction of generic competition reduced the cost of drugs for the treatment of meningitis by a factor of 14.

- It is hard to argue that HIV/AIDS does not represent a national emergency in South Africa, where it is projected to reduce life expectancy by 20 years by 2010, or in Thailand, where there are almost one million sufferers. Yet in both cases, efforts to provide cheap generic medicines have been met with legal challenges. In South Africa, the drug companies have withdrawn their objections, but only after huge amounts of public pressure. In Kenya, a quarter of the adult population is HIV-positive, but fewer than 2% receive anti-retroviral treatment. If the country were able to import the drug fluconazole, used in the treatment of cryptococcal meningitis (an opportunistic infection associated with HIV/AIDS), from Thailand, it could reduce the annual cost of treatment from over US$3,000 to US$104. But the patent holder for the drug, the Pfizer corporation, applied pressure to stop such imports taking place.

- In countries such as Mali, Tanzania, Vietnam and Colombia, pharmaceuticals account for over a fifth of total spending on public health. But this large slice of small budgets translates into tiny levels of spending on medicines per capita, ranging from 13–14 cents in countries like India and Mali, to 40–50 cents in Tanzania, and US$3 in Colombia. It is unlikely that these markets will ever generate sufficient demand to influence commercial drug innovation.

While these examples are stark and highlight a serious political problem for developing countries, it is not true to say that the TRIPs Agreement is the only problem in this area. First, many developing countries do not have IPRs in pharmaceuticals and yet have huge shortfalls in drug provision. Second, the delivery systems for drugs in many developing countries are chronically weak. Third, even at US$104 per treatment, fluconazole far exceeds available resources for drugs in many countries. Indeed, there is a danger that pricing it at US$104 instead of US$3,000 will increase expenditure to such an extent that the provision of other cheaper and simpler treatments (such as immunization programmes, and rehydration treatments for diarrhoea) will decline, resulting in net health losses for the poor.

Source for examples: Oxfam (2000).

pricing of drugs (with low prices in developing countries), strict control of parallel pricing will be necessary. Policy-makers will need to decide whether this will be a better way of serving developing countries' obvious and pressing needs than increasing flows of development assistance and continuing to permit parallel importing as an antidote to market power.

10.4 TRIPs and poverty

Changes to the TRIPs regime seem likely to impinge on poverty through three main routes: their effects on technology and growth, their effects on prices and rents and their effects on government revenues and expenditures.

10.4.1 Growth and technology

The long-run impact of any TRIPs negotiations on poverty will be critically linked to their effects on technological diffusion and hence to economic growth. If changes in the TRIPs Agreement were to result in a significantly higher level of production, marketing and dissemination of technology-based products in developing countries, then this is likely to have a beneficial impact on employment, incomes and poverty. This is particularly the case if such improvements come in crop and agricultural technology (including genetically modified crops), which would boost productivity. There is substantial evidence that the green revolution reduced poverty through increasing demand for inputs and labour, higher wages and/or lower prices – see, for example, Mellor and Gavian (1999); Mosley (1999b) and Renkow (2000).

But experience suggests that the countries that stand to gain the most are those with the capacity to absorb, modify and disseminate new technology. The poorest and smallest countries, almost by definition, have very limited capacity in this regard and are, therefore, likely to gain least from such technology diffusion (as indeed, they gain least from existing access to technology such as via reverse engineering or copying). Thus, while those large low- and middle-income developing countries that are able to adapt quickly to new technologies could benefit from TRIPs, experiencing higher industrialization and employment creation, the least developed countries seem likely to fall further behind. Moreover, middle-income countries have a much higher chance of achieving significant technical progress locally, and hence of benefiting directly from improved IPRs.

The poorest and smallest countries, having the least technological capacity, surely need strong incentives for domestic innovation, as well as access to cheap technology from abroad. While this might superficially suggest a need for preferential protection for domestic innovators, it probably does not do so in practice. At low levels of technology, patents and other IPRs are not a particularly efficient way of exploiting knowledge because of their requirements for novelty and the relatively high fixed cost of applying for patents and protecting the rights created. Thus, the national treatment element of the TRIPs Agreement is arguably not particularly burdensome to developing countries and is not worth trying to overturn.

10.4.2 Rents and prices

A poverty perspective requires attention not just to macroeconomic growth prospects but also to the distribution of growth within a country. In Chapter

4, we argued that growth is, on average, as good for the poor as for everyone else, but it is certainly important to ask whether this applies to growth arising from IPRs. One important consideration is the degree of competition within the relevant sectors of the economy. Nationally, it is desirable that monopoly rents accrue to local entrepreneurs rather than abroad, but for the poor, it makes little difference whether they are exploited by locals or by foreigners. Hence, in examining the poverty-related case for looser IPRs, governments need to assure themselves that they have the means to ensure that benefits are experienced in terms of lower prices for IPR-related goods rather than just in higher local profits.

This is another aspect of the argument above that the degree of competition in 'pre-TRIPs' markets is a key input into assessments of the costs and benefits of TRIPs. As we saw, Watal (2000) finds relatively small TRIPs-induced increases in Indian drug prices because she recognizes the Indian markets as imperfectly competitive. This reduces both the efficiency costs and the distributional inequities of strengthening IPRs. Although the experience of the green revolution should caution us against dismissing the benefits of technology simply because the direct beneficiaries are not poor, it is clearly a cause for concern if the benefits of improved technologies are captured entirely by a small group of relatively wealthy business people within a developing country.

Another important dimension identified in Chapter 4 is the effect of a trade shock on the availability of goods and services. If strengthening the TRIPs Agreement encouraged multinational companies to devote greater resources to problems that have a direct impact on poverty in developing countries, including treatments for tropical diseases and improvements in tropical agriculture, the effects could be spectacular. But as argued above, this does not seem very likely. The most vulnerable groups in these countries just do not have the purchasing power to command these companies' attention.

Public subventions to cover development-oriented research and public health programmes could, however, deliver such benefits, and should be encouraged. At first sight, such interventions might appear to be independent of TRIPs negotiations, but this is not necessarily true. If the strengthening of IPRs reduces the scientific community's interest in developing countries by increasing the financial attractions of alternative directions of research, it exacerbates the problem and raises the public costs of addressing it. Oxfam (2000) estimates that only 10% of global R&D is directed towards illnesses that account for 90% of the world-wide disease burden.

Similarly, if stronger IPRs raise the prices of known drugs in developing countries, they increase the cost of offsetting subventions. If the response to higher drug prices were just a matter of raising a little more revenue in the developed world and increasing aid flows, it might be taken lightly. But if, more plausibly, supporting research and provision in public health competed for resources within a given official assistance budget, then stronger IPRs would be imposing costs elsewhere in ways that potentially penalized the poor. It is difficult to avoid the conclusion that in the area of pharmaceuticals, the poorest developing countries will be losers from the TRIPs Agreement.

Changes in TRIPs could have a direct impact on developing country incomes through their impact on the prices of inputs into manufacturing and service firms. Higher prices for items subject to copyright and layout design (such as software, integrated chips, etc.) will extract rents from developing country firms, although this is unlikely to have a significant direct impact on the poor. Equally, job losses in factories responsible for copying activities will have a limited impact on poverty since most of the employees in such activities seem likely to be substantially better off than most poor households. On the other hand, price increases and restrictions on access to seeds and agricultural inputs will have a major impact given the poor's continuing dependence on agriculture in most countries. Moreover, if the enforcement of patenting laws puts such inputs out of the reach of poor farmers, its impact could be harsh and dramatic.

The protection of indigenous knowledge, if included in any future agreement, may help to increase income transfers to developing countries if it is effectively operationalized by specifying how such knowledge will be defined and patented. But although such knowledge may be key to the lifestyle of poor indigenous households, modern sector innovators often feel that they have little to learn from indigenous practices, so the economic value of such knowledge may be limited. Hence, developing country policy-makers need to be realistic about what they might gain through this route. More promising, perhaps, are proposals to require consent from countries of origin for the use of germplasm and genetic material. This may prove to be a valuable resource in sectors such as pharmaceuticals, although there is some controversy about this too.

10.4.3 Fiscal dimensions

An important aspect for developing country governments will be to specify to whom any rents resulting from higher IPR protection accrue. As with almost all aspects of public finance – including the changes in revenue induced by changes in growth rates and rents discussed above – they will not specifically benefit the poor unless conscious decisions are taken and enforced to channel them in that direction. Merely showing that poor countries will receive additional rents is not sufficient to show that a policy reduces poverty. Indeed, if such rents are easily appropriated by (warring) elites – as, for example, are those from oil and gems – increasing 'nature' rents could be counterproductive.

10.4.4 The enforcement of IPRs by developing countries

IP statutes are only part of the task of achieving effective property rights; they must also be enforced. This is a specialized task, requiring adequate legal machinery at home and considerable inputs of skills – especially if it is to be prosecuted abroad. Thus, a further important public policy concern is the expenditure of scarce resources on the enforcement of IPRs when development policy would mandate other priorities. Even if increased aid flows covered all the material costs of IPR enforcement and provided necessary outside expertise, there is the diversion of local bureaucratic and political effort and attention to consider.

A second consideration arises if developed countries prove much better at enforcing their rights than developing countries. Then innovators from the latter will have incentives to create their IP in the former rather than the latter. This might not be a major consideration for industrial innovations, because innovation will generally be located with the production facilities and enforced via any national system from which a patent is sought. But creative artistic work, in contrast, may be rather footloose. If developing country musicians cannot rely on their local agencies to enforce their property rights, they will be tempted to move and work in say, London or New York, where the necessary facilities are in place. This might be fine for the artists concerned, who will not be poor, but it might substantially reduce opportunities for less-prominent and less-skilled ancillary workers, some of whom may well be poor.[12]

Thus, stronger world-wide IPRs may shift productive activity towards strong enforcers and thus actually undermine creative sectors in developing countries. This is a challenge for developing country policy-makers and also for donor agencies in identifying collateral polices required to make increased openness development-friendly.

10.5 Conclusion

In conclusion, the poor are, at best, likely to suffer small losses from any strengthening of the TRIPs Agreement. The increases in prices resulting from the enforcement of IPRs must precede any substantial diffusion of technology (since innovators will wish to be sure that their IPRs are protected before investing in further marketing and dissemination) and these will lead to transfers of welfare to IP owners. If developing countries are to be successful in ensuring an ultimately pro-poor effect from extensions to the TRIPs Agreement, they will need to adopt industrial and educational policies that foster the adoption and diffusion of technology. Furthermore, their implementation of the TRIPs Agreement should encourage the widest possible dissemination of technology and enhancement of competition to ensure that the benefits are not captured only by a relatively wealthy minority.

Box 10.3 **Checklist on TRIPs**

- How important is unrequited technology transfer to you at present? How much of it can be maintained through policies such as compulsory licensing and the research exemption?

- Where technology transfer is likely to be blocked, are the poor likely to be adversely affected by price or employment changes? Or will the main losers be local monopolists?

- Would a relaxation of the TRIPs Agreement allow you to source imports significantly more cheaply, for example, certain drugs? Would the poor benefit directly or indirectly from such imports?

- What local products and activities might benefit from IP protection, for example, traditional knowledge or geographical indications? Will modifying the TRIPs Agreement help you to collect rents from these? Can you distribute them in pro-poor ways?

- How cheaply can you honour your TRIPs Agreement obligations? Would combining with other developing countries help? Can you enforce the IPRs you create?

Notes

1 Fixed costs are the minimum costs required for producing any quantity of output and are independent of the quantity produced.

2 This is true of developed as well as developing countries: Italy, for example, introduced product patents only in 1978.

3 The name of the Agreement on Trade Related Aspects of Intellectual Property Rights is actually a misnomer, since it covers IPRs whether they are trade-related or not – that is, it governs the treatment of IP regardless of whether it is traded, or affects a traded good, or whether a trading partner has expressed interest or concern over it. 'Trade-related' was a fig leaf to legitimize bringing the issue into the GATT/WTO.

4 Economic 'rents' are profits that are larger than the normal profits that would occur with competition. These rents arise from the temporary protection provided by the IPR.

5 Of course, the marginal benefit and marginal cost schedules are likely to be different for different processes and products but the basic idea of optimal protection being determined by equality of the marginal costs and benefits remains the same.

6 There are of course exceptions, notably China.

7 Fink (2001), for example, provides an analysis of how stronger patent protection in India might affect the behaviour of multinational pharmaceutical companies.

8 The United States is by far the largest beneficiary.

9 The spillovers of knowledge to people who do not produce it and the fact that person A's use of a piece of knowledge does not preclude person B from using it are the classic circumstances in which virtually all economists agree that unregulated markets will be sub-optimal. IPRs are fully recognized as a compromise between the two opposing forces of static and dynamic efficiency, as argued above.

10 The Convention defers to existing international and domestic law in the treatment of

IPRs and patents, and so strictly appears to subordinate itself to the TRIPs (CBD, Article 16.5).

11 See http://www.exim.gov/press/jul1900.html for details.

12 We are grateful to J Michael Finger of the World Bank for suggesting this issue.

11 Trade in Services

This chapter argues that:

- Services account for the bulk of world output and are the fastest growing segment of world trade, but they are still subject to myriad trade restrictions, which in many countries significantly reduce the supply and raise prices.
- Inefficient services are economically costly both directly and via their effects on other sectors.
- Many services require regulation (for example, for quality reasons) but this should be non-discriminatory and pro-competitive.
- Effective competition is the key to service efficiency, and care should be taken to ensure that trade liberalization enhances it.
- Once suitable regulatory arrangements are in place, the usual arguments made against trade liberalization – such as 'infant industries' and fear of foreign monopolies – are no more applicable to services than to goods markets.
- The Uruguay Round's General Agreement on Trade in Services (GATS) provided a framework for, but not much progress towards, liberalization in services.
- In future, developing countries should use the multilateral system to inform and support their own reforms (especially against entrenched interests) and to press for reforms in areas of export interest.
- Prominent among developing country export interests is the temporary movement of labour to provide services. If this is extended to allow the movement of relatively unskilled workers, it could be very positive for poverty alleviation.
- Some service reforms aid the poor directly, for example, those in health and education. Others may increase unskilled employment – such as tourism – or boost local efficiency and competitiveness – such as in financial services. But liberalizing some inefficient services may eliminate unskilled jobs while offering their main benefits to the relatively rich – for example, telecoms.

<u>11.1</u> Background

Services accounted for about two-thirds of global GDP in 1995, but the proportion varied greatly between developed and developing countries: 70% of GDP came from services in developed countries but only 26% in low-income countries. Developed countries account for around three-quarters of service exports while developing countries have a trade deficit in services with developed countries, except in the areas of tourism, travel and workers' remittances. But this does not mean that services are unimportant to developing countries; indeed, many small developing countries are relatively specialized in the production of services, especially tourism. Furthermore, for many developing countries, services offer a way to diversify their economies, using their comparative advantage and avoiding excessive dependence on primary commodity exports. Since many services are intensive in their use of unskilled labour, service activity is likely to offer scope for strong poverty alleviation.

Since the early 1980s, international services transactions have increased more rapidly than trade in goods, with the result that trade in services composed 20% of global trade in 1995 (see Hoekman and Primo Braga, 1997). Much of this increase has been driven by technological change, including the creation of networks such as the internet and the dramatic reduction of computing and communication costs. These developments have increased both the tradability of many services and the internationalization of physical production by facilitating co-ordination across many plants or firms.

While the OECD had initiated a number of agreements among developed countries concerning service sectors, the first multilateral agreement on services liberalization was the Uruguay Round's General Agreement on Trade in Services (GATS). This established principles for liberalizing world services trade and achieved a limited liberalization in a number of sectors. It was also the third area to establish a built-in agenda for negotiations to resume by January 2000. This agenda, work on which has already started, aims at:

- first, 'achieving a progressively higher level of liberalization'; and
- second, resolving the specific omissions from the GATS of provisions on emergency safeguards, government procurement and subsidies.

11.1.1 Modes of supply

One of the difficulties of services liberalization, especially in a multilateral framework, is simply describing and categorizing trade and trade barriers. The GATS established a useful four-fold classification, based on 'mode of supply':[1]

- *Mode 1*: cross-border supply without the presence of the company in the host country – for example, electronic information and international telephony.
- *Mode 2*: consumption abroad where consumers use the service in the supplier country – for example, tourism.

Table 11.1 Trade in services by mode of supply, 1997

Mode	Proxy used	Value (billions of dollars)	Share in total (percentages)	Share in GDP (percentages)
Mode 1 Cross-border	Balance of payments commercial services minus travel	890	41.0	3.1
Mode 2 Consumption abroad	Balance of payments travel	430	19.8	1.5
Mode 3 Commercial presence	FATS gross output in services*	820	37.8	2.9
Mode 4 Natural persons	Balance of payments compensation of employees	30	1.4	0.1
Total		2,170	100.0	7.6

*FATS is a new data concept referring to the activities of foreign affiliates.
Source: Karsenty (2000).

- *Mode 3*: services sold abroad that require the 'commercial presence' of the company in the country of transaction – for example, many financial services.
- *Mode 4*: services that need the temporary presence of people (technically known as 'natural persons') as providers in the country where the service is used – for example, construction and consultancy.

Trade statistics are notoriously difficult to derive for services, especially for modes 2–4. An inventive attempt to quantify the flows has been made by Karsenty (2000), from which Table 11.1 is taken. Karsenty estimates that cross-border and commercial presence – modes 1 and 3 – are the two main modes of trade, with movement of natural persons lagging far behind. In total, in 1997, service trade equalled 7.6% of world GDP, around a third of total world trade.

11.1.2 Barriers to trade in services

Notwithstanding the substantial increase in trade in all modes of service supply, the bulk of services are still provided locally. This partly reflects the natural non-tradability of certain services – such as government services – but it also reflects the substantial barriers to foreign provision that continue to exist in most countries. The nature and scale of such barriers vary not only from country to country but also from sector to sector and across different modes of supply. The main barriers to trade in services can be categorized into four types:

- *Quotas, local content and prohibition*: quantitative restrictions on the number of service providers or simple prohibition of service providers from other countries. For example, bilateral air service agreements specify which airlines may fly on a given route and limit the capacity permitted from third countries.
- *Price-based instruments*: tariffs in the form of entry or exit taxes, price controls by governments or subsidies to domestic companies. Examples include visa fees and official price preferences to local suppliers.
- *Standards, licensing and government procurement*: these include the need for certification or a licensing requirement by a national body or the delegation of government activities only to local companies. For example, diplomas gained from foreign education may not be recognized; and governments may require bonds or costly prudential provisions from foreign providers.
- *Discriminatory access to distribution networks*: imposing additional costs or requirements to construct infrastructure to access the network. Examples include the requirements for telephone networks and online booking for travel agencies.

Table 11.2 gives some examples of the most important barriers to the supply of services in key service sectors.

Table 11.2 Illustrative barriers to services trade, by sector

Sector	Barrier
Banking	Licensing
	Employment restrictions
	Exchange controls
	Discriminatory taxation
Insurance	Licensing
	Local incorporation
	Government procurement
	Exchange controls
Construction	Government procedure
	Tendering restrictions
	Subsidies
Air transport	Bilateral arrangements
	Subsidies
	Access to reservation systems
	Access to airport facilities
Professional services	Qualifications
	Restrictions on income repatriation
	Restrictions on partnerships

Source: Nicolaides (1989).

Unilateral reform is the most important kind of liberalization in the service sector, and in these cases, the precise terminology used to describe barriers does not matter directly: governments should merely try to devise sensible rules to regulate a particular sector. But when we come to multilateral and regional agreements, a major challenge is to characterize, codify and ultimately quantify barriers to trade in ways that permit a degree of comparability across sectors and countries. The GATS did not really solve this problem, allowing countries to bind their policies in almost any way they liked. This individualistic approach made negotiation easy if no one was pressing very hard for liberalization, but it has often left participants wondering exactly what it was that they had obtained from their trading partners. In future, a good deal more precision is likely to be called for.

11.2 The economics of services liberalization

11.2.1 The case for liberalization

The arguments for liberalizing trade in services are similar to those for trade in goods, namely that greater competition can combine improvements in the efficiency of local producers with higher quality, greater diversity and lower prices for consumers. Furthermore, services are often basic inputs to a wide range of production activities, so that restrictions are effectively a tax on, say, manufacturing activity. In these cases, improvements in supply will increase the efficiency of the rest of the economy, raising welfare and at least offering scope to reduce poverty. The positive effects that might be expected from services liberalization include:

- More efficient services, networks and infrastructures, which reduce production costs and facilitate the adoption of efficient production techniques, such as 'just in time' production.
- Upgraded infrastructure and modernized services with new technologies available from the world market.
- Improvements in a country's ability to absorb foreign direct investment (FDI).
- Enhancements in technology transfer.
- The introduction of new products.
- Reduced prices and improved product quality.

It is extremely difficult to estimate the costs of barriers to trade in services. Most countries supply little information on their barriers; the barriers tend to be both country- and sector-specific and, because services markets are often imperfectly competitive, it is extremely difficult to quantify and summarize the measures that are applied. Nonetheless, there is substantial evidence from individual countries and sectors that policies that reduce competition in service industries are very costly. In a developing country context, the losses of agricultural output due to poor transportation and storage facilities are one of the clearest examples (see Hoekman and Primo Braga, 1997).

Estimates from UNCTAD and the World Bank (1997) suggest that the prices of some business services in Uganda are very much higher than necessary. Letters of credit, for example, cost 20% of the value of the transaction to which they apply; and the total cost of transport and finance on imports is over 40%. Findlay and Warren (2000) present indices of restriction based on frequency counts of barriers and qualitative surveys in APEC countries. They find large ranges in the degree of restriction, implying that at least some countries are very restrictive.

Often the costs of such barriers are best seen when the restrictions are lifted. For example, the elimination of barriers to port services in Chile reduced operating costs by about 50% over two years (see Bennathan, 1993). And privatization and the introduction of foreign equity in telecoms companies in Argentina led to dramatic improvements in the quality and quantity of services – see *The Economist*, 6 December 1997.[2] Finally, there are estimates of the general equilibrium effects of barriers to services trade, for example, from Hertel et al. (1999). These should not be taken very seriously given the absence of good data on existing barriers, but if only because of the size of the sector, they suggest that services offer much larger gains to liberalization than either agriculture or manufacturing.[3]

11.2.2 Arguments against liberalization

Most of the apparently economic arguments against services liberalization are familiar from discussions of goods markets, as are their proponents. Developing countries in particular have expressed concern that competitiveness in the service sector depends on the capacity to adapt to new technology. Sudden liberalization, they argue, might lead to the collapse of domestic service providers with the result that services may not be provided at all or that the country may become much more vulnerable to the commercial decisions of a small number of foreign companies. In these circumstances, protection is claimed to allow domestic companies time to adapt and upgrade to world standards.

Such 'infant industry' arguments have been used by a number of developing countries, including Brazil and India, to protect their domestic markets from more mature companies from developed countries. They see protection as enhancing technological learning and capacity-building. But while this view may have force for some countries, it is hard to see how it applies in countries that have had heavily protected service sectors for many years with no substantial improvement in technological capacity. Moreover, the empirical evidence is, on balance, unfavourable. Krueger and Tuncer (1982), for example, find no general evidence of infant industry benefits in Turkey. Neither is the infant industry argument persuasive for developed countries that still maintain extremely high levels of protection in some service sectors. Of course, like other heavily protected sectors, service industries may warrant temporary transitional assistance during adjustment to a more liberal trading regime, but that is an entirely different question.

11.2.3 The importance of competition and regulation

The concern that liberalization of trade in services will lead to excessive dependence on particular foreign providers highlights a real issue. In some services, network economies create natural monopolies, while in others, traditions of public or monopoly provision remain strong. Certainly, there is little to be said for shifting to foreign-owned monopolies in these cases. (The 'little' is that they might be far more efficient technically – as in the example of Argentine telecoms.)

The appropriate policy response is not to close the border, but to accompany openness with policies to foster competition. Indeed, in terms of efficiency, competition will usually be more important than openness *per se*, but the politics of tackling entrenched supplier interests (often entrenched in the very parts of the government that are charged with regulating the sector) will frequently be easier in the context of international liberalization (see Mattoo, 2000b). In natural monopolies, competition can be enhanced by auctioning the rights to provide a service; by carefully separating the natural monopoly elements (such as the switching network in telecoms) from the competitive parts (such as the 'value added' services) and ensuring fair access to the former; and by sound regulation.[4]

Regulation is vital in many service sectors to correct the problems arising from the fact that consumers cannot readily tell the quality of the service provided (for example, a surgeon's skill or a bank's financial security). It might also be required to avoid systemic risk – the risk that failure in one firm or sub-sector unnecessarily brings down the rest. This is particularly true in financial services, but also in utilities and health. Thus, even if services are provided by foreign firms or personnel, the government still has an important role to play.

Traditionally, many sectors were self-regulating – banks, doctors and engineers, for example. This gave incumbents huge advantages and allowed them effectively to block entry to their profession and keep prices up. Thus, as part of the move towards competition, new regulatory bodies and procedures will be needed. Particularly for developing countries, these should be lean and efficient, for otherwise they become drains for skilled personnel and public funds. Part of this efficiency could come from being prepared to adopt regional or international standards or those of a major trading partner, rather than seeking to fine-tune standards to perceived local idiosyncrasies.

11.3 Services liberalization: the multilateral agenda

As noted above, the main form for liberalization of trade in services will be the unilateral actions of individual governments – there is just no other way that the detailed and time-consuming regulatory work can be done. But having said that, the multilateral framework is also important:

- First, developing countries have a strong interest in the liberalization of one of their major service exports – people – and although this

Handbook is primarily about what developing country governments can do with their own policies, we judge this of such importance that we deal with it at some length in section 11.4.1.

- Second, the GATS places certain (weak) constraints on what governments can do, especially if they have 'scheduled' a sector – that is, made it explicitly subject to GATS disciplines.
- Third, the multilateral process will condition governments' own efforts: it may make it easier politically to tackle entrenched interests; it may help to define technical solutions to various problems; and, unfortunately, it will necessarily absorb political and bureaucratic attention.

For these reasons, we need to consider both what the Uruguay Round entailed and where the current multilateral agenda in services liberalization is heading.

11.3.1 The GATS

The main general principle of the GATS is non-discrimination. This requires the application of 'most favoured nation' (MFN) treatment to all members except for listed exceptions such as regional blocs. This is known as a negative list: MFN applies except where stated explicitly. National treatment, on the other hand, is subject to a positive list – only sectors explicitly listed receive it.[5] And even this is conditional because certain restrictions can be exempted from liberalization for all services, whether 'scheduled' or not. These latter exemptions can be very far-reaching, for example, applying an 'economic needs' test that permits imports only if no domestic supplier exists.

In addition to MFN and national treatment, members can also make what are known as 'market access commitments'. These too use a positive list to define the sectors to which they apply; that is, only the sectors listed are subject to commitments on market access. For these sectors, the following restrictions are prohibited unless they have been explicitly listed in a country's Uruguay Round schedule:

- the number of suppliers;
- the total value of transactions or assets;
- the total quantity of services or service operations;
- the number of natural persons employed;
- the type of legal entity permitted; and
- the participation of foreign capital.

Other restrictions on market access are not directly controlled. However, most of them would, in fact, fall foul of the national treatment provisions, and so be prohibited via that route unless the sector in question had not been scheduled for national treatment.

It is clear that for the most part, the GATS applies only to the sectors and modes of supply that governments list (schedule). These schedules allow countries to specify limitations on both market access and national treatment both across all sectors and modes of supply and individually by sector and mode of supply. Furthermore, if a sector is not listed in a country's schedule, then no commitments apply.

The GATS distinguishes 155 sectors, each of which, in principle, has four modes of supply. Developed countries made commitments of some kind for 47% of the 620 sector-mode pairs listed by the GATS, including in over half the cases, commitments that there would be no restrictions on access. In contrast, developing countries made commitments for only 16% of the sector-mode pairs, with fewer than a half of these entailing no restrictions, while a quarter of developing countries committed to fewer than 3% of the GATS list (see Hoekman, 1996). Moreover, many 'commitments' amounted to no more than a listing of existing restrictions and policies (that is, committing only not to extend trade barriers), and in many cases, these are so complex or arcane that it is difficult to know exactly what the commitment amounts to.

The GATS also includes sector-specific annexes on the movement of natural persons, air transport, financial services, maritime transport and telecoms. These were designed to facilitate further sector-specific negotiations after the completion of the Uruguay Round in December 1993, and have led to codification and substantive liberalization in two industries:

- *Basic telecoms*: almost all countries have signed up to regulatory principles designed to ensure access to infrastructures and constrain anti-competitive behaviour by market incumbents. Many developing countries used the negotiations to accelerate the implementation of their plans to liberalize this sector (see Young, 2000). The so-called Reference Paper on Basic Telecoms developed in this negotiation to define and describe relevant competition policies has been an important template for this process. Mattoo (2000a) argues that it has important lessons for other sectors.
- *Financial services*: commitments in this sector were made by all the developed countries and countries in transition, but only 61 (of 78) developing and 6 (of 23) least-developed countries. The commitments are not particularly deep and, correctly, allow considerable regulatory activity for prudential reasons. In addition, countries have the right to introduce temporary restrictions in case of serious balance of payments or financial difficulties.

11.3.2 Service negotiations in future

Although the GATS represents a landmark in the inclusion of the services sector into the multilateral framework, there are obviously still a large number of economically harmful restrictions in place. Thus, liberalization of trade in services remains high on the agenda, both unilaterally and multilaterally. Table 11.3 lists some of issues that should feature in the latter, along with proposals for handling them to assist development efforts. The emphasis is on introducing competition, reducing the power of lobbies to frustrate competition and avoiding the use of trade barriers to support local inefficiency.

Table 11.3 Selected GATS and domestic policy issues: current status and desirable outcomes

Issue	Current status	Desirable outcome
Market access commitments under Article XVI of the GATS	Numerous restrictions, particularly on entry and foreign equity; in some cases, more emphasis on allowing increased foreign ownership and protecting foreign incumbents than on allowing new entry.	Further liberalization, with greater emphasis on eliminating restrictions on entry and promoting increased competition. Explore possibilities for formula liberalization to ease negotiating burden and reduce influence of sector lobbies.
	Limited use of the GATS to pre-commit to future liberalization, except in basic telecoms.	Wider use of the GATS to lend credibility to future liberalization programmes.
	Extremely limited market access commitments on the presence of natural persons.	Enhanced scope for the temporary, contract-related presence of natural persons.
Pro-competitive regulation (Articles VIII and IX, and the Reference Paper on Basic Telecoms)	Weak basic provisions with limited scope (Article VIII) and limited bite (Article IX), but commitment to desirable principles in the Reference Paper should contribute to enhanced competition.	Generalize the pro-competitive principles in the Reference Paper to other network-based sectors. Strengthen disciplines to deal with international cartels (for example, in transport).
		Strengthen domestic pro-competitive regulation to protect interests of consumers
Domestic regulation (Article VI)	Weak current disciplines (Article VI: 5), allow 'grandfathering' of protection through certain regulatory instruments; some success in accountancy negotiations in instituting a 'necessity test' but disappointing elaboration of disciplines on measures such as qualification requirements.[a]	Generalize the application of a necessity test to regulatory instruments in all sectors, especially where they impede developing country exports.
		Strengthen domestic regulations to remedy asymmetric information-related problems in financial, professional and other services.
		And choose economically efficient instruments to achieve universal service objectives.

Issue	Current status	Desirable outcome
	Uncertain terminology in commitments	Develop a lexicon; develop horizontal disciplines (that is, referring to one instrument across all sectors) to reduce the chances of regulatory capture.
Mutual Recognition Agreements, MRAs (Article VII)	Delicate balance (in Article VII): MRAs are allowed provided recognition is not used as a means of discrimination and third countries have the opportunity to accede or to demonstrate equivalence.	Ensure that MRAs do not become a means of discrimination. Improve quality and uniformity of domestic regulation where socially desirable, to strengthen case for foreign recognition.
Safeguards (Article X)	Limited progress to date in negotiations; no agreement on whether such a mechanism is necessary, desirable or feasible.	Create an avenue for temporary adjustment-related demands for protection, provided it is subject to strong, enforceable disciplines that prevent protectionist abuse.
Government procurement (Article XIII)	Limited progress in current negotiations; general reluctance to assume strong disciplines	Promote transparency and non-discrimination disciplines, but link to the elimination of barriers to mobility of natural persons to fulfil procurement contracts in construction and other services.s
Subsidies (Article XV)	Subject to non-discrimination requirements where national treatment commitments exist. Little progress to date.	Ensure freedom for the use of subsidies where they are the best instrument to achieve legitimate economic or social objectives
Electronic commerce	Decision not to impose customs duties, which has little meaning since quotas and discriminatory internal taxation are still permitted in many cases.	Widen and deepen scope of cross-border supply commitments on market access (prohibiting quotas) and national treatment (prohibiting discriminatory taxation) to ensure current openness continues.

a   A necessity test is the clause that permits a trade restriction only if it can be proved to be necessary for the declared objective – that is, effective and not dominated by non-trade approaches.

Sources: Low and Mattoo (2000) and Mattoo (2000a).

11.3.3 **Special circumstances, not special and differential treatment**

There is widespread agreement among governments that services liberalization has a positive role to play and should go further over the next few years. Many developing countries are liberalizing unilaterally – for example, in telecoms and business services – and a great deal of thought is going into regulatory systems. This consensus is also reflected in the WTO, where an outline for future negotiations is taking shape. As well as liberalizing, however, a number of developing country delegations are stressing their wish for 'flexibility' and 'special and differential treatment' (S&D). Some of them define these as entailing not only less liberalization, but also that policy be adapted to the stage of development of the country, and that priority be given to the main export sectors for developing countries.

S&D raises complex issues. Particularly where domestic regulation is concerned, developing countries *are* different Often they need to set up standards and regulatory arrangements from scratch; they have fewer and less reliable ways of monitoring suppliers; and their shortages of skills oblige them to seek very lean regulatory institutions. In these circumstances, premature liberalization could have serious consequences. On the other hand, in the past, S&D has basically been an excuse to undertake no liberalization, which has both imposed its own direct cost and left the developing countries marginalized in multilateral negotiations. Given the importance of services liberalization, winning and exploiting S&D in the latter sense would be highly counterproductive.

Similar arguments apply to the remaining rules issues in the services sectors: safeguards, procurement and subsidies. Some developing countries seek the right to intervene heavily in these areas (often while denying the same right to developed countries). There may well be cases for safeguards and some local preference in procurement, but an outcome that is too forgiving in these respects will leave services open to the sort of manipulation that has proved so unproductive in the goods sectors.

In short, developing countries should seek to harness the power of the multilateral negotiations to make and bind the reforms necessary to address issues of efficiency, competition and poverty. Stasis is not the answer, but neither is a 'one-size-fits-all' approach. In the end, there is no alternative to the careful analysis of particular circumstances, but it should be coupled with a clear commitment to address deep-seated inefficiencies and special interests.

11.4 **Services liberalization and poverty**

As with goods, the liberalization of trade in services can play an important role in the development of poor countries. It can increase the efficiency of existing services activities, foster productivity in user-sectors, upgrade and help to spread technology and encourage FDI – all of which are likely to be good for economic growth and poverty alleviation. This is the principle behind the argument that developing countries should not seek to use S&D and the continuing rules negotiations to avoid serious liberalization in services.

The service sector can be particularly important in terms of employment, because many services are labour-intensive. This poses both a challenge and an opportunity for developing countries. In principle, the development of the labour-intensive service sector can help to reduce poverty by generating labour-intensive growth – one of the original three prongs of pro-poor growth identified in the 1990 World Development Report (World Bank, 1990). This does require successful exporting, however, and so depends at least partly on other countries' liberalization.

The challenge is that some services in developing countries, particularly natural monopolies currently run by state-owned enterprises, are extremely inefficient and heavily overstaffed. Thus, improvements in the quality of services and reductions in prices may require substantial job losses in the short term. Where these services are predominantly consumed by relatively well-off urban populations (telephone, water and sewerage, and electricity services, for example), liberalization is likely to benefit middle-class populations at the cost of increased urban poverty. While investment resulting from better service provision is likely to improve a country's growth and employment prospects in the long term, thereby contributing to poverty reduction, governments and donors need to undertake liberalization in such sectors carefully. They need to ensure that other opportunities will arise for the affected workers and, where hardship seems likely to arise, ensure that they have effective safety nets in place.

The different modes of service delivery have different implications, particularly for the absorption of labour and consequent alleviation of poverty. Mode 4 – the movement of natural persons – offers the most direct pay-off if it can be extended to less-skilled workers. But if the workers cannot move to where the capital is, the opposite – bringing the capital to the workers under mode 3 and allowing them to export via modes 1 or 2 – may be as effective. Subject to maintaining competition in the domestic market, FDI oriented towards serving overseas markets could provide many jobs. (FDI for domestic sales may or may not boost employment, depending on whether the boost to sales that it is likely to create offsets the increase in productivity that it is likely to bring.)

Governments that are concerned about poverty reduction should focus on improving the quality and reducing the cost of the services of most importance to poor households. Transport and marketing (including basic information services) are of critical importance to the poor, as are basic health and education services and water and sanitation in urban areas. Some of these services may best be delivered through effective public provision. Others, however, would benefit from increased competition (whether between domestic or foreign suppliers). Thus, a real need is to improve the technical capacity for the analysis of competition in local markets and the regulatory capacity to liberalize in ways that are likely to enhance competition while retaining access for the poorest consumers. Box 11.1 discusses the problems of transportation to inland China. Boosting competition by allowing foreign firms to operate freight-forwarding businesses would help to open up the interior and spread China's coastal boom to the areas of greatest poverty.

Box 11.1 **Enclave development and unequal access to transport services: a case study of China**

China has experienced a rapid growth of its foreign trade since 1979, but there is a large disparity between the coastal region and the interior provinces. While inland China accounts for 63% of the country's total population and 46% of the overall income, it takes up only 17% of the foreign trade. One explanation for this may be found in the preferential treatment conferred on coastal provinces in the 1980s and early 1990s (for example, the establishment of special economic zones) or in their proximity to Hong Kong and Taiwan.

Another explanation, however, focuses on transport and logistics, specifically on the unsatisfactory state of container services. Exporters from inland China currently send goods to the ports by truck or railway, where they are containerized in special stations and sent onto the ships. The more efficient approach, preferred by multinational companies, is to use containers all the way. Because the inland penetration of containers is very low in China, inland producers are at a considerable disadvantage. Moreover, most coastal region exporters find it easier to import raw materials and intermediates from other countries across the sea rather than from the interior.

The World Bank (1996) argues that there are several reasons why inland container transport services are poor. One of them relates to the low levels of competition between freight forwarders and shipping agents – the sectors that connect shippers to shipping companies. Two state-owned enterprises hold around 80% of the market share in both freight-forwarding and shipping agencies. 'Although the Government allows major foreign shipping lines to establish their freight forwarding arms in China, they may only handle the parent companies' products. Restrictions on shipping agencies are even more sweeping: the Ministry of Commerce's 1990 Rule on International Shipping Agency bars foreign or joint venture from entering the shipping market, limiting it solely to state-owned enterprises.'

Source: World Bank (1996).

While there are many common features across service sectors, there are also many differences. Hence this chapter concludes by considering the possible poverty effects of liberalizing in three very different sectors.

11.4.1 The movement of natural persons

The focus of developing country policy-makers on this mode of service delivery is not misplaced. It is the locus of developing countries' greatest comparative advantage and the developed countries' greatest restrictions. Winters' (2000a) 'back-of-an-envelope' calculation imagines gains of US$300 billion a year to developing countries from liberalized movement of natural persons: US$60 per head for every person in the developing world.[6] Similarly, Mattoo (2000a) shows how the current success stories of developing countries exporting services, such as Indian software or Cuban health services, rely significantly on provider mobility – see Box 11.2. Despite the growing importance of cross-border electronic delivery, the movement of natural persons remains a critical part of the process in terms of such things as making contacts, maintenance and follow-up work.

But will developed countries reduce their restrictions on the movement of natural persons? The examples of the United States, United Kingdom and German responses to skill shortages in information technology show the sort of advantages that might arise from relaxing current policies and suggest the sort of allies that developing countries could find in pursuing this issue.

Box 11.2 **The experience of Indian exports of software services**

One of the most striking recent examples of a developing country service export success story is the Indian software industry, which has emerged as a significant supplier to developed country markets. Indian software exports grew from US$225 million in 1992–3 to US$1.75 billion in 1997–8. But despite the growing importance of cross-border electronic delivery of software services, the movement of natural persons remains a crucial mode of delivery. Even though its share in total Indian software exports has been declining, about 60% of Indian exports are still supplied through the temporary movement of programmers to the client's site overseas.

There are significant potential gains from further liberalization: for example, an average line of code in Switzerland (the most expensive country) is more than five times more expensive than in India (the cheapest country); but average salaries are more than eleven times higher in Switzerland.

Even though differences in labour productivity imply that a lower average salary of programmers may not necessarily translate into a lower average cost per line of software code, firms in developed countries can significantly save on development and support costs by outsourcing programming activities. With a total market for software services worth about US$58 billion in the United States, US$42 billion in Europe and US$10 billion in Japan, cost savings from outsourcing, either on- or off-plant, could be substantial (data for 1997 from WTO, 1998).

Other gains from trade liberalization for importing countries include a more competitive market structure for software services, increased choice, as countries may develop a special expertise for certain development or support services, and greater diffusion of knowledge.

But it cannot be assumed that developed countries' trade policies will automatically become more liberal through time, particularly for the movement of natural persons. In the early 1990s, the US government introduced rules that obliged foreign workers to acquire temporary work visas (H1-B visas), and limited the number of visas issued during a year to 65,000. This contributed to the relative decline of onshore services by Indian firms (see Heeks, 1998). In 1998, in response to mounting labour shortages experienced in the US information technology sector, the annual visa cap was raised to 115,000 for both 1999 and 2000. More recently, both Germany and the United Kingdom have been considering how to encourage such inflow of skilled labour.

Source: Mattoo et al. (2000).

But as noted above, little progress was made in liberalizing the movement of natural persons in the Uruguay Round. And what was agreed there – and in various regional talks like the NAFTA and the EU's Europe Agreements with East and Central European countries – is mostly concerned with relatively highly skilled workers. Thus, the United States grants NAFTA visas according to occupation, while the various services agreements guarantee the movement of 'key' personnel required for commercial presence in services and capital-intensive manufacturing. Whether such mobility favours developing countries is unclear – and whether it favours the poor in developing countries is actually rather doubtful.

When skilled personnel leave a developing country for a developed one, they typically increase their incomes significantly. This raises national income, but since skilled workers were initially not poor, it does not entail direct poverty alleviation. But if the higher incomes permit greater remittances (or perhaps taxes), there could be a positive effect. If working abroad allowed the individuals to learn greater skills, these benefits would be redoubled if they eventually returned home.

But what of those left behind? Ignoring remittances, the non-migrating workers (say the unskilled) will probably have fewer skilled workers to work with, and so suffer a loss of productivity and income. This effect will potentially be stronger if the skilled workers created externalities, via, say, innovations or demonstration effects, or if there were virtuous circles of agglomeration around significant masses of skilled workers – see, for example, Baldwin and Venables (1994). This negative view would be reversed, however, if the skilled workers generated greater externalities by being abroad – for example, by facilitating trade (see Rausch, 1999), transferring knowledge back home or, particularly, by returning home full of ideas and new abilities. It would also be reversed if the *chance* of migration led developing country residents to invest more heavily in skills so that even after the actual outflow the domestic stock of skills increased (see Mountford, 1997). Which of these arguments predominates is an empirical matter on which we have almost no information, but policy-makers need to consider all the possibilities.

The movement of low- and medium-skilled workers, on the other hand, is a far more secure route to general income growth and poverty alleviation. The income increase for those who move is likely to be proportionately larger (because developed countries are poorly endowed with such people), and by moving, they reduce the over-supply of labour at home. Moreover, far more workers would potentially be affected at the less skilled than at the highly skilled end of the spectrum. Thus, it is here that developing countries should concentrate their negotiating efforts.

The politics of achieving such a wide-ranging deal are formidable. Not only would there be practical issues to be solved – such as health cover for migrants – but it would also be necessary to overcome genuine concerns that such workers would lack rights in their host countries. Also, of course, the likely losers from such arrangements – unskilled labour in the developed countries – have been the traditional beneficiaries of protection and so seem likely to mount fierce campaigns against it.

In addition, in the name of reciprocity and national treatment, the developing countries themselves have to be prepared to accept inflows of workers as well as outflows, so they too will have political problems – from skilled elites, from traditional antagonisms and, in some cases, from their own unskilled workers. Nonetheless, the gains are such that the attempt would surely be worthwhile and, through time, the difficulties are likely to recede. Inward mobility will start to look more attractive in developed countries as the baby-boomers retire, reducing labour force growth while simultaneously increasing the demand for personal services. Box 11.3 suggests some concrete issues that might be taken up in future negotiations on this issue.

Box 11.3 **Liberalizing the movement of natural persons – what needs to be done**

Multilateral negotiations on liberalizing the movement of natural persons need to proceed on several levels. A good deal of definitional work is required to ensure that agreements are transparent and operational. This includes agreed definitions of sectors and occupations at a disaggregated level, which can then lead on to negotiations on specific sectors. These need to include quite specific market access commitments. In addition to the sectoral approach, which is necessary because sectors vary so much in detail, negotiations need to develop horizontal or cross-sectoral norms. In both sectoral and horizontal dimensions, it is necessary to extend the liberalization to low- and middle-skills levels, as these are the key to poverty alleviation.

Horizontally, four classes of continuing constraints on the movement of natural persons need to be addressed:

Immigration-related regulations concerning the entry and stay of service providers

The fundamental problem is that there is currently no separation between temporary and permanent labour movement. Even though the GATS is meant to cover only the former for delivery of services, it comes under the purview of immigration legislation. In a new round of trade negotiations, it will be important to separate the temporary from the permanent movement of labour and provide suitable provision for *short-term* mobility of workers. This might be achieved by establishing a 'GATS visa', which was fairly widely available for temporary movement. The numbers of visas could be related to specific commitments made under either modes 3 (commercial presence) or 4 (natural persons), giving the latter concrete form. For less-skilled workers, it would be possible to license firms to bring in particular numbers, charging the firms with ensuring that the migration was only temporary.

Regulations concerning the recognition of qualifications work experience and training

Detailed sector-by-sector work is required to ensure that barriers are not created by artificial distinctions in qualifications, and that due weight is attached to developing countries' less formal and on-the-job qualification routes. Where quality assurance is required, it should satisfy a 'necessity test' – that is, that the least distorting methods be chosen (for example, testing competence rather than automatically requiring retraining).

continued

Box 11.3 continued

The differential treatment of domestic and foreign personnel

For example, double taxation or migrants paying social security taxes for benefits they cannot receive. Part of this would entail abolishing the 'economic needs' test, which permits foreign workers only if no local candidates exist. Similar rules were applied to goods markets under the import-substitution regimes from the 1950s to the 1980s and were thoroughly discredited.

Regulations covering other modes of supply, particularly commercial presence, which indirectly limit the scope for the movement of natural persons

Rules controlling the establishment of foreign firms – for example, on establishing branches or on staffing by local persons – reduce the opportunities or people who might otherwise move abroad temporarily.

Source: Chanda (1999).

11.4.2 Financial services

Although the delayed Uruguay Round Agreement on financial services instituted a fair amount of liberalization, there is plainly room for more. The direct poverty consequences of financial liberalization are negligible. The poor just do not transact in the kinds of markets involved: they do not directly use commercial financial institutions and the very small-scale lending and insuring that does affect them is of no interest to the commercial sector.

There may be indirect effects, however. Cheap and effective financial services, including payments mechanisms, raise the competitiveness of existing firms and, more importantly, facilitate new transactions and opportunities. If financial and e-commerce liberalization allow small farmers and craft workers better access to the market, the benefits could be huge – see Box 12.5 in Chapter 12 on opening up trade in manufactures via communications technology.

Of course, concern is frequently expressed about the monopoly power of multinational companies in the financial services sector operating in developing countries, and it is indeed a problem to be guarded against. But the poor are currently very often the victims of local financial institutions that are both monopolistic and inefficient. Competition would be very likely to help them. Moreover, it is open to governments to impose some form of universal service requirement as a condition for licensing, so long as it satisfies national treatment. This may be useful in extending financial services to rural areas, although policy-makers should recognize that trying to impose costly branch networks on banks could undermine their effectiveness elsewhere, or even their willingness to operate at all. Box 11.4

suggests that liberalization is unlikely to be sufficient to bring finance to the poor, but that it might be a useful contributory policy.

The experience of the 1990s strongly suggests that premature financial liberalization can be dangerous in terms of boom and eventual bust in the financial system. The poor are probably only small participants in the boom, but will often suffer significantly in the bust. Thus pro-poor considerations reinforce the current conventional wisdom that sound regulatory structures and macro policies need to be in place prior to financial liberalization. It should, though, be noted that nothing in the GATS Protocol on Financial Services constrains sound prudential regulation. The issue is merely one of timing.

Box 11.4 Financial liberalization and credit for the poor in Africa

Mosley (1999a) estimates the impact of financial liberalization on access to rural credit in four African countries: Uganda, Kenya, Malawi and Lesotho. Domestic financial liberalization, through giving up control of interest rates and removing credit subsidies, has led to higher real interest rates, but other than Uganda, has not translated into higher levels of savings, or increased access to rural credit.

In Uganda, average estimated credit disbursements to the agricultural sector showed a marginal increase from US$116 million three years prior to liberalization to US$123 million three years after the liberalization; while in Malawi, the number declined from US$121 to US$109 million over the same periods of time either side of liberalization. Using sample survey data, Mosley reports that between 1992–7, the percentage of sampled households with access to rural credit rose in Kenya and Uganda from 13.1% and 9.2% to 25% and 21% respectively, but fell in Malawi from 12% to 8%. Access to credit by the poorest 10% (by income) remained unchanged or fell marginally in all four countries.

Commercial and foreign banks have been reluctant to step into the informal lending sector despite the higher rates in informal lending. In Mosley's words, this is probably 'due to high levels of subjective risk, supplemented with ignorance and a shortage of individuals able to act as go-betweens and present the financial results of micro-finance institutions in a form digestible by commercial banks'. Informal sector and rural lending is still carried out by traditional money-lenders, NGOs and government agencies.

Mosley also shows that financial innovation in rural areas and the development of financial institutions catering to the poor strongly improve access to rural credit and lower poverty. Examples of successful micro-finance institutions include the PCEA Chogoria and the Rural Enterprise Program in Kenya and the CCEI/Gatsby Trust Scheme in Cameroon. Other examples are Bolivia's BancoSol and Bank Rakyat Indonesia.

These micro-finance institutions offer savings and credit services on commercial terms to marginal households and use peer pressure as a substitute for collateral in loan repayments and recovery. They have managed to sustain high loan recovery rates,

continued

Box 11.4 continued

cover costs and make profits, with lending rates that lie between those of commercial banks and informal money-lenders. Formal institutions can reach small lenders and borrowers by forging links with informal and micro-finance agents, thereby lowering information costs and developing community-based contract enforcement mechanisms. On the other hand, simply privatizing state micro-finance agencies can prove disastrous as illustrated by the collapse of the MRFC in Malawi.

Source: Mosley (1999a).

11.4.3 Tourism

Tourism is an important sector for many developing countries, especially the smallest ones. It is also a sector that lends itself to international trade (especially via commercial presence for international hotel and travel companies) and for which poverty is an important dimension. Hoekman's (1996) results suggest that 'hotels and restaurants' is the sector with the highest coverage of commitments by developing countries, whereas the transportation sector's commitments are among the lowest.

Tourism can play a very important role in the process of development and can be an important source of income for the poor. In 1997, developing countries received 30.5% of world international tourist arrivals; for most middle-income countries and half the low-income countries, tourism was either large (2% of GDP or 5% of exports) or growing fast (by 50% or more over the period 1990–7). This set includes all but 1 of the 12 countries that are home to 80% of the world's poor (see Ashley et al., 2000).

Tourism can generate income for the poor in several different ways:

- wages from formal employment;
- earnings from selling goods and services – food, construction, etc.;
- dividends and profits from domestic companies; and
- collective income from community or government activities.

Of course, developing countries receive only part of the gross expenditure on tourism. The leakage back to developed countries averages around 55% of tourism expenditure, rising to 75% in the case of Gambia. There are four main reasons for this leakage, according to Ashley et al. (2000):

- imported skilled labour;
- imports of luxury goods, food and other goods and services;
- repatriation of profits by foreign companies; and
- the important role of marketing, transport and other services based in the originating countries.

Developing country commentators sometimes argue that squeezing this leakage is an easy source of increased revenue, but the potential bounty can easily be overestimated. Tourist industries are fairly concentrated, but it is not clear that they are exploitative. Besides, in the absence of a developing country cartel, which is more or less inconceivable, it is not clear that individual developing countries could redress the balance. Moreover, from a pro-poor perspective, shifting developed country rents back to developing countries is not important: very little of the return accrues to the poor. Thus, policy attention needs to be directed towards how tourism affects poverty directly, not to distributive battles. As regards the former, three developing countries have proposed an Annex to the GATS loosely paralleling the pro-competitive thrust of the Reference Paper on Basic Telecoms – see Box 11.5.

As well as generating incomes and broadening horizons and opportunities, tourism also has a number of direct and indirect negative effects on poverty. In particular, tourism can exacerbate the losses due to market failures arising from the presence of externalities and public goods. For example, environmental degradation, prostitution, overburdened female workers, limitation of access to natural resources, disrupted networks or cultural damage are all potential negative effects of tourism. Ashley et al. (2000) also suggest losses due to the volatility of tourism incomes and the diversion of labour from other activities. But these are essentially market issues, which in the absence of specific market failures are taken into account correctly by private decisions. Similarly, Ashley et al.'s strictures about tourism diverting policy-makers' attention or capital investment apply equally to any new activity, and indicate no market failure *per se*.

But given the legitimate policy worries stemming from market failure, tourism probably needs a consciously pro-poor strategy to maximize the poor's access to jobs and tourist markets and to protect other resources from over-exploitation. Ideally, poor and local people should participate in devising a tourism strategy. This requires human, financial and social capital, but it also requires political courage by the central authorities.

Most of what is required for pro-poor tourism is purely domestic; it is

Box 11.5 **Tourism proposal**

The Dominican Republic, El Salvador and Honduras have put forward a Draft Annex on Tourism for the GATS. It does not contain specific provisions for liberalization of tourism services but rather, recognizing the wide range of services involved in tourism, suggests provisions on competitive safeguards, which build on the Reference Paper on Basic Telecoms.

The objective is to legitimize measures to prevent anti-competitive practices, such as the discriminatory use of information networks, ancillary services to air transport, predatory pricing or the allocation of scarce resources; and the abuse of dominance through exclusivity clauses, refusal to deal, tied sales, quantity restrictions or vertical integration. There are also provisions on consumer safeguards and for sustainable development of tourism.

Source: Mashayekhi (2000)

affected by the GATS only in that policy must not discriminate between domestic and foreign, or between different foreign, providers. The permitted market access tools allow all of the interventions required to manage congestion.

A GATS liberalization would preclude restrictions on foreign nationals working in hotels and would require care over any controls over foreign ownership. Blanket bans on FDI, limits on the total number of hotels (domestic and foreign) or regulation to enforce local environmental constraints would all be permitted, but arbitrary licensing restrictions on foreign entrants would not. In return, by offering assurances to investors, a GATS liberalization may boost investment and tourist activity, which, subject to the sort of management outlined above, would very probably have a positive impact on poverty alleviation.

11.5 Conclusion

Services compose a major part of every economy and trade in them is generally rather restricted. There are large potential gains from increasing the degree of competition in services markets, and trade liberalization, either unilateral or multilateral, offers one of the best tools for doing so. A more liberal trading environment should reduce the costs and increase the quality of services used in the domestic economy and open up opportunities for profitable exporting.

Liberalization does not entail eliminating necessary regulation in services markets, but merely ensuring that the regulations are pro-competitive and non-discriminatory. Service sectors differ among themselves just as much as goods sectors, and policy-makers will need to consider their own markets individually. Many sectors seem to offer scope for strongly pro-poor liberalizations, but there is a possibility that in others, the poor are suppliers (workers) rather than users, and complementary policies will be necessary to avoid the adverse poverty effects of increased unemployment. The three sectors we have analysed here suggest the sort of analysis that will be useful in exploring these issues. Developing countries have a strong interest in liberalizing the movement of natural persons. Box 11.6 presents the usual checklist for policy-makers.

Box 11.6 **Checklist on services liberalization**

- Identify those basic services for which liberalization reduces prices and that are very important for the poor – for example, transport, health and education, water and sanitation – and liberalize them unilaterally, subject to safeguarding universal service provisions where necessary.
- Identify cases where competition will drastically reduce unskilled employment, and ensure that the conditions are in place to reabsorb the labour quickly.
- Do your regulations and competition law ensure that there is competition in domestic markets?
- Is the government's important role in assuring the quality and security of services, especially for poor consumers, conducted lightly, efficiently and non-discriminatorily?
- Does poor service provision constrain efficiency and competitiveness? If so, liberalize the offending sectors, especially where doing so would increase unskilled employment.
- Push for further liberalization in those service sectors of export interest, especially in the case of natural persons.
- How can you use the multilateral process to help tackle entrenched interests that are stunting development?

Notes

1   Nicolaides (1989) discusses how to define a service.
2   Moreover, these gains have occurred despite worries that the new firms have great monopoly power and hence have not been entirely consumer-orientated or pro-poor (see Consumers International, 2000).
3   The size of the initial barriers is by far the most critical input into computable estimates of the costs of protection, far more important than the sizes of the elasticities assumed by researchers.
4   In auctions, a degree of local preference may be warranted to reflect the greater ease of regulating local firms, but it should be modest and granted only where the case for it is explicit and soundly-based.
5   National treatment in the context of services is defined as treatment no less favourable than that accorded to like domestic services and service providers; the treatment is not necessarily identical since in some cases that might actually worsen the conditions for competition for foreign-based firms.
6   Suppose that when a worker moves from a low- to a high-income country, he or she could make up a quarter of the wage gap between the two countries (that is, assume that three-quarters of observed wage gaps are due to differences in individual characteristics, and hence would persist even after people started to work in the rich countries). Suppose also that 50 million additional developing country people worked abroad in any year, equivalent to an increase of about 5% in developed countries' populations. With a wage gap of, say, US$24,000 a year, the gains would be US$300

billion a year. (Labour costs per manufacturing worker, which are an indicator of productivity, were about US$32,000 in the United States in 1990–4, compared with US$1,192 in India, US$1,442 in Lesotho, US$5,822 in China and US$6,138 in Mexico; high-income countries' population was 927 million in 1997 – see World Bank, 1999d).

12 Liberalizing Manufacturing Trade

This chapter argues that:

- Manufacturing is an important sector of virtually every economy. It is heavily protected in most developing countries and parts of it are subject to major barriers in developed countries.
- Manufacturing is a natural sector for inclusion in a future round of multilateral trade negotiations, but this should not preclude unilateral action as well.
- Liberalization of trade in manufactures promises improvements in resource allocation and enhanced productivity growth, but the conditions have to be in place for firms to respond to new threats and opportunities.
- Some workers might lose from liberalization, and safety nets may be needed for affected workers. There may be a case for phasing a liberalization over time.
- Not all job losses cause poverty, however: depending on the operation of labour markets (including the informal sector), workers may get new jobs quickly at equal or better wages. And of course, there will probably also be job gains.
- The abolition of the Multi-Fibre Arrangement will benefit developed countries (that liberalize) and potential exporters of clothing; but those developing countries that have no comparative advantage in the sector will lose.

12.1 Background

Manufacturing is an important sector of almost every economy. Table 12.1 reports the shares of manufacturing in GDP and imports and exports of goods by region and income class. East Asia is the region that is most

Table 12.1 Shares of manufacturing in GDP, exports and imports, 1997
(percentages)

	GDP	Exports	Imports
Lower middle income	29	57	70
Upper middle income	21	54	77
East Asia and the Pacific	33	72	75
Europe and Central Asia	na	53	66
Latin America and the Caribbean	21	46	79
Middle East and North Africa	14	19	68
South Asia	19	76	54
Sub-Saharan Africa	17	na	na
High income	21	81	75

Note: The World Bank's 'high income' category includes OECD members, Hong Kong, Singapore, various oil states and several small countries that are not normally classified as 'developed', such as Bermuda, Reunion and French Guiana.

Source: World Bank (1999d).

heavily dependent on manufacturing and the Middle East and North and sub-Saharan Africa the least dependent. But in terms of export shares, the developed countries lead. Employment in manufacturing is also important, although it usually accounts for a smaller share of total employment than manufacturing's share of GDP. This is because manufacturing is relatively skill- and capital-intensive.

Manufacturing also plays an important role in development theory, often being characterized as the *sine qua non* of development. The development of manufacturing capability behind tariff walls was the immediate aim of the – now substantially discredited – import-substitution model of development (see, for example, Krueger, 1997 or Bruton, 1998).

Manufacturing also figured prominently in the history of post-war trade liberalization. The GATT's first seven (pre–Uruguay) rounds of multilateral trade negotiations focused primarily on reducing barriers to trade in industrial goods. These resulted in substantial reductions in average tariff rates over the last 40 years such that the average tariff on manufactured goods imported by developed countries from other developed countries is now only 0.8%. This focus reflected the interests of the developed countries, who at the time, dominated GATT membership and were heavily committed to manufacturing exports.

In contrast, the poorest developing countries were regarded primarily as commodity producers and importers of manufactures with, therefore, relatively little interest in the reduction of other countries' tariffs on manufactured goods. In addition, of course, most developing countries were not members of the GATT and those that were members were exempted from offering concessions on their own tariffs by 'special and differential treatment' (S&D – see Chapters 8 and 11).

This position has changed dramatically in the last 30 years. In 1965,

Figure 12.1 The structure of developing country exports of manufactures: share in total exports and share sold to developing countries

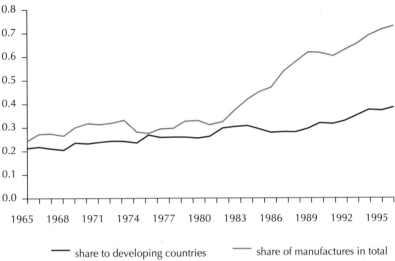

Source: Hertel and Martin (2000).

manufactures made up only around a quarter of developing countries' merchandise exports, but by 1996, manufactures accounted for almost three-quarters of developing countries' merchandise exports (see Hertel and Martin, 2000). Figure 12.1 shows how the commodity shares of merchandise exports from developing countries have changed since 1965 and the dramatic growth in importance of manufactured exports since the early 1980s.

Despite the reductions in tariffs in recent years, there are still substantial barriers to manufacturing exports, especially in developing countries – see Table 12.2. This is important for two reasons:

- First, tariffs impose costs on the protected country in terms of consumer welfare and inefficient allocation of resources.
- Second, the rapid growth of 'South-South' trade – almost 40% of developing countries' exports of manufactures were destined for other developing economies in 1995 (see Hertel and Martin, 2000) – means that developing countries are penalizing each other in terms of lost export markets, scope for specialization, etc.

Table 12.2 Pattern of protection in manufactures, 1995

Exporting region	Importing region	
	Developed countries (%)	Developing countries (%)
Developed countries	0.8	10.9
Developing countries	3.4	12.8
World	1.5	11.5

Source: Hoekman and Martin (1999).

In addition, developed countries still maintain protection against the types of manufactured goods supplied by developing countries. The average tariff on the latter's bundle of exports is four times higher than that on the set of manufactures imported from other developed countries. This protection is compounded by the presence of tariff peaks and tariff escalation in developed countries, particularly in those products of most export potential for developing countries.

The consequence of these high tariffs is that developing countries still pay a tax for access to the markets of other countries. Of a theoretical global tariff revenue from trade in manufactures of US$190 billion (calculated as the product of imports and the applicable tariff rate summed over all manufactured commodities and countries), developing country exporters are liable for US$80 billion (about 45%, or twice their percentage share of world income). Of this, US$57 billion arises from tariffs on imports into developing countries, that is, tariffs on 'South-South' trade.

In addition to tariff barriers, there remain a number of non-tariff barriers to manufactured goods. The most important of these are developed country barriers to developing country exports from the textiles and clothing sector as sanctioned by the Multi-Fibre Arrangement (MFA). This suggests that the manner and speed with which the commitments to remove these barriers by 2005 undertaken in the Uruguay Round's Agreement on Textiles and Clothing (ATC) are implemented is of crucial importance to developing countries. Furthermore, developing countries also frequently impose non-tariff barriers on manufactured imports with damaging effects on their own economies. For example, India maintains 'core' non-tariff barriers on all 85 categories in a broad classification of imports, and Brazil on 48 categories – see Finger and Schuknecht (2001).

The principal costs of manufacturing protection fall on the protecting country itself, a fact that should provide quite enough incentive for trade liberalization for developing country governments seeking to maximize national income. Protection also hurts the exporters whose trade it cuts, and here too, developing countries are the main losers. They should seek concessions not only in developed countries, but also among themselves. Finally and very importantly, manufacturing protection penalizes other sectors, especially agriculture. Exchange rates that are overvalued in order to obtain cheap industrial inputs (prioritizing imports of capital goods for industry) and barriers to imports of manufactured goods all draw resources out of agriculture and towards an inefficient manufacturing industry. This implies that removing the protection of manufactures is likely to provide a major boost for agriculture in developing countries, the sector on which the poor tend to be most dependent.

12.2 The economics of trade restrictions on manufacturing

There is no built-in agenda for the multilateral liberalization of manufacturing tariffs, but there are many opportunities for benefits to both developed and developing countries from further liberalization. Consequently, there is growing support for its inclusion in future trade negotiations. This section reviews the agreements for reducing tariffs and, in particular, for liberalizing trade in textiles.

12.2.1 Tariffs

The traditional welfare economics of tariffs is well documented.[1] Tariffs reduce the welfare of the country that imposes them by distorting the allocation of resources away from other products, the production of which would maximize national income at world prices. Although producers gain from tariff protection, consumers lose and their loss is not fully compensated by producer gains and the revenue generated by the tariff. This is because of two types of efficiency losses: production by high-cost firms who could not compete at world prices; and the inability of some consumers to afford the good at the tariff-inclusive price, when they could have afforded it at the world price.

Tariffs also act as an implicit form of export taxation since, by raising the price of imports, they encourage the production of import-substitutes relative to the production of exports. Tariff liberalization therefore helps to raise consumer real incomes, reduce the welfare losses associated with inefficient levels of production and consumption, and boost exports through redistribution of resources from inefficient industries to the competitive export sector. A case of successful manufacturing development

Box 12.1 Trade liberalization in Sri Lanka

Sri Lanka's economic liberalization began in 1977. Athukorala and Rajapatirana (1998) analyse the effects of trade liberalization on domestic industry, identifying overall positive effects:

'Five key findings emanate from the study that have general validity for other newcomers to industrialization among developing countries. First, the economic liberalization, which was neutral among activities, was largely successful in changing the structure of industry, raising both the output and the export growth rate of manufactures. Second, as trade barriers were reduced, resource allocation improved, with greater utilization of labour per unit of output... There was also significant total factor productivity growth following the economic liberalization. Third, industrial growth and export success were closely related to private foreign direct investment, which increased in response to policy changes welcoming foreign investment. Fourth, the liberalization of imports increased access to better-quality and cheaper intermediate inputs, reducing the reliance on state-owned enterprises, which had provided high-cost, low-quality inputs before the liberalization. Finally, a more stable macroeconomic environment during the early phase of the economic liberalization, along with the absence of ethnic conflict during the later phase, would have led to even better performance.'

Source: Athukorala and Rajapatirana (1998).

predicated on trade and other liberalization is Sri Lanka – see Box 12.1.

Of course, trade liberalization does increase competition in the import-competing sector of the domestic economy, as Box 12.2 describes in the case of Tanzania. This may put inefficient domestic firms out of business, releasing the resources necessary for the efficient sectors and firms to expand. But at least temporarily, it may also have negative effects in terms of employment.

Tariffs on manufactures in developing countries are the first cause of concern. A second concern is the tariffs faced by the exports of developing countries, particularly developed countries' tariff peaks. The higher the tariff, the more strongly developing countries' exports are cut back (and, perhaps, their prices depressed), and the more production is switched away from the goods subject to such peaks. Since the tariff peaks occur in precisely those industries in which developing countries have a strong comparative advantage, this implies that they face large welfare costs. But as noted above, tariffs on trade between developing countries also frustrate the exploitation of comparative advantage and reduce incomes.

A third cause of concern is developed countries' tariff escalation in which duties are low on imports of primary or unprocessed goods, but escalate according to the degree of processing in the imported good. This clearly discourages a developing country from processing activity for exports. Thus, while development strategies in many countries aim to upgrade production processes in order to capture a larger share of the value added, tariff escalation pushes in the opposite direction. In technical terms, tariff escalation leads to high rates of 'effective protection' – see Box 12.3.

Box 12.2 **Tanzania: liberalization in manufactures and the competitive environment**

Tanzania has been implementing trade reform since the early 1990s, abolishing most quantitative restrictions, reducing and rationalizing tariffs and liberalizing the exchange rate regime. A survey carried out in 1995 across 83 manufacturing enterprises shows that trade liberalization appears to have been associated with increased competition, benefiting exporters but posing concerns for firms that compete with imports. Because relatively few firms specialize in exports, only 23% of the manufacturing firms reported beneficial effects of liberalization. While exporting firms could increase prices, especially after the removal of the anti-export bias and the devaluation that accompanied exchange rate liberalization, a significant proportion of firms reported increased competition from imports, constraining their ability to increase prices. The net effect of these changes is not clear from the survey, but given that Tanzania clearly does not have comparative advantage in manufacturing, it is notable that a quarter of manufacturing firms gained from liberalization.

Source: Grenier et al. (1999).

Box 12.3 Tariff escalation and the rate of effective protection

Effective protection is defined as the proportionate increase in value added that protection permits: that is, $(V-V^*)/V^*$, where V is value added per unit of output under the tariff regime and V^* the same under free trade. Value added is the value of an output less the value of all the intermediate or material inputs that it uses. It is what is left over to provide incomes for labour, capital and taxes. If an output tariff raises the value of a unit of output by more than input tariffs raise the value of inputs, value added at domestic prices is increased and resources are attracted into the sector concerned.[1] If world prices imply value added of, say, $10, while protection permits, say, $15, the labour and capital contributing the value added in the protected country would earn 50% more as a result of protection. Alternatively, they could afford to become 50% less efficient than world producers and yet still survive.

Tariff escalation biases protection against the production of final goods in developing countries, the sectors where most of the value added is concentrated. Thus, it allows the protected developed countries to maintain high value added in sectors that are inefficient when evaluated at world prices.

---

1 Of course, factors respond to the differences in returns across sectors, so strictly, the analysis needs to look at effective protection in all sectors simultaneously to predict resource flows.

12.2.2 The Multi-Fibre Arrangement (MFA)

Manufactured goods are also subject to a large number of non-tariff barriers, most importantly in textiles and clothing. Until the Agreement on Textiles and Clothing (ATC), the textiles and clothing trade was regulated by the MFA, which provided a multilateral framework for discriminatory quantitative restrictions against 35 developing countries and economies in transition (see IDS, 1999c). Although a schedule for the elimination of these quotas in now in place (see Table 12.4), most of these restrictions still exist. The myriad bilateral quotas between developed and developing countries contained in the MFA have resulted in a highly inefficient allocation of resources at a global level. Faini et al. (1995) identify two main sources of inefficiency:

Inefficient allocation across producers
Restrictions reallocate production from low- to higher-cost suppliers in four ways:

• reallocation from constrained exporters to domestic suppliers;
• reallocation from constrained exporters to unconstrained exporters;
• reallocation between different constrained exporters; and
• inefficient allocation between firms in constrained exporting countries.

These inefficiencies reduce exports and output by efficient producers with corresponding declines in incomes and employment. Since much of the labour involved is unskilled, the poverty implications could be very great.

Of course, the reallocations will tend to increase the output of higher-cost firms and countries, such as those that have the quotas to supply developed country markets but would no longer be competitive in a free market, such as Hong Kong. Thus, the MFA creates jobs in some places, although almost certainly fewer jobs than it destroys elsewhere. Overall, it imposes losses of billions of dollars worth of welfare in developing countries.

Inefficient allocation among importing countries
Market segmentation also leads to inefficient allocation of goods between consumers. There are two ways in which this can occur:

- reallocation among consumers located in different constrained importing countries due to the MFA's arbitrary segmentation of import markets; and
- reallocation from consumers in constrained importing countries towards consumers in importing countries that have not negotiated or imposed any restrictions.

One of the relative benefits claimed for restricting imports via bilateral quotas rather than tariffs is that it permits developing country exporters to share the rents created by restricting trade. In fact this benefit is often overestimated – see the careful analysis by Krishna and Tan (1998), which suggests that exporters receive only between a third and a half of the rents created. Moreover, as de Melo and Winters (1993) have shown for footwear, even full rents do not necessarily compensate for the losses of income due to the frustration of comparative advantage.

12.3 Progress on liberalizing trade in manufactures

12.3.1 Tariffs

At the close of the Uruguay Round, 130 countries or customs areas had agreed to tariff bindings or reductions. The average trade-weighted tariff on all industrial products from all sources was reduced by 38% (see Safadi and Laird, 1996). But there were substantial variations depending on the type of good. Table 12.3 shows current trade, average tariffs after the Uruguay Round and tariff reductions for commodity groups that concern developing countries. Looking at the developed countries' imports from developing countries, there were substantial proportional reductions in tariffs on wood, pulp, paper and furniture, metal products and non-electric machinery. But these reductions tended to be concentrated in areas that already had low tariffs. In particular, tariff reductions in the areas of most importance to developing countries – including textiles and clothing, leather, rubber, footwear, travel goods and transport equipment – fell far below the one-third reduction intended and important tariff peaks remain. For example, 52% of the United States' textile and clothing imports are subject to tariff rates of between 15–35% (see Panagariya, 1999a).[2]

Table 12.3 Trade value, post-Uruguay Round average tariffs and tariff cuts on imports of industrial goods

	Developed countries' imports from developing countries			Developing countries' imports from developing countries			Developing countries' imports from developed countries		
	Trade US$ billion, 1988	Average tariff (percentage) Post-Round average tariff %	Tariff reduction %	Trade US$ billion, 1988	Average tariff (percentage) Post-Round average tariff %	Tariff reduction %	Trade US$ billion, 1988	Average tariff (percentage) Post-Round average tariff %	Tariff reduction %
Fish and fish products	7.7	5.0	22	0.3	15.9	49	0.8	8.7	74
Wood, pulp, paper and furniture	11.5	1.5	59	1.7	7.3	17	6.6	9.6	49
Textiles and clothing	30.0	11.1	16	1.6	21.1	21	7.8	20.7	23
Leather, rubber, footwear and travel goods	16.9	6.1	13	1.2	8.2	31	2.9	18.5	19
Metals	23.8	0.8	66	5.4	8.5	16	18.1	13.5	28
Chemicals and photographic supplies	7.1	2.7	41	2.9	9.2	25	27.7	13.0	30
Transport equipment	7.9	3.9	15	0.9	10.6	9	13.0	21.8	17
Non-electric machinery	11.6	1.2	59	1.9	10.2	26	36.8	14.4	24
Electric machinery	25.7	2.4	39	1.7	14.0	21	23.3	16.0	25
Mineral products	17.9	1.0	38	2.1	8.1	14	9.9	9.4	17
Other manufactured articles	11.3	2.0	57	1.0	8.8	16	13.9	13.9	27
Industrial products (excluding petroleum)	171.5	3.9	28	20.9	10.3	21	160.8	14.7	25

Note: the details in this table differ from those in Table 12.2 for several reasons. These are based on detailed analysis of a selection of 47 countries and are weighted by trade flows from the period 1987–91. Table 12.2 relies on more aggregate tariff data with estimates for all countries in the world and is weighted up by 1995 data.

Source: de Paiva Abreu (1996).

Table 12.3 also reports developing countries' average tariffs on imports from both developed and other developing countries. Developing countries' tariffs are much higher than those of developed countries, even in textiles and clothing in which they have comparative advantage. In terms of tariff reductions, developing countries made smaller percentage cuts, but given their higher base rates, their degree of import liberalization (the reduction in the post-tariff import price) was significantly greater. Thus, for example, developed countries cut tariffs on non-electrical machinery by 59% from 3% (not reported in the table) to 1.2%, a fall in the import price of 1.7%. Developing countries, on the other hand, cut theirs (on developed countries) by 24% from 18.9% to 14.4%, a fall in the import price of 3.8%. It is the sizes of these percentage declines in import prices that truly reflect the degree of import liberalization and which determine the economic effects of a reform.

Table 12.3 shows clearly the similarities in the developing and developed countries' patterns of protection – and just how far the former still are from free trade.

The Uruguay Round also saw a substantial increase in the number of tariffs that were bound. Tariffs have been bound on all but 1% of imports of industrial products to developed countries. Similarly, transition economies have bound 96% of their tariffs. Developing countries, on the other hand, have only bound 61% of their tariffs, although this was still a substantial increase from 13% prior to the beginning of the Round (see de Paiva Abreu, 1996).

12.3.2 The Agreement on Textiles and Clothing (ATC)

One of the major achievements of the Uruguay Round was the agreement to end the MFA, which will be phased out in four stages. At every stage, a percentage of imports based on the 1990 volume of imports must be included for liberalization according to the schedule shown in Table 12.4.

Thus, 33% of the volume of imports has already been integrated (that is, made subject to normal WTO principles) while two-thirds remain subject to MFA quotas. For the products still subject to quotas, the ATC specifies that the quotas must be increased every year at the rates given in Table 12.4. The textiles and clothing sector is divided into four groups: tops and yarns, fabrics, made-ups and clothing. Some items of every group must be included in the liberalization at every stage. Furthermore, the liberalization is binding and final for each WTO member (see Spinanger, 1999).

Table 12.4 The four stages of ATC liberalization

Stage	Date	Minimum volume integrated (%)	Remaining quota growth rate (%)
Stage 1	1 January 1995	16	16
Stage 2	1 January 1998	17	25
Stage 3	1 January 2002	18	27
Stage 4	1 January 2005	49	All items integrated

Source: Reinert (2000).

As Table 12.4 shows, the schedule of liberalization is heavily back-loaded with most of the liberalization happening at the very end of the ten-year transition period. There have been loud complaints that minimal liberalization has resulted from the implementation of the ATC so far, since importing countries have weighted their liberalization towards products that were not under restraint in their country, have little value added, or are of little interest to developing countries. In addition, tariffs remain high and, in some cases, importing countries have used transitional safeguards or applied anti-dumping and other WTO-legal restrictions against textiles and clothing.[3] The United States in the initial two stages has met its obligation to integrate 33% of its textiles and clothing categories into GATT in a way that has eliminated only 1% of its MFA restrictions, while the EU has eliminated 7% and Canada 14% (see Finger and Schuknecht, 2001).

Several commentators have noted that the inclination of the importing countries to leave most of the meaningful liberalization of textiles and clothing until the very end of the transition period raises concerns about the political feasibility of the implementation of the final stage – see, for example, Martin and Winters (1996) and Baughman et al. (1997). Wang and Winters (2000) suggest that developed countries should make a public and binding commitment that the MFA abolition will be made genuinely and in good faith by 2005 (that is, with no new restrictions such as frequent anti-dumping duties). They also suggest that developing countries should make clear that if its abolition is not handled in this way, there would be no case for their signing a new trade agreement.

At least in terms of aggregate economic welfare, the trade liberalization agenda on manufacturing is straightforward. Some of it requires multilateral action, but by no means all:

* honest abolition of the MFA;
* reductions in tariff peaks (especially in clothing) and tariff escalation, mainly in developed countries; and
* major reductions in developing countries' tariffs and non-tariff barriers.

12.4 Manufacturing and poverty: multilateral liberalization and poor countries

The impact of further reductions in manufacturing tariffs on poverty can be examined from two different perspectives. First, there is the potential impact of further multilateral tariff reductions on *poor countries*. And second, there is the potential impact of a domestic reduction in manufacturing tariffs on *poor groups* within a developing country. We consider each in turn.

Hertel and Martin (2000) have examined the potential gains associated with further tariff liberalization in a future round of multilateral trade negotiations based on the widely used Global Trade Analysis Project (GTAP) model of global trade (see Hertel, 1997). Their model contains 19 commodities and 28 regions, explicitly including many of the larger developing countries (India, Korea, Indonesia, Malaysia, the Philippines, Singapore and Hong Kong, Thailand, Vietnam, China, Taiwan, Mexico, Argentina, Brazil and Chile) while aggregating the remaining developing countries into regions (South Asia not including India, the rest of South America, economies in transition, the Middle East, the rest of North Africa, the South African Customs Union, sub-Saharan Africa other than SACU, and the rest of the world).

Hertel and Martin predict that a 40% cut in industrial product tariffs world-wide would generate an increase in global trade volume of US$380 billion – about 4.7% of merchandise and non-factor service trade in 1995. Most strikingly, they suggest that three-quarters of the welfare gains would accrue to developing countries (in contrast to the benefits from agriculture and services liberalization, most of which accrue to the developed countries).

These gains would primarily accrue to East and South Asian countries, with the greatest proportionate gains predicted for Vietnam, the Philippines, Singapore and Hong Kong, and China. This is because these countries have the highest tariffs and/or the largest manufacturing sectors to liberalize. In other words, the benefits arise mainly from countries' own liberalizations via the improvements in domestic resource allocation. The changes in border prices induced by liberalization – rises in export prices as partners reduce their tariffs and increases in import prices as a country reduces its own – are, on balance, much less important. This is because the effects are in general not large and because they tend to be offsetting in a multilateral liberalization.[4]

Independent of negotiated liberalization, Maizels (2000) compares the terms-of-trade of developing and developed countries trading with the United States for the period 1981–95. He suggests that developing countries suffered a marked deterioration relative to developed countries. This is mainly due to the fact that developing countries export low-tech products to the United States (compared to the high-tech products that other developed countries export), and that these are subject to constant competitive pressure as new sources of supply arise. This effect is independent of any trade liberalization and points to the need for developing country entrepreneurs to be active in seeking new products and new production techniques.

Developed countries' trade liberalization in manufactures, particularly in textiles and clothing, is likely to provide large benefits to those developing countries whose factor endowments give them a comparative advantage in the production of manufactured goods, especially if they themselves liberalize sufficiently to let their export sectors expand. This will primarily benefit countries with large and relatively well-educated labour forces. Since these include countries such as China and, potentially, India, which contain very large numbers of poor people, liberalization is likely to have an important impact in reducing the global numbers of poor people.

But countries with a comparative advantage in natural resources or with less well-educated labour forces are likely to gain less from further liberalization of manufactures. This applies to a large number of poor countries in sub-Saharan Africa, as well as some countries in Latin America.

Indeed, in cases where such countries have previously had preferential access to developed country markets, liberalization may erode such preferences. Furthermore, the quotas under the MFA forced some exporters to dispose of above-quota surpluses at low prices in other developing countries. Liberalization in developed countries may therefore raise the prices faced by developing countries that import textiles and clothing.

Thus, although further multilateral liberalization of manufactures could yield large global gains, these gains will be unevenly distributed. The likely distribution suggests that global poverty will be reduced, but some poor countries may gain little and could even lose. One response is to argue that any further liberalization should be accompanied by measures to assist developing countries that may be negatively affected to adjust accordingly. Another is to observe that if these countries themselves liberalize, and if agriculture and services are liberalized as well as manufactures, the gains will be more evenly spread.

12.5 Manufacturing and poverty: domestic liberalization and poor groups

The highest tariffs on manufactures are imposed by developing countries, and the greatest welfare gains are likely to be obtained by reducing these tariffs. But a concern with the poverty effects of liberalization might lead to a somewhat more nuanced view of the liberalization of trade in manufactures. As with other forms of liberalization, manufactures liberalization will affect poverty through its impact on the prices faced by poor households, through employment and wage effects and through government revenue and expenditure effects. In addition, it will potentially have dynamic effects via its effects on productivity. Of these, the effects on employment are probably the most significant in the short run and those on productivity in the long run.

12.5.1 Prices

The price effects of tariff reductions on manufactured goods are likely to be smaller than those of agricultural liberalization since manufactures constitute a much smaller proportion of the expenditure of poor households than food. Nonetheless, the real income effects can be important, especially when the reductions concern goods of particular importance to the poor, such as clothing and manufactured inputs to agricultural production. Household surveys and poverty profiles suggest that poor households consume both traded and non-traded (locally produced) manufactures. The price effects of liberalization will have an important positive impact when such non-traded goods are close substitutes for their traded equivalents and where the markets for each are relatively well integrated. Conversely, where local markets are poorly integrated and local goods differentiated from the goods subject to tariffs, the impact on poverty through price effects will be more muted. As noted in Chapter 4, the biggest effects will occur if manufacturing liberalization makes new goods available. When reform entails removing quantitative restrictions and prohibitions, such effects could well dominate the outcome.

12.5.2 Jobs

It is also important to understand how the characteristics of the country determine the impact of tariff liberalization. A manufacturing liberalization in isolation will tend to reduce manufacturing activity in favour of agriculture and services. If manufacturing was inefficient (because protected), this is likely to boost welfare and income, and if it was also capital-intensive, liberalization is likely to boost wages. There are also likely to be technical efficiency benefits. High levels of protection shield inefficient local industries from international competition, and a reduction in such protection will help to increase competition and force firms to improve the efficiency of their operations and to lower prices for consumers.

But if manufacturing industry is extremely inefficient by world standards, such liberalization is likely to lead to considerable job losses in the short term. This is particularly true if the enterprises had initially been state-owned, as in Eastern Europe or China. For example, in Chile, Edwards and Edwards (1996) find a positive relationship between the degree of liberalization in a sector and the probability of its (former) workers being unemployed, and that workers in those sectors that suffered greater reform tended to have longer unemployment spells.[5]

Conversely, of course, liberalization opens up new opportunities in manufacturing or elsewhere, which might permit strong poverty alleviation in the medium term. Harrison and Revenga (1998) find that in their sample, overall employment *increased* following trade liberalization in all except the transition economies (where so much else was happening).

The extent to which job losses will lead to an increase in poverty, or job gains to a reduction, depends on three factors:

The structure and importance of manufacturing industry
Clearly, the poverty effects of liberalization will depend in part on the contribution of manufacturing to the country's GDP. As Table 12.1 showed, there are large variations in this. Several East Asian countries – Malaysia, Korea and China, for example – have manufacturing shares of GDP of over 30%. At the other extreme, in sub-Saharan African countries outside the Southern African Customs Union, manufactures account for only 11% of GDP.

The structure of manufacturing industry also matters. In many developing countries, formal manufacturing-sector jobs are relatively well paid and so it is likely that the holders of such jobs will be substantially better off than people working elsewhere. Consequently, temporary unemployment among such workers may have a small impact on absolute poverty because they will have assets to cushion themselves.[6]

Conversely, in countries in which the 'typical' manufacturing employee is low-skilled and relatively poor, temporary unemployment may have a stronger direct impact on poverty. In addition, employment in different manufacturing sectors can be strongly gender biased, so that the employment and unemployment effects of liberalization can be quite different for men and women. Thus, to determine the poverty effects of liberalization, it is important to have a profile of the employees who are most likely to be adversely affected.

Labour market flexibility

Even where liberalization does result in redundancies of poor workers, the long-term impact on poverty will depend on the speed with which such workers can obtain other forms of employment and the wages they command there. Consequently, the structure and flexibility of the local labour market is a key determinant of whether a negative shock is transmitted into increased poverty. Unfortunately, there is remarkably little research on labour turnover in developing countries (see Matusz and Tarr, 1999). The evidence from developed countries suggests that adjustment is surprisingly rapid in most circumstances (see Jacobsen, 1978). If this is also true in developing countries, then transitional unemployment resulting from liberalization may not result in significant increases in poverty in the short term.

But this is by no means certain if the pre-liberalization jobs used very sector-specific skills and/or were highly protected. Rama and MacIsaac (1999) find that employees displaced from the Ecuadorian Central Bank in 1994 had regained on average only 55% of their pre-dismissal salaries after 15 months despite generally low unemployment levels. Mills and Sahn (1995) find that the average unemployment duration of Guinean public sector workers laid off in the period 1985–8, was over two years, with fully 30% of them still unemployed in 1992.[7] Thus, in determining the poverty effects of liberalization, it is important to ascertain the re-employment prospects of the affected workers.

Considering the poverty effects of long-run employment change (either positive or negative) requires information on both 'before' and 'after' wages. Winters (2000c) discusses India's early reform of manufacturing trade. This was accompanied by an increase in formal manufacturing jobs (at wages well above poverty levels), but a larger decline in informal manufacturing jobs paying 'poverty-line' wages. Winters speculates that this pattern arose because a real exchange rate depreciation of over 10% reduced activity in non-tradable manufacturing, which also happens to be concentrated in the informal sector.

The increase in formal jobs presumably reduces poverty. But whether the informal sector decline increases poverty depends on whether the unemployed obtain new informal-sector jobs at about the same wage or fall back on subsistence activities that may have paid even lower wages. Unfortunately, including in the Indian case just cited, we do not generally have such information. Box 12.4 reports further on the reform of India's

Box 12.4 Liberalization in the formal cotton sector in India

Trade liberalization has consequences for both the formal and informal sectors, but even in the formal sector, the effects on workers differ depending on the competitiveness in the industry. Kambhampanti and Howell (1998) analyse the effects of trade reform on formal-sector employment in the cotton industry in India. They find that trade reform reduced the employment in the formal sector through a reduction in the number of firms and a shift towards more capital-intensive technologies. Thus, it has reduced the number employed in the sector and, presuming that informal wages are below formal ones, hurt some of the workers. Furthermore, the reform did not affect the wages of those workers who remained, because these are determined in an institutional framework that is largely free of market forces. But the authors also find that the increased capital-intensity in the sector has improved labour conditions for the workers remaining employed, through the enhancement of health and safety conditions.

The net effect on poverty of those reforms depends on whether the losers of jobs found new ones and whether the gains to those remaining employed pulled their households out of poverty. There are no obvious answers to these questions in the study.

Source: Kambhampanti and Howell (1998).

formal cotton sector. In considering both of these examples, it is important to note that changes in manufacturing are likely to have only small effects on overall poverty rates and prevailing wages in India. Formal manufacturing employs about 1.2% of the work-force and informal manufacturing another 5–6%.

The overall reform programme
Manufacturing liberalization is rarely undertaken on its own in developing countries. Often in the past, such liberalization was undertaken as part of a comprehensive package of reforms implemented with the assistance of international donors. If this is the case, it is important to take account of how the overall impact of the reform programme may change the poverty effects of liberalization in manufactures.

Specifically, unemployment resulting from a given manufactures liberalization may have a different impact on poverty if the economy is simultaneously subject to other large negative shocks through, for example, stabilization measures. If a series of large negative shocks reduces aggregate demand sufficiently to discourage investment and labour turnover, then this may undermine the supply response in the sectors 'winning' from trade liberalization. Such traps can be important in developing countries with relatively thin markets, particularly if the initial shock has a strong impact on employment in a single locality.

A contrary problem might arise if reform fails to address serious inflexibilities in the labour market. For example, in the early 1990s, the response of Polish manufacturing to a huge devaluation was initially muted because the state-owned enterprises would not release labour (see Winters and Wang, 1994). Only when new hard budget constraints were imposed on these firms did they release the labour to newer, smaller and more dynamic firms. Preserving state-sector jobs kept people notionally off the unemployment register, but did not prevent poverty because wages were eroded (and often not paid) and employment services (such as health care) collapsed.

Given the potential poverty effects of unemployment associated with manufactures liberalization, there is a good case for increased investment in mechanisms to cushion the shocks faced by poor workers who are made redundant. In developed countries, this is achieved through unemployment insurance. But comprehensive unemployment insurance is generally not practical or affordable in developing countries. More appropriate are policies designed to assist re-entry to the work-force plus a basic safety net for those who need it.

In targeting resources at the poor, there is a balance to be struck between helping individuals who are poor because of inherent characteristics (the very young, the very old, the sick or the disabled) or because of a lack of productive assets (notably land and education), and those who are transitorily poor because of an adverse shock such as unemployment.[8] Assistance to the last category should focus on assisting unemployed workers to find alternative forms of employment. There may also be a case for programmes that help households to maintain a basic level of livelihood in the transitional period. But given that employment shocks are not necessarily the most important form of economic shock for poor households in developing countries, such programmes should be carefully designed to ensure that they reach the most vulnerable.

12.5.3 Government revenue

Another effect of manufactures liberalization on poverty comes through its impact on government revenue and expenditure. Of the estimated US$189 billion of tariff revenue collected by developing countries in 1995, US$150 billion comes from tariffs on manufactured goods, compared with US$34 billion from agriculture and US$5 billion from minerals and energy tariffs (see Hertel and Martin 1999; and McDougall et al., 1998). Manufacturing tariffs therefore represent the most important source of tariff revenue for developing countries and trade taxation accounts for a high percentage of government revenue for many of the poorest countries. So liberalization of manufactures could in principle have a negative effect on government revenues (see Deacon, 2000).

But evidence from many countries suggests that liberalization, at least in its initial stages, need not deplete revenues. Much depends on the design of the liberalization and the manner in which it is implemented. Ebrill et al. (1999) set out circumstances in which revenue is likely to be least affected by trade reform and may even increase. These are cases where:

- trade policy was initially very restrictive;
- liberalization involves measures such as replacing quantitative restrictions with equivalent or lower tariffs;
- liberalization is accompanied by measures to reduce exemptions and increase compliance; or
- liberalization takes place in a stable macroeconomic environment (see McKay et al., 2000)

The first three of these are typical characteristics of unreformed manufacturing sectors.

Finally, liberalization of manufacturing tariffs is often undertaken as part of a systematic restructuring of manufacturing industry. Such restructuring will often result in a reduction or removal of existing subsidies. While this may compound the poverty effects mentioned above, it may also release funds, which can be spent on appropriately targeted measures to cushion the negative impact of restructuring and improve the supply response to liberalization. Where subsidies have supported a small number of relatively well-paid jobs in formal manufacturing, it is likely that the redeployment of such funds to tackle poverty directly will have a much more positive impact on the poor than the original subsidies.

12.5.4 Growth

Traded manufactures include intermediate inputs and capital equipment, as well as final consumption goods. We have already described how tariffs on intermediate goods influence the effective rate of protection for final outputs, but modern theory focuses on a different aspect of intermediates. One view stresses how a plentiful and widely varied supply of intermediate goods fosters technical efficiency and higher outputs by allowing a greater degree of specialization in production. A second view argues that access to modern intermediate and capital goods is the key to technical progress, for they both embody new technology and stimulate users to find new applications.

There is evidence for both views (see Chapter 2) although it is not totally unambiguous. If they are correct, however, the most important long-run effect of manufacturing liberalization on poverty will be via its effects on growth. Frequently, the workers who make direct use of sophisticated imports will not be poor – indeed, writers such as Abramovitz and David (1996) stress the importance of workers' skills if technology is to be absorbed. But the overall growth of the economy will increase incomes in general, and the evidence suggests that this significantly helps the poor. In addition, liberalization may increase the returns to acquiring skills, which may also raise long-run incomes.

Related to the argument that manufacturing liberalization boosts growth is the impact of liberalization on productivity in the manufacturing sector itself. As discussed before, liberalization increases competition, which in turn might be expected to increase productivity. There is evidence that openness increases productivity at the sector level, although the productivity increase does not affect all the firms within the sector – see, for example, McKay et al. (2000) who summarize the evidence. Choudhri and Hakura (2000) suggest that for low-growth (traditional) manufacturing sectors, increased international trade has little or no effect on productivity growth. But this result may just reflect the experience of developed countries, since their sample includes both rich and poor countries.

12.5.5 Ensuring that liberalization of trade in manufactures is pro-poor

Although it generally improves aggregate welfare, the liberalization of manufactures is not inherently positive or negative for poverty alleviation. Thus, it is important for it to be accompanied by complementary policies to ensure that the poor obtain the maximum possible benefit. This may, of course, involve moving out or keeping out of manufacturing, but in many cases, some sub-sectors will be viable, if only to supply local markets. For these sub-sectors, especially in the poorest countries, the real issue is how to encourage the necessary improvements in manufacturing productivity and upgrading. Openness will provide the opportunity and stimulus, but may usefully be combined with domestic policies to encourage the enhancement of skills, the provision of suitable local transport and communications infrastructure, improvements in the provision of utilities and business services, flexibility in labour markets and so on (see Wood and Jordan, 2000).[9]

The need for such complementary policies does not necessarily mean that liberalization should be slow – delay is neither economically nor politically desirable in many circumstances. But it does suggest that policy-makers should think hard about who is going to be hardest hit by the liberalization of manufactures and put measures in place to protect them in the short term and enable them to switch activities in the long term. They also need to ensure that firms have the legal and technical abilities to adjust to new challenges and opportunities.

Policy-makers' thinking about the liberalization of manufactures should pay particular attention to the impact on the informal sector. The poor are often involved in informal manufacturing activities (as well as petty trading and the provision of non-traded services). The impact of manufactures liberalization on such activities will generally mirror the impact on the formal sector. On the one hand, increased unemployment resulting from redundancies in the formal sector will increase the numbers of workers in the informal sector, increasing competition and putting downward pressure on wages. On the other hand, the liberalization may provide opportunities for new informal-sector activities to provide complementary inputs and services to the sectors or consumers advantaged by the liberalization.

Again, appropriate complementary policies may help the poor working in the informal sector to gain the maximum benefit possible from the liberalization. These policies will include the facilitation of small-scale business services. In particular, one key gap between the informal and formal sectors is the 'knowledge gap': formal-sector firms typically have access to far more and far better information about their markets than informal-sector firms.

Box 12.5 illustrates the benefits of improving communication, either via the internet or by providing telephone contacts. Such improvements reduce transaction costs and therefore help to expand the domain (and therefore the size) of the market. They empower poor people to exploit their manufacturing ability better and thus offer the potential to enhance incomes significantly. Measures such as these call for greater market integration through 'internal' liberalization, suggesting that they will be the natural complement to traditional 'external' trade liberalization if the benefits of the latter are to reach the poor.

Box 12.5 Reaching the market

The World Bank (2001) gives several examples in which improving communications have transformed trade in manufactured goods:

Virtual Souk expands market access for artisans in the Middle East and North Africa

Artisans in the Middle East and North Africa have always crafted high-quality products using traditional techniques and ancestral know-how. But shrinking local markets and difficulties in gaining access to more lucrative national and international markets are leading to a gradual disappearance of culturally-rich crafts – and with them an important source of income for poor people.

The Virtual Souk is bucking this trend. Since 1997, this internet-based marketplace has been providing direct access to international markets for several hundred artisans from Egypt, Lebanon, Morocco and Tunisia, many of them women. Online sales have soared, reaching markets around the world. Through the Virtual Souk, artisans gain access to opportunities for empowerment, capacity-building and income generation.

Cellular phone technology gives bargaining power to women in Bangladesh

A subsidiary of Grameen Bank, Grameen Telecom operates a village pay-phone programme that leases cellular telephones to selected bank members, mostly women in rural areas, who use the telephone to provide services and earn money. Today, around 2,000 village pay-phones are in place. These phones have helped lower the cost of information gathering. This can be seen in lower prices for poultry feed, more stable diesel prices, and less spoilage of perishable goods due to more precise shipment dates. Women providing the phone services have gained confidence and new status as 'phone ladies'. Telephone users include both rich and poor, but poor people make more calls for economic reasons.

Sources: World Bank (2001); for Virtual Souk see www.peoplink/vsouk/; for the Grameen Telecom cellular phone programme, see Burr (2000).

But greater market integration also has risks. The better integrated the domestic economy, the greater the transmission of shocks. As vulnerability is a key component of the experience of poverty, integration may need to be complemented by measures to enhance the security of the poor, for example, health insurance, micro-credit, pension schemes, and food- and cash-for-work. The appropriate set of measures will depend on the range and nature of the shocks to which poor households are subject. The key point, however, is that liberalization should take into account the ability of poor households to cushion themselves from any resulting negative shock, without at the same time undermining the incentives to adjust.

12.6 Conclusion

Liberalizing manufactured trade is an important goal for the next round of multilateral trade talks and for countries acting unilaterally. It can clearly foster poverty alleviation by enhancing growth and productivity and by improving resource allocation. It could also, however, increase poverty among particular groups. Box 12.6 summarizes the discussion in the form of a checklist for policy-makers.

Box 12.6 **Checklist on manufacturing liberalization**

- Is your country a net gainer from textile and clothing liberalization – that is, does it have plentiful and reasonably-educated labour? Will you lose low-priced imports as the MFA is relaxed?
- Will the removal of tariff peaks and tariff escalation allow you to process goods more fully before export? Will this processing create jobs for the poor or reduce demand for unskilled labour relative to capital and more skilled workers?
- Will manufacturing trade reform reduce prices and increase the availability of goods to poor households?
- Are firms able to expand to exploit new opportunities? Do they have the technical and institutional ability to adjust to increased competition and exploit new opportunities, including for improving technology?
- Will your own liberalization squeeze domestic manufacturing? Will any contraction fall heavily on poor workers or workers who support poor families via remittances?
- Are workers in expanding sectors receiving higher incomes than they did previously? How rapidly are displaced workers likely to find new jobs? At what wages? These questions require insight into informal and rural labour markets as well as the formal manufacturing sector.
- Will liberalization increase or decrease revenue? Must any falls impinge on programmes of importance to the poor?
- Are safety nets in place for workers distressed as a result of liberalization?

Notes

1   See Winters (1991), for example, for a more detailed exposition.
2   Finger et al. (1996) also give statistics on the tariff concessions given and received in the Uruguay Round. Their figures differ a little from those reported here due to slight differences in coverage and methodology.
3   See Reinert (2000) for details on the safeguard provisions of the ATC.
4   In fact, the methods used in GTAP arguably exaggerate these terms-of-trade effects, especially for small countries.
5   Greater reform implies higher initial tariffs which, in turn, imply lower initial efficiency relative to world standards.
6   This conclusion should be treated with care since well-paid employees in developing countries can sometimes be responsible for remitting incomes to a large number of dependent friends and families. Thus, unemployment among 'relatively wealthy' workers can have strong indirect poverty effects if remittances are an important source of income for households.
7   In neither case, however, are we dealing with people who were initially very poor.
8   See Chapter 3 for an elaboration of the characteristics of the poor in developing countries, and Chapter 7 for a discussion of transitory versus chronic poverty.
9   Some potential domestic measures can be considered as industrial policy. There is a debate about the effectiveness of industrial policy and the extent to which it is constrained by the WTO – see Chapter 13.

13 Export and Domestic Subsidies

This chapter argues that:

- Subsidies provide a means of addressing market failures and hence of increasing aggregate incomes.
- But in addition to the difficulties of identifying the market failures themselves, subsidies also pose formidable administrative problems of ensuring that they are not captured by interest groups, and that international subsidy wars do not break out.
- Export subsidies will generally raise the domestic prices of the subsidized goods; production subsidies may do so according to circumstances. Their effect on poverty depends on the net consumption positions of poor households.
- Subsidies can also affect factor prices, with subsidies to industrial sectors favouring returns to capital and skilled labour over returns to the unskilled.
- The cost of financing subsidies could also have adverse effects on the poor.
- The WTO has disciplines on export and production subsidies, but they are not very strong for poor countries.
- The WTO does not prohibit subsidies for regional development, factor use or consumption, which are likely to be the most important components of a subsidy programme aimed at helping the poor.

13.1 Background

All economists recognize that markets sometimes fail. For example, some activities create 'externalities' whereby one person (or firm) is affected by another's actions other than via the market. In other cases, there are 'public goods' in the technical sense that one person's consumption does not preclude another from consuming the same unit (for example, using a piece of knowledge) and no one can be prevented from (or avoid) consuming the good (for example, clean air or loud music). These market failures mean that market outcomes are generally sub-optimal and that policy intervention could improve matters. If the problem is that a good or service is underprovided by the market, that intervention could be a subsidy, of which there are many useful examples, including the provision of defence, primary education or public health services.

Where economists agree less is over how effective governments are at identifying cases for subsidies and implementing them effectively – in other words, whether governments also fail – and if they do, the relative sizes of government and market failure. Among the potential problems are that subsidies can serve to support inefficiency rather than to increase output; that firms behave strategically (by under-investing, for example) in order to win subsidies; that subsidies can merely disguise transfers to favoured clients; and that the possibility of getting subsidies leads firms to use resources to lobby for them rather than actually producing goods.

At the international level, a further difficulty is that if one government subsidizes an industry, it could have a severe impact on competing firms in another country. This may be globally harmful if the latter is the country with true comparative advantage in the sector, but even if it is not, the subsidies induce adjustment costs there and could start a subsidy war. It is for this last reason that subsidies have fallen under the purview of the GATT and now the WTO.

The Uruguay Round Agreement on Subsidies and Countervailing Measures (ASCM) introduced much clearer rules on what constituted a subsidy and when the international community wished to constrain their use. Developing countries have found their discretion to use export and production subsidies limited by the new rules and have in some cases come to resent the changes. There have been proposals to revise the ASCM, although they have not been pressed particularly hard either by governments or by policy commentators. Nonetheless, subsidies are one of the areas in which developing country policy-makers need to consider their options as they develop negotiating positions to aid their battle against poverty.

In fact, few subsidies have had to be dismantled because of the ASCM, but the scope for new ones has been reduced. Opinions differ about whether the current regime represents a serious constraint on anti-poverty policy or a welcome respite from potentially damaging rent-seeking activity. On the one hand, subsidies can help to address market failures in developing countries and so assist both static and dynamic efficiency. On the other hand, economists are divided about whether subsidies are an important part of development policy; and even where subsidies may boost aggregate income, their distributional effects may be very regressive. Moreover, several types of subsidy, such as those on consumption, wages or regional development, remain free of international control. This chapter discusses the arguments surrounding subsidies and concludes that from a poverty perspective, there is little case for changing the rules.

13.2 The economics of subsidies

The immediate effects of subsidies are easy to describe. A subsidy increases the incentive to undertake the subsidized activity, which has effects on prices and/or quantities in related markets. The price and quantity outcomes may, in turn, have an impact on factor incomes and/or consumer welfare. And, of course, subsidies cost money.

These effects mean that subsidies shift real income around between economic agents. The contentious part of the analysis of subsidies is determining whether the sum of these changes in income is positive, that is, whether the subsidy increases overall welfare/real incomes. This hinges around whether the subsidy is curing an existing economic distortion or creating a new one. In this section, we consider the ways in which subsidies might affect the various determinants of poverty outlined in the conceptual framework developed in Chapter 4.

13.2.1 The price effects of subsidies and the possibility of WTO complaints

An export subsidy increases firms' incentives to export, and so will potentially affect both production and the allocation of goods between home and export markets. For a small country that sells at given world prices, export subsidies do not reduce export prices; rather, they divert sales from home to export markets. Firms will prefer to export rather than sell in the domestic market because the former pays a subsidy. This tends to raise the domestic prices of exportable goods because it reduces domestic supply, and may even drive them off the domestic market altogether if the export incentive is large enough. In the extreme case, in which an identical good is sold at home and abroad and there are no imports, an export subsidy in a small country will raise the domestic price by the full amount of the subsidy. If home and export goods are imperfect substitutes in production, the domestic price rises will be attenuated, but are still likely to be positive. Whether price increases help or hurt the poor depends, as ever, on whether they are net purchasers or sellers of the goods concerned.

A production subsidy to exportable goods that are sold in either the domestic or foreign market will not, in the simple case, increase domestic prices. This is because the subsidy will not change the relationship between (fixed) export prices and domestic prices. But if output increases while domestic sales do not (because their price is unchanged), exports will be higher. For a genuinely small country (a so-called 'price-taker' on world markets), these exports will have no discernible effect on any other exporter, but otherwise, it is possible that another WTO member might complain about the increase in subsidized sales. If the subsidized goods are differentiated between home and export varieties (and there are no imports), some of the subsidy is likely to be passed on to domestic consumers in terms of lower prices.

A production subsidy to domestic import-competing goods will not reduce domestic prices if identical imports continue at fixed world prices. But it will do so if goods are differentiated, and therefore not perfect substitutes, or if the subsidies are large enough to eliminate imports altogether. In these cases, some other WTO member will be losing sales and may find it worthwhile to complain.

A production subsidy to final non-traded goods is likely to reduce domestic prices somewhat and may, in developing countries, be a way of increasing the variety of goods available to consumers. Since by definition, no other WTO member is supplying these goods, such subsidies seem unlikely to attract WTO partners' interest. A production subsidy to non-traded intermediate goods might affect trade patterns, however, if it financed a reduction in the prices of traded final goods. Examples of this include subsidizing energy prices, which might make energy-intensive exports very competitive – witness EU and US concern over Russia's aluminium exports in the early 1990s.

13.2.2 Factor markets

Subsidies raise producer prices and increase the incentive to produce the subsidized good. Their resulting effects on factor prices depend on how factor markets operate. In order that a subsidy does not lead to an infinite increase in output, there needs to be at least one factor that is limited in supply and whose price rises. The extreme case is Ricardo's analysis of agricultural rent in the nineteenth century. Here, land is the fixed factor and an increase in output prices causes other, mobile factors of production to move into agriculture at their prevailing prices. The fixed factor, land, experiences an increase in return but, of course, no increase in the quantity used, while the mobile factors, including labour (particularly the unskilled) gain higher employment but no increase in wages. As we observed in Chapter 4, whether that does workers any good depends on whether they were earning the prevailing agricultural wage before moving. What we do know is that landowners (who are not usually poor) gain.

In fact, in developing countries, subsidies are paid less frequently to agriculture than to industry where, in the short run, the fixed factor is capital (possibly including human capital and intangibles such as reputation). In the longer run, the higher returns might cause capital to flow into the favoured sector, reducing its rate of return there and shifting the benefits of the subsidy towards labour in terms of either wage or employment rises. If, however, there are explicit or implicit barriers to entry in the subsidized sector (which is likely if governments are concerned to limit the financial commitment associated with their subsidy policies) the benefits will remain with incumbent capital.

Moreover, any long-run increase in the capital stock in the subsidized sectors has to come from somewhere. It will be supplied through declines in other sectors' investment or decreases in current consumption or increases in international debt. The first potential outcome highlights the general equilibrium aspects of subsidies. Unless overall employment and the capital stock increase, switching activity into one sector shifts it out of another; the net benefits of such policies depend on the relative merits of the two sectors, and the effect on factor prices depends on differences in factor intensities, as shown in Chapter 4. For example, if subsidies are used to boost 'modern' industries, which are capital- and skilled-labour-intensive, they are likely to increase profits and the skill premium and reduce unskilled wages.

13.2.3 Domestic distortions

If an economy has no market failures or distortions – in other words, if all prices reflect marginal social costs[1] and there are no constraints – the market achieves the optimum allocation of resources by itself, and subsidies reduce welfare by moving the economy away from the optimum. If, on the other hand, there are market failures, subsidies can provide a means of overcoming them and increasing welfare. Economic theory – Bhagwati (1968), for example – suggests that in this case, subsidies should be applied as close as possible to the distortion that requires a countervailing measure.

For example, suppose that an urban minimum wage reduces manufacturing employment, and hence manufacturing output, below optimum levels. Abolishing the minimum, or introducing a wage subsidy to offset its effects on employers, would correct the distortion precisely and allow other market decisions to generate optimality. A subsidy to production would increase output as desired, but since it would not affect relative factor prices, it would leave firms operating too capital-intensively and lead to the employment of more capital as well as more labour. Thus, it would be 'second-best'. A tariff on manufactured imports would have the same effects on producers as the production subsidy, but in addition, it would raise prices to consumers, adding a further unattractive distortion. It would be 'third-best'.

Similar analysis pertains to all the other allocative distortions that might exist. For example, a labour market externality whereby firms cannot reap all the benefits of the training they provide (a positive externality) should be tackled via a wage subsidy or the public provision of training. A capital market failure making it unduly difficult for firms to borrow should be tackled directly by capital policies, not output subsidies. Environmental benefits from production (such as farmers maintaining biodiversity in the countryside) should be funded directly not via higher output prices. By the same token, if exporting generates positive spillovers not available from home sales, exports should be subsidized. Thus, the case for subsidies being beneficial amounts precisely to showing that such market failures and spillovers exist and that the proposed subsidy is the best way of tackling them.

As long as factor or environmental subsidies do not impinge disproportionately on trade, they should not be considered items of trade policy and are, consequently, not subject to WTO disciplines. Export subsidies, on the other hand, clearly are – see below.

13.2.4 **Technology and growth**

The main claim made for subsidies in the context of development is the 'infant industry' argument – that subsidies facilitate learning, technology acquisition, and dynamic comparative advantage that cannot be appropriated by private agents and hence will not be paid for by any individual firm. These are just specific cases of the externalities discussed above. Commentators such as Amsden (1989) and Wade (1990) argue that interventions, including implicit or explicit subsidies, lay behind the economic 'miracles' in Korea and Taiwan, and Amsden (forthcoming) extends the argument to a much broader set of countries.

Their case is that by carefully targeted (strategic) subsidies, these governments were able to stimulate key sectors, which both became efficient in their own right and provided positive spillovers to other sectors. In other words, the government was able to provide critical co-ordination of a sort not available through merely market-generated interactions. If this is true, and if there were no alternative means of co-ordinating sectors or generating human capital, subsidies would be an important part of the long-term fight against poverty, for, as observed above, growth is probably the most important single factor behind permanent poverty reduction. Table 13.1 shows the prevalence of subsidy policies in Asian economies.

But the case for sector-specific subsidies, as opposed to general policies facilitating learning and the development of enterprise, is not unchallenged – see, for example, Krueger (1990a). Lee (1996) and Kim (2000) argue that trade-oriented interventions reduced growth and technical progress in Korea. And Panagariya (2000) observes that despite its plethora of export subsidies and incentives, India achieved strong export growth only when it liberalized its imports.

The 'anti' school focuses on the ineffectiveness of subsidies in encouraging dynamism and efficiency (subsidies can reduce rather than enhance the incentive for efficiency) and the more immediate regressive impact of supporting capital and entrepreneurs. In part, the effectiveness of subsidies depends on the ability of the government to encourage recipient firms to be efficient and dynamic through other means. This ability varies substantially from country to country, with the East Asians apparently far ahead of most others.[2] Of course, the poverty case for subsidies also depends on the ability of governments to ensure that any resulting growth is moderately pro-poor. Thus, even to their advocates, the trade-offs surrounding subsidies hinge substantially around other policies and issues of governance.

13.2.5 **Government revenue and expenditure**

The most direct cost of – and greatest discipline on – subsidy use is the money that they cost the government. Subsidies have to be financed by increased taxation or reduced expenditure elsewhere, and if raising money is costly, this increases the deadweight losses of subsidies beyond the allocative effects already discussed.

Table 13.1 Export-oriented subsidies in Asia

Type of subsidy	India	Malaysia	Bangladesh	Philippines	Thailand	Republic of Korea	Singapore	Indonesia	Hong Kong	Japan
Subsidies affecting production										
Credit subsidies	Y	Y	Y	na	Y	Y	Y	Y	Y	Y
Input subsidy	Y	Y	Y	N	Y	Y	N	Y	na	Y
R&D assistance	Y	Y	Y	Y	Y	Y	Y	Y	Y	Y
Pricing and marketing arrangements	Y	Y	Y	Y	Y	Y	N	Y	na	na
Regional assistance	Y	Y	Y	Y	Y	Y	Y	N	na	Y
Subsidies affecting exports										
Export cash subsidies	N	N	Y	Y	Y	N	N	N	N	N

Y= Yes; N= No.
Source: Singh (1996).

Moreover, in considering the poverty effects of subsidies, governments need to consider how they will be financed in order to avoid indirectly harming the poor. Sometimes, successful subsidies become less costly through time – firms start to stand on their own feet – but more often, they become more costly as the subsidized activity expands. A notable example is the EU's Common Agricultural Policy.

13.2.6 Shocks and vulnerability

Subsidies are not likely to have positive effects on long-run price and income stability, but they might help to alleviate short-term negative shocks. If world price slumps or import surges lead to major negative shocks for local firms, temporary subsidies might be an appropriate response. Before resorting to them, however, a government would need to be confident that the shock was only short-term (and most governments – in both developed and developing countries – have proved very bad at making this judgement), and they must have a good reason why private markets could not provide the safety-net. But if these conditions were met, a subsidy may avoid serious adjustment strains, including redundancy for poor workers who would then slip into poverty. If such temporary subsidies were industry-specific and disrupted trade patterns, they could lead to complaints in the WTO.

13.2.7 The problem of administering subsidies

The biggest challenge of subsidies is to control them. There are probably many cases where market failures or adverse shocks could usefully be addressed with subsidies if the government had the information necessary to identify them and the political means to reject inappropriate requests for support. But the precise outcome of an intervention often depends on things that governments cannot observe or know with certainty, and this immediately puts the policy process at the mercy of interested parties. And it is not only bribery and corruption that lead to the private capture of public policy, but also the democratic processes of information sharing, discussion and norm-creation between governments and firms.[3]

Sufficient effort might overcome the information and governance problems of subsidy policy, but it is costly. Moreover, by signalling a willingness to subsidize, a government is encouraging lobbying, and the mere act of establishing the public and private institutions necessary to examine trade interventions objectively induces a flow of requests for intervention, which absorbs labour that would be better employed otherwise. Thus, the cost side of the subsidy ledger contains not only the allocative and fiscal costs of individual subsidies, but the risk of policy bias and the costs of managing the inevitable flow of requests for support once the practice is established.

13.3 Subsidies in the Uruguay Round

The Uruguay Round's Agreement on Subsidies and Countervailing Measures (ASCM) was an innovative and far-reaching agreement on subsidies and the rights to act against them. The disciplines it imposes on a developing country depend partly on whether its GDP per head is below US$1,000 per year, loosely, whether it is classified as 'least developed'. Hence, interests in the ASCM and its renegotiation may not be uniform across all developing countries. Furthermore, the ASCM does not apply to agriculture and services.

The subsidies part of the ASCM distinguishes four groups of producer subsidies: prohibited, actionable, non-actionable specific (exempt) and non-specific. The last group covers horizontal (non-sector-specific) subsidies offered to all firms meeting certain objective criteria (such as size or number of employees), and it lies outside the scope of the ASCM; that is, non-specific subsidies are permitted under WTO law.[4] The third group, non-actionable specific subsidies, includes those for research and development (R&D), regional development or the implementation of environmental legislation. There is a requirement to consult with trading partners if they claim that such subsidies prejudice their interests, but there is explicitly no recourse to dispute settlement over them. Thus, the WTO constrains only the first two categories of subsidies.

13.3.1 Prohibited subsidies

The ASCM indicates that by the end of the transition period (2000 for developing countries and 2003 for least-developed countries) subsidies conditional on export performance (export subsidies) or on using domestic rather than imported inputs (domestic input subsidies) will be prohibited for developed and developing countries. For the least-developed countries, export subsidies will still be permitted, subject to a test that a country does not account for more than 3.25% of world trade in the subsidized commodity. It is open to any developing country to request WTO permission to maintain a pre-existing subsidy beyond the transition period, but not to introduce new ones under such dispensations.

Prohibited subsidies can be the subject of complaints to the WTO and its subsequent dispute settlement procedure, which can call on countries to dismantle them. There is no requirement on the part of the complainant to prove that it is injured by the subsidy, and until the subsidy is removed, the complainant can presumably impose a countervailing duty (subject to its legal processes for introducing such duties, which usually require the proof of injury). But countervailing action is not permitted if either:

- the target country accounts for less than 4% of the complainant's imports of the good in question *and* developing countries with shares below 4% account for less than 9% collectively; or
- the subsidy is below 2% of the value of the product (the *de minimis* condition).

One of the strengths of the ASCM is its clarity about what constitutes a prohibited export subsidy. In addition to the obvious cash transfers, its illustrative list contains currency retention schemes that offer a bonus to exports, rebating direct taxes, excessive remission of indirect taxes on inputs, and subsidizing inputs. This list leaves little doubt that subsidies are interpreted pretty strictly.

13.3.2 Actionable subsidies

All remaining specific subsidies are actionable by countervailing duties including, in principle, subsidies on non-traded goods. Imposing countervailing duties on exports from developing countries requires the complainant country to prove:

- serious prejudice to their interests;
- the 'nullification or impairment' of its benefits under the WTO;[5] or
- injury.

Serious prejudice is sufficient to justify action only for subsidies exceeding 5% of value, for debt write-offs and when governments cover operating losses (other than as a one-off case for social reasons). It can include cases where the complainant feels that it has lost exports as a result of the subsidy – either to the subsidizing country or another. For all other subsidies, 'impairment' can be claimed to arise only on exports to the subsidizing country and 'injury' can only be claimed from damage done by exports from the subsidizing country. Actions are governed by the same market share and *de minimis* rules as prohibited subsidies.

13.3.3 Consumption and factor subsidies

Finally, consumption subsidies that are applied even-handedly to domestic and imported supplies are not restricted by the WTO rules, provided that they are not specified in such a way as to be obviously discriminatory and they do not affect the prices of tradable goods in a significant way. Thus, for example, food subsidies, household energy subsidies or health and education programmes are not vulnerable to action.[6]

Similarly, factor use subsidies – for example, to the wages of workers taken directly off the unemployment register – are not covered by the ASCM, unless they are configured in ways that make them *de facto* subsidies to specific sectors. In the latter case, a nullification complaint could be registered.

13.4 Possible negotiating issues

Reform of the ASCM is not particularly high on most countries' agenda for the next round of trade negotiations, possibly because they recognize the small probabilities of achieving movement. Broadly speaking, developed countries wish to tighten up on the disciplines, while developing countries seek to relax them in order to allow a wider range of interventions. Among the proposals from the latter are:

- permitting export subsidies in developing countries by making them non-actionable or via the relaxation of the *de minimis* or export competitiveness thresholds;
- prohibiting all developed country subsidies while permitting more or less all developing country ones (see UNCTAD, 1999a);
- including certain horizontal subsidies under the ASCM, making some currently permissible ones actionable (such as R&D and environmental subsidies), and some currently actionable ones permissible (for example, those to foster economic diversification and to permit more generous tax and tariff rebate schemes);
- allowing complementary measures like export credit and insurance schemes below market rates, concessional tax and duty provisions and export-processing zones (see Bora et al., 2000); and
- allowing more favourable rules for graduation (and its reverse) around the US$1,000 GDP per head limit.

It is interesting that among academics, even advocates of activist policies argue that the current WTO rules leave enough scope for what they consider to be satisfactory policy mixes (see Lall, 1999; and Amsden, 2000). Thus, they do not appear to press for relaxation of the rules, but rather see the issue in terms of avoiding refinements to the rules that would preclude policies that were potentially beneficial. Amsden (2000), for example, argues that constraints on regional, environmental and R&D subsidies would be adversely constraining. Similarly, if horizontal (non-sector-specific) subsidies, such as those to small firms and general training programmes, were constrained, many people would believe that development programmes would suffer. So even though such subsidies generally accrue directly to the non-poor, such commentators see them as long-term contributors to poverty alleviation. Indeed, if 'subsidy' were interpreted so widely as to incorporate any government intervention that costs money and benefits firms, most economists would accept that a complete ban would be harmful.

Thus, the ASCM has a number of 'loopholes', which may allow developing countries to apply industrial policy measures. But they can be used by developed countries as well. Thus, for developing countries, the possibility of subsidy competitions (war) in these areas might appear to reduce their value. And even if developed countries forgo certain subsidies, there is still scope for competition among developing countries.

<u>13.5</u> Subsidies and poverty

Changes in subsidy rules will have *direct* effects when they change the treatment of particular goods by developing country governments. They may possibly also have *systemic* effects, changing those countries' policy regimes and private sector behaviour. In addition, developing countries may be affected by *trade* effects arising from changes in the supply of subsidized imports or competing exports from other countries.

These three components need to be considered separately. Governments that actively pursue changes in the subsidy rules presumably have in mind changes in their treatment of at least some goods and thus must consider the direct effects. Other governments may have no such intentions, but will still need to consider trade effects and, unless they have credible domestic constraints preventing their exploiting all the room (rope?) that the WTO permits them, systemic effects.

13.5.1 Direct effects

Price effects

As noted in section 13.2.1, subsidies may raise, lower or leave unchanged the prices faced by domestic residents for particular goods and services. The prohibited classes – export and local input subsidies – will raise domestic prices and have adverse effects on domestic consumers/users. Hence, unless the subsidized goods are produced in significant amounts by the poor, such subsidies are likely to worsen poverty. Thus, negotiators need to know which set of circumstances will apply to particular goods and poor households' net supply positions for those goods. As always, the latter are likely to vary both geographically – perhaps on the basis of rural/urban differences – and in other dimensions as well. When considering local input subsidies, it should also be remembered that if the final goods are sold on markets in which prices are fixed by competition from identical traded goods, the subsidies will not be passed on to consumers/users of those goods, and so there will be no offsetting consumer benefits there.

Subsidies to all inputs of a kind (that is, regardless of their origin) are potentially actionable rather than prohibited under WTO. They can be useful anti-poverty tools if the input markets are badly flawed, as is sometimes claimed of those for agricultural inputs used by poor farmers. It is worth recording, however, that such input subsidies are frequently associated with constraints on the selling prices of the final goods, and experience suggests that farmers would often be better off if the whole package were scrapped. Hence, provided that care is taken to ensure that the subsidies and final price restrictions are lifted together, constraints on the use of subsidies might shift policy to a better stance.

Subsidies to non-traded local final goods may reduce consumer prices (while raising producer prices) and increase the availability of goods; thus, they could also be useful in tackling poverty. As noted above, they are currently unlikely to be targeted by partners' actions under WTO rules; their discipline is largely a domestic matter, and should not be made subject to deeper disciplines in any future negotiations. Production subsidies to traded goods, on the other hand, are likely to have smaller positive effects and are, anyway, already candidates for countervailing measures from trading partners.

Factor market effects

To the extent that they increase the returns to an activity, subsidies will increase the demand for the factors that undertake it. Given that in developing countries, subsidies accrue more to industry than to agriculture, the direct benefits are more likely to accrue to capital, and possibly skilled labour, than to the unskilled labour that is of most relevance to poverty. If capital is fixed and the subsidized production is capital-intensive, then real wages may actually fall. If on the other hand, labour markets are segmented and manufacturing wages determined exogenously, the poor may reap some benefit from industrial subsidies in terms of increased employment in manufacturing at above-poverty wages. The balance of these effects will vary from case to case, depending not only on the features of the subsidized sector, but also on those from which it bids away resources and on how the subsidy is financed. There is certainly no presumption that subsidies are pro-poor in this allocative, static, sense.

Revenue and dynamics

Subsidy programmes are likely to have serious revenue implications and the method of their finance is likely to have a major impact on their poverty implications. Thus, for example, Ravallion and Van de Walle (1991) find that changing the financing assumptions reverses conclusions about the poverty effects of Indonesian rice reforms. In particular, reducing rice subsidies benefits the poor if the fiscal savings are redistributed to consumers in terms of an equal payment per person, but not if the redistribution is less progressive.

On the dynamic effects of subsidies, opinions differ, as noted above. Quite clearly, if subsidies successfully address learning or capital market issues, they will eventually have pro-poor effects via economic growth. Nearly all economists would agree that there is scope to correct market failures in developing countries, but whether governments would be able actually to achieve this through the sort of policies that are currently discouraged by the ASCM is moot. A specific case probably needs to be made that this is so.

Adjustment: compensating and complementary policies

If future trade negotiations introduced changes to the subsidy rules that required a further dismantling of existing subsidies, they would have to allow reasonable adjustment periods. To avoid severe short-term adjustment strains, governments should make full use of these by starting to adjust early and announcing the inevitability of the subsidies disappearing. For subsidies subject to unfavourable dispute settlement rulings or countervailing duties, adjustment may need to be faster, but even here developing countries may be able to negotiate reasonable periods. If not, direct compensatory policies for the adversely affected poor may be warranted.

Attention also needs to be paid to the possibility that markets are completely undermined by the changes. This was the case in Zambia's reform of maize marketing in the early 1990s. The private trading firms that replaced the state marketing board discontinued the implicit subsidies to remote areas entailed in pan-national pricing, and just ceased to purchase from such areas, causing considerable hardship (see Chapter 9; and Winters, 2000c). Merely removing a subsidy without changing institutions so dramatically is much less likely to generate such nasty surprises, but the possibility still needs to be guarded against.

13.5.2 Systemic effects

The dangers of a 'subsidies culture' arising from too relaxed an attitude towards subsidies has already been discussed. Such systemic effects can only serve to hurt the poor, for in any tacit political dealings, they are at a huge disadvantage relative to other players.

The same applies, although for different reasons, on a global scale. The WTO prohibition on export subsidies is a means of avoiding subsidy competition between governments. Such competitions would not only lead to the transfer of rents to powerful companies that can play governments off against each other, but they would almost certainly harm poorer countries, which could not afford large stakes. Thus, even if there appear to be direct benefits from individual subsidies, developing country governments are beneficiaries of general prohibitions because the global systemic effects would be so disastrous for them. In summary, while subsidies might appear to be a useful tool for addressing some short-term poverty problems, the long-run systemic problems associated with unrestricted subsidization count very strongly against them.

13.5.3 Trade effects: developed country subsidies

The opposite side of the subsidy coin is the supply of subsidized imports to developing countries. In pure theory, cheaper imports are advantageous and so any constraints on other countries' subsidies would be costly. If, on the other hand, subsidies increase the fluctuations in import prices or import availability, or if they exacerbate market failures in areas such as learning or achieving economies of scale by domestic producers, constraints would be welcome. How these effects impinge on poor households depends, of course, on the factors discussed in Chapter 4 and, by reversing their signs, we can see how using countervailing duties to offset them will affect the poor.

OECD countries do not generally subsidize their exports or production very heavily and so this is not an issue that requires general attention by developing country policy-makers. But it is important in particular cases. The most notable of these is agriculture, which we considered in Chapter 9. But it is also potentially relevant in products such as coal, steel and shipbuilding. These industrial sectors are of export relevance to some developing countries, but they are probably not of great significance for poverty, because they are neither heavy users of unskilled labour nor big budget items for the poor.

13.5.4 **Administering anti-subsidy policies**

Developing countries are almost certainly net beneficiaries of a set of simple and clear rules for subsidies, coupled with semi-automatic and *prima facie* remedies. Allowing more subsidies and relying on domestic investigation to eliminate undesirable ones may look desirable from an exporting point of view. But a systemic effect of such an approach would be that developing countries would have to establish domestic procedures to deal with allegedly subsidized imports. The WTO rules are long on procedure, and hence rather costly; if success in WTO dispute settlement relies on procedural correctness, the need for care and resources is redoubled. The cost of creating the means to pursue countervailing or anti-dumping duties is not only the cost of the establishment, but the fact that its existence will tend to invite a stream of requests for protection, which will also absorb resources in the private sector.

Even on the export side, discretion or a lack of clarity is costly; defending subsidy actions in the WTO is very demanding of official time, as well as of pure cash, and so the clearer are the lines *ex ante*, the less likely are such costs to be incurred. Extracting skilled manpower from the economy to staff bureaucratic exercises is equivalent to reducing the set of factors available for unskilled – poor – workers to work with. Thus, even putting aside the diversion of official attention from pro-poor policies such as welfare and education programmes, it is likely to reduce the unskilled wage.

13.6 **Conclusion**

That governments need to intervene in economies to correct market failures is not disputed. Indeed, the Uruguay Round explicitly recognizes a role for subsidies in developing countries. So a WTO rule that prohibited intervention would clearly be quite inappropriate. What is less clear is what subset of subsidies might best be subject to WTO attention. On the one hand, subsidies can help to offset market failures arising from learning, credit and reputation effects and over the adoption of technology. On the other hand, these problems are often better addressed by other more general means, and it is difficult for governments to distinguish between good and bad cases for intervention. Thus, even recognizing that markets are failing, permitting such subsidies might ultimately be counterproductive, especially given the calls on skilled manpower that they make. Moreover, even if subsidies are welfare-improving overall, there is real uncertainty about whether they will be pro-poor, especially in the short term.

There is thus a rather weak poverty case for pressing for a relaxation of subsidy disciplines for developing countries. Rather, governments need to seek other solutions for the market failures they have, including possibly making use of the scope that the WTO still permits for non-specific production subsidies, for certain specific subsidies and for consumption subsidies.

At the same time, there is not much of a case for tightening current disciplines. The Uruguay Round regime precludes almost all cases where developing country subsidies could cause material injury to developed country exports or import-competing interests, and prevents the worst of the damage that countries could do to themselves by the careless use of subsidies. Further tightening would possibly close off avenues for useful intervention by governments that can administer subsidies well, and would unduly constrain domestic policy. This is certainly not an argument for unrestrained subsidization within the current limits. But it does recognize that on occasions, governments need to intervene to overcome market failures or address critical distributional issues. A far more productive focus for negotiation efforts would be to introduce the disciplines of the ASCM into the agricultural arena, where developed country subsidies do far more direct harm to the poor.

Box 13.1 **Checklist on subsidies**

- Will subsidies (or their elimination) raise or lower consumer prices? What are poor households' consumption levels for those goods?
- How will subsidies affect producer prices? Will the changes be transmitted to factors of interest to the poor, especially unskilled labour? In many cases, the benefits will accrue to owners of land and capital and skilled workers.
- If subsidies were permitted, could you distinguish good from bad cases for subsidies? Could you enforce performance conditions on recipients of subsidies?
- Where subsidies have anti-poverty objectives, why are production or export subsidies preferable to consumption or factor subsidies?
- Are there more direct ways than subsidies of tackling market failures?
- Can subsidies be financed in a pro-poor fashion?
- Could you survive a subsidy war?

Notes

1   The marginal social cost represents the real cost for society of producing an extra unit of output. It can be different from the private marginal cost because it includes the positive and negative effects that production imposes on society. For example, in the case of an activity that pollutes a river, the private cost will not include the cost for society of pollution, while the social cost will include both the cost of production and the cost from polluting.
2   Amsden argues that this ability is the key to successful policy intervention.
3   Witness the prominent role of the private sector in the formation of US trade policy, fostered substantially by the requirement that the Administration consult the private sector widely on all negotiations.
4   Subject to a requirement that the criteria and the administration of such subsidies do

not reintroduce *de facto* specificity by focusing the assistance on particular firms or activities.

5   This means that benefits that it reasonably expected from a liberalization negotiated under WTO were frustrated by the subsidy. The replacement of a prohibitive tariff by a subsidy designed to keep imports out would be an impairment of the benefits expected from the tariff reduction and so would be actionable even in the absence of imports. This would not be true, however, of the *maintenance* of a pre-existing subsidy as tariffs came down.

6   Health and education policies might be affected by bindings under the GATS, but that has no subsidies chapter at present – see Chapter 11.

14 Anti-dumping

This chapter argues that:

- Anti-dumping duties (ADDs) are ordinary protection with a great public relations programme.
- When developing country exports are hit with ADDs, exporters suffer; when the exporters voluntarily increase their prices to head off the threat of ADDs, they may or may not suffer, but their workers almost certainly will. Whether these workers are poor or not varies, of course.
- The ease with which developed countries can impose ADDs has a deterrent effect on developing country exports well beyond the set of exports that actually face them.
- Unfortunately, it is unlikely that WTO negotiations will reduce the use of ADDs in the near future.
- Developing countries are starting to use ADDs more frequently and their effects are generally damaging for the poor.
- ADDs favour profits over wages and the jobs they preserve are unlikely to involve the poor. The price increases they induce, on the other hand, are more likely to hurt the poor. By absorbing skilled labour (both public and private), anti-dumping regimes reduce the productivity and wages of unskilled labour.
- Developing country ADDs are unlikely to put pressure on developed countries to negotiate on their ADDs.

14.1 Background

Price discrimination among markets within a country is a normal commercial practice. It is not necessarily harmful and should be subject to policy intervention only if its effect is predatory, that is, if it is intended to undermine competing firms and then create a dominant position. Between

292

countries, however, price discrimination, in which export prices fall below the prices of the same goods sold in the home market, is termed 'dumping'. This practice has been subject to policy restraint on criteria that allow much more intervention than in domestic markets, for at least 100 years.[1] Moreover, in recent years, the benchmark against which the export price is compared has been broadened – from the home price in the exporting country to so-called 'normal value', which can also be based on production costs. This further extends the reach of anti-dumping policy. Current practice, validated in the Uruguay Round Agreement on Anti-Dumping, is that 'if an enterprise is found to be dumping its products and if such dumping is causing injury to the domestic industry in the importing country, the importing WTO Member can impose a countervailing [anti-dumping] duty on the imports up to the maximum extent of the margin of dumping' (see Lal Das, 1999).

The first step in the establishment of an anti-dumping duty (ADD) is a complaint about dumping by a domestic industry to its government. The government then investigates the claim and grants protection if it is persuaded both that dumping is taking place and that the dumping is causing 'injury'. The 'margin of dumping' (roughly the extent to which dumping price falls below 'normal value') and the 'injury margin' (the price increase that would eliminate injury) must be calculated and, either singly or jointly, they determine the ADDs that must be levied. As documented by a number of researchers – Finger (1993), for example – the rules for calculating these margins have gradually been relaxed to such an extent that ADDs are now applied far more frequently than economic analysis suggests is warranted.

In fact, ADDs have proliferated in the last 30 years to such an extent that that they have become the preferred means of legalized emergency protection in developed countries. Between 1987–97, there were 2,196 anti-dumping investigations – 391 of which were initiated by the United States, 383 by Australia, 355 by the EU, and 188 by Canada (see Tharakan, 1999). But while the main users of anti-dumping measures have been the developed countries, their usage by developing countries has increased dramatically during the 1990s, particularly in Mexico (which initiated 188 investigations between 1987–97), Argentina (123), Brazil (97), South Africa (88), India (55) and Korea (53).

14.2 The economics of anti-dumping

Predatory pricing occurs when an enterprise sells a good at below marginal cost in order to eliminate competition and gain monopolistic power to raise prices. It is widely recognized as being anti-competitive and thus potentially welfare-reducing, and all extant domestic competition policies make provision to act against it. By the same token, international predation should be actionable, although the number of cases in which a single firm, or even all the firms in a single country, can squeeze all the competition out of the world market is likely to be very limited. International predation does not, however, justify current anti-dumping practice, because it would be possible to use domestic competition law to counter it.

In practice, predation appears to be very rare. The US law of 1916, which permits triple damages for dumping if predation can be proved, has been used only once and then unsuccessfully. Bourgeois and Messerlin (1998) suggest that even the most generous interpretation would find signs of predation in just 2% of EU anti-dumping cases over the period 1980–97. Thus, the fact that import prices are lower than domestic prices is almost always due to the competitiveness of foreign industry rather than to predatory pricing. To apply ADDs in these cases is essentially to resort to ordinary tariffs, penalizing competitive foreign industries with a view to protecting domestic producers at the expense of consumers. (Tariffs raise the prices of imports, allowing domestic suppliers to raise their prices and hence transferring income from domestic consumers/users to less competitive domestic producers, and causing an overall national economic loss.)

The UK National Consumer Council estimates that in 1990, EU ADDs on consumer electronic goods cost consumers £1,170 million – roughly 5% of total (projected) consumer expenditure on electronic goods (see Grimwade, 1996). The US International Trade Commission (1995) estimates that in 1991, the total economic losses associated with US ADDs and 'countervailing duties' (duties designed to offset foreign subsidies) were about US$1.5 billion. These ADDs and countervailing duties covered approximately US$9 billion of imports. But as we argue below, the real effect of ADDs is their deterrent effect, of which we have no estimates other than that it must certainly exceed these direct effects.

ADDs can be used like ordinary protection to address domestic firms' difficulties with competitive imports because the tests for determining the presence of dumping and injury are so forgiving that they can be satisfied in huge numbers of cases. In this regard, the Uruguay Round Agreement on Anti-dumping (strictly the 'Agreement on the Interpretation of Article VI of the GATT') was less than constructive, because it explicitly validated a number of biases in procedure that had previously been used but were of doubtful legality. This matters because importing governments that are unsure of their ground legally are likely to prosecute cases less vigorously and to accept less draconian settlements than are confident ones.

Among the practices permitted by the WTO are:

- the construction of 'normal value' where the exporter's domestic price data are unavailable or held to be unreliable;
- the use of artificially high profit margins in such 'normal value' calculations;
- a very broad definition of injury; and
- the use of 'best available information' on exporters' costs if real data cannot be provided on the very tight deadlines permitted. ('Best available' typically means as provided by the complaining domestic firm, which is hardly likely to be a disinterested source.)

Anti-dumping has two subtle features that greatly increase its cost. First, a substantial amount of evidence shows that the mere act of investigating a claim of dumping significantly reduces imports. In other words, even firms that are subsequently found not to have been dumping respond to the case by reducing exports, as do firms from other countries supplying the same goods. What makes this worse is the fact that obtaining anti-dumping protection is relatively straightforward, at least in particular sectors such as bulk chemicals and steel. This means that the mere existence of the anti-dumping law will have a trade-reducing (and hence an investment-reducing) effect: exporters will not aggressively seek markets and will thus forgo opportunities for investment and sales because they fear that success will just be met by restriction.

Second, the threat of an anti-dumping action ending with ADDs can provide leverage on an exporter to make a commitment that it will not export below a minimum price. Accepting such commitments is a legal way of suspending an anti-dumping investigation, and it is extremely attractive to everyone except domestic consumers. Instead of having their exports taxed at the border, exporters essentially tax them themselves and keep the revenue. For domestic firms, competition is mitigated, which was the purpose of the anti-dumping action in the first place. And for the importing government, the fact that exporters share the benefits of the higher price paid by consumers makes them far less likely to oppose the imposition of trade restrictions.

ADDs have other attractions too (see Finger, 1996):

- Unlike other WTO-legal measures, they permit discriminatory action – indeed, an almost infinite degree of discrimination is possible, since, in principle, a good could be taxed differently for every plant of the same firm (see Messerlin and Reed, 1995). This is very important politically: firms and governments can pick off competition from politically weak countries or from new suppliers threatening established trade links without discomforting powerful partners.
- In practice, the 'injury test', which determines whether a domestic firm has been hurt by the imports, is softer than that for other kinds of contingent protection (such as safeguards under Article XIX of the GATT).
- The rhetoric of foreign unfairness is a vehicle for building a political case for protection. Finger (1993) describes anti-dumping as 'ordinary protection with a great public relations program'.
- Unlike safeguards, ADDs require no compensation to be made to the adversely affected trading partner. This is perhaps the most important attraction of ADDs from the perspective of importing countries.

Anti-dumping measures are applied unevenly. They show quite a strong correlation with the exporting firm's degree of competitiveness; they are concentrated in 'sunset' industries;[2] and they are more commonly used against countries that are held either to have non-market economies or which are not members of the WTO (see Ehrenhaft et al., 1997). Moreover, they seem to be influenced by currency fluctuations and the business cycle:

according to Knetter and Prusa (2000), the number of anti-dumping complaints in Australia, Canada, the EU and the United States rises during periods of exchange rate appreciation (when import prices fall) and reductions in GDP growth (when the economy is in recession). Table 14.1 gives the country and sectoral breakdown of EU anti-dumping activity over 1980–97.

In some cases, firms in developed countries can escape the worst effects of ADDs by investing directly in the taxing country, thus keeping or even increasing their market share – see Box 14.1 on the Kodak–Fuji rivalry. But firms in developing countries will not generally have enough resources to invest in other countries, and therefore will tend to suffer more from the restrictions.[3]

Given the powerful economic arguments against the use of ADDs, explanations of their proliferation have focused on political economy dimensions. Concentrated industry lobby groups are more effective in putting across their arguments to importing governments than are dispersed

Table 14.1 EU anti-dumping cases by target country and sector, 1980–97

Target country	No. of cases
OECD	194
Asian 'tigers'	74
Eastern Europe	184
China	69
Other developing countries	135
Total	*656*
Of which Main sectors (by ISIC)	
351 Inorganic chemicals	205
371 Iron and steel	85
383 Electrical machines	81
321 Textiles	64
383 Non-electrical machines	41

Source: Bourgeois and Messerlin (1998).

Box 14.1 An example of tariff-jumping foreign direct investment (FDI)

In 1993, Eastman Kodak made an anti-dumping complaint in the United States against imports of photographic paper coming from Fuji Photo Film in Japan and the Netherlands. Kodak claimed that it was being injured by Fuji's 300% dumping margin. The claim led to a suspension agreement by which Fuji 'voluntarily' reduced its exports to the United States substantially. But the anti-dumping agreement also seems to have led Fuji to invest in the United States, creating a plant in 1996. Less than a year later, Fuji had the largest share in the US market.

Source: Blonigen (2000).

consumer organizations. Furthermore, protectionist lobbies tend to argue that dumping practices are destroying domestic industry and local employment, and very often public opinion is sympathetic to this argument. Consequently, consumer organizations are reluctant to campaign strongly on such issues for fear of being seen to favour foreign producers over domestic employment.

14.3 Anti-dumping today

Anti-dumping was one of the most contentious issues during the Uruguay Round, and the resulting Agreement arguably one of the least liberal. Since then, complaints have continued to be voiced by the victims of ADDs and by the majority of commentators. But far from declining, the use of ADDs has spread to developing countries. While many governments would like to see further international restrictions on the use of ADDs, most recognize that it is politically implausible to expect much progress in the near term.

14.3.1 The Uruguay Round Agreement on Anti-Dumping

The Uruguay Round Agreement on Anti-dumping modified the existing rules on anti-dumping in both a procedural and substantive fashion. The Agreement made procedures more formal and demanding, partly in the interests of transparency and partly to reduce the discretion that governments had to manipulate the process, to either raise or lower the chances of imposing ADDs. In principle, these procedural requirements can be exploited by firms on both sides of an anti-dumping investigation. But in practice, they have two potentially adverse effects for developing countries:

- First, as victims of anti-dumping suits, they need to devote similar resources to the procedural game as do the plaintiffs, who are normally large companies from developed countries.
- Second, if they become more frequent users of ADDs themselves, they will be required to devote substantial public resources to the process, especially since violations of procedure can be used to get the WTO to strike down ADDs in dispute settlement.

The cost of anti-dumping (including its economic costs) may discourage developing countries from using ADDs more widely, which would be all to the good. Just as likely, however, given the huge political attractions of anti-dumping, is that it will just entail the expenditure of more resources on policies that almost invariably harm developing country economies and their poor.

The main measures on anti-dumping agreed in the Uruguay Round and hence currently applicable under the WTO are:

- Clearer, but arguably looser, rules for calculating margins, including specifying when constructed values can be used.
- Exhortation to compare prices fairly (for example, by using the same

method to average domestic and export prices), but with permission not to do so if a justification is offered.

- An anti-dumping case has to be terminated if the margin of dumping is less than 2% or if the exporter's share of imports is less than 3%.
- Cumulating imports from more than one country in order to determine injury is subject to tighter conditions. (Cumulation facilitates the finding of injury because it permits the importing country to add together imports from several sources in order to show the pressure on its industry.)
- ADDs must be terminated after no more than five years unless a review shows that such termination would lead to the resumption of the dumping behaviour. But there is no time limit on such reviews.
- The WTO's dispute settlement arm will handle dispute settlement on ADDs, but only in an attenuated way (see Lal Das, 1999). In all other subjects in the WTO Agreements, the panel is expected to 'make an objective assessment of the matter before it, including an objective assessment of the facts of the case and the applicability of and conformity with the relevant covered agreements' (Article 11 of the Dispute Settlement Understanding). But for anti-dumping, the panel is restricted solely to determining whether the national authorities of the country imposing the anti-dumping measure established the facts properly and whether they evaluated the facts in an unbiased and objective manner. If they did, then the decision of the national authority may not be overturned, even if the panel disagrees with it.

Finger (1996) concludes that the Uruguay Round represents a victory for the users of anti-dumping, not the victims, and since the conclusion of the Round, we have seen a huge proliferation in anti-dumping law. Most developing countries now have anti-dumping laws, whereas ten years ago they did not. We have also seen the spread of the actual use of ADDs to developing countries, with certain middle-income countries becoming major users. The Uruguay Round has done nothing to discourage the use of ADDs in developed countries, and in any future downturn in economic activity, we can expect to see their use pick up again to historical levels.

14.3.2 Prospects for limiting anti-dumping

The case for negotiating a rollback of ADDs, limiting them to the most egregious cases, is overwhelming economically. But it is widely recognized that the United States is unwilling to contemplate changes to the present regime.[4] Indeed, during the late 1990s, the United States went to considerable lengths to avoid any discussion of anti-dumping in the WTO, even under the heading of competition policy, which is, after all, the locus for the only respectable case for anti-dumping policy. Neither does the EU wish to raise this issue, although it has not been as adamant. Overall, therefore, the chances of serious negotiations on this topic are small.

One issue that should be considered, however, is whether the proliferation of ADDs makes sense for developing countries. Economically, it does not, but it has been argued that proliferation may be a way of bringing the developed countries to the negotiating table. On the whole, this stratagem seems likely to backfire. One view of anti-dumping is that it is a way of governments enforcing tacit private arrangements to keep prices up. It is thus a tool to favour firms over consumers, and the firms involved (who basically call the tune) are not particularly bothered whether enforcement is by developed or developing country governments. Moreover, the major developed countries have plenty of ways of countering small developing countries' anti-dumping actions that they do not like and they are, in any case, likely to be little affected by them.

Thus, outside the few large developing economies, ADDs are likely to confer very little negotiating power on developing countries. On the other hand, ADDs impose high costs on consumers and the economy as a whole in developing countries, and use up scarce administrative resources. They are almost certainly bad for the poor.

There is no question that slipping into an anti-dumping war in which developed and developing countries both escalated their use of ADDs to discipline the other would be wholly destructive. The present anti-dumping regime casts a long shadow of deterrence over much potential trade. But if the process showed signs of breaking out of its current bounds in terms of sectors and procedures to justify ADDs, that shadow would lengthen considerably.

Article 15 of the Agreement on Anti-dumping states that developed countries must give special consideration to developing countries when considering ADDs. But to date, the Article has not been translated into a more constructive approach by developed countries. Nevertheless, it could be a starting point for future negotiations to create clear limits on the use of ADDs against developing countries.

14.4 Anti-dumping and poverty

14.4.1 Developed countries' anti-dumping actions

Anti-dumping actions limit the access of developing countries to developed country markets, especially in products where poor countries are most competitive. For this reason, stronger restrictions on the use of anti-dumping policies in developed countries would boost industrialization and employment creation in developing countries. Moreover, as noted above, the extent of the benefit far exceeds the current rather small proportion of trade that is actually subject to ADDs.

There is an argument that compared to other forms of emergency protection, anti-dumping allows exporters to reap a higher share of the rents created because it is normally sympathetic to self-imposed export price increases. This may be true if the protection is inevitable, but it ignores the fact that anti-dumping is so comfortable a policy that its existence encourages more rather than less protection. Moreover, while it may be the case that increasing export prices while freezing or reducing quantities increases income flows, it is no recipe for market development. The rents created encourage corruption – or at least managed trade – and almost certainly do not filter through to the workers, poor or not. The restrictions on quantities prevent the expansion of competitive sectors and hence tend to curtail the earnings or employment of the abundant factors of production, including unskilled labour.

14.4.2 Developing countries' anti-dumping actions

When developing countries use anti-dumping procedures, the effect on poverty is still more direct. ADDs will almost always sharply increase domestic prices ; and the resulting effects on poverty will depend on the extent to which the poor consume the good in question, their ability to purchase substitutes, and the extent of competition in the domestic market.

It is possible that the poor could have a production interest in the goods protected by ADDs, but on the whole the industries where ADDs are most prevalent are not those that use high proportions of unskilled labour in developing countries. In addition, anti-dumping will absorb skilled administrative labour in what is a socially non-productive activity, and not only in the government but also within the private sector, as firms seek to prepare watertight cases for protection. As noted in Chapter 13, such absorption reduces the real wage of other factors of production, specifically unskilled labour.

It needs to be asked whether ADDs could ever be useful in preventing short-term adjustment strains for fundamentally sound industries, that is, whether ADDs could be a useful emergency measure. The answer is 'no'. This is not because short-term protection against import surges is never warranted (although it is warranted less often than many governments claim) but because, relative to other approaches to emergency protection such as safeguards, anti-dumping is inefficient. It encourages discrimination (and so fosters buying from more rather than less expensive suppliers) and it fosters artificial increases in import prices. Moreover, it is attractive to firms and bureaucracies and is thus likely to generate a more active protection policy than other measures would. So even on this score, ADDs have very little to offer developing countries or their poor.

An important area where developing countries might impose ADDs and countervailing duties is agriculture. Developed countries are selling food at prices below cost and this can certainly injure domestic farmers. As Chapter 9 demonstrated, the impact of such duties on the poor is ambiguous depending, *inter alia*, on whether the country is a net food importer or exporter, and the net consumption positions of the poor. But agriculture is governed by the Agreement on Agriculture (AoA) rather than the Agreement on Anti-dumping and the ASCM.

A final issue concerning anti-dumping and poverty relates to labour standards. Some lobbying groups in developed countries have claimed that developing countries use 'social dumping' to boost their exports via their lack of standards (labour, environmental or quality) and the existence of very low wages. Standards are analysed in Chapters 15 and 16, but in the context of this chapter, such dumping would only really be an issue if wages in the export sector were clearly lower than in the rest of the economy. This is not clear at all, and in most exporting sectors of the economy, wages are higher than average, invalidating the idea of social dumping.

14.5 Conclusion

With the gradual liberalization of trade under the GATT/WTO, anti-dumping procedures have become the main protectionist tool used by developed countries against the visible exports of developing countries (outside agriculture and textiles). The prospects for a future removal of these barriers are not good because of the resistance of developed countries.

Developing countries are responding by increasing their own use of anti-dumping measures. The relative ease with which such WTO-legal discriminatory actions can be implemented raises the prospect of a retaliatory spiral threatening the liberal world trading regime. But even without retaliatory spirals, ADDs have nothing to offer developing countries or their poor. Anti-dumping action carries the usual costs of protection, plus some additional ones arising from its discriminatory and market-fixing nature. It wastes skilled labour and diverts the private sector into seeking protection rather than improving productivity.

Even if there are no negotiated limits to anti-dumping in the near future, developing countries would do well to curb their own use of this tool. Certainly, they should not try to use it as a negotiating lever against developed countries, for it will probably be ineffective and costly.

Box 14.2 **Checklist on anti-dumping**

- Are your exports *actually* constrained by others countries' ADDs? (Ask companies for concrete examples rather than general impressions to establish this.)
- Are the poor heavily involved in producing exports that suffer from ADDs?
- How many skilled people would be involved in seeking and administering your own ADDs?
- How would your own anti-dumping actions affect prices of interest to the poor?
- Would your own ADDs really persuade the United States and the EU to negotiate the issue at the WTO?

Notes

1   See Finger (1993) on the history and economics of anti-dumping.
2   That is, industries that are likely to be in long-term decline due to a country's lack of comparative advantage in the sector.
3   Such tariff-jumping FDI is frequently held to be an advantage of ADDs, but this is actually far from clear. Investment induced by trade restrictions is certainly less efficient than the trade would be and may well be worse for welfare in absolute terms.
4   An interesting interpretation of this is that the United States' intransigence arises because its trade policy has, in effect, been privatized (see Finger and Nogues, 2000): US negotiating positions have to be determined with private sector committees and regular reports on negotiations made back to these groups. Research has suggested quite close parallels between membership of these committees and contributions to the PACs (Political Action Committees), which funnel private funds to politicians.

15 Labour Standards

This chapter argues that:

- Labour standards can be strongly beneficial for developing countries and the poor, because they can enhance the living conditions of the poor and increase economic efficiency.
- But they need to be appropriate to a country's level of development and they must command widespread support within society. Otherwise, standards can harm the poorest, who will be left out of the regulated sectors.
- Although there are moral and economic arguments to support the adoption of labour standards, there is no clear reason to tie these standards to trade negotiations and the imposition of trade restrictions.
- Non-trade measures will provide more efficient ways to improve labour conditions than trade sanctions. These include educational programmes and the promotion of civil society institutions; some may require developed countries to provide resources and technical assistance.
- Unilateral trade liberalization will interact with standards, changing the incentives for introducing standards (usually raising them) and, in turn, being influenced by standards in its effects.

15.1 Background

This chapter reviews the arguments for linking international trade and labour standards and finds them generally unpersuasive. In particular, it seems unlikely that establishing links between the two concepts will improve poverty alleviation. The chapter also discusses the connection between labour standards and unilateral trade reform, and appropriate ways of seeking to achieve core labour standards, especially with respect to child labour.

The term 'labour standards' covers a very wide range of rights and requirements. Maskus (1997) provides a useful four-fold classification:

- *Basic rights*: which include rights against slavery, physical coercion, discrimination and exploitative child labour.
- *Civic rights*: which include freedom of association, collective bargaining and expression of grievances.
- *Survival rights*: which include the rights to a living wage, limited hours of work, information about hazards of the job and compensation for accidents.
- *Security rights*: which include rights against arbitrary dismissal and rights to retirement and survivors' compensation.

Some of these rights may clearly be termed 'basic' or 'core' labour standards in the sense that the principles they embody command universal respect as a matter of humane treatment of workers. Adherence to others, on the other hand, depends on the level of development of a country, with some poor countries choosing not to implement some of the more costly labour standards. In 1998, the International Labour Organization (ILO) – the international body that oversees labour standards – defined core labour standards applicable to all member countries (ILO, 1998b):

- freedom of association and the effective recognition of the right to collective bargaining;
- the elimination of all forms of forced or compulsory labour;
- the abolition of exploitative child labour;
- and the elimination of discrimination in respect of employment and occupation.

These core labour standards, which are held to represent a minimum set of rights for all people, have become the focus of a fierce debate. There is little disagreement that labour standards are a legitimate and useful tool for governments. Societies certainly have the right (and perhaps the duty) to regulate themselves in such areas, and given that labour standards can be a means of helping the poorer and weaker members of society, they can certainly be pro-poor. But the standards need to be appropriate to a country's level of development: standards set too high will tend to hurt the poorest because they fall outside their ambit. Moreover, to be legitimate, and hence effective, the standards need to command wide support within the society they affect.

This suggests that the current debate is not about labour standards *per se* but about whether internationally determined and enforced standards are appropriate for developing countries and their poor.

15.1.1 Why is this an issue now?

Globalization has led to developed countries facing competition from developing countries in products that use unskilled labour intensively. Concurrently, over the last two decades there have been declines in the real wages and/or levels of employment of unskilled workers in developed countries. Although the evidence suggests that these declines are probably more to do with skill-biased technological change than with international trade (see, for example, the Symposium in *The Journal of Economic Perspectives*, 9(3), 1995), and although the declines now seem to have attenuated, the existence of lower labour standards in many developing countries than those prevailing in developed countries has led some labour groups and developed country governments to blame 'unfair competition' and 'social dumping'.

Simultaneously, the growth of information and communication technologies has given consumers in developed countries far more information about the poor conditions of workers in developing countries and the weak enforcement of human rights in some countries. Maintenance of such conditions is regarded as morally reprehensible by people who view labour standards as basic human rights and who, therefore, see such standards as universal principles that should apply equally to all countries at all times (see Sapir, 1995). This has led to calls by NGOs and labour organizations for action to improve working conditions in developing countries and, in some cases, for sanctions to be imposed against countries that violate core labour standards.

The ILO has numerous conventions on labour standards (see Section 15.3) but they are not binding on member countries unless they voluntarily ratify them. Even then, the Organization has little capacity to enforce the conventions, so their provisions are not always respected in the countries that have ratified them. Consequently, both labour groups seeking protection from competition and civil society groups wishing to put an end to labour practices of which they disapprove, have advocated the use of trade measures to persuade countries to adopt a minimal set of labour standards.

In particular, the United States has been active in promoting the inclusion of a 'social clause' into the WTO Agreements, which would permit the discriminatory exclusion of imports from countries that fail to respect core labour standards. Labour standards were also the subject of the side agreement to the NAFTA that President Clinton used to assuage labour groups' opposition to the NAFTA's passage through the US Congress (see Anderson, 1995a). Similar approaches have been taken by the EU with the Protocol on Social Policy annexed to the Maastricht treaty in 1992 and the social and labour clauses in the Cotonou Agreement (with the ACP countries) and the Euro–Med Agreements (with Mediterranean countries).

But most developing countries are strongly opposed to the inclusion of any form of social clause in the WTO Agreements since they regard this as back-door protectionism, designed to increase the costs associated with their most important source of comparative advantage – cheap labour. Indeed, the failure to agree on whether and how social and labour standards might be included in the WTO agenda for the next round of multilateral trade negotiations was one of the causes of the failure of the Seattle ministerial meeting in 1999.

15.2 The economics and politics of linking labour standards and trade

Five principal arguments have been proposed in favour of linking trade measures to labour standards: the 'unfair advantage' argument; the 'race to the bottom' argument; the 'morality' argument (see Sapir, 1995); the 'legitimacy' argument; and the 'enforcement' argument.

15.2.1 Unfair advantage

The unfair advantage argument states that lower labour standards in developing countries give them an unfair competitive advantage over countries with higher standards. Proponents of this argument call for the creation of a 'level playing field' to ensure 'fair trade'. But the economics of this argument are of doubtful merit. The level of labour standards adopted in different countries clearly depends on their income levels. Developed countries, for example, had far worse labour standards than their current levels when they had the same per capita income as today's developing countries. So developing countries understandably regard it as somewhat hypocritical of developed countries to criticize them for poor labour standards. Basu (1999) cites the UK Select Committee Report of 1831–2 on details of child labour, and shows that no continental region in the world currently has higher rates of child labour than Britain did in the middle of the nineteenth century.

Even if the desirability of some harmonization of labour standards (or at least some minimum standards) were to be accepted, the imposition of trade restrictions in pursuit of them is likely to be welfare-reducing. The economic case for the optimality of free trade is not altered by the existence of different standards in different countries, so long as they genuinely reflect differences in social attitudes. And if this condition is not met, then that is a matter for domestic policy not trade policy (see, for example, Bhagwati and Hudec, 1996; and Maskus, 1997). Diversity of standards in itself is not an argument for interfering with trade.

Moreover, the argument that developed countries suffer excessive (if not unfair) competition from developing countries with low labour standards is actually rather weak. In fact, the imposition of core labour standards in developing countries is as likely to enhance as to reduce their economic efficiency. Swinnerton (1997) argues that the application of core labour standards prohibiting forced labour and discrimination and allowing freedom of association and collective bargaining is likely to enhance economic efficiency in an economy regardless of its level of development. This view implies that the absence of core standards confers no competitive benefits on developing countries and that developed country concerns on this score are therefore misguided (see Martin and Maskus, 1999). Of course, this does not mean that the incorporation of such standards within a multilateral trade agreement would be necessarily welfare-enhancing.

The position over child labour is slightly more complex insofar as short-term competitiveness is concerned. But it is important to note that there are virtually no goods that are produced both in the United States and by child labour in developing countries. In other words, child labour provides almost no direct competition to US workers (see Basu, 1999).

15.2.2 Race to the bottom

The flip-side of the 'unfair advantage' argument is the fear that lower labour standards in developing countries will lead to a 'race to the bottom' as developed countries feel obliged to loosen their own standards in order to compete. Similarly, it is often argued that footloose capital will withdraw from high-standard (and therefore high-cost) countries and invest in those with lower standards in order to maximize their profits. The solution would then lie in some form of coordinated standard setting between countries in order to avoid a global reduction in standards.

While these are serious concerns in principle, the empirical evidence provides very little support for a race to the bottom. If lower standards did indeed attract greater foreign direct investment (FDI), there would be a correlation between these two variables across different countries; Rodrik (1996) shows that no such correlation exists. And Aggarwal (1995) finds no association between US FDI and poor labour standards in developing countries or any indication that export success in developing countries is due to cost advantages based on inadequate core labour standards. In general, the existing empirical literature does not support the contention that a race to the bottom is taking place.

Moreover, if there were a race to the bottom, it would presumably be strongest between developing countries rather than between them and developed countries. This is because developing country locations are better substitutes for each other (and therefore subject to greater mutual relocation) than are developed and developing country locations. But if this were the case, there would be pressure for coordination and harmonization of labour standards from the developing countries themselves, which, in fact, is the very opposite of what we observe. This point is particularly relevant for issues of child labour where, as indicated above, there is almost no direct competition with developed country workers.

15.2.3 Moral arguments

The third major argument in favour of linking trade and labour standards is that breaches of core labour standards are morally reprehensible and that trade measures should therefore be used to force countries to comply with them. One version of this argument suggests that trade sanctions should be applied in order to dissociate oneself from the activities of the offending party – that there should be 'no truck with the devil'. But trade measures are typically justified as a means of applying pressure on the offending party to change its labour standards with the intention that such changes should improve the welfare of the affected workers. Thus, the validity of this argument depends crucially on the actual impact of the proposed trade measures on the welfare of the workers and general welfare in the affected country.

Maskus (1997) provides a detailed set of theoretical models showing the likely impact of different types of intervention on welfare in the affected countries. In particular, he shows that measures that benefit one sector may simply shift the problem to another: for example, forcing the introduction of union rights into the exportable goods sector could raise wages there but reduce wages in other sectors, or generate unemployment. In general, the impact of trade restrictions implemented by foreign countries depends on the circumstances and could easily backfire if their goal is to improve the situation of workers with limited rights. Much depends on such issues as whether the sector in question is labour-intensive, whether it is the exportable goods sector, and what linkages there are to the informal or residual employment sectors.

Certainly, the few empirical examples of the application or the threat of application of restrictions based on labour standards suggest that such measures may have unforeseen negative effects. For example, in 1995, the Bangladesh garment sector attracted US media attention for the use of child labour for exports to the United States. The response to the resulting, well-intentioned, consumer pressure was the immediate dismissal of thousands of child workers – see Box 15.1. Even with subsequent initiatives to help these children go to school, most have not done so and many are working in much more exploitative jobs, including child prostitution (see DfID, 1999).

Box 15.1 Senator Harkin and the garments industry in Bangladesh

Research for the Department for International Development (DfID) shows how the imposition of certain labour standards can have undesirable effects. The garments industry has been a major success story for Bangladesh, demonstrating the potential for industrial growth and poverty reduction through labour-intensive export development. The legal age for employment in the industry is 14, but until 1992, many children younger than this were working in the garment factories. In 1992, Senator Harkin of the United States introduced a bill aimed at banning the import of items produced by children.

The sentiment behind this bill was admirable: that the West should not benefit from the products of child labour and that the ban would help to combat child labour. But its effect on children's lives was disastrous. Under the threat of the bill, the Bangladesh Garments Manufacturers and Exporters Association (BGMEA) announced the elimination of child labour by 31 October 1994. 50,000 children were dismissed. Since the children had been working to earn money to contribute to their own survival, their dismissal left them in even worse circumstances than the conditions of their labour. Most of the children were forced into even more dangerous employment – including prostitution – in the informal sector, and many families, dependent on children's income, faced even greater poverty.

Source: Crawford (2000).

15.2.4 **Legitimacy**

While the pure economic arguments for linking trade and labour standards are weak, some commentators use political economy arguments. One concerns the legitimacy of the world trading system. For example, both the International Confederation of Free Trade Unions (ICFTU) and Sir Leon Brittan, former External Affairs Commissioner of the European Commission, argue that it is important to build popular support for the multilateral trading system. They argue that this requires a mechanism for linking trade policies with labour concerns (see Brittan, 1995 and ICFTU, 1999), a view that was clearly shared by the Clinton administration in the United States. Rodrik (1997) makes a similar case.

Given its widely accepted contribution to post-war growth and prosperity, any threat to the world trading system is a serious issue. But its actual legitimacy is not likely to be enhanced by encumbering it with instruments and tasks that belong elsewhere. There needs to be an analytical justification for introducing such tasks and some prospect that they will produce successful outcomes. To charge the trading system with raising world-wide labour standards could threaten its very existence if it proved incapable of delivering.

Rollo and Winters (2000) see this argument as one of the main reasons for resisting the advent of a WTO 'social clause'. Instead, the perception that the trading system can assist on labour standards needs to be addressed politically. Developed country electorates should be informed of the trade-offs actually involved and their governments should locate the debate in the appropriate institution – the ILO – even if this involves confronting the problems of devising an enforcement mechanism for rules that most countries in the world do not support.

15.2.5 **Enforcement mechanisms**

Finally, there is a political argument that is rarely explicitly invoked, but which arguably lies behind most of the 'trade and...' agenda – see Rollo and Winters (2000). It is that the WTO has the best enforcement mechanism in town and, if you care deeply enough about something, it is worth co-opting this mechanism to your own agenda. There is an obvious truth in this, but before it can be used to justify public policy, it needs to be shown that some suitably large proportion of the relevant population shares the objective. And that share of the population needs to include those people who will bear the cost of the policy. Moreover, the possible costs of linking trade and non-trade issues in terms of other forgone objectives need to be balanced against the benefits.

It is widely believed that the strength of the WTO's enforcement mechanisms would make a WTO-based social clause more effective in securing changes in labour standards than the current ILO-based efforts, which rely on 'naming and shaming'. Rodrik (1997), for example, argues that trade restrictions can provide strong incentives to improve labour standards. He believes that they are likely to be effective despite their efficiency costs if there is an institution to check that the measures applied are not protectionist in intent and that there is compensation to developing countries in order to mitigate the negative effects of the measures.

But some fear that the formal inclusion of labour standards into trade agreements would be a 'slippery slope' because it would be extremely difficult in practice to create effective safeguards to prevent such measures being used for protectionist purposes (see Bhagwati, 1995, for example). They argue that the proliferation of provisions within the WTO Agreements that legitimize discrimination based on differences between countries' domestic policies threatens to undermine the core principles underpinning the multilateral trading framework – most favoured nation (MFN) treatment of other countries and national treatment of foreign companies. The way in which anti-dumping duties have come to be used to protect domestic industries in the absence of predatory behaviour is a stark warning in this respect (see Chapter 14). Others – Rollo and Winters (2000), for example – argue that since labour standards are so contentious, bringing them into the WTO could endanger progress in all the other areas in which the organization is active. If labour standards were one of the main reasons for the failure of the Seattle ministerial meeting in 1999, there could hardly be a better illustration of this danger.

15.3 Existing approaches to labour standards

Labour standards have been the responsibility of the ILO since 1919, when the organization was formed as an outgrowth of the Treaty of Versailles in a climate of considerable concern about the use of inadequate labour standards to gain competitive export advantage. The organization has a tripartite structure with representation from labour, business and government in each member country.

The ILO's first major function is to promote higher international labour standards through the preparation of a series of conventions, of which there are more than 180 (see Maskus, 1997). Ratification of these conventions is sporadic, partly because some countries simply disagree with some conventions, but also because some conventions are regarded as too inflexible, not allowing for legitimate national variations in labour practices even if they are relatively minor. Table 15.1 lists the conventions that cover core labour standards, along with the number of countries that had ratified them by 2001.

Most ILO conventions have been widely ratified by member countries. Moreover, in many instances, the failure to ratify a convention does not necessarily imply the lack of equivalent legislation in the country in question. Conversely, however, several countries that have ratified conventions have failed to implement their provisions in practice.[1]

The second major function of the ILO is to serve as a clearing house and publicity mechanism for complaints about both governmental and private actions that contravene national obligations in labour standards. The process through which this is done depends on persuasion and peer pressure. A Committee of Experts issues interpretations on the operation of

Table 15.1 The ILO's core labour standards conventions

Convention number	Title	Date	Number of adherents
Convention 29	Forced Labour Convention	1930	158
Convention 105	Abolition of Forced Labour Convention	1957	156
Convention 100	Equal Remuneration	1959	153
Convention 111	Discrimination (Employment and Occupation)	1958	151
Convention 138	Minimum Age	1973	111
Convention 182	Worst Forms of Child Labour	1999	89
Convention 87	Freedom of Association and Protection of the Right to Organize	1973	137
Convention 98	Right to Organize and Collective Bargaining	1949	149

Source: Singh and Zammit (2000), ILO (2000) and www.ilo.org.

various conventions. Subject to these findings, the ILO compiles documents on each country's compliance with conventions it has ratified (see Maskus, 1997). Complaints about country practices are considered and the ILO's findings are publicized, but until very recently no sanctions beyond public opinion existed. In 1999, however, the ILO excluded Myanmar from its proceedings for its persistent use of forced labour. In December 2000, it approved the imposition of sanctions for the same reason, requiring other members to review their dealings with Myanmar to ensure they were not abetting the use of forced labour. This increased activism, coupled with the fact that the recent improvements in information and communications technologies and the burgeoning activities of NGOs have made 'naming and shaming' more effective than ever, mean that ILO is becoming a more potent force in raising labour standards.

15.4 Current negotiating positions on trade and labour standards

The issue of establishing a formal link between minimum labour standards and trade restrictions has a long history – see, for example, Charnovitz (1987) and Woolcock (1995). But with the exception of Article XX(e), which allows countries to ban imports produced with prison labour, the WTO Agreements make no formal linkage between trade measures and labour standards.[2] Nevertheless, at the end of the Uruguay Round, the US and French negotiators managed to ensure that the issue of labour standards would remain on the agenda for future multilateral negotiations. And US insistence on its inclusion was one of the key points of disagreement at the Seattle ministerial meeting in 1999.

   In contrast to the United States, the EU in October 1999 agreed a position on trade and labour standards that proposes the creation of a Joint ILO/WTO Standing Working Forum on Trade, Globalization and Labour Issues, to promote a better understanding of the issues involved. And the EU

Council has confirmed the EU's opposition to sanctions-based approaches.

Developing country governments are almost universally opposed to the introduction of labour standards into the WTO, some very vehemently indeed. But in some middle-income developing countries, there are certain constituencies that are in favour, such as organized labour.

The ILO also has considerable misgivings about the inclusion of a social clause in the procedures of the WTO. In response to the debate over whether and how social considerations might be linked to trade, it has set up a Working Party on 'The Social Dimensions of the Liberalization of Trade', but this group has also excluded consideration of sanctions-based measures.

15.5 Labour standards and poverty

This section argues that appropriate labour standards can promote poverty alleviation and help to share the benefits of globalization more evenly. But such standards should be the business of domestic not international politics. Pressure via trade sanctions could very easily backfire and hurt the poor, who will often tend to fall outside the protections that labour standards offer.

15.5.1 Standards can be pro-poor

The effective and universal implementation of the core labour standards on forced labour, discrimination, freedom of association and collective bargaining is likely to reduce poverty in all countries. This is simply because these standards are so basic that their enforcement is not likely to incur any substantial economic cost (indeed, if anything, they are likely to improve economic efficiency), but they would prevent the most egregious forms of exploitation. And, as so often, the poor – the weakest – have most to gain from limits on the powerful.

But making the implementation of core labour standards 'effective and universal' is extremely difficult. If enforcement is partial, it is likely to worsen poverty because employment will shift from regulated sectors to unregulated ones, pushing down real wages, safety standards and job security in the latter. Since it is in these sectors that the poor are mostly found, the effect would be doubly bad: displacement would increase the numbers subject to poor conditions and low wages and the resulting decline in conditions would hurt those already in poverty.

The enforcement of standards with respect to child labour presents a more complicated problem. Poverty is likely to increase if child labour were to be effectively prohibited altogether, since this would remove from very poor households an additional source of income and a means of mitigating risk. Furthermore, since such a prohibition could not easily be enforced, it is likely that it would result in a displacement of child workers from poor conditions in monitored sectors of the economy to even worse conditions in other, informal or illegal, sectors.

At the same time, there are clear benefits to the poor from measures to prevent the exploitation of children. The difficulty, of course, is in the definition of exploitation. It is necessary to determine whether a child's employment is in the best interests of the child, given the feasible alternatives available to that child (see Swinnerton, 1997), and to give thought to policies other than simply outlawing child labour. The appropriate policy will depend on such matters as the quality and availability of education and administrative arrangements for monitoring child labour, all of which will depend, in turn, on a country's level of development.

The implementation of labour standards that are higher than the core labour standards will have different implications for different countries, depending on the relative size of two opposing effects on poverty. For the poorest retained workers who are subject to improved conditions, poverty will decrease as they benefit from the new standards; but employers are also likely to reduce the overall levels of employment to reflect the new higher cost. Since low-paid workers are typically the most vulnerable in the workplace, the imposition of such standards is likely to increase unemployment and poverty among the poorest segments of the population. Thus, there is a tension between promoting poverty reduction through growth by allowing countries to exploit their lower costs of production and the socio-political process within all countries in which workers attempt to improve their working conditions.

15.5.2 The link between labour standards and trade

Linking trade and core labour standards in the WTO would probably raise compliance with such standards in exportable-goods industries because of the effective threat of trade sanctions. But the poverty-reducing potential of such action is likely to be overwhelmed by the negative spillovers to other sectors and the adverse poverty effects of the trade measures themselves. Since for many developing countries, growth through greater integration in the global economy is an important means of poverty reduction, trade sanctions could be highly deleterious.

Furthermore, there is a very strong possibility that the introduction of any trade and labour standards linkages would be exploited by protectionist interests in wealthier countries. Experience of the operation of anti-dumping law suggests that once legal provisions for discriminatory action are available, they will be extensively used. Thus, from a poverty-reduction perspective, as well as that of aggregate income in developing countries, it is almost certainly best that no linkage is permitted between trade and labour standards under the auspices of the WTO.

15.5.3 How labour standards and trade liberalization influence one another

This Handbook is primarily concerned with the way in which the benefits of international trade and trade liberalization are distributed and, in particular, with the impact of liberalization on poverty. The existence of binding labour standards will undoubtedly have an influence, but in quite subtle ways. For example, too high a set of standards could constrain responses to liberalization by curtailing competitiveness and thus limiting the degree of poverty reduction achieved. On the other hand, appropriate standards may help to ensure that more of the benefits are shifted down to the weak and poor than would occur in unregulated markets. Determining which of these forces predominates requires information on local labour markets, as discussed in Chapter 4. This is typically much more readily available to those in the countries concerned than to international commentators.

How will unilateral trade liberalization affect labour standards? To the extent that standards are costly (and that demands for better standards increase with income), opening up is likely to enhance standards – at least for labour-abundant countries whose real wages increase with trade. The increase in competition may make firms more cautious about standards but this is likely to be important mainly for middle-income rather than low-income countries. Furthermore, the structural changes induced by liberalization may shift workers towards less standards-conscious sectors (especially if the public sector contracts), although it is likely that this will be accompanied by increased wages in these sectors. Governments may therefore feel that they want to complement liberalization with raising standards, but they should be careful not to prevent the adjustment that liberalization requires.[3]

15.5.4 Domestic policy is the key

It is in developing countries' interest to adopt some type of 'social floor', not only because of moral arguments but also because it could help to reduce poverty and increase economic efficiency. Nevertheless, the adoption of this social floor needs to be done willingly, gradually and according to the economic and administrative capacity of developing countries. The key is domestic rather than international policy: formulating appropriate regulations that command widespread respect, and designing effective enforcement mechanisms that both improve standards and recognize the need for productive, competitive employment. The economics of labour standards suggest that non-trade forms of intervention will be more effective than trade sanctions in achieving poverty reduction. Many of these call for resources and technical assistance, and many commentators argue that developed countries concerned about developing country standards should pursue these avenues rather than promoting trade sanctions. We illustrate these for the case of child labour, but the approaches and ideas apply equally to most labour standards issues.

15.5.5 Policies on child labour and poverty

The most important non-trade approaches to improved child labour standards include:

Targeted educational programmes

Probably the single most effective method for tackling the specific problem of child labour is to support targeted educational programmes designed to lower the cost of education and improve its quality. This helps to encourage poor families to withdraw their children from the workforce and put them into schooling because of the long-term benefits both to the child and to the household. Often part-time schooling, which allows a combination of work and school, will be the optimal strategy. Boxes 15.2 and 15.3 cite two examples of (fairly) successful education programmes.

Poverty alleviation programmes

Poor labour standards are directly associated with poverty. This is particularly true for child labour, where poverty forces families to use the additional income from child labour to supplement income and mitigate risk. Thus, adequate safety nets and anti-poverty programmes, as well as

Box 15.2 What ever happened to Senator Harkin's 50,000?

Nobody knows exactly what happened to most of the 50,000 children laid off in Bangladesh after Senator Harkin's 1992 bill – see Box 15.1. But for 10,500 there has been a positive outcome. A Memorandum of Understanding was signed in July 1994 between the BGMEA, the ILO and UNICEF, with support from the government of Bangladesh and the US Department of Labour.

Under the Memorandum, no child under 14 was to be recruited to work in garment factories, but children already working would not be pushed out until a school programme was in place for them. The school programme (funded by UNICEF and the BGMEA) provides for former child workers to be traced and placed in schools run by NGOs. The children are paid a monthly stipend of TK300 (about US $6) to compensate for loss of earnings (although this is less than half of what they could hope to earn if they were working). In addition, the BGMEA agreed to offer employment to other members of the child's family – if there was anyone old enough. The programme also undertook to provide support, such as credit and training, for income-generating activities and to provide lunch to the children at school, depending on the availability of other sources of donor funds.

Surprise monitoring reports suggest that the project has had a positive impact: a baseline survey in 1995 found 43% of factories employing children; according to October 1998 reports, this figure has fallen to 3%. In response to the progress made to date, the US Ambassador has recently announced that he will be supporting the case for a 30% increase in the US garment imports quota for Bangladesh.

In the end, a disastrous situation, caused by well intentioned but ill-considered international interventions to combat child labour, has been turned to some good. Much has been learnt, and what was essentially a salvage exercise has provided some models for future projects. But paying stipends will never be sustainable, and there are still the other 39,500 children who 'fell through the net' and were never traced by the project.

Source: Crawford (2000).

Box 15.3 **Local education initiatives cut child labour**

Children working on the fruit farms of Pernambuco and Bahia, Brazil, to supplement their families' incomes were exposed to dangerous agrochemicals, unable to attend school and, in some cases, lacked even the most basic health care and nutrition. The Rural Workers Union of Petrolina conceived a scheme to provide the children with non-formal education and train them in skills that would help them find better jobs in the future. A garden school and a non-formal education centre were created to prepare the children to join the public school system. The two communities involved supported the programme by donating land for the horticultural training sessions and by building the education centre. 80 children targeted by the programme enrolled in schools.

Source: ILO (1998a).

rising incomes in general, will help to reduce the resistance to improved labour standards. The latter are often enthusiastically embodied into law once they become economically feasible norms.

Promoting civil society
Improved labour standards typically result from a process of social and political struggle. Direct measures to enhance capacity among civil society organizations can therefore help to promote higher standards (although it should be noted that higher standards for relatively better-off workers, which raise labour costs and increase unemployment, may not enhance the welfare of poorer workers in the informal economy).

Improving child labour conditions
Sometimes it is better to improve rather than ban child labour – see, for example, Box 15.4 on a scheme from Turkey.

Box 15.4 **Child street workers in Ankara**

The city authorities have come to the aid of child workers on the streets of Ankara, Turkey, by creating a local centre in which they find sympathetic social support and receive nutrition, health aid, education and personal care. This is backed by a mobile unit of specialists equipped to follow the children into their working environment. Nearly 100 children have been placed in jobs linked to formal apprenticeship schools. Some of them benefit from vocational training provided at the centre. Shoeshiners have been moved from the hazards of the open streets to work in the protected locations of public buildings, hospitals and business centres. The police are co-operating by adopting a more understanding approach with the youngsters and ensuring their security in the workplace.

Source: ILO (1998a).

Supporting international efforts
Supporting international efforts, such as the ILO's International Programme for the Elimination of Child Labour, can help to ensure appropriate improvements in labour standards without jeopardizing the growth prospects of countries based on their comparative advantage.

Among other approaches to child labour that have been suggested but which are subject to at least some reservations are:

Product labelling schemes
Providing information on how goods are produced allows consumers to make their own judgements about the value that they place on labour standards in other countries. In principle, this can lead to an economically efficient outcome. But there are significant problems with the administrative capacity needed to run effective labelling schemes, and conceptual difficulties with defining precisely what such a label should say. Moreover, if meeting the conditions on the label is costly, labelling could be a disadvantage for small and poor producers.

Ethical trading initiatives
Ethical trading initiatives encourage buyers to work with their suppliers to improve labour standards. Such positive forms of encouragement can help to ensure that improved standards are associated with enhanced productivity to the benefit of all parties. But there is a danger that the costs of verifying ethical standards are too high in the cases of small enterprises and poor workers, so that developed country traders, mindful of their reputations, restrict their business to larger and more accessible suppliers that can be monitored easily. In this way, well-meaning ethical trading schemes can actually impose considerable costs on the poor.

15.6 Conclusion

Using the trading system to encourage or enforce labour standards has been one of the most important areas of trade friction between developed and developing countries. Despite the economic and moral arguments for supporting the adoption of some type of labour standards, the rationale for linking them to trade is weak. Appropriate labour standards can benefit developing countries and their poor, but they must be consistent with the country's level of development. If they are too ambitious, they are likely to harm the poor.

Moreover, even if internationally agreed standards are appropriate to a country, it is unlikely that trying to use trade policies to force them on an unwilling government will be effective. Too often trade sanctions backfire and hurt the very people they are intended to help. Instead, other forms of intervention (which might require technical assistance or resources from developed countries), such as training programmes or promoting civil society, are likely to be more effective in improving working conditions in developing countries without increasing labour costs excessively.

Box 15.5 Checklist on labour standards

- Would your export or other industries lose sales if core labour standards were externally enforced? What alternatives exist for the displaced workers?
- Does your country satisfy the requirements of core labour standards? Can you apply higher standards?
- Will higher standards achieve wide application, or will they lead to a (poor) underclass who fall outside the ambit of the law?
- Are standards 'too high', *de facto* constraining economic activity and adjustment?
- Have you established other non-trade measures to promote minimum labour conditions?
- Are domestic firms willing to collaborate in improving labour conditions?
- Can domestic firms take advantage of fair trade initiatives or labelling schemes at the same time as improving labour conditions?

Notes

1   See Maskus (1997) for a more detailed analysis of these conventions.
2   This was not true of the Havana Charter, which was intended to create an International Trade Organization after the Second World War. It did exhort members to take actions to eradicate unfair labour conditions.
3   There are cases where standards have been reduced, as in Chile, but in this case, official standards offered workers more formal protections than were economically justified and far more than core standards called for.

<u>16</u> Environmental Standards

This chapter argues that:

- The poor are commonly very vulnerable to environmental degradation. But in general, correcting the problem is a matter of domestic policy that should be quite independent of international trade.
- International competitiveness and comparative advantage should be defined only after the costs of environmental damage have been taken into account.
- Once private costs reflect social costs, there is no reason to expect international trade to be environmentally damaging: even where it is damaging, the returns in terms of extra income generated by trade will outweigh the environmental costs incurred.
- The policy challenge in this situation – again, domestic – is to ensure that the costs (damage) and benefits (income) accrue substantially to the same people, in other words, that the 'polluter pays'.
- Even with appropriate domestic policies, some environmental problems may spill over from one country to another. These call for international co-operation – multilateral environmental agreements – but only very rarely are trade restrictions warranted.
- The WTO Agreements contain a number of provisions permitting intervention on environmental grounds but they require that as far as possible, interventions should reduce trade as little as is consistent with achieving their aims and that they be non-discriminating between domestic and foreign producers and between different foreign producers.
- Trade liberalization can exacerbate poverty through its environmental effects, but if domestic environmental policy is sound, there is no presumption that it will do so. Policy-makers need to consider the possible linkages, however, and pre-empt extreme problems by using compensatory and complementary policies.

<u>16.1</u> Background

Increasing incomes and greater access to information, particularly in developed countries, have led to heightened public concern about environmental problems, including climate change, ozone depletion, deforestation and the loss of biodiversity. Similarly, in developing countries, concern is growing over air, water and land pollution arising from economic development. Environmental pollution is of particular concern to the poor who are often forced to live on marginal or degraded land and may thus be more vulnerable to changes in their natural environment than are richer people. In addition, the poor have few resources to invest in ensuring that the environmental resources to which they have access are used sustainably and few means to mitigate the impact of pollution and environmental degradation on their livelihoods.

Environmental problems can be usefully divided into two types: domestic, in which the damage is contained within the borders of a country; and trans-boundary, in which the damage affects more than one country. The emergence of global environmental problems such as global warming and ozone depletion has led to a growing recognition of the interdependence of the global environment and the conclusion of around 200 multilateral environmental agreements.

Box 16.1 **Mexican tuna and Indian shrimps**

Mexico asked for a GATT dispute settlement panel in 1991 after the United States banned its tuna exports because the rate of dolphin deaths per Mexican net dropped exceeded that of US fishermen. The panel concluded in Mexico's favour, ruling that Article XX of the GATT does not allow restrictions protecting natural resources outside the jurisdiction of the country making the restriction. But a recent dispute over shrimps has taken 'case law' further. The United States requires that all wild shrimp sold on its territory must be caught using nets with devices to exclude turtles. The restriction amounts to an effective ban on shrimp imports from India, Malaysia, Pakistan and Thailand, who appealed to the WTO. The United States justified its policy by reference to the Bonn Convention on Migrating Species, the Biodiversity Convention, and the Convention on International Trade in Endangered Species of Wild Fauna and Flora (CITES). The disputes panel found that the US measure amounted to an unjustifiable discrimination between countries, and therefore did not comply with the conditions outlined in Article XX. The United States appealed and the Appellate Body, overturning the findings of the panel, agreed that the US law was covered by an exception to WTO rules for measures relating to the conservation of exhaustible natural resources. But it concluded that the way in which the United States had implemented the measures was discriminatory. The United States had offered technical assistance and a three-year phase-in period for certain Latin American countries, but the complainants were allowed only four months.

Source: IDS (1999b).

The increasing integration of the world economy through international trade and investment has given rise to concerns about the impact of trade on the environment and calls for the incorporation of environmental clauses in international trade agreements. Such clauses could specify the processes which must (or must not) be used in the production of certain products and legitimize the exclusion of goods from countries failing to adopt the same standards. See Box 16.1 for examples of the use of such clauses by the United States to try to prevent tuna imports from Mexico and shrimp imports from India, Pakistan, Malaysia and Thailand.

Developing countries have generally opposed the inclusion of environmental standards in trade agreements since they regard it as an implicit form of protectionism and an attempt by developed countries to impose their environmental standards on others. The next round of trade negotiations will thus have to resolve whether and how considerations of the links between trade and the environment can be incorporated into the WTO Agreements.

16.2 The economics of trade and environmental standards

The economics of incorporating domestic environmental standards into trade agreements are very similar to the economics of incorporating labour standards into trade agreements (see Chapter 15). Many of the same classes of arguments used in favour of linking trade measures to labour standards are used to support a linkage to environmental standards, including: the 'unfair advantage' argument; the 'race to the bottom' argument; the 'morality' argument (see Sapir, 1995); the 'legitimacy' argument; and the 'enforcement' argument. In addition to these, we explore an argument based on international spillovers, which is specific to environmental standards, plus two widely discussed 'principles' of environmental policy, the 'polluter pays' principle and the 'precautionary' principle.

16.2.1 Unfair advantage

The unfair advantage argument states that lower environmental standards in developing countries give them an unfair competitive advantage over countries with higher standards. Proponents of this argument call for the creation of a 'level playing field' to ensure 'fair trade'. But the economics of this argument are weak. The level of environmental standards adopted in different countries clearly depends on their income levels. Developed countries, for example, had far worse environmental standards than their current levels when they had the same per capita income as today's developing countries. So developing countries understandably regard it as somewhat hypocritical of developed countries to criticize them for poor environmental standards.

Furthermore, there is considerable evidence that environmental damage does not increase indefinitely with income; Rather, it displays the 'environmental Kuznets curve' shown in Figure 16.1.[1] At low levels of development, most countries produce relatively little pollution. As growth raises incomes, pollution intensity[2] rises as countries switch to more polluting activities. But after a certain level of income, changes in economic structure, demands for improved environmental standards and improvements in technology result in a lowering of pollution intensity. The turning point will be different for different pollutants and for some pollutants, notably carbon dioxide, the main greenhouse gas, there is no evidence that the turning point has been reached (see Nordström and Vaughan, 1999).

This argument assumes that countries' choices of environmental standards depend on their relative valuations of income and environmental degradation. Developing countries seeking to meet the basic needs of their populations may, understandably, place a higher relative valuation on economic development over environmental protection than developed countries. Harmonization of environmental standards across countries is therefore likely to be strongly welfare-reducing. Indeed, the application of any universal standard will be welfare-reducing if the standards applied by each country individually were the result of informed social choice in each society. But clearly, there may be countries where the chosen standards are not the result of a transparent and representative decision-making process. Thus, as with labour standards, there may be a case for the application of 'core' or basic minimum standards to improve welfare. Even here though, it is debatable whether trade-related restrictions are likely to yield significant environmental benefits.

Perroni and Wigle (1999) use a model of world trade to explore the implications of various trade-related approaches to global warming. They show that both trade-related process standards and tariff-based policies are rather ineffective in reducing global emissions. Furthermore, as with labour standards, the economic case for the optimality of free trade is not altered by the existence of different standards in different countries.[3]

Figure 16.1 Pollution intensity and economic development

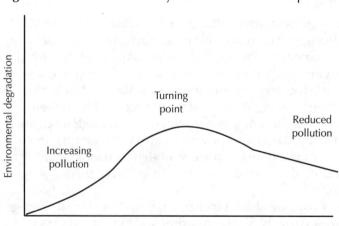

16.2.2 **The polluter pays principle**

There is one aspect to the 'unfair trade' argument that does have some economic basis. This concerns the different implementation of the 'polluter pays principle' by different countries.

Polluter pays is a well-established principle of environmental policy. Economically, it merely states that public policy should seek to make polluters recognize and pay for their anti-social activities by ensuring that they pay the full marginal social cost of their activities – that is, the private cost of production (as they always pay) plus the (external) cost they impose on society by polluting. The marginal external cost associated with a unit of pollution will differ across countries because of differences in the capacity of the environment to absorb pollution. Consequently, the polluter pays principle is entirely consistent with the existence of widely different environmental standards between countries: it merely states that polluters should pay the full marginal social cost of their activities within their own country.

But the manner in which environmental policy is implemented varies greatly between countries. Some make efforts to ensure that polluters do pay according to an estimate of the costs that they impose on society, while others fail to enact such policies, thereby providing their producers with an implicit subsidy. This is not a subsidy arising from countries' adoption of lower standards; rather, it arises from their failure to ensure that polluters bear the cost of the chosen standard. Of course, like all other subsidies, the welfare cost of such a policy is borne principally by countries providing the subsidy (it is their environment that is polluted) and the welfare benefit accrues primarily to consumers in other countries who receive goods or services at lower prices.

Although the Agreement on Subsidies and Countervailing Measures (ASCM) permits subsidies to improve and protect the environment, countries might feel that they have reasonable grounds for complaining against implicit subsidies resulting from polluters *not* paying. This is a treacherous area, however, because it could lead to protection based on any number of claimed implicit subsidies (see Sinner, 1994). In any case, environmental subsidies can be challenged in the WTO if they cause demonstrable injury to producers in other countries, so the case for incorporating additional trade measures to counter such implicit subsidies is weak.

16.2.3 **Race to the bottom**

The flip-side of the 'unfair advantage' argument is the fear that lower environmental standards in developing countries will give rise to a 'race to the bottom' as developed countries feel obliged to loosen their standards in order to compete. The solution would then lie in some form of co-ordinated standard setting between countries in order to avoid a global reduction in standards. Similarly, it is often argued that footloose capital will withdraw from high-standard (and therefore high-cost) countries and invest in countries with lower standards in order to maximize their profits.

These are serious concerns, since the emergence of a race to the bottom is clearly theoretically possible (see Klevorick, 1997). If a race to the bottom is occurring, we should observe evidence of this in the following areas, but in fact we hardly do so at all:

- *The pattern of trade*: tougher regulation should restrict output and exports.
- *The allocation of foreign direct investment (FDI)*: lower regulations might cause FDI to flow out to 'pollution havens'.
- *Plant location*: multinational companies may relocate their plants to take advantage of lower environmental standards.
- *Profitability*: tighter regulation might reduce the profitability of firms.[4]

16.2.4 Moral arguments

A major argument in favour of linking trade and environmental standards is that the adoption of lower standards (such as catching tuna with nets that also kill dolphins) is morally reprehensible and trade measures should therefore be used to force countries to raise their standards.

This argument is invalid if the conventional economic view is taken: that individuals and societies know what is best for them and make choices accordingly. Thus, if a country's socio-political process results in a lower set of environmental standards that are consistent with the preferences and natural resource endowments of that country, most economists would argue that the chosen standards maximize welfare and that any attempt to force the country to adopt different standards would reduce welfare.

Thus, the moral argument in favour of linking trade to environmental standards relies either on the assertion that the socio-political process in other countries does not properly reflect the wishes of the people (that is, that they would choose higher standards if they had a chance), or that the people 'don't know what is good for them' (that is, that their welfare will improve if higher standards are imposed against their will). Both views raise serious problems of interference with national sovereignty.

16.2.5 The precautionary principle

A central tenet of many environmental agreements is the 'precautionary principle'. This states that where science does not give a clear verdict about the possible negative environmental impact of a particular policy, governments are entitled to take precautionary measures against potential risks to the environment, health and safety, provided that such measures are based on sound science and not taken for protectionist reasons.

The precautionary principle should not conflict with trade agreements *per se*. But there are instances where there is no consensus of scientific opinion on an issue, making it possible for some governments to apply restrictions based on the precautionary principle, while others believe that the restrictions are discriminatory. The dispute between the United States and the EU over hormones in beef is a case in point. The dispute panel's interpretation of the WTO Agreements generally means that harm must be proven scientifically before a restriction is legitimate, whereas strict application of the precautionary principle would shift the burden of proof onto those claiming that the restriction is illegitimate.

16.2.6 Legitimacy

While the pure economic arguments for linking trade and domestic environmental standards are weak, some commentators argue that it is necessary to include environmental standards in trade agreements in order to ensure their legitimacy in the eyes of a sceptical public. These arguments have been made by environmental organizations, unions and politicians, and they exactly mirror similar arguments for the inclusion of labour standards (see Chapter 15; and Brittan, 1995).

But, as argued in Chapter 15, the legitimacy of the international trading system depends not only on its inclusion of topics popular with the electorates of some countries, but also on equity between countries and its ability to continue to deliver growth and prosperity. Encumbering trade agreements with instruments and tasks designed to achieve non-trade objectives runs the risk of reducing the effectiveness of such agreements in promoting improvements in global welfare through greater openness and international trade (see Rollo and Winters, 2000).

16.2.7 Enforcement mechanisms

Many of those advocating the linkage of trade and environmental standards in trade agreements do so because they regard the WTO enforcement mechanism as more powerful than the mechanisms available through multilateral environmental agreements. They therefore wish to 'co-opt' the WTO enforcement mechanism to their own agenda. As Ekins et al. (1994) argue, 'trade policies may be among the only available instruments whereby countries that agree among themselves not to damage the global environment can prevent others from doing so'.

While there is clear merit in this argument, it can only be used as a basis for public policy if a large proportion of the countries involved share the same environmental objective. In other words, countries have to be satisfied that the agreement being pressed on them is efficient (in the sense that no other arrangement can achieve the same result at lower cost) and that it is equitable in its burden-sharing (see Bhagwati, 1995).

Moreover, some fear that the formal inclusion of environmental standards in trade agreements would be a 'slippery slope' because it would be extremely difficult in practice to put in place effective safeguards to prevent such measures being used for protectionist purposes (see Bhagwati, 1995, for example). They argue that the proliferation of provisions within the WTO Agreements that legitimize discrimination based on differences between countries' domestic policies (whether environmental policies or anything else) threatens to undermine the core principles underpinning the multilateral trading framework – most favoured nation (MFN) treatment of other countries and national treatment of foreign companies.

16.2.8 International spillovers

The arguments made so far concern domestic environmental issues – those where the perpetrator and victim of the damage reside wholly within the same country. But there are also cross-border spillovers, whereby activity in country A directly affects country B's environment. Regional examples include acid rain or river pollution, while global examples include ozone depletion, global warming and, arguably, loss of biodiversity.

Where the problem is international, the solution is also international. It does not necessarily entail restricting international trade, but it does call for international co-operation and at least raises the possibility that one country should discipline another. If international trade itself was the problem, intervention on trade would be legitimate, but that is a rare occurrence. For example, there might be a ban on international trade in harmful products as a supplement to domestic bans if moving the products were dangerous. But if the concern is about international transportation, it is the transportation that should be taxed (made to pay its full social cost), not the trade. This is because the aim is to encourage cleaner forms of transportation, not to prevent goods from moving *per se*.

The arguments above about the race to the bottom and moral imperatives essentially seek to turn local environmental issues into international ones by inferring links between different countries' actions. In part, the legitimacy of these cases depends on the conviction with which those links can be made, and their strength relative to issues of national sovereignty and self-determination.

16.3 Environmental standards in the WTO Agreements

The WTO Agreements already contain several provisions dealing with environmental issues – see Box 16.2 for the main ones. In addition to these provisions, there is a Committee on Trade and Environment, which is the principal site for environment-related discussion, analysis and proposals within the WTO.

16.4 Multilateral environmental agreements

While domestic environmental problems call for domestic measures, international ones call for international solutions, usually in the form of multilateral environmental agreements. Three major environmental agreements – the Convention on International Trade in Endangered Species of Wild Fauna and Flora (CITES), the Basle Convention on the Control of Trans-boundary Movement of Hazardous Wastes and their Disposal, and the

Box 16.2 **WTO rules for environmental protection**

Examples of provisions dealing with environmental issues in the WTO Agreements include the following:

- **The Rule of Exceptions (Article XX)**: which allows exceptions for measures 'necessary to protect human, animal or plant life or health' and 'relating to the conservation of exhaustible natural resources', if such measures are made effective in conjunction with restrictions on domestic production or consumption. The word 'environment' is not expressly found in Article XX, but the text has been interpreted as general environment protection. But 'measures must not constitute arbitrary or unjustifiable discrimination between countries where the same conditions prevail' nor should they be a 'disguised restriction to international trade'.

- **The Technical Barriers to Trade (TBT) Agreement**: which specifically covers environmental protection and recognizes the legitimacy of government policies to this end. Any tighter standards imposed in pursuance of this objective must be scientifically justified and necessary to achieve legitimate objectives. The Agreement provides that in addition to the two conditions imposed by Article XX, environmental standards should not create unnecessary obstacles to trade, and countries can seek resolution of disputes that may arise.

- **The Sanitary and Phyto-sanitary Agreement (SPS)**: which was negotiated in the Uruguay Round and specifically mentions the environment, in broadly the same terms as the TBT Agreement.

- **The ASCM**: which specifies that subsidies provided for the adaptation of existing facilities to new environmental requirements cannot have countervailing measures imposed by a partner country. Subsidies are allowed for up to 20% of firms' costs in adapting to new environmental laws.

- **The Agreement on Agriculture (AoA)**: which exempts payments made to farmers under government environmental or conservation programmes from the general requirement to reduce subsidies.

- **Intellectual property**: under the TRIPs Agreement Article 27, governments can refuse to issue patents that threaten human, animal or plant life or health, or risk serious damage to the environment.

- **Article 14 of the GATS**: which exempts policies to protect human, animal or plant life or health from normal GATS disciplines under certain conditions.

Source: IDS (1999b).

Montreal Protocol on Substances that Deplete the Ozone Layer – contain trade-related provisions – see Box 16.3. With the first two, trade-related provisions are included because trade is a primary cause or supporting factor of the environmental problem itself. But in the case of the Montreal Protocol, trade provisions are included primarily as a mechanism to ensure the compliance of other member and non-member states with the agreement.

Box 16.3 **Key multilateral environmental agreements with trade-related provisions**

The 1973 Convention on International Trade in Endangered Species of Wild Fauna and Flora (CITES): this prohibits trade in certain species (for example, rhino horn, tiger products, ivory) in order to protect threatened animals from extinction.

The 1987 Montreal Protocol on Substances that Deplete the Ozone Layer (Amended in 1990, 1992 and 1995): this aims to reduce the production and use of ozone-depleting substances.

The 1989 Basle Convention on the Control of Trans-boundary Movement of Hazardous Wastes and their Disposal: this allows states to prohibit the importation of hazardous wastes.

One source of concern is the compatibility of multilateral environmental agreements with international trade agreements. Although there has never been a formal complaint based on a conflict between an environmental agreement and the GATT/WTO, there is clearly potential for such a conflict. One approach would be to give environmental agreements precedence over trade agreements in instances where there might be conflict. Thus, the parties to the NAFTA give the three environmental agreements in Box 16.3 precedence if there is any conflict between their trade obligations under the environmental agreement and the NAFTA (see Esty, 1994). A key issue for the next round of trade negotiations will be to find an adequate mechanism of ensuring consistency between multilateral environmental agreements and WTO obligations.

WTO provisions on the environment contain a 'necessity' clause: the trade restriction is legitimate only if there are no alternative less trade-distorting policies available. The NAFTA adopts a weaker test: rather than requiring that there are no less WTO-inconsistent means of achieving the stated environmental objective, the NAFTA merely requires parties to search for less trade-intrusive policies that are 'equally effective' and 'reasonably available'. The next round of trade negotiations is therefore likely to debate whether to reduce the size of the hurdle that must be overcome for countries to justify trade-limiting environmental programmes.

16.5 The current status of negotiations

The outcome of the Seattle WTO ministerial meeting has given more urgency to the debate about trade and the environment, and some countries are pushing for the inclusion of the issue in future negotiations. Work within the WTO Committee on Trade and Environment has been extensive and, although discussions between the NGOs and governments have revealed important disagreements on this issue, some potential areas of agreement have been identified. Sampson (1999) identifies the following issues as the most important for negotiation:

'Win-win' scenarios
In sectors where trade restrictions are harmful for the environment, their removal can improve developing countries' market access. The WTO Committee on Trade and Environment identifies fisheries and agriculture as such 'win-win' sectors.

Standards and testing
Countries should be allowed to adopt the standards needed for domestic policy objectives as currently agreed in the SPS and TBT Agreements (see Box 16.2), but at the same time, some countries want to raise global standards. These ambitions need to be reconciled.

Prominent among the issues here is the role that developing countries play in standard-setting institutions. They clearly have interests in ensuring that international standards address their concerns and are appropriate to their circumstances. But given their critical shortages of skilled labour, it is far from clear that they can afford to provide inputs at anything resembling the levels of developed countries. Indeed, finding ways in which developing countries can have a fair level of influence on the nature of such international public policies without unduly diverting their scarce resources from other development objectives is a major challenge in the global governance debate – see Winters (2001) on the trade aspects of this.

A further complication is the high cost of proving compliance with technical and health standards. Given that most importing governments insist that this be done only by bodies that they have approved, the provision of testing is not 'contestable', and unless approval is granted quickly, freely and with complete objectivity, the dangers for bias and excess charges are clear. Moreover, since obtaining authorization is a fixed cost, testing can impinge disproportionately heavily on suppliers that are small and poor.

The precautionary principle
There is a need to resolve the use of the precautionary principle in risk assessment and standard setting with the more traditional requirement for clear scientific evidence of a hazard.

Environmental labelling
Some countries are keen to incorporate 'eco-labelling' schemes in the WTO Agreements. But such schemes can impose large administration and implementation costs on developing countries.

Production and process methods
Some environmentalists seek to discriminate depending on whether a given production process is environmentally friendly or not, while the WTO Agreements are based on the principle of non-discrimination between

different sources of the same product. This precludes policies discriminating by methods of production if it cannot be determined which method was used merely by examining the product itself.

Existing multilateral agreements
There is a need to clarify the relationship between and precedence of existing multilateral environmental agreements with WTO rules.

Two further issues are important to developing country interests in international environmental policy:

Traditional knowledge and biodiversity
This issue is about how developing countries can be compensated for the use of 'traditional' endowments and whether they should be able to protect them in some way. This is briefly discussed in Chapter 10.

Domestically prohibited goods
This is the issue of whether countries should have the right to export goods that they ban at home. In principle, there would seem to be little objection to this if the importer is fully informed and willing to accept them, although as noted above, some commentators have reservations about how developing country governments actually determine their countries' willingness. On the other hand, it might be argued that an importing government should be able freely to reject imports of goods that are banned from use or sale in the exporting country.[5]

The above list indicates that developing countries will need to work hard to ensure that further negotiations on trade and environment reflect their priorities. In order to achieve this goal, many developing countries will need technical assistance to identify the implications of proposed measures for their development.

16.6 Environmental standards, trade and poverty

This section argues that the effects of environmental damage on the poor will be negative, but if environmental protection imposes costs in terms of forgone income, the effects may be worse. Each case needs to be assessed on its merits. But if domestic policies are correct, there is no reason to expect the effects on the environment of trade liberalization to be adverse or for the poor to be hit disproportionately.

16.6.1 The poor are more vulnerable

The poor rely more heavily on (and are therefore more vulnerable to) their natural and physical environment than most other segments of society. For example, the poor are affected badly by air pollution from inefficient wood-burning stoves, from land degradation resulting from deforestation and the use of marginal lands, from lack of access to clean water supplies and decent sanitation. They draw a larger proportion of their income than the rich from common natural assets that are more vulnerable to over-exploitation than private assets. The poor are also likely to have poorer access to health care when environmental pollution causes illness and, of course, they have fewer resources with which to afford curative care.

The poor are also affected by global environmental problems. Although most poor countries are affected relatively little by ozone depletion, many may suffer significant losses from global warming as a result of rising sea levels, increased levels of disease and greater desertification. The poor are often forced to live in marginal areas prone to flooding, desertification, infestation by a variety of disease vectors (for example, malarial or tsetse fly-ridden areas) or subject to unreliable rainfall patterns. These areas are often the same areas most at threat from global environmental change so that the poor are likely to lose disproportionately from global environmental threats.

The details of the link between environmental damage and the poor will vary across countries just like the linkages between trade and poverty. For example, in some countries, industrial air pollution will be critical; elsewhere, it will be desertification as a result of slash-and-burn agriculture. Policy-makers should identify the areas in which environmental vulnerability has its worst poverty effects. Then, quite independently of international trade, they should try to address the critical problems via such policies as creating property rights (to encourage conservation), taxing damage, providing information and, if necessary, promulgating regulations.

It is always possible that correcting the incentives for managing the environment worsens some poor households' income position. In these cases, the search for compensatory and complementary policies will be very important. Indeed, experience suggests that environmentally damaging activities (such as poaching) will not stop until the poor perpetrators can find (or are provided with) alternative sources of income.

Even following all of this, some environmental issues will be more important for poverty alleviation than others, and policy-makers need to identify these and be aware that trade liberalization may exacerbate them, just as it can have unfortunate distributional consequences. But if the correct incentives are in place domestically, there is no reason to expect particularly or systematically bad outcomes from trade.

16.6.2 Trade policy and the environment

The promotion of sustainable development, including higher environmental standards for the types of pollution and environmental threats faced by poor people, is a key component of poverty alleviation. Hence, it is desirable that international trade contributes to such goals where possible. Increased trade can have both positive and negative effects on the environment. By promoting growth, trade liberalization can cause an increase in pollution as the scale of production in a country increases. And if a country has a comparative advantage in 'dirty' industries, trade liberalization will encourage a greater degree of specialization in such activities and so increase pollution in that country.

But growth is often accompanied by technological improvements that reduce emissions and by greater demands for improved environmental standards. Moreover, global pollution will frequently be reduced by countries following their comparative advantage. For example, allowing agricultural production to relocate from land-scarce countries (such as Europe and Japan) to land-abundant ones that require less intensive cultivation methods (such as the Americas and Australasia) will reduce fertilizer use.

In addition, if comparative advantage in dirty industries is based on countries' ability to absorb high pollution loads, then international specialization may increase global pollution but reduce its welfare cost, by redistributing it to areas better able to handle higher levels of pollution. This argument assumes that countries' willingness to accept such pollution takes account of the full social costs of the pollution, but if so, the benefits of the additional income generated will outweigh the environmental costs in aggregate. Even then there may be distributional or poverty problems if the incomes accrue to one group and the pollution to another. Again, this comes back to ensuring that polluters pay the full social marginal cost of their activities. So if trade liberalization increases activity by dirty industries, governments must ensure that those industries pay for the extra pollution they cause. If after paying, those industries are no longer profitable, the expansion should not have occurred – that is, the country did not have a genuine comparative advantage in the dirty industries once it costed the pollution properly. Such industries should not expand with trade.

The issue is basically one of domestic pricing (possibly using taxes to charge for pollution). Once proper pricing is in place for domestic resources, if dirty industries find themselves unprofitable, they should contract. The country does not have comparative advantage in dirty industries and it should not regret (in aggregate) that they do not expand following trade liberalization. If on the other hand, after paying the full cost of pollution, the dirty industries are still internationally competitive, their expansion represents a valid trade-off between pollution and income.

Furthermore, it is important to remember that trade policies have general equilibrium effects and these might have an environmental dimension. Policies that discourage exports of 'clean' goods and services – such as excessive regulation on service exports – could divert exports and production into dirty sectors – for example, the traditional 'heavy' industries such as mining and iron-working.

Of course, the success, or otherwise, of an industry will affect prices and factor markets in the ways discussed in previous chapters, and these effects may be either pro- or anti-poor. All that we have argued here is that once pollution is properly costed, the analysis of the poverty effects of trade liberalization are the same as before.

Overall, the impact of trade liberalization on the environment and on the costs of environmental degradation will depend on the detailed characteristics of each particular country. But, even if the impact of trade on the environment differs from country to country, environmental objectives should not, in general, be used to justify a move away from the principle of non-discrimination in international trade. This is because, in almost all circumstances, there are alternative policies that will have a more positive impact on the environment at lower welfare cost. For example, emission taxes (or auctioned permits) are the most effective method of dealing with pollution because they directly address the problem at source. If they are impractical, then taxes on the inputs that give rise to the pollution are the next least-harmful form of intervention, followed by taxes on the output of the activity. Using trade policy is generally the least effective and most costly method of reducing pollution, because although it provides incentives to reduce pollution, it has all sorts of other unintended consequences such as curtailing consumption or distorting factor use.

Furthermore, permitting discrimination against foreign products on the basis of environmental standards raises the risk of arbitrary protection. There are clauses allowing discriminatory treatment in the WTO Agreement on Anti-dumping and these have led to widespread discrimination and negative welfare consequences for the countries concerned; the inclusion of an environmental standards clause in trade agreements might run exactly the same risk. Such actions would be extremely harmful to growth in several developing countries. In particular, they are likely to have a negative impact on countries with a comparative advantage in resource-based industries, including many of the poorest countries in sub-Saharan Africa and Latin America. Reducing growth in these countries is likely to increase rather than reduce poverty, and given the strong cycle of degradation between poverty and environmental damage, this is likely to have a negative rather than a positive impact on their environments.

16.6.3 Alternatives to trade sanctions

If poverty reduction through sustainable development is the policy aim, then one of the most important policies must be to provide technical assistance to developing countries in the implementation of the multilateral environmental agreements to which they have already agreed. This is likely to have a much greater positive effect on both the environment and poverty alleviation than punitive trade-based measures.

Technical assistance may include such elements as research and policy-making capability and establishing testing facilities. But for most developing countries, the most direct aspect of technical assistance is technology transfer. If correcting environmental externalities at reasonable cost depends on technological solutions, such corrections may not be available in developing countries, either because the technologies require skills that they lack or the purchase of equipment or permissions that they cannot afford. In this sense then, technical assistance implies relaxing these constraints. The Montreal Protocol on the reduction of ozone-depleting emissions is explicit that developing countries will be given access to technologies necessary for abatement, but it has frequently been argued that insufficient progress has been made in this direction. A particular problem revolves around proprietary technologies, for which developed country governments have been reluctant to pay royalties on behalf of developing country members of the convention.

The arguments above suggest that one of the few 'legitimate' political arguments for discrimination based on environmental standards would be where the environmental standard chosen by a country does not, in fact, reflect the social choice that would be made by its people were they to be consulted. While discriminating on this basis is treacherous – few countries can claim that all political choices are genuine reflections of the will of the people – it suggests that one important positive measure would be to support the development of civil society organizations (such as environmental NGOs, the press and other media) that promote debate and the formation of social consensus on environmental issues. In particular, this may help to ensure that the views of the poor are reflected in the environmental standards a country chooses.

16.7 Conclusion

Environmental problems are primarily matters of domestic policy and therefore, as in many other areas, the appropriate policies depend on the detailed characteristics of each country. By improving international resource allocation, trade liberalization will benefit the environment in many countries. But since some countries must have comparative advantage in dirty activities, trade liberalization and further specialization can also increase environmental damage in others. But if domestic policies are formulated correctly – that is, if polluters are made to pay the full social costs of the environmental damage they cause, then overall welfare will be higher despite the greater pollution. Moreover, there is then also no presumption that the effects on poverty felt through the environment will be any worse than those felt through other routes. The real danger arises if the benefits from polluting activities are captured by the non-poor, while the costs of the resulting environmental degradation fall on the poor. Finally, trans-boundary pollution and genuinely international environmental problems are also of significant concern to many developing countries. But these are better handled via multilateral environmental agreements than by trade policy and sanctions.

Box 16.4 **Checklist on environmental standards**

- What are your principal environmental problems? What domestic policies – such as pollution taxes or defining property rights – would address them?
- Can you improve the linkages between civil society and policy-makers to ensure that environmental policies accurately represent social choices?
- Do you suffer or create international environmental spillovers? What sort of multilateral environmental agreement would address them?
- Are your domestic policies constrained by their potential effects on international trade? If so, look for domestic market failures to explain why the costs and benefits of expanding an activity are not equal at the margin.
- Does trade exacerbate your environmental problems? Is this because some domestic activity is incorrectly priced?
- If domestic policies are correct, how does the trade-induced environmental problem impinge on the poor? As with all such effects, can you use compensation or complementary policies to alleviate its effects?
- Which of your exports might be vulnerable to others' environmentally driven trade restrictions? What multilateral environmental agreements might help to avoid these?

Notes

1   The 'environmental Kuznets curve' is due originally to Grossman and Krueger (1995).
2   Pollution intensity is the quantity of pollution per US$ of output or income.
3   See, for example, Anderson (1995a).
4   In general, studies of the pattern of trade show either small or insignificant effects of environmental regulation on exports and output. And studies of the allocation of FDI show very little support for the existence of pollution havens (see Eskeland and Harrison, 1997) although there is some evidence that US FDI in chemical industries are influenced by weak environmental regulation (see Xing and Kolstad, 1998). Similarly, although surveys of multinationals provide some support for a race to the bottom (see UNCTAD, 1993), studies based on what companies actually do (as opposed to what they say) show little support for relocation resulting from lower environmental standards (see Mani et al., 1997; Mani and Wheeler, 1999; and Metcalfe, 2000). Finally, studies examining profitability generally show a positive rather than a negative relationship between environmental performance and profitability due to new market opportunities created by environmental compliance and induced efficiency gains (see Repetto, 1995; and Cohen and Fenn, 1997). Overall, the empirical evidence provides very little support for a race to the bottom based on environmental standards.
5   The recent WTO dispute between France and Canada on asbestos hinged around this question and the panel upheld the French ban on imports.

17 Competition Policy

This chapter argues that:

- Competition is an important ally in the fight against poverty, because it constrains the exercise of market power.
- Open borders generate strong competition in some sectors but an effective competition policy can be important in others.
- But competition policy is costly, and it may also slow down poverty alleviation because it absorbs a great deal of skilled labour.
- A multilateral agreement on competition policy may assist developing country governments to achieve their competitive policy goals, but not if it heavy-handedly imposes institutional requirements or appears to be more concerned with market access than with domestic efficiency and equity.
- International agreement to discipline hard-core cartels should be pro-poor, but the number of such cases is likely to be quite small.
- Competition policy is potentially a very useful tool for fighting poverty, but governments need to weigh the benefits of an international agreement against its costs.

17.1 Background

Competition policy is a 'set of measures and instruments used by governments to determine the conditions of competition that reign in the market – antitrust policy, competition law, deregulating activities, etc.' (see Hoekman and Holmes, 1999). It strictly includes not only competition law, aimed, for example, at controlling the abuse of monopoly power, but also policies that facilitate competition, such as providing standards for goods, privatizing state enterprises and opening markets. Competition policy is primarily a domestic issue, concerned with regulating domestic markets and domestic firms. By curbing the power of major producers or distributors and helping to bring the benefits of competition to consumers, it is generally quite strongly pro-poor.

With the increase in economic interdependence, however, issues of competition and anti-competitive practices have spread beyond the purely domestic scene and competition policy has acquired an international dimension. Specifically, it has been proposed as a topic for negotiation and action in the WTO, and it is this link that brings it into a handbook on trade liberalization and poverty. Thus, although competition policy has an important role to play in domestic development policy, other than periodically observing this fact, we shall concentrate here only on the aspects of competition policy that are associated with trade liberalization, especially those that may figure in WTO debates. These mainly concern the competition law issues – preventing the abuse of market power. Such abuse may occur in the domestic distribution of importable goods or in markets for non-tradable goods, both of which should be amenable to purely domestic competition policy. There is also, however, the possibility of international abuses of market power, which raises the scope for international competition policy involving some kind of co-ordination or multilateral agreement to enhance competition.

Before discussing international competition policy, however, we should note a very important connection between a developing country's trade and competition policies, quite independent of the WTO. A liberal trade policy – freely importing a good at the world price – is one of the most potent antidotes to domestic monopoly (and often, domestic monopolists are among the most potent opponents of trade liberalization). It is true that foreign competition may encourage domestic firms to merge in defence, but the open border prevents them from exploiting their larger sizes and smaller numbers. In this sense – an important practical one – a good trade policy removes some of the need for competition policy because it makes markets 'contestable'.

17.1.1 Why is this an issue now?

There are several motives behind the efforts to start international negotiations on competition policy (which are led mainly by the EU). First, as noted, there is a concern to control the international abuse of market power. Second, both international and domestic competition policy are likely to be enhanced if there are more effective arrangements for international information exchange and co-operation. Third, multilateral negotiations may provide a political context in which developing countries can start to develop their own competition policies for purely domestic objectives, and may also provide blueprints and information to help the process.

Multilateral competition policy is also frequently seen as an adjunct to market access negotiations – to try to ensure that restrictions on competition do not undermine (technically, 'nullify or impair') the benefits of trade liberalization negotiated under the WTO.[1] For example, if a country reduces its tariff in a sector where a domestic firm controls the distribution chain, foreign competitors will still have difficulties accessing the market. Thus, to be welfare-improving, as well as to be attractive to trading partners, a trade reform may need to be accompanied by the removal of anti-competitive practices.

Intra-EU competition policy has played this role for EU members, and has been seen as an important bulwark for intra-EU trade liberalization in the past. In fact, market access considerations are far more important for developed countries than developing countries: for example, they lay at the heart of the Fuji–Kodak WTO dispute between the United States and Japan. The United States, however, is not an enthusiast for multilateral talks on this issue: it fears that any agreement would be weak and prefers to exert unilateral pressure abroad and to assert policy autonomy at home.

The attitudes of developing countries to competition policy and to international talks on the issue are varied. As developing country governments have become more favourably disposed towards markets, the shortcomings of their current competition policy arrangements have become more evident, and have also been better appreciated by multilateral and bilateral advisers. Thus, many developing country policy-makers are now beginning to contemplate the virtues of competition policy, both unilaterally and, to the extent that it helps them to achieve domestic goals, multilaterally.

But developing countries as a whole could be characterized as enthusiastic only about international rules to discipline cross-border anti-competitive practices – international competition policy – not about multilateral rules on domestic competition policy. Although it is difficult to define a precise dividing line between these two aspects, they lie at opposite ends of the spectrum. The former commands quite wide support among developing countries as a means of addressing a perceived market failure. The latter, on the other hand, is generally viewed rather passively and, whenever it starts to resemble a 'one-size-fits-all' approach, with hostility. Somewhere in between is the view that a multilateral framework may help developing country governments to construct appropriate domestic laws and institutions.

The potential effects of enhanced competition policy on poverty are mixed. Competition is very important in developing countries in ensuring reasonable prices and trading conditions for consumers, small farms and businesses. And fostering the 'rule of law' over the exercise of market power is also likely to be very constructive. Thus, effective competition policy can make quite an important contribution to poverty alleviation. But effectiveness is far from certain and may come at considerable expense (especially in terms of skilled labour). Hence, developing country governments need to consider the trade-offs involved in moving beyond the first step of just opening the economy up to international competition.

It is also not clear to what extent the chances of improving domestic competition policy will be enhanced by international negotiations, not least because being so strongly redistributive, competition policy needs strong domestic legitimacy, and it is not certain that international negotiations help to achieve this. Using competition policy to address international market abuses could have significant poverty effects, but the frequency with which it can be used in this way is likely to be quite low. Moreover, although there is now much greater sensitivity to the issue than in the Uruguay Round, especially in the EU, there is still a danger that internationally negotiated competition policy obligations could be quite burdensome bureaucratically. All of this suggests that while developing country governments need to think seriously about their own competition policy goals, and about how international talks could enhance these, they should approach such talks with a realistic view of the relative costs and benefits.

Competition policy already overlaps with several other WTO issues. In the area of TRIMs, for example, domestic and export performance requirements can be seen as 'second-best' policy measures designed to neutralize multinational companies' more objectionable practices like price fixing or market allocation (see Chapter 18). The 'first-best' measure would be an adequate competition policy capable of directly regulating these practices. Similarly, anti-dumping duties can only really be justified in terms of countering anti-competitive predatory pricing (see Chapter 14).

17.2 The trade-offs in competition policy

Competition policy seeks to address private practices that limit effective competition. The main issues are generally agreed to be those presented in Table 17.1, although the approaches adopted to deal with them differ, even among developed countries. Competition is highly desirable, but competition policy may be expensive and difficult to implement effectively, so governments need to assess the trade-offs carefully both in aggregate and for the poor. Sometimes, open borders are the best a country can expect to achieve in this area.

The benefits of competitive markets are widely appreciated. If companies do not compete fully because of market power, prices are higher, resource allocation is more inefficient and the distribution of income is disturbed. It is widely appreciated that in some markets, public intervention might be required to achieve competition. Moreover, a pro-competitive public policy might be twice blessed, for as well as the direct benefits, there would be a strong message about the rule of law, the even-handedness of the law, the need for transparency and accountability within business, and a general focus on efficiency and fairness. Thus, few would contest that developing countries must eventually develop competition policy disciplines, just as today's developed countries have had to do.

But two questions need to be answered before setting off down this route. The first is whether an effective competition policy is feasible. The political difficulties of introducing and enforcing competition policy are great, for it potentially puts governments in direct conflict with their major producers. At the very least, careful political work is required to build a coalition of

Table 17.1 Targets of competition policy: the main anti-competitive practices

	Restrictive objectives	Welfare effects	Examples
Horizontal restraints	Price fixing Market or customer allocation Reduced production or sales	Increase prices Limit competition Can reduce production costs and increase welfare effects	Export cartels Market sharing arrangements Technology arrangements Pricing agreements
Vertical restraints	Market dominance through: – resale price maintenance – refusal to deal – exclusive dealing – reciprocal exclusivity – tied selling – predatory pricing – quantity fixing – territorial exclusivity	Depending on market structure, if the vertical restraint allows for entry in the market, it can be welfare improving – but it is likely to limit entry and exit, foster the abuse of powers and increase prices	Control of production and distribution chain Restricted access to networks

Source: UNCTAD (1999b).

consumers and user industries (usually the small and medium-sized enterprises within them) to support competition policy. If it is unsuccessful, the policy might never get underway, or worse, it might be 'captured' by the very firms it is designed to discipline. Avoiding these pitfalls and getting the right degree of independence between competition policy authorities and the government requires careful balancing. (Too close to the government risks political interference, whereas too independent risks non-accountability and capture.)

The second question is at what stage does competition policy become worthwhile. Much of competition policy relies on sophisticated law and economics and is very demanding of skilled labour. Moreover, if the government has an effective policy, the private sector will almost certainly wish to employ its own specialists to protect its rights.[2] The drain of such resources out of the production sector will be costly – not least to other factors of production (notably unskilled labour) with which they would otherwise combine.

In all developed countries, competition policy has evolved gradually over time. In its proposals for an international agreement, the EU has hinted that the first stages might usefully entail transparency, non-discrimination, international co-operation and action against hard-core cartels (see, for example, European Union, 2000). Incrementalism of this kind is clearly desirable, and the EU's list of priorities is sensible. It is not, however, innocuous: 'transparency' is defined as including 'due process' and 'effective domestic remedies', the two elements that are most skill-intensive.

For some countries, trade liberalization might be the best, or the only, way of achieving competition on domestic markets. It is cheap to administer and for small markets, provides the only way to reconcile scale and competition. It is true that open borders cover only a subset of markets and also that trade liberalization may increase the earnings of international cartels. (Where cartels exist, tariffs worsen the plight of the consumer by further raising the prices they face, but at least they have the virtue of clawing back some of the monopoly rents for the importing government.) Hence, both domestic and international competition policy may need to follow liberalization. But that does not stop trade liberalization from being a very constructive first step towards effective competition.

It is sometimes argued that competition policy is a prerequisite for trade liberalization. Where the domestic sector is potentially internationally competitive, there may be a case for introducing domestic competition policy before trade liberalization in order to boost local efficiency prior to the full onslaught of competition. In general, however, potentially efficient firms will still be recognizable when the competition is international, and they will have even greater incentives to improve their performance. Moreover, trade liberalization implies that some sectors must decline (to zero in small economies) so that delaying liberalization on the grounds that the domestic sector must be given time to prepare to compete is not likely to be constructive in general.

Finally, even putting aside resource issues (and their consequences for unskilled and poor workers), it is important to recognize that international competition policy or a multilateral agreement on domestic competition policy could harm developing countries. This depends very much on the details, but Hoekman and Holmes (1999) assess the welfare effects for developing countries of certain stylized elements of competition policy that might figure in negotiations – see Table 17.2. They conclude that most have ambiguous effects on developing countries.

- Competition standards may have benefits, but they may be costly to implement.
- A non-violation dispute settlement in the WTO can facilitate the resolution of certain competition policy frictions, but it can be difficult to implement because the WTO cannot affect the national application of antitrust law.[3]
- The prohibition of cartels may have positive effects in terms of global efficiency, but developing countries may benefit from their own export cartels.
- The adoption of procedural norms may be beneficial, but their enforcement in developing countries is uncertain and/or costly: complex procedure benefits those with the deepest pockets.

Table 17.2 Options for a competition policy agreement: the effects on a developing country

Option	National welfare
1. Minimum substantive standards of antitrust law	+/–
2. Expand the scope to bring non-violation complaints	+/–
3. Introduce antitrust criteria in anti-dumping	+
4. Give a greater transparency and 'discovery' role to the WTO	+
5. Prohibit export cartels	+/–
6. Adopt procedural and due process norms	+/0

Note: + indicates a positive impact, – a negative impact, and 0 no impact. More than one symbol indicates a range of outcomes is possible.

Source: Hoekman and Holmes (1999).

17.3 Progress on multilateral approaches to competition policies

Competition policy is on the multilateral agenda in terms of both domestic policy regimes and an international agreement to discipline international anti-competitive behaviour. Positions differ widely, however, between developed and developing countries as well as within each group, so the agenda is still actually very fluid.

17.3.1 Competition aspects of the WTO Agreements

The United States started the interest in the cross-border effects of anti-competitive practices in the 1940s, when it complained about Japanese and German export cartels during the inconclusive negotiation of the International Trade Organization. Developed countries, especially the United States, have since pursued cross-border competition policy objectives mainly via unilateral procedures based on retaliation and via bilateral procedures, although some attempts have been made at the multilateral level to agree competition rules in the OECD and UNCTAD. The WTO already covers aspects of competition policy in many of its Agreements, as Table 17.3 shows. Such sectoral provisions are likely to stay and may be extended, but the big debate is about whether the WTO should have more general ('horizontal') rules concerning national competition law and its enforcement.

In 1996, the WTO created a Working Group to study the relationship between trade and competition policies, and negotiations on competition policy were expected to be launched at some point. But the lack of consensus became evident from the beginning of the investigations, and in its first report at the end of 1998, the Working Group suggested continuing with the discussions. As of mid-2001, it is unclear whether competition policy will form part of any round of trade negotiations in the near future.

Table 17.3 Competition policy dimensions of existing WTO Agreements

Item	Articles	Link with competition
General Agreement on Tariffs and Trade (GATT)	Article II:4	Restrictions on import monopolies
	Article III	Maintenance of competitive conditions independent of actual trade effects
	Article VI	Condemnation of dumping and predatory pricing
	Article XI	Prohibition of government use of most quantitative import and export restrictions and prohibitions
	Article XVII	Restrictions with respect to state trading enterprises
	Article XX(d)	Restrictions on general exemptions
	Articles XXIII:1(b)	Competitive assessment of government measures
	Article XXIII	Non-violation nullification and impairment
Agreement on Safeguards	Articles 11:1(b) and 11:3	Need to enhance rather than reduce competition during structural adjustment programmes
General Agreement on Trade in Services (GATS)	Article 7	Recognition of another member's licensing to avoid licensing, certification or related requirements as a barrier to entry
	Article 8	MFN obligation for monopolies whether public or private
	Article 9	Imposes consultation and co-operation with other countries in sectors where competition is restrained
Commitments in Financial Services	Paragraph 1	List of monopoly rights and commitment to reduce and eliminate such rights
	Paragraph 10.1	Reduce restrictions on the operation of financial services suppliers
	Paragraph 10.2	Ensure national treatment to foreign financial service providers
Annex on Telecommunications		Allow service providers of other members access to public telecoms networks
Reference Paper on Basic Telecoms		Maintain adequate measures to prevent anti-competitive practices of major suppliers
Agreement on TRIPs	Article 8	Prevent the abuse of intellectual property rights restraining trade
	Article 22	Limit trademarks and geographical indicators that would result in public confusion
	Article 31(k)	Considering anti-competitive practices in compulsory licensing
	Article 40	Recognition that some licensing practices restrain trade and impede technology diffusion
Agreement on Technical Barriers to Trade	Articles 3, 4 and 8	Ensure that technical regulations and standards are not trade restrictive

Item	Articles	Link with competition
Agreement on Preshipment Inspection	Article 2	Rules for preshipment inspection entities
Agreement on Subsidies	Articles 6 and 18	Regulation of market displacement, price undercutting and voluntary undertakings
	Article 15	Examination of trade restrictive practices and competitions in determination of injury
Agreement on TRIMs		Introduce provisions on competition policy in TRIMs
Agreement on Government Procurement		Transparency in government procurement decisions

Source: OECD Joint Group on Trade and Competition (1999).

17.3.2 EU and US differences

The lack of consensus arose from different views about competition policy both among the developed countries and between developing and developed countries. Within the developed countries, the United States and the European Union have very different approaches to competition policy – see Table 17.4. The United States relies heavily on *per se* prohibitions (ruling out certain practices) and structural indicators (for example, on firms with dominant shares of the market). In contrast, the European Union tends towards the *rule of reason* (asking what the outcome of a practice is) and behavioural restraints (for example, focusing on the abuse of a dominant position rather than the position itself). Behavioural restraints maintain discretion and can clearly permit cases where apparently non-competitive forms actually improve welfare, for example, by enhancing technical advance. The cost of this, however, is a lack of clarity for firms and potential inconsistency (and possible bias) in application.

Internationally, the United States seeks co-operation, but is strongly opposed to either a binding WTO agreement that would constrain its domestic policies or a superficial one that would not constrain other countries. The EU, on the other hand, strongly supports the inclusion of competition policy as a separate item in the WTO Agreements, based partly on its own favourable experience of a supranational competition regime. Its proposals are for a flexible 'bottom up' agreement, in which countries accept some core principles and then adopt further specific obligations as and when they become ready to do so – see, for example, various EU submissions to the WTO: European Union (1999, 2000 and 2001).[4]

The EU would not seek the harmonization of competition law, but

Table 17.4 Major differences between EU and US competition policies

EU competition policy	*US antitrust laws*
Excludes small companies.	No special treatment for small companies.
Special section in law on state-owned companies.	No special treatment for state-owned companies, since there are few state-owned companies in the United States.
Integrating the markets of the member states into a union-wide market is an objective of EU competition policy. Agreements that contribute to the existence of different national markets are therefore prohibited (for example, granting exclusive selling rights in a specific country). The EU is inclined to have a more positive judgement on mergers or joint ventures that unite companies from different countries.	The US market is already highly integrated. Agreements that grant territorial exclusivity along state lines are usually seen as efficient and pro-competitive and are therefore allowed. Mergers of firms from different states are subject to the same control as mergers within a state.
Strictly prohibits most vertical agreements.	More tolerant view of vertical agreements, on the grounds of efficiency.
The definition of a relevant market is narrower than in the United States.	The definition of a relevant market is broader than in the EU.
Companies have a dominant position if they have a 40% market share.	Companies have a dominant position if they have a 70% market share.

Sources: Wood (1996) and Paasman (1999).

advocates the following principles:

- a requirement to adopt a competition policy and law;
- agreement that the law should be based on core principles, such as most favoured nation (MFN), non-discrimination, national treatment and transparency;
- recognition of the different needs of countries at different stages of development;
- consensus in handling matters such as hard-core cartels and market dominance;
- co-operation and information sharing; and
- a commitment to enhanced technical assistance.

As noted, this is a perfectly sensible approach, and could assist developing countries to develop their own competition policies, but it is not innocuous, for transparency certainly entails significant resource costs.

After an initial lack of enthusiasm, Japan and the newly industrialized countries of East Asia have also moved towards considering a multilateral agreement. But they argue that prior to introducing international competition policy, WTO members should dramatically scale back contingent protection measures like anti-dumping.

17.3.3 Developing countries

Developing countries differ considerably in the details of their views. But a number of them attended a roundtable discussion arranged by the UK Department for International Development (DfID) and the Commonwealth Secretariat in July 2000, which agreed that the WTO was a credible forum for the negotiation of a multilateral framework agreement on competition principles. Although they argued the need for more discussion of the core elements, supporters of such an agreement agreed something rather similar to the EU position just set out.[5] In addition, they accepted the need for an implementation framework, including a peer review mechanism, and a dispute settlement mechanism, although the details of the latter would require careful consideration and would depend on the nature of the agreement itself.

Among the benefits that the supporters saw in such an agreement were that it could help to drive developing countries' domestic agendas, strengthen political will and underpin domestic legislation to deal with domestic and cross-border restrictive business practices. They also thought that an agreement could identify principles and practical ways of co-operating on cross-border and international matters, in particular on international cartels and restrictive practices by multinationals.

For developing countries as a whole, using competition policy as a means to enhance domestic competition or as an adjunct to market access are perceived as mainly developed country issues. Their long-held aim of 'controlling' multinationals clearly falls under its rubric, however, and could potentially mobilize substantial support for such an agreement. Such control is clearly desirable in some cases, but developing country negotiators need to be realistic about what is achievable. The wide set of issues and deep interference in commercial affairs that are sometimes mentioned under this heading are far too draconian for developed countries to accept, and could anyway damage essential multinational investment in developing countries. The EU in particular argues for discipline on hard-core cartels, some of which damage developing country interests. But this is much narrower than 'controlling' multinationals, and it is not clear how much an international agreement would increase existing EU ability and willingness to act against cartels.

17.3.4 Prospects

Despite the proponents' arguments and the expressed enthusiasms for a multilateral agreement on competition policy, several factors make its establishment look difficult:

- The diversity of existing national competition policies makes it difficult to implement multilateral rules that would change very much.
- There is a widespread concern over national sovereignty.
- The WTO deals with country policies but cannot interfere in private actions regulated by national law, as much of competition policy requires.
- There are valid doubts about how far an agreement would benefit developing countries.

17.4 Competition policy and poverty

There are four main routes by which competition policy could impinge on poverty in developing countries: enhancing competition; disciplining international cartels and multinationals; disrupting industrial policy; and accelerating institutional development. Among these, the first is by far the most promising.

17.4.1 Encouraging domestic competition

As noted above, competition promises considerable advantages in terms of growth and poverty alleviation, as a way both to assist consumers/users in getting value for money and to force producers to become more efficient. In both ways, it is likely to raise the real incomes of the poor. In addition, the transparency conferred by a clear competition policy could also stimulate inflows of investment. Trade liberalization is a great stimulus to effective domestic competition, and in many markets can be sufficient to reap all its gains, but developing countries will eventually also need to progress down the road of competition policy in order to cover non-tradable sectors.

Subject to the reservations surrounding feasibility and cost, this should happen sooner rather than later. Moreover, although competition policy is essentially a domestic concern, an international agreement coupled with technical assistance could provide useful templates and political impetus for such reforms. A lack of competition usually operates to the advantage of those powerful enough to exploit it – multinationals, local magnates, elite labour groups, etc. – so the number of times that competition policy undermines a practice that actually helps the poor is likely to be very small. And it is also important to recognize that governments have means of stimulating competition other than competition policy; in particular, local abuses of market power can be tempered by supporting a wide variety of civil society actions against the perpetrators, which may be much more effective locally than government competition policy.

17.4.2 Developed country export cartels and multinationals

The global merger wave implies an increase in the monopoly power of large firms and multinationals. In addition, the increase in foreign direct investment (FDI) has been accompanied by an expansion in the acquisition of companies at a more local level. Developing countries find it more difficult than developed countries to deal with multinationals and domestic subsidiaries, and to regulate the unequal competition between multinationals and domestic companies. Hence, an effective international competition policy has more apparent attractions for developing than for developed countries – see Box 17.1.

The effect of multinationals' market power on poverty is potentially very broad. The direct price effects are that poor households could face higher consumer prices, which might be especially important in the case of food, and that monopsonistic buying will drive down the prices of exports. In addition to their immediate effects on those concerned, these adverse terms-of-trade effects will reduce national income (lower wages and/or profits) and almost certainly cut government revenue. Monopsonistic employers of labour may reduce wages and employment below competitive levels, although, so far, this is not a problem that has figured in international discussions of competition policy.

The key issue in the treatment of market power is determining whether abuse has actually occurred. There is a tendency sometimes to attribute all of developing countries' dissatisfaction with the trading system to 'monopoly power'. But with the standards of proof currently used in developed countries' domestic competition policy, the number of situations that international competition policy could rectify is probably rather small.

The EU lays great stress on the argument that an international agreement

---

Box 17.1 Why international monopolies are a special problem for developing countries

- To determine whether there has been an international abuse of a dominant position (that is, the exertion of monopoly power), information is required on such issues as market structure and costs, and this is difficult for developing countries to garner without the co-operation of multinationals' 'home countries'. For example, determining abuse may require access to pricing and cost information from the countries where the multinationals have their headquarters.
- Export cartels typically take actions and decisions outside the country whose market they are exploiting. That country's government will be hard pressed to reverse those decisions, even if they get to find out about them.
- Once abuse has been identified, an individual developing country government might be unable to discipline the offending company; for example any compensatory tariff increase it makes might be referred to a WTO dispute panel if the monopolist's 'home' government backs it.
- Victims of predatory pricing by an export cartel often have no access to a court system to restrain the cartel.

Source: Gleckman and Krut (1994).

would permit stronger disciplines on international cartels. It will clearly help in this direction, but by how much is actually unclear. Most effective international cartels will have either production or sales in developed countries and hence could already be disciplined under their domestic law. And if the prosecution of such cartels requires information from developing countries, this could be provided without the need for an agreement. Thus, if developed countries were concerned about their firms exploiting developing countries, they could generally act already. If they currently choose not to, it is not certain that they would do so in response to actions or requests initiated by developing countries under an international agreement. And certainly, a developing country government tackling a cartel of developed country firms will need to invest heavily in procedure in order to persuade the developed country government to co-operate.

A further important qualification on disciplining international cartels is that the benefits must be passed onto the poor in terms of lower prices. Merely transferring rents from international to domestic firms will offer little poverty alleviation.

Nonetheless, an international agreement permitting stronger disciplines on international cartels could send an important signal to the firms involved of the seriousness with which the international community treats their behaviour. In addition, it might strengthen the hand of regulators and policy-makers within developed countries who do wish to use existing competition policies to discipline the activities of their own companies even where the costs of such activities predominantly fall outside their jurisdiction.

The effective prevention of export cartels could, conceivably, impinge on developing countries from the other side of the equation. Particularly in primary commodities, developing countries may be able to turn the terms of trade in their favour by cartel action, and this would be ruled out by international competition policy. In practice, however, this is probably not a major loss because developing countries have found it difficult to manage such cartels in the past, and if one were successful, the developed countries probably already have quite enough instruments to undermine it.

17.4.3 Industrial policy

Constraints on domestic competition policies could conflict with industrial policies in developing countries, which, to some commentators, would represent a significant constraint. Whereas competition policy is primarily defined in terms of static efficiency, industrial policies ostensibly focus on dynamic efficiency. 'Infant industry' protection often calls for reduced domestic competition (for example, in the development of 'keiretsu' in Japan), as firms capabilities are developed. According to this view, developing countries need a flexible competition policy that allows industrial policies to be aimed at the long-term growth of productivity (see Singh and Dhumale, 1999). The need to maintain investment may, they argue, require the steady growth of profits and therefore co-operation between government and domestic companies and a limitation of domestic competition.

The net effect on the poor is again difficult to disentangle, not least because there is considerable controversy about the efficacy of 'infant industry' protection in the first place (see Chapter 13). Domestic protection would trigger higher prices in the short and medium term. Successful industrial policy, on the other hand, would benefit the poor in the longer run in terms of income, prices and possibly employment. Government revenue would also benefit from successful development.

The different stresses that different economists lay on competition and industrial policies reflect deep differences in views about development itself. But once we think of the international trading environment, the question may be a bit of sideshow. Industrial policies are already subject to some WTO discipline – via TRIMs, for example (see Chapter 18) and the ASCM (see Chapter 13) – and if an anti-competitive action impairs a voluntarily given tariff liberalization, it may already be actionable under a non-violation complaint. In addition, any internationally negotiated competition agreement is likely to include sufficient exceptions and reservations that any currently WTO-consistent interventions are likely to remain so for a long time.

In fact, the EU proposal to allow members to record a number of exceptions to competition policy disciplines under an international agreement could mean that many of the agreement's domestic advantages are vitiated. To sign an agreement but then exempt all the critical sectors would be easy politically but costly economically. It runs the risk of creating all the bureaucracy but forgoing most of the substantive gains of an agreement, increasing the chances of a negative outcome overall.

17.4.4 Institutions

The progressive tightening of competition rules and the cultivation of institutions to manage competition policy will both enhance market functioning and market access in developing countries, and facilitate their general institutional development. The effects on the poor will potentially be very positive for they are major beneficiaries of the creation of markets and of policies that curb the powers of small elites.

But the process of creating a competition policy must be adapted to the developing countries' priorities, being both flexible and gradual. The development of competition policy takes time and is only one of many steps in the development process. For example, competition authorities are recent arrivals even in some EU countries like Spain or Portugal. Attempting to implement overly sophisticated institutions in developing countries would very probably be costly and ineffective because of the countries' inability to staff and manage them effectively. Enforcing competition requires rare technical and political skills, and poor competition authorities could be part of the problem not part of the solution. In the context of international negotiations, the extension of competition policies to developing countries will, at the very least, need technical assistance from developed countries and plenty of time. And any attempt to harmonize standards and procedures for developing countries and developed countries would be wholly inappropriate.[6]

In addition, policy-makers need to ask whether competition authorities represent an appropriate use of available labour in economies with skills shortages. As skilled labour is drawn off for these regulatory tasks, the net losers will be owners of other factors of production, which have fewer resources to work with. Thus, poor, unskilled workers will pay for competition policy as well as benefit from it. There is a trade-off to be made.

Clearly, the trade-off depends on the effectiveness of competition policy and its costs, and some people have argued that a rudimentary competition authority would not absorb many resources. This is clearly a matter for further study, but it is important to allow for the fact that skills will be absorbed not only in the authority itself but also in the private sector to engage with it. Moreover, an international agreement calling for 'due process' almost certainly demands levels of input, analysis and legal activity close to those found in developed countries. This is especially true when, as some hope, the authorities will be dealing with companies that have their headquarters in developed countries. And it is likely to be far more expensive than the first steps towards competition policy that developing countries might take in a purely domestic context.

Finally, competition policy is strongly redistributive and intrusive into domestic politics. If international negotiations provide impetus and political cover for developing country governments to develop their own competition policy, they could aid institutional development. But if on the other hand, governments appear to be establishing competition authorities at the behest of outside interests and in order to ensure market access for foreigners, rather than as organic solutions to local problems, those authorities will have to fight hard for legitimacy. Thus, effectiveness is not assured even if major resources are devoted to the task. Indeed, by weakening local ownership and responsibility, an appearance of external pressure could undermine institutional development and be positively costly.

<u>17.5</u> Conclusion

It is useful to distinguish two aspects of competition policy:

Domestic competition policy
This considers domestic violations of competition that harm consumers; at the same time, it must create a proper environment for the growth and competitiveness of domestic companies in developing countries. Well executed, domestic competition policy offers strong potential for poverty alleviation, because it redresses the asymmetries between the powerful and the weak. Ideally, domestic competition policy should evolve gradually and organically in response to local needs, although the process may be aided by a multilateral agreement. But international pressure, if it is too strong, will

be counterproductive and damaging to the poor. And competition policy is not the only, or necessarily always the best, way to promote domestic competition.

International competition policy
This seeks to redress the balance between large companies – basically multinationals – and developing country governments. It relies on some kind of multilateral co-operation, co-ordination or supervision. This could be based on a very basic agreement on a code of conduct for multinationals, and on technical, informational and operational co-operation between multinationals' 'home' countries and developing countries. Multilateral competition policy will probably not entail very activist policies, and will probably not discipline many companies, but it would offer developing countries some assurances against their worst fears of exploitation.

Both domestic and international competition policy could assist the pursuit of poverty alleviation by reducing consumer prices and increasing national income. In general, however, the links are not particularly strong. An important corollary to competition policy negotiations would be for developing countries' governments to identify sectors where the lack of competition affects the poor most powerfully and act on these directly. They also need to ensure that any competition policy they create is lean and efficient and not a serious drain on finite stocks of skilled labour.

Box 17.2 Checklist on competition policy

- Is anti-competitive behaviour at home hurting the poor? In which sectors?
- Can you act directly in these sectors using current institutions rather than instituting new policies and institutions?
- Could you operate formal domestic competition policy disciplines, which typically require deep processes? Would this be the best use of highly-skilled labour?
- Would an international initiative help achieve your domestic competition policy goals?
- Can you identify specific instances in which foreign monopoly power hurts your economy?
- Could you muster the evidence of abuse sufficiently well to bring a case under such an agreement?

Notes

1   Market access was the first motivation mentioned in the EU's proposal for negotiating competition policy at the WTO's ministerial meeting in Seattle in 1999 (European Union, 1999). Since then it has probably become less significant in EU thinking.
2   It is difficult to think of a single case of law-based competition policy that is not accompanied by private legal activity.
3   Non-violation disputes are those in which a WTO member claims that its advantages under the WTO have been compromized by another's actions, even though the latter has violated no WTO rule.
4   The EU seems keen to have a multilateral rather than a plurilateral agreement: the former requires all WTO members to sign even if they have different substantive obligations, whereas the latter pertains only to the subset of WTO members that explicitly chooses to join it.
5   See the DfID minute of this roundtable discussion, DfID (2000c).
6   No country is currently recommending this directly, but following experience in the Uruguay Round, it is well to state it explicitly.

18 Investment and Trade Related Investment Measures (TRIMs)

> ***This chapter argues that;***
>
> - Investment is a critical element of development; foreign direct investment (FDI) can also be very important.
> - Trade-related investment measures (TRIMs) are interventions designed to influence the behaviour of foreign companies.
> - TRIMs are usually designed to compensate for a distortion in the economy, aiming to offset its effect or at least to gain a share of the rents it creates. Policy is usually best aimed at removing the distortion, but if this is impossible, a TRIM may boost national income.
> - If TRIMs stimulate economic growth, they may help poverty alleviation, but their direct effects are more likely to be negative than positive for the poor.
> - An international investment agreement might increase confidence in developing countries' policies towards multinational companies. But it could also constrain legitimate public policy objectives, and developing countries can, anyway, pursue good investment policies unilaterally.
> - An agreement to prevent bidding wars between countries seeking to attract FDI by offering concessions would benefit developing countries, which typically do not have deep pockets from which to fund such activities

18.1 Background

International investment is an important route by which developing countries can become more deeply integrated into the world economy. The most important – and currently most sought-after – element of investment is foreign direct investment (FDI), which potentially offers developing countries access to finance, technology, design and marketing outlets. Over the past ten years, the inflows of FDI to developing countries have increased five-fold, and now represent a third of global cross-border intra-firm investment – US$158 billion out of US$489 billion in 1996–8 (see IDS, 1999a). But it is worth noting that most of these FDI flows have gone to just six developing countries – Brazil, China, India, Indonesia, Mexico and Korea – which now account for a half of all inward investment stock in developing countries.

As we saw in Chapter 11 on the GATS, investment can be a substitute for international trade – an alternative way for a firm to supply an overseas market. But for essentially historical reasons, investment was entirely excluded from the GATT: FDI was not a major issue in the 1940s, and besides, given the predilection for planning at that time, governments were quite unable to contemplate the possibility that they would not want to manage such matters as firm ownership and location. Over time, this attitude has changed and, particularly during the 1990s, governments have sought to codify their investment relationships through bilateral investment treaties (of which there are nearly 2,000 today), regional arrangements and a proposed Multilateral Agreement on Investment (MAI), though this was effectively abandoned in 1998.

Since this Handbook is concerned with trade liberalization, we do not pursue these arrangements in detail here, although they are amenable to the same sort of analysis as we have used for trade issues, especially trade in services. But we must deal with one aspect of investment: trade-related investment measures (TRIMs). These refer to situations in which governments' enthusiasm to manage inflows of FDI in order to apply industrial policy or pursue development objectives spills over into interference with trade above and beyond normal border measures. Such interventions were always contrary to the GATT, but until the 1990s, they never faced effective discipline *de facto* – another tacit indicator of the interventionist attitude towards investment. During the 1990s, however, the warmer attitude towards FDI led many governments to relax their conditions for inward investment, and hence to the unilateral relaxation of many TRIMs. In addition, TRIMs figured in the Uruguay Round, resulting in the TRIMs Agreement, which reiterated the disciplines on two classes of TRIM and made explicit the means to enforce them.

TRIMs are among the most explosive of all the current disagreements about the implementation of the Uruguay Round that divide developing and developed countries. The TRIMs Agreement called for countries to register existing TRIMs in 1995 and phase them out over five to seven years. Most users of TRIMs failed to do the former. And now that the five years have elapsed and attitudes towards implementation have relaxed a little, they are struggling to decide whether or not to admit that they actually have been operating TRIMs and ask for an extended phase-out. Nearly all of these sensitive cases concern regulations requiring the use of local parts in the motor vehicles industry – an industry that has received special treatment over the years from virtually every government.

The TRIMs agenda relates to poverty in two ways:

- First, there are arguments about whether or not TRIMs raise national income and, so by extension, whether they increase the opportunities for poverty alleviation and income generation among the poor.
- Second, TRIMs may directly affect prices, wages and employment, although how frequently among the poor is moot.

18.2 The economics of TRIMs

TRIMs are requirements imposed on foreign investors by host countries in order to shape investment and the behaviour of foreign firms according to domestic industrial priorities. They are typically used as part of broader economic policy regimes designed to pursue such goals as industrialization, technology development and diffusion, skill acquisition and entrepreneurship, local employment, regional development and export expansion (see Maskus and Eby, 1990). But as noted above, TRIMs can distort and restrict trade and some of them are now subject to effective WTO disciplines.

Most East Asian countries have used TRIMs at some stage of their industrialization process, especially performance requirements. The measures used included local content requirements, export performance targets, foreign exchange restrictions, licensing restrictions, mandatory local participation and trade balancing (see Bora et al., 2000). FDI has been highly beneficial in East Asian countries, and it has been argued that these measures, implemented selectively at some stages and complemented with fiscal incentives (tax holidays or subsidies), have helped to spread the positive effects of FDI around the economy. But despite the general success of these economies, there is no direct evidence that the benefits of TRIMs exceed their distortion costs.

Greenaway (1992) suggests three main functions for TRIMs:

- *Resource allocation targets*: to shape the allocation of resources according to host government objectives, for example, by ensuring that the investment is neutral with respect to the balance of payments (that is, that it does not import more inputs than the value of its exports) or that it guarantees the utilization of domestic labour.
- *Dynamic targets (called insurance targets by Greenaway)*: to ensure that part of the benefit from multinational companies' investment will stay in the country and that the multinational will reinvest profits in the host country.
- *Rent-shifting targets*: to redistribute part of the surpluses generated by the investment away from the multinational and towards domestic residents.

The main restrictive measures used can be divided in two groups: requirements implemented at the first stage of the production process –

input TRIMs; and requirements applied at the final stage of the production process – output TRIMs. Table 18.1 summarizes the most common forms.

Some TRIMs work essentially as tariffs, while others are equivalent to quotas. For example, local content requirements have similar resource allocation effects to tariffs on intermediate goods, raising the effective price paid by the final goods producer (see Low and Subramanian, 1996). This is because the local content requirement can force the producer to use a higher-cost local input rather than a cheaper imported alternative. Trade balancing and foreign exchange balancing requirements, on the other hand, have the effect of restraining imports and therefore act as quantitative restrictions.

18.2.1 **TRIMs as correctives to market failures**

Economic theory suggests that capital searching for higher rates of return will flow from developed to developing countries. Under perfect competition, complete markets and free trade, such capital flows are unambiguously beneficial, and companies' decisions about whether to serve foreign markets through trade, temporary presence, direct investment or licensing of local companies will be made purely on the basis of cost and efficiency (what Julius, 1994, calls 'modal neutrality').

But the real world contains numerous distortions and exploiting these is one of the principal activities and *raisons d'être* of multinationals. Indeed, in countries with large internal markets, trade barriers are (often intentionally) a major incentive for FDI, allowing a foreign company to obtain the rents from serving a protected market. Host-country governments might attempt to limit the monopoly power of large multinational investors or, more commonly, to share some of the rents created by imposing conditions on their operation. Thus, the case for TRIMs is based on the theory of the 'second-best': where there is already a distortion (such as a tariff), then the additional implementation of a TRIM may be welfare-enhancing relative to the *status quo*. For example, if monopoly profits are created in the domestic market, the government might transfer some of them to locals by insisting on local equity participation. If protection causes exchange rate overvaluation, welfare might be enhanced by insisting on some level of export performance.

There are caveats, however. First, not all TRIMs are welfare-improving, even relative to the *status quo*. For example, Greenaway (1992) and Balasubramanyam (1991) suggest that while minimum export requirements and local equity requirements can be welfare-improving via export expansion and tax revenue increases, local content requirements are welfare-reducing, giving more protection than a tariff or a subsidy. Particularly where the objective is difficult to monitor, such as fostering technology transfer or training local entrepreneurs, TRIMs may be quite ineffective. For example, Blomstrom et al. (1994) show that technology requirements typically do not lead to transfer of useful technologies, while vigorous product market competition and facilitating technology absorption via education do.

Table 18.1 The most common TRIMs

Instrument	Intended effect
Input TRIMs	
Local content requirements	Specify that some proportion of value added or intermediate inputs is locally sourced
Trade balancing requirements	Link imports of one product to export performance of some other
Laws of similars	Require multinationals to use local substitutes for imported inputs if a similar component is locally manufactured
Limitations on imports	Limit the amount of goods and services that the company can import as inputs in the production process
Foreign exchange restrictions	Constrain investor in terms of the amount of intermediate inputs that can be imported
Local equity participation	Specifies that some proportion of the equity must be held locally
Local hiring targets	Ensure specified employment targets are hit
Expatriate quotas	Specify a maximum number of expatriate staff
National participation in management	Specifies that certain staff must be nationals or sets a schedule for the 'indigenization' of the management
R&D requirements	Commit multinationals to investment in research and development
Technology transfer	Commits multinationals to local use of specified foreign technology
Output TRIMs	
Minimum export requirements	Specify a certain proportion of output to be exported
Trade balancing requirements	Mandate that imports are a certain proportion of exports
Export controls	Specify that certain products may not be exported
Market reserve policy	Specifies that the local market is reserved for local producers
Product mandating requirements	Oblige the investor to export the mandated product from the host country only
Licensing requirements	Oblige the investor to license production of output in the host country
Technology transfer	Commits multinationals to a specified embodied technology

Source: Greenaway (1992).

Second, even given the distortion whose effect is to be offset, the TRIM may not be optimal. For example, if the problem were domestic monopoly sales, a (perfectly WTO-legal) excise tax would be a more efficient way of claiming some of the rent than a complex local content requirement.

Third, if the cause of the distortion is policy, the use of a TRIM will always be worse than the 'first-best' solution of removing both the distortion and the TRIM.

The assessment of TRIMs is more complex where they are ostensibly addressing intrinsic rather than policy-driven market failures. Domestic policies could almost always be designed to address the market failure directly, but it is possible that when administration costs and the political economy difficulties that beset domestic interventions are taken into account, a TRIM would be temporarily useful. For example, the compulsory licensing of a multinational's technology may alleviate competition policy problems; or restrictions on types of personnel may overcome failures in the market for training and education. This is certainly not a *carte blanche* for TRIMs, but it does suggest that, on occasions, a coherent case may be made for them.

In summary, TRIMs are a second-best policy aimed at extracting part of the rent earned by multinationals investing in distorted policy environments. This explains the high correlation between the usage of these measures and import protection or investment incentives, and suggests that TRIMs are part of industrial policy strategies. This linkage with investment incentives, often in the form of tax reductions, makes the impact of TRIMs difficult to quantify, because they entail agreements between governments and companies that both parties have an interest in keeping confidential. It also explains why TRIMs do not kill off investment flows. In a world where there is competition for the allocation of FDI, restrictions can only be applied if they are accompanied by other generous benefits. Indeed, as McCulloch (1990) points out, TRIMs are really a problem of uncompleted trade liberalization: with full liberalization and competitive multinationals, price competition would not allow countries to impose TRIMs and also compete in the market.

18.3 The current status of TRIMs

18.3.1 The legacy of the Uruguay Round

Since TRIMs can act as tariffs or quotas, they were targets for liberalization in the Uruguay Round negotiations. TRIMs were found to violate GATT disciplines under at least two articles:

- Local content and trade balancing requirements violate Article III (national treatment), which requires the equal treatment of foreign and domestic goods once the former have passed the border.
- Trade balancing, foreign exchange balancing and domestic sales requirements were identified as quantitative restrictions and therefore in violation of Article XI, which prohibits quantitative restrictions.

The TRIMs Agreement tackled these classes of policy in three main ways:

- A timetable for the elimination of TRIMs that violate Articles III and XI of the GATT – two years for developed countries, five years for developing countries and seven years for the least-developed countries (a period that, in this case, can be extended).
- The requirement to notify the WTO of such TRIMs 90 days before their application in order to check their consistency with WTO disciplines.
- The establishment of a committee to study TRIMs and monitor the implementation of the Agreement.

The TRIMs Agreement is interesting in the narrowness of its coverage. It prohibits TRIMs that violate Articles III and XI, but allows export performance requirements, which could have equally trade-distorting consequences. This seems particularly anomalous given that export subsidies in industrial sectors *are* prohibited by the ASCM (see Chapter 13). In negotiation, this outcome reflected the efforts of the larger developing countries, which were keen to be able to continue to 'charge' companies for access to their home markets by insisting on exports that would not be made on commercial criteria (see Low and Subramanian, 1996). The developed countries, representing the multinationals, presumably found these TRIMs less burdensome than others, and so did not resist this exception.

The more 'dynamic' TRIMs, such as those dealing with technology transfer, labour training or the employment of local labour, are also potentially just as distorting as the banned ones. But they do not violate any part of the GATT, and so while they might figure in future negotiations of an investment agreement, and while they should clearly be considered for unilateral removal on economic grounds, they did not feature in the Uruguay Round. This is in contrast to the services sector, in which countries can bind themselves not to impose training or employment conditions on incoming firms.

18.3.2 Unilateral policy

Even where measures are not subject to WTO disciplines, countries should think hard about using them. The need for export conditions is often essentially a reflection of exchange rate overvaluation, which, if this is a long-run problem, is likely to be indicative of distortions elsewhere in the economy. An industry that can sell domestically while importing components enhances welfare as long as it is facing the appropriate relative prices in domestic and foreign markets (that is, facing an appropriate exchange rate). Similarly, the case for other detailed interventions against multinationals mostly relies on there being other distortions that they are exploiting – for example, competition policy failures or investment incentives – and addressing these directly is a better long-run policy than using TRIMs.

18.3.3 **An investment agreement?**

All of these issues should really fall under the heading of investment policy, and whether or not international agreements exist, developing country governments should seek to establish satisfactory environments for FDI. These reside primarily in sound economic policy and secure domestic institutions in areas such as the rule of law, property rights and dispute resolution. More specifically in the investment area, they entail guaranteeing basic rights to operate commercially within the context of local law (that is, national treatment) and to move capital, earnings and essential personnel freely across the border.

There is no case for penalizing foreign companies, but neither is there a case for subsidizing them. Many commentators see FDI as a way of encouraging modernization and, indeed, it can play an important role. But the benefits of FDI can be overestimated, and, particularly if they get into bidding wars, developing countries risk losing all the benefits of inward investment to the multinationals themselves. Agosin and Mayer (2000) find, for example, that FDI flows do not always help to increase total investment: in some Latin American countries, they may have crowded out domestic investment.

The potential contribution of an international agreement on investment is three-fold:

Ending restrictions on establishment
First, the MAI, as opposed to nearly all bilateral investment treaties, sought to curtail the ability of governments to restrict inward investment to particular sectors; that is, outside a set of clearly defined sectors, it sought to create (limited) rights of establishment for multinationals in member countries. In principle, such rights will have a beneficial impact on investment. Moreover, the management of such establishment is rarely an important tool of economic development. Just as in developed countries where there are still calls for limitations on foreign ownership (and occasionally actual limits), it usually represents an attempt to protect influential domestic firms from competition.

But although controls on establishment are rarely a force for good, international restrictions on their use would be a serious incursion into domestic sovereignty and offer a significant hostage to fortune in restricting governments' ability to manage their economies even in ways that respect national treatment. *De facto*, this was the perception of developed countries in the MAI negotiations, for they listed all sorts of exceptions to establishment, including, for example, such sectors as mineral water bottling in Wisconsin. In behaving in this way, developed country governments essentially showed that they were not ready for an agreement (see Henderson, 1999). Developing country governments may well want to desist from restricting establishment to certain sectors, but they can always do so unilaterally.[1]

Establishing policy credibility
The second area in which an international investment agreement might

contribute is to give credibility to developing countries' promises to treat multinationals fairly once they have established. An agreement opens governments up to punishment if they violate it and so increases the incentives for 'good' behaviour. An international agreement would help governments establish credibility in their treatment of multinationals, not so much by defining good policy, as by this threat to punish transgressions. It would essentially trade-off higher incentives to maintain good policy against the danger that genuine public policy needs would sometimes be undermined.

On the policies themselves – for example, commitments not to expropriate property, to allow divestment and full commercial control, etc. – developing countries already have all the power necessary to pursue them. Thus, if their domestic procedures are sufficiently credible to reassure investors, an international agreement offers little additional mileage. Domestic credibility could arise from things like clear public acknowledgement of the benefits of multinationals and of stable policies towards them, full transparency, using 'high-level' laws rather than administrative fiat to define policy, and sound macroeconomic and trade policies.

Avoiding competition for investment
Third, and potentially more importantly, an international agreement on investment might be able to control the competition to attract FDI through artificial incentives. This game is essentially what economists call a 'prisoner's dilemma' in which everyone has an incentive to cheat (subsidize) but in which everyone would be better off if no one cheated. International agreements are more or less the only way out.

At present, there is not much prospect of an international agreement on investment emerging. As Henderson (1999) argues, the failure of the MAI negotiations in 1998 shows that the developed countries are not willing to commit to the sort of disciplines that they wish to impose on developing countries. Hence, any agreement that emerged in the near future would be wholly asymmetric or, more likely, so weak as to confer almost no additional credibility on developing country regimes. Some commentators, especially from the EU, argue for a so-called 'bottom-up' agreement that provides a framework and then allows developing countries to adopt specific obligations in their own time. This might reconcile current reluctance with future progress, but is not likely to lead quickly to substantive policy changes.

18.4 TRIMs and poverty

Investment, industrialization and growth will, in general, help to reduce poverty, so ultimately the impact of TRIMs on poverty depends on how successful the measures are in promoting such growth. A number of commentators have argued that in a second-best world, certain TRIMs can be welfare-enhancing elements of an industrial strategy. Thus, for example, if monopoly is inevitable, there may be benefits to insisting on the incoming multinational training local labour or using general-purpose technologies that have positive spillovers elsewhere in the economy.

The direct effects of TRIMs on poverty, however, seem more likely to be neutral or adverse. The willingness to intervene in these detailed ways is likely to produce strong protectionist pressures from local firms, and indeed from the multinationals concerned, which will constantly be seeking to renegotiate the terms on which they operate. Many TRIMs merely serve to support inefficient domestic industries, often removing from them the incentives to modernize and compete. The industries concerned are not likely to be major employers of unskilled labour; indeed, given the plausibility of the arguments about learning industrial skills, the beneficiaries will frequently be at the top end of the skill spectrum. Thus, TRIMs may well divert skills toward the protected sectors and away from co-operation with unskilled labour; if so, they would reduce the real wages for the unskilled.

Neither is there a plausible case to be made that TRIMs are needed to reduce the prices faced by the poor. Governments could, in principle, make it a condition of establishment that multinationals serve some part of the poor community at affordable prices, but they do not. Rather, TRIMs mostly serve to increase prices by reducing efficiency, which either hurts the poor or leaves them indifferent if they make no use of the goods that are protected.

Some measures, such as local equity requirements, can help to reduce poverty by raising tax revenues and the redistribution of these revenues to the poor through public expenditure. But since most TRIMs act as disincentives to production, they are often complemented by investment incentives, which work in the opposite direction by reducing tax revenues.

<u>18.5</u> Conclusion

In short, poverty alleviation is likely to be helped only by the best of growth-enhancing TRIMs. Given that there are good substitutes for most of these, there is little reason to fear that controls on, or unilateral reductions in, TRIMs will be bad for the poor. Most current TRIMs are probably anti-poor or neutral at best. Developing countries do need to devise good regimes for inflows of investment for this can be an important component of development. But such regimes comprise sound policies and institutions, not bidding wars to attract FDI followed by efforts to claw back some of the gains by imposing TRIMs.

International agreements could help to control bidding wars for FDI, but currently there is little prospect of their doing so. International and bilateral donors could also help in devising good policies towards FDI, but this is essentially a matter for advice and technical assistance, not binding substantive policy agreements. Creating a good environment for investment is an area in which developing countries are essentially on their own, needing to rely on domestic policy-making capacity rather than international agreements to tie their hands.

Box 18.1 **Checklist on TRIMs**

- Does your economy suffer market failures that are exploited by multinationals? Can these be addressed directly?
- Would a TRIM address the problem without unduly raising domestic costs?
- Do your TRIMs siphon skilled labour off into protected sectors and reduce unskilled wages?
- What do TRIMs do to the prices faced by the poor?
- Would an international investment agreement enhance credibility and so boost inflow of investment? Can you not induce such credibility unilaterally?

Notes

1   In addition and very importantly, the MAI was seen as imposing a set of rights for multinationals without imposing a set of obligations, which was very negatively perceived by developing countries, as well as a large number of international NGOs.

Glossary

Note: *Italic* entries in the text indicate that the term is included in the glossary.

ACP: African, Caribbean and Pacific countries, a specific group of 77 (mostly) former colonies given special treatment by the *EU*.

ADDs: Anti-dumping duties – see *anti-dumping*.

Aggregation and disaggregation: Aggregation is adding up data referring to small units (such as firms) into those referring to larger groups (such as the agricultural sector or the whole economy). The latter are known as aggregates. Disaggregation is breaking up larger groups into smaller groups.

Anti-dumping: Dumping is selling exports at below 'fair value' – usually interpreted as the price of the goods on the exporter's home market or an estimate of the cost of production. Anti-dumping is a policy used by importing governments designed to counteract dumping, for example, by imposing duties or negotiating price increases.

AoA: Agreement on Agriculture, part of the Uruguay Round Agreement.

APEC: Asia-Pacific Economic Co-operation, a group of economies clustered around the Pacific, including the major ones of the United States, Japan and China, which is seeking to reduce the barriers on their trade to zero by 2020. They meet at head of government level annually and coordinate a number of trade initiatives between themselves.

ASCM: Agreement on Subsidies and Countervailing Measures, part of the Uruguay Round Agreement.

Asymmetric information: Asymmetric information describes a situation where different market participants have different amounts of information about a proposed transaction. It is frequently sufficient to prevent the transaction from occurring, that is, to create a *market failure*. For example, only the seller of a used car can know whether it is a good or bad one. Buyers mistrust sellers when the latter claim their cars are good and, expecting the worst, will not pay the value of a good one. As a result, there is no market for good used cars.

ATC: Agreement on Textiles and Clothing, part of the Uruguay Round Agreement.

Border prices: The prices of goods at the border of a country. For imports, they include the cost of the goods plus the insurance and freight required to get them to the border (the so-called cif price). The prices do not include tariffs.

Budget constraints, soft and hard: The budget constraint says that the expenditure of a consumer, firm or country cannot exceed its ability to finance it. Finance may involve borrowing or selling assets, although over time these too are constrained by the fact that borrowing must be repaid. Hard budget constraints are where the budget constraint is applied rigorously; soft budget constraints are where they are not, for example, where governments regularly bail out loss-making firms.

Capital, capital-intensive: Capital comprises long-lasting productive assets – for example, buildings or machinery (physical capital), land or resources (natural capital), skills (human capital), knowledge (intangible capital) or social conventions (social capital). Financial capital refers to financial assets. Capital-intensive goods use relatively large amounts of capital in their production; c.f. *labour-intensive*.

Cartel: A cartel is an arrangement between firms to control a market – for example, to fix prices or limit competition between members of the cartel.

CITES: Convention on International Trade in Endangered Species of Wild Fauna and Flora, which agrees rules for trading such species, up to and including a complete ban on all trade.

Comparative advantage: A country has a comparative advantage in producing a good if its *opportunity cost* (in terms of other goods forgone) for doing so is lower than other countries. Comparative advantage predicts that in a well-functioning world economy, countries will export goods in which they have a comparative advantage; that trade follows comparative advantage is a *necessary condition* for global efficiency. Every country has comparative advantage in something – the product for which it is least inefficient relative to the rest of the world.

Competition policy: Competition policy is designed to protect and stimulate competition in markets – for example, through restrictions on mergers, bans on *cartels* and the prevention of price fixing. Some commentators include broader policies such as free trade and access to patent information under the general heading.

Computable general equilibrium (CGE) models: CGE models are mathematical characterizations of the economy, used to predict the effects of shocks in *general equilibrium*.

Consumer surplus: Consumer surplus is the *welfare* that a consumer gains from consuming a good over and above the price they pay for that good.

Consumption and income smoothing: When income varies over time, consumers typically try to 'smooth' consumption by saving when times are good and drawing on savings when they are bad. They may also try to rearrange their activities to make their flow of income smoother.

Contestability: A market is contestable if new suppliers can enter it easily. The threat of such entry is a discipline on the incumbent suppliers and can prevent prices from rising far above costs, because any excess profits will be rapidly followed by entry.

Contingent protection: Contingent protection is protection that is available automatically under certain circumstances (contingencies). It includes *anti-dumping* duties and countervailing duties (to offset *subsidies*).

Deadweight loss: Deadweight loss is the loss of economic *welfare* to society as a whole with no offsetting gains.

Decoupling: Decoupling is when subsidies to producers (usually farmers) are unrelated to production, and provide no incentive to increase production; in contrast, simple subsidies per unit of output tend to increase production.

Dependency ratio: A dependency ratio is the ratio of dependents per household earner.

Disciplines (WTO):   WTO rules are often referred to as disciplines on the behaviour of governments.

Discrimination: Discrimination in international trade involves treating different partners differently, for example, offering some preferred partners lower tariffs. Non-discrimination is the absence of such behaviour.

Disputes settlement (WTO):   WTO has formal procedures for settling trade disputes. These include consultations between the parties, the establishment of a three-person panel to advise on the WTO-consistency of the disputed practices and an Appellate Body to review panel decisions. It is all overseen by a Dispute Settlement Body (DSB), a council comprising a representative from every WTO member.

Distortions: Distortions are a policy or phenomenon that prevents markets from operating properly, for example, a tax, a minimum wage or an *externality*.

Domain of trade: The domain of trade is the range over which a good or service is traded – usually conceived of as a geographical range.

Dynamic effects: Analysis and results in which time matters – for example, through the order in which or the speed with which things happen – are called dynamic effects. The way an economy adjusts to a shock and the determination of its long-run growth rate are both dynamic issues – c.f. *static effects*.

Econometrics: Econometrics is the application of statistical methods to economics. Economists postulate a particular view of the world, express it mathematically in terms of observable data and unobservable parameters of behaviour, and then use statistics on the observables (data) to estimate the unobservables and/or test whether the view they started with really describes the world (that is, whether it explains the data reasonably).

Economies of scale: Economies of scale measure the relationship between production costs per unit of output and the number of units produced. If such costs are constant, we have constant returns to scale. If costs fall as output increases, we have increasing returns.

Effective protection: Effective protection is defined as the proportionate increase in value added that protection permits: that is, $(V–V^*)/V^*$, where V is value added per unit of output under protection and V^* the same under free trade. Value added is the value of an output less the value of the intermediate, or bought-in, inputs that it uses. It is what is left over to provide incomes for labour, capital and taxes.

Efficiency: Technical efficiency is when a firm (or other agent) obtains the maximum output from a given bundle of inputs. Allocative efficiency is when an agent or a country is allocating its resources over goods or activities such that, subject to its *budget constraint*, it maximizes economic welfare. Efficiency can refer to either consumption or production. Dynamic efficiency entails that over time, economic *welfare* is maximized, which is rather loosely interpreted as meaning that economic growth is maximized.

Efficiency losses: *Efficiency* losses are the losses of economic welfare due to inefficiencies of either an allocative (see *resource allocation*) or technical nature.

Elasticity: Elasticity is the ratio between the proportional (percentage) change in one variable and the proportional (percentage) change in another. For example, the price elasticity of demand is the percentage change in demand divided by the percentage change in price causing it. A cross-price elasticity refers to changes in demand for one good induced by changes in the price of another. Income elasticity is the percentage change in demand divided by the percentage change in income causing it.

Endogenous: A variable is endogenous to a model if it is determined by the model – strictly, arising from the workings of the system.

Endogenous growth: Endogenous growth is a form of economic analysis where the long-run rate of economic growth is determined by some feature of the system. In early economic theory, economic growth was exogenous in the long run, relating only to countries' population growth and rate of technical progress, which were presumed to be *exogenous*.

Endowments: Endowments are what economies have 'naturally' in terms of population, land, natural resources and, in some views of the economy, capital.

Equilibrium: Equilibrium is the outcome of a process from which there is no incentive to move – that is, at which, given the constraints they face, no one would wish to change their behaviour.

EU: European Union.

Euro–Med Agreements: The Euro–Med Agreements are the agreements signed or proposed between the EU and other countries in the Mediterranean – for example, Cyprus, Tunisia and Turkey. They cover financial aid and general co-operation, and offer the parties preferential access to each others' markets for international trade.

Europe Agreements: The Europe Agreements are the agreements between the EU and the countries of Central and Eastern Europe. They are like the *Euro–Med Agreements* but extend further and deeper to cover issues such as trade in services and the harmonization of standards.

Exemptions: Exemptions arise where imports are exempted from tariffs for some reason.

Exogenous: An exogenous variable is one that arises from outside the system, that is, it is not determined by the model under consideration.

Export restrictions: Export restrictions are where exports are restricted by administrative regulation. Export taxes also restrict exports, but are not usually included within this definition.

Export subsidies: Export subsidies are where governments pay exporters a supplement for each unit they export.

Externalities: Externalities arise where one agent's (a person, firm or country) behaviour affects another's welfare or profit other than via the price mechanism.

Factor markets: Factors of production include labour, capital, land and natural resources. Factor markets are where these are traded and thus, in the absence of controls, where their prices and employment are determined.

FDI: Foreign direct investment is investment by firms in one country in activities located in another, where the investor has (a measure of) direct control over the activities. It contrasts with buying a small part of the equity or debt of a foreign firm (portfolio investment), which confers no direct control.

Fiscal policy: Fiscal policy is policy concerning taxation and the overall balance of government taxation and expenditure.

Fixed costs: Fixed costs are those costs of production that are fixed regardless of the volume of production.

Formal sector: The formal sector comprises firms that have been formally incorporated and thus are legally recognized as firms.

Free rider: A free rider benefits from something but does not contribute towards its cost. The 'free-rider problem' occurs where a good or service is underprovided by the market because each agent hopes that others will provide it and so allow them to free-ride. In the extreme case, no one provides it. Free-riding is a particular problem for *public goods*.

GATS: General Agreement on Trade in Services, one of three Agreements administered by the *WTO*.

GATT: General Agreement on Tariffs and Trade, one of three Agreements administered by the *WTO*. The GATT refers only to trade in goods and was originally signed in 1947. It was embodied in a Secretariat and representative missions from member governments located in Geneva and the term GATT was sometimes used to refer to these rather than the agreement per se. In 1995, the WTO was created out of the embodiment of the GATT, inheriting many of its procedures, practices and traditions, and the GATT reverted to being just an agreement whose substantive work was overseen by the WTO.

General equilibrium analysis: General equilibrium is where everything affects everything else. In particular, general equilibrium analysis recognizes economy-wide *budget constraints* – for example, that labour used for one purpose cannot be used for something else.

Generalized System of Preferences (GSP):   The GSP is a system whereby developed countries charge below normal (*MFN*) tariff rates on imports from developing countries.

Green revolution: The green revolution was a process that took place during the 1960s and 1970s in which new varieties of grains with vastly higher yields were introduced.

GTAP: The Global Trade Analysis Project, based at Purdue University in the United States. It provides data and models for *computable general equilibrium modelling*.

Heckscher–Ohlin: Heckscher–Ohlin is a theory of international trade in which trade is determined solely by differences in countries' *endowments* of *factors of production*.

HIPC: Heavily indebted poor countries. The HIPC Initiative is the scheme whereby the IMF and the World Bank write down the debts of those countries on certain conditions.

Human capital: Human capital is the skills and knowledge of the workforce. It is regarded as a type of capital because it is long-lived, productive and created by accumulation – the characteristics of *capital* in general.

ILO: International Labour Organization.

IMF: International Monetary Fund.

Imperfect competition: Markets in which there are a limited number of sellers are described as imperfectly competitive. Sellers can charge a price above *marginal cost*, although they may not make excess profits because this margin might be absorbed by *fixed costs*.

Import substitution: Import substitution is a theory of and approach to development that focuses on providing domestic substitutes for all imported manufactures. In general, it is held to have failed badly over the 1960s, 1970s and 1980s.

Income effects: The effect of a price change on a consumer's real income is called an income effect. It depends on how large the price change is and how much the consumer is spending on that good. (The more they spend, the larger the income effect.)

Income elasticity: Income elasticity is the percentage increase in expenditure on a good induced by a 1% increase in income.

Income elasticity of demand: See *elasticity*.

Increasing returns to scale: See *economies of scale*.

Infant industry arguments: Infant industry arguments suggest that industries must be protected from import competition while they are establishing themselves. The problems are that protection frequently induces inefficiency and that it does not address the fundamental *market failures* that cause industries to fail to develop.

Input-output (I-O) matrix: An I-O matrix reports for each industry how much input from various industries (including itself) is required per unit of its output. I-O matrices also report inputs of factors of production as well.

International Development Targets: The International Development Targets were goals agreed internationally for the reduction of poverty by 2015. See Box 3.4.

IP/IPRs: Intellectual property/intellectual property rights.

Irreversability: Irreversability is where decisions, once taken, cannot be reversed, that is, the initial position cannot be restored – for example, baking a cake.

Labour-intensive: Industry X is more labour-intensive than industry Y if it uses more labour per unit of capital than does industry Y. Y is said to be capital-intensive.

Labour market flexibility: When labour markets are relatively flexible in allowing people to change jobs, firms to hire and fire workers and wages to change.

Lomé Agreement: The Lomé Agreement was between the *EU* and the *ACP* countries over trade, aid and general cooperation. It offered the ACP countries preferential access to EU markets. It was replaced by the Cotonou Agreement in 2000.

LSMS: Living Standards Measurement Survey, a series of household-level surveys of living standards. The surveys are conducted by governments, but World Bank advice helps to improve their quality, make them somewhat comparable, and disseminate them.

Macro (economics): Macroeconomics involves analysis at the level of the whole economy – for example, total exports, national income.

MAI: Multilateral Agreement on Investment – negotiated during the 1990s under the auspices of the OECD but abandoned in 1998.

Marginalism (costs, benefits and revenues): Most economic analysis concerns 'the margin' – whether a little more of this is worth having a little less of that. The marginal utility of something is the extra utility (*welfare*) gleaned by consuming a tiny bit more of it. Marginal cost (MC) is the cost of producing one unit more of a good. The margin is interesting because it is the key to *optimization*. If the MC of a good exceeds the price for which it can be sold, a firm would increase its profits by producing less (that is, it should scale back production slightly); if the MC is below the price, it should produce the marginal unit (that is it can increase profits by increasing production). Thus, the firm is maximizing profits when MC equals price.

Market dominance/power: A firm has market power if it can influence the price it receives for its goods or services by managing the quantity supplied. Dominance by a firm implies high degrees of power, certainly in excess of those of other firms in the market.

Market failure: Market failure is a generic term for conditions that cause markets to fail to deliver *Pareto-optimal* outcomes. They may cause the complete absence of a market (for example, under *asymmetric information*) or cause market outcomes to be sub-optimal (for example, with *distortions*).

MFA: Multi-Fibre Arrangement, negotiated under the GATT since the 1960s to manage trade in textiles and clothing. It relies on quantitative restrictions.

Micro (economics): Microeconomics involves analysis of individual units/agents (such as households, firms), usually making use of the economist's standard tool of *optimizing* something subject to constraints.

Monopoly: Monopoly is where there is only one seller (the monopolist) of a good. This seller can exploit their position to raise prices.

Monopsony: Monopsony is where there is only one buyer (the monopsonist). This buyer can exploit their position to lower the prices they pay.

Moral hazard: Moral hazard is the danger that if a contract promises payment on certain conditions, people change their behaviour to make those conditions more likely – for example, not taking care of insured goods.

Most favoured nation (MFN): MFN is the 'normal', non-discriminatory, tariff charged on imports of a good. In commercial diplomacy, exporters seek MFN treatment – that is, the promise that they get treated as well as the most favoured exporter. If all exporters have this clause, everyone is treated equally and there is no discrimination.

Multiplier effects: Under certain circumstances (mainly where there is under-employment), an extra $1 of spending generates more than $1's worth of extra output and incomes – it has a multiplier effect. Person A spends $1 on B's output; B spends some of that on C's output; C spends some of that ...etc.

NAFTA: North American Free Trade Agreement, between Canada, Mexico and the United States.

National treatment: National treatment is where imported goods and services, once they have entered a country and paid any tariff due, are treated in exactly the same way as national goods. In particular, they face the same internal taxes and no additional restrictions.

Natural monopoly: A natural monopoly exists where technological factors make it economic to have only one supplier – for example, gas and telephone lines into individual dwellings.

Natural persons: Natural persons are ordinary people – this is a piece of legal jargon.

Necessary condition: A is a necessary condition for B if you cannot have outcome B without having condition A.

Network economies: Network economies are where the value of a good or service increases as more people acquire or use it. For example, there is no point in having the only telephone in the world – there is no-one to call.

NGOs: Non-governmental organizations, typically charities and campaigning groups.

Nominal rates of protection: Nominal rates of protection are the proportion by which the (tariff-inclusive) internal price of an import exceeds the *border price*.

Non-discrimination: The absence of *discrimination*.

Non-tariff barriers (NTBs): NTBs is a catch-all phrase describing barriers to international trade other than the tariffs – for example, quotas, licensing, voluntary export restraints.

OECD: Organization for Economic Co-operation and Development.

Oligopoly: Oligopoly is where there are only a few sellers. Oligopolists typically have less market power than monopolists, but can still usually raise the price above costs.

Openness: Openness is the extent to which a country is open to goods, services or factors from the rest of the world. See section 2.1 for some specific measures of openness.

Opportunity cost: The opportunity cost of good or activity A is what you forgo to get it. For example, what a firm could have produced with the resources that it actually used to produce product A.

Optimization: Optimization is the process of trying to maximize or minimize something (for example, profits and cost respectively). Constrained optimization – optimization subject to constraints – is the heart of economics – for example, maximizing welfare subject to a *budget constraint* or maximizing output subject to using only the resources that are available.

Panel data: Panel data refer to data-sets that include observations on several units over more than one time period.

Pareto efficiency/improvements: Pareto efficiency is a situation in which one economic agent (for example, an individual or a country) can be made better off only at the expense of making another agent worse off. A Pareto improvement is where at least one agent is made better off and no-one is made worse off.

Partial equilibrium analysis: Partial equilibrium analysis is where one market is studied in isolation on the assumption that nothing that happens in it materially affects any other market. It is strictly appropriate only for very small markets.

Path-dependency: Path-dependency is the situation whereby the final equilibrium reached depends on the path taken to reach it through time. In most pieces of analysis, economists first locate the final equilibrium of a market or economy and then argue that ultimately, any path will lead to it. Path-dependency depends on things like *irreversability*.

Perfect competition/imperfect competition: Perfect competition (in the sense of 'complete' competition) is an idealized state in which competition is so fierce that no firm has market power and there are no excess profits for the marginal firm. It is a useful analytical tool for economists because it is usually simple to analyse and, in fact, many markets do approach this state in practice over the long run.

Political economy: Political economy draws attention to the political motivations in economics, especially the way in which income distribution rather than efficiency motivates economic behaviour.

Prebisch–Singer view of development: The Prebisch–Singer thesis is that the price of primary commodities relative to manufactures declines inexorably through time. This motivates a focus on industrialization and often a strategy of *import substitution*. Recently, economists have also noted the tendency for the prices of simple *labour-intensive* manufactures produced by developing countries to decline relative to those of other manufactures.

Predatory pricing: Predatory pricing is the practice of reducing prices so far that rival firms are driven out of business and then raising prices again to exploit the resulting *monopoly power*.

Price discrimination: Price discrimination is the practice of charging different customers different prices for something in order to exploit their different degrees of enthusiasm for it – for example, lower off-peak fares exploit workers' need to travel in the rush hour, while allowing less important personal travel to take place at other times. Price discrimination is not necessarily harmful.

Price fixing: See *cartels*.

Price takers: Economic agents are price takers if they cannot affect the prices at which they trade – loosely, they have no market power.

Production subsidies: Production subsidies are supplements paid to producers per unit of output.

PRSP: Poverty Reduction Strategy Papers – a tool of World Bank strategizing – see section 7.7.

Public goods: A public good is one that is 'non-rival' and 'non-excludable'. Non-rival means that A's consumption does not preclude (or even hinder) B's consumption – for example, receiving a radio broadcast. Non-excludable means everyone has to consume the same amount – for example, a very loud radio broadcast on a crowded beach. Markets cannot generally provide the optimal amount of public goods. Non-excludability means that no-one has the incentive to pay for them – see the *free-rider* problem. Non-rivalry means that, once a *public good* exists it is *efficient allocatively* to let everyone use it freely (for nothing) and hence it raises no revenue.

Quantitative restrictions: Quantitative restrictions are barriers to trade where the volume or value of imports is restricted administratively.

Quotas: Quotas are the amounts permitted under *quantitative restrictions* (for example, of imports).

R&D: Research and development are activities or expenditures designed to create new or improved products or processes.

Real wages: Real wages are wages corrected for the price level – notionally what money wages (known as nominal wages) will actually buy. Real wages are usually measured by dividing nominal wages by the retail price index. The 'producer real wage' is how many units of his output a worker receives in wages. It is essentially the nominal wage divided by the price of the particular output and reflects the real cost of employment to the employer.

Rents: 'Economic rents' are payments for a service that are not strictly required for the provision of that service. Rents are essentially 'excess' payments over the cost of producing the services (including, of course, an allowance for normal profits).

Rent-seeking: Rent-seeking is political activity by economic agents (which nonetheless absorbs economic resources) designed to allow them to claim part of a particular rent.

Resource allocation: Resource allocation refers to the way resources are allocated over activities or consumption – for example, the allocation of factors of production over industries or of consumer budgets over consumer goods.

SACU: Southern African Customs Union, comprising Botswana, Lesotho, Namibia, South Africa and Swaziland.

Safeguards: Safeguards are the arrangements under the GATT whereby countries can use tariffs to stem temporarily the flow of imports if they are causing injury to domestic producers.

Safety net: A safety net aims to ensure that everyone achieves a minimal level of consumption.

Second best: Imagine an economy in which N conditions are *necessary* to achieve optimality. The general theorem of second best states that if not all of these can be met, it may not be optimal to meet some of them. Thus, if a tariff is the only *distortion* in a small economy, removing it will improve economic welfare, but if other conditions for optimality are violated (for example, there is a minimum wage or an *externality*), that is no longer certain. Second best does <u>not</u> mean that we can say nothing: it means that specific cases must be considered individually. When general rules of economic policy are promulgated, their proponents are not usually saying that second best problems are inconceivable, but that they judge them empirically to be unimportant.

Second-round effects: Second-round effects are generated when shocks in one market are spread to others as producers and consumers change their behaviour – for example, switching to a cheaper substitute.

Sequencing: Sequencing is the order in which policy changes are introduced.

Social capital: Social capital is 'capital' that exists in the fabric of a society – that is, in the way that it conventionally behaves. Since these behaviours aid production, they are like physical, financial or human capital, and they also take time to build up and erode. Examples include the convention that people support each other in times of need, help each other harvest crops without entering a wage relationship and do not steal each others' livestock. Conventions are much more efficient than formal contracts because they require less enforcement.

Social costs: Social costs include the costs borne by all members of a society. Private costs are those borne by the parties making the decisions or causing the costs. The difference is the *externality*.

Social dumping: Social dumping is alleged if countries can sell abroad very cheaply by virtue of having very low (arguably exploitative) labour standards.

Special and differential treatment (S&D):   S&D is a term in the GATT to indicate that developing countries are treated differently and less demandingly than developed countries. For example, they receive preferential market access under the Generalized System of Preferences, have to make fewer offers in tariff negotiations, and are allowed to subsidize exports.

Specialization: Specialization means concentrating production on particular goods or services. 'Complete' specialization entails producing only one or a few goods and nothing of many.

Spillovers: Spillovers occur when one cannot exclude others from benefiting from your own economic activity – for example, knowledge spillovers occur when the new knowledge generated by research and development *(R&D)* is obtained by those who did not invest in the R&D.

SPS: Agreement on the Application of Sanitary and Phyto-sanitary Measures, concluded in the Uruguay Round.

Stabilizations: Stabilizations are the processes of trying to cure macro-economic imbalances such as large government or balance of payments deficits. Almost always, this requires austerity measures because the imbalances arise from an excess of spending over income.

Static effects: Analysis and results that are independent of real time are called static effects. They may represent the immediate impact of something or the very long-run outcome when all adjustment has been worked out.

Stolper–Samuelson theorem: Stolper–Samuelson is a theorem arising from the *Heckscher–Ohlin* theory of trade. It states that provided that a good is actually produced in a country, an increase in its price will increase the real wage or return of the factor used intensively in its production and reduce the real wage or return of another factor.

Structural adjustment: Structural adjustment is the term used to describe the process of establishing macroeconomic stability under IMF programmes (see *stabilization*) plus efforts to reform incentives to increase long-run efficiency often overseen by the World Bank. The latter often include policies like privatization, trade reform and fiscal reforms.

Subsidies: Subsidies are payments to offset some of the costs of an activity, for example, *export subsidies, production subsidies* and consumption subsidies.

Substitution effects: Substitution effects are the effects of a change in the price of one good on the demand for itself and other goods, other than that operating through the *income effect*. They reflect how far one good is substitutable for another.

Sufficient condition: A is a sufficient condition for B if the presence or existence of A ensures outcome B.

Sunk costs: Sunk costs are a *fixed cost* that, once incurred, cannot be recovered.

Tariff bindings: In GATT negotiations, countries commit themselves not to raise particular tariff levels. We refer to these as tariff bindings and to the committed maximum as the bound tariff.

Tariff equivalent: Sometimes an *NTB* can be quantified in terms of a tariff equivalent – the tariff that would have the exact same effect as the NTB.

Tariff escalation: Tariff escalation is where the tariff increases as a good becomes more processed. Escalation discourages imports of more processed varieties of the good (discouraging foreign processing activity), and offers domestic processors positive levels of *effective protection*. See Box 12.3.

Tariff peaks: Tariff peaks are particularly high tariffs, usually on narrowly defined goods.

Tariff rate quotas (TRQs): Tariff rate quotas occur where a good is subject to a tariff, but a certain quantity of it (the 'quota') is admitted at a lower tariff. They are mainly applied to agricultural trade.

Tariffication: Tariffication involves converting *NTBs* into their *tariff equivalents*. The Uruguay Round Agreement of the GATT tariffied developed countries' agricultural NTBs and bound tariffs at the resulting rates.

TBT: Agreement on Technical Barriers to Trade, concluded in the Uruguay Round of the GATT/WTO.

Terms of trade: The terms of trade measure the ratio of export prices to import prices. An increase potentially makes a country better off because it can buy more imports per unit of exports. The income terms of trade is the ratio of the total value of exports to import prices – that is, how many units of imports a country can buy with its exports.

Thin markets: Thin markets have few buyers and sellers. These markets typically have volatile prices because shocks require big adjustments by this small number of agents in order to restore *equilibrium*.

Time-series: Time-series data describe a variable through time. When several such data series are available, special techniques of time-series analysis allow *econometricians* to analyse them in powerful ways.

Trade Policy Review Mechanism (TPRM): The TPRM is part of the WTO. It involves publishing surveys of members' trade policies – ranging from every two years for the largest members to every ten for the smallest.

Trade adjustment assistance: Trade adjustment assistance is the collective name for schemes to offer special assistance to people or firms hurt by a trade reform.

Trade creation: Trade creation occurs when a policy liberalization encourages trade, allowing imports to displace less efficient local production and/or to expand consumption that was previously thwarted by artificially high prices.

Trade diversion: Trade diversion occurs when a trade reform discriminates between different trading partners and results in a less efficient (higher cost) source displacing a more efficient (lower cost) one. This can happen if the former is freed from barriers that continue to face the latter.

Traded and tradable goods: Traded goods are those that are actually traded. Tradable goods are those that are potentially tradable even if no trade is actually occurring. Non-traded goods or services are those sort that are not actually traded. Non-tradables are those that really could not be traded even in principle – for example, some government services, and very low value but bulky goods such as top-soil.

TRAINS database: Trade Analysis and Information System database from UNCTAD.

Transfer: A transfer of money or welfare from one economic actor to another – for example, from producers to consumers or from government to households.

TRIMs: Trade-related investment measures, and the common name of the Uruguay Round Agreement on such measures.

TRIPs: Trade-related aspects of intellectual property rights. An agreement on TRIPs was concluded under the Uruguay Round and constitutes the third agreement overseen by the *WTO* in addition to the *GATS* and the *GATT*.

UNCTAD: United Nations Conference on Trade and Development.

UPOV: International Union for the Protection of New Varieties of Plants.

Value added: Value added is the value that is added by *factors of production* as they process a good. Value added is the source of the incomes earned by factors. It is measured as the value output minus the value of all bought-in (or produced) inputs.

Value chain analysis: Value chain analysis involves careful study of the relations between different stages of production of a good, including market structures.

Variable costs: Variable costs are the costs of production that vary with the volume of production.

Variable levies: Variable levies are tariffs that vary so that whatever the border price of an import, its tariff-inclusive price equals or exceeds a pre-determined level. Much used in the EU's Common Agricultural Policy, variable levies are now, strictly speaking, banned by the WTO.

VAT: Value added tax.

Volatility: Volatility is the propensity of something to vary through time – usually referring to short-run random variation in both directions.

Welfare: Welfare is the 'enjoyment' that consumers are inferred to gain from their consumption. While welfare cannot be measured directly, economists can make inferences about changes in it by analysing behaviour – for example, bundle of goods A is preferred to bundle B but bundle C is preferred even more. Gradually, this allows them to build up a representation of behaviour that allows them to value outcomes as if they were measured in money terms.

WIPO: World Intellectual Property Organization.

WTO: World Trade Organization, created in 1995 as the successor to the GATT. It administers three agreements – the *GATT*, the *GATS* and *TRIPs* – and also deals with *disputes settlement* and the *Trade Policy Review Mechanism*.

Bibliography

Abramovitz, M. and P.A. David (1996), 'Convergence and Deferred Catch-up: Productivity Leadership and the Waning of American Exceptionalism', in *The Mosaic of Economic Growth*, edited by R. Landau, T. Taylor and G. Wright, Stanford: Stanford University Press.

Addison, T. and L. Demery (1985), 'Macro-Economic Stabilisation, Income Distribution and Poverty: A Preliminary Survey', London: Overseas Development Institute.

Adelman, I. and S. Robinson (1978), *Income Distribution Policy in Developing Countries*, Oxford: Oxford University Press.

Ades, A. and R. Di Tella (1997), 'National Champions and Corruption: Some Unpleasant Interventionist Arithmetic', *Economic Journal* 107, pp. 1023–42.

Ades, A. and R. Di Tella (1999), 'Rents, Competition and Corruption', *American Economic Review* 89, pp.982–93.

Agarwal, B. (1994), *A Field of One's Own: Gender and Land Rights in South Asia*, Cambridge: Cambridge University Press.

Aggarwal, M. (1995), 'International Trade, Labor Standards, and Labor Market Conditions: An Evaluation of the Linkages', US International Trade Commission, Working Paper 95–06.

Agosin, M. and R. Mayer (2000), 'Foreign Direct Investment in Developing Countries. Does it Crowd in Domestic Investment?', UNCTAD Discussion Paper No. 146, February 2000.

Ahmad, E. and N.H. Stern (1991), *The Theory and Practice of Tax Reform in Developing Countries*, Cambridge: Cambridge University Press.

Alwang, J. and P.B. Siegel (1999), 'Labor Shortages on Small Landholdings in Malawi: Implications for Policy Reforms', *World Development* 27, pp. 1461–75.

Alwang, J., P.B. Siegel and S.L. Jorgensen (1996), 'Seeking Guidelines for Poverty Reduction in Rural Zambia', *World Development* 24, pp. 1711–23.

Amsden, A. (1989), *Asia's Next Giant: South Korea and Late Industrialization*, New York and Oxford: Oxford University Press.

Amsden, A.H. (2000), 'The Rise of the Rest: Late Industrialisation Outside the North Atlantic Area', mimeo, Amherst College, Mass.

Anderson, K. (1995a), 'The Entwining of Trade Policy with Environmental and Labour Standards', Adelaide: Centre for International Economic Studies, University of Adelaide.

Anderson, K. (1995b), 'Lobbying Incentives and the Pattern of Protection in Rich and Poor Countries', *Economic Development and Cultural Change* 43, pp. 401–24.

Anderson, K., Erwidodo and M.D. Ingco (1999), 'Integrating Agriculture into the WTO: The Next Phase', paper for the WTO/World Bank conference on 'Developing Countries in a Millennium Round', September 1999, Geneva (www.worldbank.org/research/trade/archive.html/).

Anderson, K. and R Tyers (1989), *Agricultural Trade Liberalisation: Implications for Developing Countries*, Paris: OECD.

Appleton, S. (1998), 'Changes in Poverty in Uganda, 1992–1996', Centre for the Study of African Economies Working Paper 98/15, Oxford University.

Ashley, C., C. Boyd and H. Goodwin (2000), 'Pro-poor Tourism: Putting Poverty at the Heart of the Tourism Agenda', Overseas Development Institute, Natural Resource Perspectives 12.

Athukorala, P. and S. Rajapatirana (1998), 'Economic Liberalization and Industrial Restructuring: The Sri Lanka Experience', World Bank Current Studies in Industry, International Economics, Macroeconomics and Growth.

Bacchetta, P. and H. Dellas (1997), 'Firm Restructuring and the Optimal Speed of Trade Reform', *Oxford Economic Papers* 49, pp. 291–306.

Baffes, J. and J. Meerman (1998), 'From Prices to Incomes: Agricultural Subsidization without Protection?', *World Bank Research Observer* 13, pp. 191–211.

Balasubramanyam, V.N. (1991), 'Putting TRIMs to Good Use', *World Development* 19, pp. 1215–24.

Baldwin, R. and A.J. Venables (1994), 'International Migration, Capital Mobility and Transitional Dynamics', *Economica* 61, pp. 285–300.

Ballard, C.L., J.B. Shoven and J. Whalley (1985), 'General Equilibrium Computations of the Marginal Welfare Costs of Taxes in the United States', *American Economic Review* 75, pp. 128–38.

Banerjee, A., D. Mookherjee, K. Munshi and D. Ray (2000), 'Inequality, Control Rights and Rent Seeking: Sugar Cooperatives in Maharashtra', *Journal of Political Economy* 109, pp. 138–90.

Barrett, C.B. (1998), 'Immiserized Growth in Liberalized Agriculture', *World Development* 26, pp. 743–53.

Barro, R. J. and X. Sala-i-Martin (1995), *Economic Growth*, New York: McGraw-Hill.

Basu, K. (1999), 'Child Labor: Cause, Consequence, and Cure, with Remarks on International Labor Standards', *Journal of Economic Literature* 37, pp. 1083–1119.

Baughman, L., R. Mirus, M.E. Morkre and D. Spinanger (1997), 'Of Tyre Cords, Ties and Tents: Window-Dressing in the ATC?' *World Economy* 20, pp.407–34.

Baulch, R.J. (1997), 'Transfer Costs, Spatial Arbitrage, and Testing for Food Market Integration', *American Journal of Agricultural Economics* 79, pp. 477–87.

Baulch, R.J. and J. Hoddinott (2000), 'Economic Mobility and Poverty Dynamics in Developing Countries', *Journal of Development Studies* 36, pp. 1–24.

Bautista, R.M. (2000), 'Agriculture-based Development: A SAM Perspective on Central Vietnam', Washington DC: Trade and Macroeconomics Division, International Food Policy Research Institute.

Ben-David, D., H. Nordstrom and L.A. Winters (2000), 'Trade, Income Disparity and Poverty', WTO Special Study No.5.

Bennathan, E. (1993), 'Deregulation of Shipping: Lessons from Chile', in *Regulatory Reform in Transport: Some Recent Experiences. A World Bank Symposium*, Washington DC: World Bank.

Besley, T. (1995), 'Non-market Institutions for Credit and Risk Sharing in Low-income Countries', *Journal of Economic Perspectives* 9, pp. 115–27.

Besley, T. and R. Kanbur (1993), 'The Principles of Targeting', in *Including the Poor*, edited by M. Lipton and J. Van der Gaag, Washington DC: World Bank Regional and Sectoral Studies.

Bhagwati, J. (1968), *The Theory and Practice of Commercial Policy: Departure from Unified Exchange Rates*, Princeton: Princeton University Press.

Bhagwati, J. and R.E. Hudec (1996), *Fair Trade and Harmonization: Prerequisites for Free Trade? Volume 1: Economic Analysis*, Cambridge, Mass. and London: MIT Press.

Bhagwati, J. (1995), 'Trade Liberalisation and 'Fair Trade' Demands: Addressing the Environmental and Labour Standards Issues', *World Economy* 18, pp.745–59.

Bigsten, A. et al (1998), 'Exports and Firm-level Efficiency in the African Manufacturing Sector', mimeo, Centre for Study of African Economies, Oxford University.

Binswanger, H. and E. Lutz (2000), 'Agricultural Trade Barriers, Trade Negotiations and the Interests of Developing Countries', paper for the UNCTAD X High-level Round Table on 'Trade and Development: Directions for the Twenty-first Century', February 2000, Bangkok .

Birdsall, N. and J.L. Londoño (1997), 'Asset Inequality Matters: An Assessment of the World Bank's Approach to Poverty Reduction', *American Economic Review* 87, pp. 32–7.

Blomstrom, M., A. Kokko and M. Zejan (1994), 'Host Country Competition and Technology Transfer by Multinationals', *Weltwirtschaftliches Archiv* 130, pp. 521–33.

Blonigen, B.A. (2000), 'Tariff Jumping Anti-dumping Duties', NBER Working Paper No. 7776.

Booth, D., F. Lugngira, P. Masanja, A. Mvungi, R. Mwaipopo, J. Mwami and A. Redmayne (1993), *Social, Economic and Cultural Change in Contemporary Tanzania: A People Oriented Focus*, Stockholm: Swedish International Development Authority.

Bora, B., P. J. Lloyd and M. Pangestu (2000), 'Industrial Policy and the WTO', *World Economy* 23, pp. 543–59.

Boskin, M. J. and C.E. McLure. (1990), *World Tax Reform: Case Studies of Developed and Developing Countries*, San Francisco: ICS Press.

Bourgeois, J.M. and P.A. Messerlin (1998), 'The European Community Experience', in Brookings Trade Forum 1998, edited by R.Z. Lawrence, Washington DC: Brookings Institution.

Bourguignon, F. (1991), 'Optimal Poverty Reduction, Adjustment, and Growth', *The World Bank Economic Review* 5, pp. 315–38.

Bourguignon, F., W. Branson and J. de Melo (1992), 'Adjustment and Income Distribution: A Micro-Macro Model for Counterfactual Analysis', *Journal of Development Economics* 38, pp. 17–39.

Bourguignon, F., J. de Melo and A. Suwa (1991), 'Distributional Effects of Adjustment Policies: Simulations for Archetype Economies in Africa and Latin America', *The World Bank Economic Review* 5, pp. 339–66.

Bourguignon, F., P. Fournier and M. Gurgand (2000), 'Distribution, Development and Education in Taiwan, 1979–1994', mimeo, World Bank.

Bowen, H.P., A. Hollander and J.M. Vianne (1998), *Applied International Trade Analysis*, Ann Arbor: Michigan University Press.

Brandao, A. and W. Martin (1993), 'Implications of Agricultural Liberalization for the Developing Countries', *Agricultural Economics* 8, pp. 313–43.

Brander, J.A. and B. J. Spencer (1994), 'Trade Adjustment Assistance: Welfare and Incentive Effects of Payments to Displaced Workers', *Journal of International Economics* 36, pp. 239–61.

Brandolini, A. and G. D'Alessio (2000), 'Measuring Well-being in the Functioning Space', paper for the 26th General Conference of the International Association for Research in Income and Wealth, August/September 2000, Cracow, Poland.

Brittan, S. (1995), 'How to Make Trade Liberalisation Popular', *World Economy* 18, pp. 761–7.

Bruno, M., M. Ravallion and L. Squire (1996), 'Equity and Growth in Developing Countries: Old and New Perspectives on the Policy Issues', World Bank Policy Research Working Paper No. 1563.

Bruton, H. J. (1998), 'A Reconsideration of Import Substitution', *Journal of Economic Literature* 36, pp. 903–36.

Burr, C. (2000), *Grameen Village Phone: Its Current Status and Future Prospects*, Geneva: International Labour Organization.

Burtless, G. (1995), 'International Trade and the Rise in Earnings Inequality', *Journal of Economic Literature* 33, pp.800–16.

Canagarajah, S., D. Mazumdar and X. Ye (1998), 'The Structure and Determinants of Poverty Reduction in Ghana, 1988–1992', mimeo, World Bank.

Castro-Leal, F., J. Dayton, L. Demery and K. Mehra (1999), 'Public Social Spending in Africa: Do the Poor Benefit?' *World Bank Research Observer* 14.

Chambers, R. (1989), 'Editorial Introduction: Vulnerability, Coping and Policy', *IDS Bulletin* 20, pp. 1–7.

Chambers, R. (1995), 'Poverty and Livelihoods: Whose Reality Counts?' *Environment and Urbanization* 7, pp. 137–204.

Chambers, R. (1997), *Whose Reality Counts? Putting the First Last*, Intermediate Technology Publications.

Chanda, R. (1999), 'Movement of Natural Persons and Trade in Services: Liberalizing the Temporary Movement of Labour under the GATS', mimeo, ICRIER, New Delhi, presented to Global Development Network, December 1999, Bonn.

Charnovitz, S.(1987), 'The Influence of International Labour Standards on the World Trading Regime: A Historical Overview', *International Labour Review* 19, pp. 65–81.

Chen, S. and M. Ravallion (1996), 'Data in Transition: Assessing Rural Living Standards in Southern China', *China Economic Review* 7, pp. 23–56.

Choudhri, E.U. and D.S. Hakura (2000), 'International Trade and Productivity Growth: Exploring the Sectoral Effects for Developing Countries', *IMF Staff Papers* 47, pp. 30–53.

Christian Aid (1999), 'Fair Shares? Transnational Companies, the WTO and the World's Poorest Communities', *Christian Aid Policy Report* 11.99.

Cohen, M. and S. Fenn (1997), 'Environmental and Financial Performance: Are They Related?' Department of Economics, Vanderbilt University.

Colman, D. and D. Roberts (1994), 'The Common Agricultural Policy', in *The Economics of the European Union: Policy and Analysis*, edited by M. Artis and N. Lee. Oxford and New York: Oxford University Press.

Consumers International (1999), 'WTO Rules And Food Security', Consumers International Trade Briefing Paper No. 9, September 1999.

Consumers International (2000), 'Services at the WTO', Consumers International Trade and Economics Briefing Paper No. 3, November 2000.

Corden, W.M. (1990), 'Protection, Liberalization and Macroeconomic Policy', in *Trade Liberalization in the 1990s*, edited by H.W. Singer, N. Hatti, and R. Tandon, New Delhi: Indus Publishing Company.

Cornia, G.A. (1999), 'Liberalization, Globalization and Income Distribution', WIDER Working Paper 157:21.

Cornia, G.A., R. Jolly and F. Stewart. (1987), *Adjustment with a Human Face*, Oxford: Clarendon Press for the United Nations Children's Fund.

Correa, C. (1999), *Intellectual Property Rights, the WTO and Developing Countries. Implications and Implementation Options for Developing Countries: The TRIPS Agreement and Policy Options*, London: Zed Books.

Coulombe, H. and A.D. McKay (1996), 'Modeling Determinants of Poverty in Mauritania', *World Development* 24, pp.1015–31.

Crawford, S. (2000), 'The Worst Forms of Child Labour: A Guide to Understanding and Using the New Convention', University of Edinburgh, February 2000, paper for DfID.

CUTS (1999), 'Conditions Necessary for the Liberalisation of Trade and Investment to Reduce Poverty', Final Report to DfID, August 1999.

Datt, G. and M. Ravallion (1996), 'How Important to India's Poor is the Sectoral Composition of Economic Growth', *The World Bank Economic Review* 10, pp. 1–25.

de Haan, A. and S. Maxwell (1998), 'Poverty and Social Exclusion in North and South', *IDS Bulletin* 29.

de Janvry, A., M. Fafchamps and E. Sadoulet (1991), 'Peasant Household Behaviour with Missing Markets: Some Paradoxes Explained', *Economic Journal* 101, pp. 1400–17.

de Janvry, A., M. Fafchamps, M. Raki and E. Sadoulet (1992). "Structural Adjustment and the Peasantry in Morocco: A Computable Household Model", *European Review of Agricultural Economics* 19, pp.427–53.

de Janvry, A. and E. Sadoulet (1993), 'Rural Development in Latin America: Relinking Poverty Reduction to Growth', in *Including the Poor*, edited by M. Lipton and J. Van der Gaag, Washington DC: World Bank.

de Maio, L., F. Stewart and R. van der Hoeven (1999), 'Computable General Equilibrium Models, Adjustment and the Poor in Africa', *World Development* 27, pp. 453–70.

de Melo, J. and L.A. Winters (1993), 'Do Exporters Gain from VERs?' *European Economic Review* 37, pp. 1331–49.

de Paiva Abreu, M. (1996), 'Trade in Manufactures: The Outcome of the Uruguay Round and Developing Country Interests', in *The Uruguay Round and the Developing Countries*, edited by W. Martin and L.A. Winters, Cambridge: Cambridge University Press.

Deacon, B. (2000), 'Globalisation and Social Policy: The Threat to Equitable Welfare', UNRISD Occasional Paper No. 5.

Deardorff, A.V. and R.M. Stern (1994), *The Stolper–Samuelson Theorem: A Golden Jubilee*, Ann Arbor: University of Michigan Press.

Deaton, A. (1997), *The Analysis of Household Surveys: A Microeconometric Approach to Development Policy*. Baltimore and London: John Hopkins University Press for the World Bank.

Decker, P.T. and W. Corson (1995), 'International Trade and Worker Displacement: Evaluation of the Trade Adjustment Assistance Program', *Industrial and Labor Relations Review* 48, pp. 758–74.

Defourny, J. and E. Thorbecke (1984), 'Structural Path Analysis and Multiplier Decomposition within a Social Accounting Matrix Framework', *Economic Journal* 94, pp. 111–36.

Deininger, K. and P. Olinto (2000), 'Asset Distribution, Inequality, and Growth', World Bank Policy Research Working Paper No. 2375.

Delgado, C.L., J. Hopkins, V. Kelly; with P. Hazell, A.A. McKenna, P. Gruhn, B. Hojjati, J. Sil, and C. Courbois (1998), 'Agricultural Growth Linkages in Sub-Saharan Africa', IFPRI Research Report 107, Washington DC.

Demery, L. and L. Squire (1996), 'Macroeconomic Adjustment and Poverty in Africa', *The World Bank Economic Review* 11, pp. 39–59.

Dercon, S. (1998), 'Change in Poverty in Rural Ethiopia 1989–1995: Measurement, Robustness Tests and Decomposition', mimeo, Centre for the Study of African Economies, Oxford University.

Dervis, K., J. de Melo and S. Robinson (1982), *General Equilibrium Models for Development Policy*, Cambridge: Cambridge University Press.

Devereux, S. (1993), 'Goats before Ploughs: Dilemmas of Household Response Sequencing during Food Shortages', *IDS Bulletin* 24, pp. 52–9.

DfID (1999), 'Trade, Labour Standards and Development: Where Should They Meet?' DfID Background Briefing Note.

DfID (2000a), *Eliminating World Poverty: Making Globalisation Work for the Poor*. London: Cm 5006, Her Majesty's Stationery Office.

DfID (2000b), 'Poverty Reduction Strategies', DfID Background Briefing, April 2000.

DfID (2000c), 'Round Table on Competition Policy and Law: Their Role in Pro-Poor Development', mimeo, DfID

Dixit, A.K. and V. Norman (1980), *Theory of International Trade : a Dual General Equilibrium Approach*, Welwyn: Nisbet.

Dixit, A.K. and V. Norman (1986), 'Gains From Trade without Lump-sum Compensation', *Journal of International Economics* 21, pp. 111–22.

Dollar, D. (1992), 'Outward-oriented Developing Economies Really do Grow More Rapidly: Evidence from 95 LDCs, 1976–1985', *Economic Development and Cultural Change*, pp. 523–44.

Dollar, D. and A. Kraay (2001), 'Growth Is Good for the Poor', World Bank Policy Research Working Paper No. 2587.

Dollar, D. and R. Gatti (1999), 'Gender Inequality, Income and Growth: Are Good Times Good for Women?', Policy Research Report on Gender and Development Working Paper Series No. 1, World Bank, Washington DC.

Easterly, W. and A. Kraay (2000), 'Small States, Small Problems? Income, Growth, and Volatility in Small States', *World Development* 28, pp. 2013–27.

Ebrill, L., J. Stotsky and R. Gropp (1999), 'Revenue Implications of Trade Liberalization', IMF Occasional Paper 180:42.

Edwards, S. (1986), 'The Order of Liberalization of the Current and Capital Accounts of the Balance of Payments', in *Economic Liberalization in Developing Countries*, edited by A.M. Choksi and D. Papageorgiou, Oxford: Blackwell.

Edwards, S. (1998), 'Openness, Productivity and Growth: What Do We Really Know?' *Economic Journal* 108, pp. 383–98.

Edwards, S. and A. Cox Edwards. (1996), 'Trade Liberalization and Unemployment: Policy Issues and Evidence from Chile', *Cuadernos de Economia* 33, pp. 227–50.

Ehrenhaft, P.D., B. Hindley, C. Michalopoulos and L.A. Winters (1997), 'Policies on Imports from Economies in Transition : Two Case Studies', World Bank. Europe and Central Asia Region. Country Department III. Studies of Economies in Transformation 22:65.

Ekins, P., C. Folke and R. Costanza (1994), 'Trade, Environment and Development: The Issues in Perspective', *Ecological Economics* 9, pp. 1–12.

Elbehri, A., M.D. Ingco, T.W. Hertel and K. Pearson (1999), 'Agriculture and WTO 2000: Quantitative Assessment of Multilateral Liberalization of Agricultural Policy', paper for the WTO/World Bank conference on 'Agriculture and the New Trade Agenda in the WTO 2000 Negotiations', October 1999, Geneva.

Elson, D. (1991), *Male Bias in the Development Process*, Manchester: Manchester University Press.

Esfahani, H.S. (1991), 'Exports, Imports, and Economic Growth in Semi-industrialized Countries', *Journal of Development Economics* 35, pp. 93–116.

Eskeland, G. and A. Harrison (1997), 'Moving to Greener Pasture? Multinationals and the Pollution-haven Hypothesis', World Bank Policy Research Working Paper 1744.

Esty, D.C. (1994), 'Making Trade and Environmental Policies Work Together: Lessons from NAFTA', *Aussenwirtschaft* 49, pp. 59–79.

European Union (1999), 'EC Approach to Trade and Competition. Preparations for the 1999 Ministerial Conference', Communication from the European Community to the Working Group on the Interaction Between Trade and Competition Policy WT/GC/W/191.

European Union (2000), 'The Development Dimension of Competition Law and Policy', Communication from the European Community to the Working Group on the Interaction Between Trade and Competition Policy WT/WGTCP/W/140.

European Union (2001), Communication from the European Community to the Working Group on the Interaction between Trade and Competition Policy WTO WT/WGTCP/W/160.

Evans, D. (1999), 'Options for Regional Integration in Southern Africa', mimeo, Institute of Development Studies.

Faini, R., J. de Melo and W. Takacs (1995), 'A Primer on the MFA Maze', *World Economy* 18:113–135.

Falvey, R. (1999), 'Factor Price Convergence', *Journal of International Economics* 49, pp. 195–210.

Falvey, R. and C..D. Kim (1992), 'Timing and Sequencing Issues in Trade Liberalisation', *Economic Journal* 102, pp. 908–24.

FAO (1995), Impact of the Uruguay Round on Agriculture, Rome: FAO.

Feenstra, R.C, and G. Hanson (1995), 'Foreign Investment Outsourcing and Relative Wages', in *Economy of Trade Policy: Essays in Honour of Jagdish Bhagwati*, edited by R.C. Feenstra, G.M. Grossman and D. Irwin, Cambridge, Mass. and London: MIT Press.

Feenstra, R.C., Dorsati Madani, T. Yang and C. Liang (1997), 'Testing Endogenous Growth in South Korea and Taiwan', NBER Working Paper No. 6028.

Fernandez, R. and D. Rodrik (1991), 'Resistance to Reform: Status Quo Bias in the Presence of Individual-specific Uncertainty', *American Economic Review* 81, pp. 1146–55.

Findlay, C. and T. Warren (2000), 'Measuring Impediments to Trade in Services', in *GATS 2000: New Directions in Services Trade Liberalisation*, edited by P. Sauvé and R.M. Stern, Washington DC: Brookings Institution Press.

Finger, J.M. (1991), 'Development Economics and the GATT', in *Trade Theory and Economic Reform*, edited by J. de Melo and A. Sapir, Oxford: Blackwell.

Finger, J.M. (1993), *Anti-dumping: How it Works and Who Gets Hurt*, Ann Arbor: University of Michigan Press.

Finger, J.M. (1996), 'Legalized Backsliding: Safeguard Provisions in GATT', in *The Uruguay Round and the Developing Countries*, edited by W. Martin and L.A. Winters, Cambridge: Cambridge University Press.

Finger, J.M., M.D. Ingco and U. Reincke (1996), *The Uruguay Round: Statistics on Tariff Concessions Given and Received*, Washington DC: World Bank.

Finger, J.M. and J. Nogues (2000), 'WTO Negotiations and the Domestic Politics of Protection and Reform', paper for CEPR conference on 'The World Trading System Post Seattle: Institutional Design, Governance and Ownership', July 2000, Brussels .

Finger, J.M. and L. Schuknecht (2001), 'Market Access Advances and Retreats since the Uruguay Round Agreement', in *Developing Countries and the WTO*, edited by B. Hoekman and W. Martin, Oxford: Blackwell.

Finger, J.M. and P. Schuler (2000), 'Implementation of the Uruguay Round Commitments: the Development Challenge', *World Economy* 23, pp. 511–25.

Finger, J. M. and L.A. Winters (1998), 'What Can WTO Do for Developing Countries,' in *The WTO as an International Organization*, edited by A.O. Krueger, Chicago: Chicago University Press.

Fink, C. (2001), 'How Stronger Patent Protection in India Might Affect the Behavior of Transnational Pharmaceutical Industries', World Bank Policy Research Working Paper 2352.

Fontana, M. and A. Wood (2000), 'Modeling the Effects of Trade on Women, at Work and at Home', *World Development* 28, pp. 1173–90.

Foster, J.E., J. Greer and E. Thorbecke (1984), 'A Class of Decomposable Poverty Measures', *Econometrica* 52, pp. 761–66.

Frankel, J.A. and D. Romer (1999), 'Does Trade Cause Growth?' *American Economic Review* 89, pp. 379–99.

Gereffi, G. (1999), 'International Trade and Industrial Upgrading in the Apparel Commodity Chain', *Journal of International Economics* 48, pp. 37–70.

Gibbon, P. (1998), 'Peasant Cotton Cultivation and Marketing Behaviour in Tanzania since Liberalisation', Copenhagen: Centre for Development Research.

Gisselquist, D. and Harun-ar-Rashid (1998), 'Agricultural Inputs Trade in Bangladesh: Regulations, Reforms and Impacts', mimeo, World Bank.

Gleckman, H. and R. Krut (1994), 'Business Regulation and Competition Policy: The Case for International Action', Christian Aid Discussion Paper 41.

Glewwe, P. and G. Hall (1998), 'Are Some Groups More Vulnerable to Macroeconomic Shocks than Others? Hypothesis Tests on Panel Data from Peru', *Journal of Development Economics* 56, pp. 181–206.

Goldin, I. and O. Knudsen (1989), *Agricultural Trade Liberalisation: Implications for Developing Countries*, Paris: OECD.

Goldin, I., O. Knudsen and D. van der Mensbrugghe (1993), *Trade Liberalisation: Global Economic Implications*, Paris: OECD.

Goldin, I. and D. van der Mensbrugghe (1995), 'The Uruguay Round: An Assessment of Economywide and Agricultural Reforms', in *The Uruguay Round and the Developing Countries*, edited by W. Martin and L.A. Winters, Cambridge: Cambridge University Press.

Greenaway, D. (1992), 'Trade Related Investment Measures and Development Strategy', *Kyklos* 45, pp. 139–59.

Greenaway, D. and C. Milner (1991), 'Fiscal Dependence on Trade Taxes and Trade Policy reform', *Journal of Development Studies* 27, pp. 95–132.

Greenaway, D. and C. Milner (1993), *Trade and Industrial Policy in Developing Countries: A Manual of Policy Analysis*, Ann Arbor: University of Michigan Press.

Greenaway, D., W. Morgan and P. Wright (1998), 'Trade Reform, Adjustment and Growth: What Does the Evidence Tell Us?', *Economic Journal* 108, pp. 1547–61.

Grenier, L., A. McKay and O. Morrissey (1999), 'Competition and Business Confidence in Manufacturing Enterprises in Tanzania', CREDIT Research Paper 99/2, University of Nottingham.

Grimm, M. (2001), 'Macroeconomic Adjustment, Sociodemographic Change, and the Evolution of Income Distribution in Cote D'Ivoire: A Decomposition by Microsimulation', paper for the WIDER Development Conference on Growth and Poverty, May 2001, Helsinki.

Grimwade, N. (1996), 'Anti-dumping Policy after the Uruguay Round - An Appraisal', *National Institute Economic Review*, pp. 98–105.

Grootaert, C. and R. Kanbur (1995), 'The Lucky Few Amidst Economic Decline: Distributional Change in Cote d'Ivoire as Seen Through Panel Data Sets, 1985–88', *Journal of Development Studies* 31, pp. 603–19.

Grosh, M.E. (1993), 'Administrative Costs and Incidence in Targeted Programs in Latin America: Towards Quantifying the Trade-off', mimeo, World Bank.

Grosh, M. and P. Glewwe (2000), *Designing Household Survey Questionnaires for Developing Countries: Lessons from 15 years of the Living Standards Measurement Study*, Washington DC: World Bank.

Grossman, G.M. and E. Helpman (1991), *Innovation and Growth in the Global Economy*, Cambridge, Mass.and London: MIT Press.

Grossman, G.M. and A.B. Krueger (1995), 'Economic Growth and the Environment', *Quarterly Journal of Economics* 110, pp. 353–77.

Guillaumont, P., S. Guillaumont Jeanneney and J-F. Brun (1999), 'How Instability Lowers African Growth', *Journal of African Economies* 8, pp. 87–107.

Haddad, L., J. Hoddinott and H. Alderman (1997), 'Introduction: The Scope of Intrahousehold Resource Allocation Issues', in *Intrahousehold Resource Allocation in Developing Countries*, edited by L. Haddad, J. Hoddinott, and H. Alderman, Baltimore: John Hopkins University Press.

Haddad, L., J. Hoddinott and H. Alderman (1997), *Intrahousehold Resource Allocation in Developing Countries*, Baltimore:Johns Hopkins University Press.

Haddad, L., M.T. Ruel and J.L. Garrett (1999), 'Are Urban Poverty and Undernutrition Growing? Some Newly Assembled Evidence', *World Development* 27, pp. 1891–904.

Haddad, M. and A. Harrison (1993), 'Are There Positive Spillovers from Direct Foreign Investment? Evidence from Panel Data for Morocco', *Journal of Development Economics* 42, pp. 51–74.

Haggblade, S., P. Hazell and J. Brown (1989), 'Farm-nonfarm Linkages in Rural Sub-Saharan Africa', *World Development* 17, pp. 1173–201.

Handa, S. and D. King (1997), 'Structural Adjustment Policies, Income Distribution and Poverty: a Review of the Jamaican Experience', *World Development* 25, pp. 915–30.

Hanmer, L. and F. Naschold (1999), 'Can the International Development Targets Be Met? A Preliminary Report', London: Overseas Development Institute.

Harrison, A. (1996), 'Openness and Growth: A Time-series, Cross-country Analysis for Developing Countries', *Journal of Development Economics* 48, pp. 419–47.

Harrison, A. and G.H. Hanson (1999a), 'Who Gains from Trade Reform? Some Remaining Puzzles', *Journal of Development Economics* 59, pp. 125–54.

Harrison, A. and G.H. Hanson (1999b), 'Trade Liberalization and Wage Inequality in Mexico', *Industrial and Labour Relations Review* 52, pp. 271–88.

Harrison, A. and A.L. Revenga (1998), 'Labor Markets, Foreign Investment and Trade Policy Reform', in *Trade Policy Reform: Lessons and Implications*, edited by J. Nash and W. Takacs, Washington DC: World Bank.

Harrison, G.W., T.F. Rutherford and D.G. Tarr (1996), 'Quantifying the Uruguay Round', in *The Uruguay Round and the Developing Countries*, edited by W. Martin and L.A. Winters, Cambridge: Cambridge University Press.

Hathaway, D.E. and M.D. Ingco (1996), 'Agricultural Liberalization and the Uruguay Round', in *The Uruguay Round and the Developing Countries*, edited by W. Martin and L.A. Winters, Cambridge: Cambridge University Press.

Hazell, P. and B. Hojjati (1995), 'Farm/non-farm Growth Linkages in Zambia', *Journal of African Economies* 4, pp. 406–35.

Heeks, R. (1998), 'The Uneven Profile of Indian Software Export', Development Informatics Working Paper No 3, Institute for Development and Management, University of Manchester.

Henderson, D. (1999), *The MAI Affair: A Story and its Lessons*, London: Royal Institute of International Affairs, International Economics Programme.

Henson, S., R. Loader, A. Swinbank and M. Brehahl (1999), 'The Impact of Sanitary and Phytosanitary Measures on Developing Country Exports of Agricultural and Food Products', paper for the WTO/World Bank conference on 'Agriculture and the New Trade Agenda in the WTO 2000 Negotiations', October 1999, Geneva.

Hertel, T.W. (1997), *Global Trade Analysis: Modeling and Applications*, Cambridge: Cambridge University Press.

Hertel, T.W., P.V. Preckel and J.A.L. Cranfield (2000), 'Multilateral Trade Liberalisation and Poverty Reduction', paper presented to the Swedish Parliamentary Commission on Global Development (Globkom), Purdue University.

Hertel, T.W., K. Anderson, J.F. Francois, B. Hoekman and W. Martin (1999), 'Agricultural and Non-agricultural Liberalisation in the Millennium Round', paper for the WTO/World Bank conference on 'Agriculture and the New Trade Agenda from a Development Perspective', October 1999, Geneva.

Hertel, T.W. and W. Martin (1999), 'Developing Country Interests in Liberalizing Manufactures Trade', World Bank and Purdue University.

Hertel, T.W. and W. Martin (2000), 'Liberalising Agriculture and Manufactures in a Millennium Round: Implications for Developing Countries', *World Economy* 23, pp. 455–69.

Hertel, T.W., W.A. Masters and A. Elbehri (1998), 'The Uruguay Round and Africa: A Global, General Equilibrium Analysis', *Journal of African Economies* 7, pp. 208–36.

Hindley, B. (1987), 'Different and More Favourable Treatment', in *The Uruguay Round: A Handbook for the Multilateral Trade Negotiations*, edited by J.M. Finger and A. Olechowski, Washington DC: World Bank.

Hoekman, B. (1996), 'Assessing the General Agreement on Trade in Services', in *The Uruguay Round and the Developing Countries*, edited by W. Martin and L.A. Winters, Cambridge: Cambridge University Press.

Hoekman, B. and K. Anderson (1999), 'Developing Country Agriculture and the New Trade Agenda', *Economic Development and Cultural Change* 49, pp. 171–80.

Hoekman, B. and P. Holmes (1999), 'Competition, Policy, Developing Countries and the WTO', *World Economy* 22, pp. 875–93.

Hoekman, B. and W. Martin (1999), 'Some Market Access Issues for Developing Countries in a Millennium Round: Results from Recent World Bank Research', *Cuadernos de Economia* 36, pp. 947–78.

Hoekman, B. and C.A. Primo Braga (1997), 'Protection and Trade in Services: A Survey', *Open Economies Review* 8, pp. 285–308.

Hood, R. (1998), 'Fiscal Implications of Trade Reform', in *Trade Policy Reform: Lessons and Implications*, edited by W. Takacs and J. Nash, Washington DC: World Bank.

Hulme, D. and P. Mosley (1996), *Finance Against Poverty*, London: Routledge.

Humphrey, J. (1999), 'Globalisation and Supply Chain Networks: The Auto Industry in Brazil and India', mimeo, Institute of Development Studies, Sussex.

IDS (1996), 'Introductory PRA Methodology Pack', mimeo, Institute of Development Studies, Sussex.

IDS (1999a), 'International Investment Treaties and Developing Countries', Institute of Development Studies, Trade and Investment Background Briefing 9.

IDS (1999b), 'Trade and Environmental Standards', Institute of Development Studies, Trade and Investment Background Briefing 8.

IDS (1999c), 'Trade Protection in the Textile and Clothing Industries', Institute of Development Studies, Trade and Investment Background Briefing 4.

IDS (2000), 'Poverty Reduction Strategies: A Part for the Poor?' Institute of Development Studies Policy Briefing Issue 13.

IDS, University of Edinburgh and Active Learning Centre Glasgow (2000), 'DfID Poverty Guidance', mimeo, DfID.

IFAD (1999a), *Assessment of Rural Poverty in West and Central Africa*, Rome: Africa I Division Project Management Department, IFAD.

IFAD (1999b), *Regional Assessment: Supporting the Livelihoods of the Rural Poor in East and Southern Africa*, Rome: Africa II Division, IFAD.

IFAD (2001), *IFAD Rural Poverty Report*, Oxford: Oxford University Press.

ILO (1998a), 'Child Labour: Targeting the Intolerable', International Labour Conference, 86th Session 1998 Report VI (1), Sixth Item on the Agenda, Geneva: ILO.

ILO (1998b), 'Declaration on Fundamental Principles and Rights at Work', mimeo, Geneva: ILO.

ILO (2000), *ILOLEX: ILO Database on International Labour Standards*, Geneva: ILO.

IMF (1999), 'Review of Social Issues and Policies in IMF-Supported Programs', paper prepared by the Fiscal Affairs and Policy Development and Review Departments, August 1999, International Monetary Fund.

Ingco, M.D. (1996), 'Progress in Agricultural Trade Liberalization and Welfare of Least-Developed Countries', Washington DC: International Trade Division, International Economics Dept, World Bank.

Ingersent, K.A., A.J. Rayner and R.C. Hine (1995), 'Ex-post Evaluation of the Uruguay Round Agriculture Agreement', *World Economy* 18, pp. 707–28.

International Confederation of Free Trade Unions (ICFTU) (1999), 'ICFTU Comments on Preparations for the 3rd Ministerial Conference of the WTO'.

Jacobsen, L.S. (1978), 'Earning Losses of Workers from Manufacturing Industries', in *The Impact of International Trade on Investment and Employment*, edited by W. Wald, Washington DC: US Government Printing Office.

Jalan, J. and M. Ravallion (1998), 'Determinants of Transient and Chronic Poverty: Evidence from Rural China', Washington DC: World Bank.

Jalan, J. and M. Ravallion (1999), 'Are the Poor Less Well Insured? Evidence on Vulnerability to Income Risk in Rural China', *Journal of Development Economics* 58, pp.61–81.

Journal of Economic Perspectives (1995), Symposium on Income Inequality and Trade. *Journal of Economic Perspectives* 9, pp. 15–80.

Julius, D. (1994), 'International Direct Investment: Strengthening the Policy Regime', paper for the IIE Conference on 'Managing the *World Economy* of the Future: Lessons from the First Fifty Years after Bretton Woods', Washington DC: World Bank.

Kambhampanti, U. and J. Howell (1998), 'Liberalisation and Labour: The Effect on Formal Sector Employment', *Journal of International Development* 10, pp. 439–52.

Kanbur, R. (1987), 'Structural Adjustment, Macroeconomic Adjustment and Poverty: A Methodology for Analysis', *World Development* 15, pp. :1515–26.

Kanbur, R. (2001), 'Economic Policy, Distribution and Poverty: The Nature of Disagreements', paper presented to the Swedish Parliamentary Commission on Global Development (Globkom) on 22 September 2000.

Kaplinsky, R. (2000), 'Globalisation and Unequalisation: What Can Be Learned from Value Chain Analysis?' *Journal of Development Studies* 37, pp. 117–46.

Kapstein, E. (1998), 'Trade Liberalization and the Politics of Trade Adjustment Assistance', *International Labour Review* 137, pp.501–16.

Karsenty, G. (2000), 'Assessing Trade in Services by Mode of Supply', in GATS 2000: New Directions in Services Trade Liberalization, edited by P. Sauvé and R.M. Stern, Washington DC: Brookings Institutions Press.

Karunaratne, N.D. (1998), 'Trade Liberalization in Thailand: A Computable General Equilibrium (CGE) Analysis', *Journal of Developing Areas* 32.

Killick, T. (1993), *The Adaptive Economy: Adjustment Policies in Small, Low-Income Countries*, Washington DC: World Bank.

Killick, T. (1995), 'Structural Adjustment and Poverty Alleviation: An Interpretative Survey', *Development and Change* 26, pp. 305–31.

Killick, T. (1998), 'Adjustment, Income Distribution and Poverty in Africa: a Research Guide', paper for the African Economic Research Consortium, London: Overseas Development Institute.

Kim, E. (2000), 'Trade Liberalization and Productivity Growth in Korean Manufacturing Industries: Price Protection, Market Power, and Scale Efficiency', *Journal of Development Economics* 62, pp. 55–83.

Klasen, S. (1999), 'Does Gender Inequality Reduce Growth and Development? Evidence from Cross-country Regressions', Policy Research Report on Gender and Development Working Paper Series No. 7. World Bank, Washington DC.

Klevorick, A. (1997), 'Reflections on the Race to the Bottom', in *Fair Trade and Harmonization: Prerequisites for Free Trade?*, edited by J.N. Bhagwati and R.E. Hudec, Cambridge, Mass. and London: MIT Press.

Knetter, M.M. and T.J Prusa (2000), 'Macroeconomic Factors and Anti-dumping Filings: Evidence from Four Countries', NBER Working Paper 8010.

Knight, J.B. (1976), 'Devaluation and Income Distribution in Less Developed Economies', *Oxford Economic Papers* 28, pp. 208–27.

Kochar, A. (1995), 'Explaining Household Vulnerability to Idiosyncratic Income Shocks', *American Economic Review* 85, pp. 159–64.

Kraay, A. (1998), 'Exports and Economic Performance: Evidence from a Panel of Chinese Enterprises', mimeo, World Bank, Development Research Group.

Krishna, K.M. and L.H. Tan (1998), *Rags to Riches: Implementing Apparel Quotas under the Multi-fibre Arrangement*, Ann Arbor: Michigan University Press.

Krueger, A.O. (1990a), 'Asian Trade and Growth Lessons', *American Economic Review* 80, pp. 108–12.

Krueger, A.O. (1990b), 'Asymmetries in Policy Between Exportables and Importables Competing Goods', in *The Political Economy of International Trade: Essays in Honour of Robert E. Baldwin*, edited by R.W. Jones and A.O. Krueger, Oxford and Cambridge, Mass.: Blackwell.

Krueger, A.O. (1997), 'Trade Policy and Economic Development: How We Learn', *American Economic Review* 87, pp. 1–22.

Krueger, A.O. , M. Schiff and A. Valdes (1992), 'Agricultural Incentives in Developing Countries: Measuring the Effect of Sectoral and Economy-wide Policies', *Development Economics* 2, pp 127–43.

Krueger, A.O. and B. Tuncer (1982), 'An Empirical Test of the Infant Industry Argument', *American Economic Review* 72, pp. 1142–52.

Lal Das, B. (1999), *The World Trade Organisation: A Guide to the Framework for International Trade*, London, New York and Penang: Zed Books and Third World Network.

Lall, S. (1998), 'Technological Capabilities in Emerging Asia', *Oxford Development Studies* 26, pp. 213–43.

Lall, S. (1999), *The Technological Response to Import Liberalisation in Sub-Saharan Africa*, London: Macmillan Press.

Lanjouw, P. and M. Ravallion (1998), 'Benefit Incidence and the Timing of Program Capture', World Bank Policy Research Working Paper 1956, World Bank,Washington DC.

Lawrence, R.Z. and R.E. Litan (1986), *Saving Free Trade: A Pragmatic Approach*, Washington DC: Brookings Institution.

Lee, J. (1996), 'Government Interventions and Productivity Growth', *Journal of Economic Growth* 1, pp. 391–414.

Leidy, M.P. (1994), 'Trade Policy and Indirect Rent Seeking: A Synthesis of Recent Work', *Economics and Politics* 6, pp. 97–118.

Levinsohn, J., S. Berry and J. Friedman (1999), 'Impacts of the Indonesian Economic Crisis: Price Changes and the Poor', NBER Working Paper No. 7194.

Lewis, J.D., S. Robinson and K. Thierfelder (1999), 'After the Negotiations: Assessing the Impact of Free Trade Agreements in Southern Africa', Washington DC: Trade and Macroeconomics Division, International Food Policy Research Institute.

Lindland, J. (1997), 'The Impact of the Uruguay Round on Tariff Escalation in Agricultural Products', *Food Policy* 22, pp. 487–500.

Liu, A., S. Yao and R. Greener (1996), 'A CGE Model of Agricultural Policy Reform in the Philippines', *Journal of Agricultural Economics* 47, pp. 18–27.

Löfgren, H. (1999), 'Trade Reform and the Poor in Morocco: A Rural-Urban General Equilibrium Analysis of Reduced Protection', Washington DC: Trade and Macroeconomics Division, International Food Policy Research Institute.

Lopez, R., J. Nash and J. Stanton (1995), 'Adjustment and Poverty in Mexican Agriculture: How Farmers' Wealth Affects Supply Response', World Bank Policy Research Working Paper 1494.

Low, P. and A. Mattoo (2000), 'Is There a Better Way? Alternative Approaches to Liberalization under the GATS', mimeo, World Bank.

Low, P. and A. Subramanian (1996), 'Beyond TRIMs: A Case for Multilateral Action on Investment Rules and Competition Policies?', in *The Uruguay Round and the Developing Countries*, edited by W. Martin and L.A. Winters, Cambridge: Cambridge University Press.

Lutz, M. (1994), 'The Effects of Volatility in the Terms of Trade on Output Growth: New Evidence', *World Development* 22, pp. 1959–75.

Lutz, M. and H.W. Singer (1994), 'The Link Between Increased Trade Openness and the Terms of Trade: An Empirical Investigation', *World Development* 22, pp. 1697–709.

Maizels, A. (2000), 'The Manufactures Terms of Trade of Developing Countries with the United States, 1981–97', Queen Elizabeth House Working Papers Series 36.

Mani, M., S. Pargal and M. Huq (1997), 'Does Environmental Regulation Matter? Determinants of the Location of New Manufacturing Plants in India 1994', World Bank Policy Research Working Paper 1718.

Mani, M. and D. Wheeler (1999), 'In Search of Pollution Havens? Dirty Industry in the World Economy, 1960–1995', in *Trade, Global Policy, and the Environment* edited by P.G. Fredriksson, Discussion Paper No. 402, World Bank, Washington DC.

Martin, W. and K. Maskus (1999), 'Core Labor Standards and Competitiveness: Implications for Global Trade Policy', mimeo, World Bank.

Martin, W. and L.A. Winters (eds.), (1996), *The Uruguay Round and the Developing Countries*, Cambridge: Cambridge University Press.

Mashayekhi, M. (2000), 'GATS 2000 Negotiations. Options for Developing Countries', Trade-Related Agenda, Development and Equity Working Papers 1, South Centre.

Maskus, K. (1997), 'Should Core Labor Standards Be Imposed through International Trade Policy?' World Bank Policy Research Working Paper 1817.

Maskus, K. (1998), 'The International Regulation of Intellectual Property Rights', *Weltwirtschaftliches Archiv* 134, pp. 186–208.

Maskus, K. (2000a), 'Intellectual Property Issues for the New Round', in *The WTO After Seattle*, edited by J.J. Schott, Washington DC: Institute for International Economics.

Maskus, K. (2000b), *Intellectual Property Rights in the Global Economy*, Washington DC: Institute for International Economics.

Maskus, K. (2000c), 'Regulatory Standards in the WTO: Comparing Intellectual Property Rights with Competition Policy, Environmental Protection, and Core Labor Standards', World Bank Policy Research Working Paper, No. 1817, World Bank, Washington DC.

Maskus, K. and D.R. Eby. (1990), 'Developing New Rules and Disciplines on Trade-Related Investment Measures', *World Economy* 13, pp. 523–40.

Maskus, K. and M. Penubarti (1995), 'How Trade-related Are Intellectual Property Rights?' *Journal of International Economics* 39, pp. 227–48.

Mattoo, A. (2000a), 'Developing Countries in the New Round of GATS Negotiations: Towards a Pro-Active Role', *World Economy* 23, pp. 471–90.

Mattoo, A. (2000b), 'Financial Services and the WTO: Liberalisation Commitments of the Developing and Transition Economies', *World Economy* 23, pp. 351–86.

Mattoo, A., C. Fink, C. Neagu and R. Rathindran (2000), *Services Handbook*, Washington DC: World Bank.

Matusz, S.J. and D. Tarr (1999), 'Adjusting to Trade Policy Reform', World Bank Policy Research Working Papers 2142.

McCalman, P. (1999), 'Reaping What You Sow: An Empirical Analysis of International Patent Harmonization', mimeo, University of California, Santa Cruz.

McCulloch, N. and R.J. Baulch (1999), 'Assessing the Poverty Bias of Economic Growth: Methodology and an Application to Andhra Pradesh and Uttar Pradesh', Institute of Development Studies, Institute of Development Studies Working Paper 98.

McCulloch, N., R.J. Baulch and M. Cherel-Robson (2000), 'Poverty, Inequality and Growth in Zambia during the 1990s', Institute of Development Studies Working Paper 114.

McCulloch, N. and R.J. Baulch (2000), 'Simulating the Impact of Policy upon Chronic and Transitory Poverty in Rural Pakistan', *Journal of Development Studies* 36, pp. 100–30.

McCulloch, N., M. Cherel-Robson and R.J. Baulch (2000), 'Growth, Inequality and Poverty in Mauritania, 1987–1996',Institute of Development Studies.

McCulloch, R. (1990), 'Investment Policies in the GATT', *World Economy* 13, pp. 541–53.

396 *Trade Liberalization and Poverty: A Handbook*

McDougall, R.A., A. Elbehri and T.P. Truong (1998), *Global Trade Assistance and Protection: the GTAP 4 Data Base*, Centre for Global Trade Analysis, Purdue University.

McGee, R. (2000), 'Analysis of Participatory Poverty Assessment (PPA) and Household Survey Findings on Poverty Trends in Uganda', mimeo, Institute of Development Studies.

McKay, A. (1999), 'Methodological Issues in Assessing the Impact of Economic Reform on Poverty', in *Evaluating Economic Liberalization*, edited by M. McGillivray and O. Morrissey, London: Macmillan Press.

McKay, A., L.A. Winters and A.M. Kedir (2000), 'A Review of Empirical Evidence on Trade, Trade Policy and Poverty', A Report to DfID) prepared as a Background Document for the Second Development White Paper.

Mellor, J. and S. Gavian (1999), 'The Determinants of Employment Growth In Egypt - The Dominant Role of Agriculture And the Rural Small Scale Sector', mimeo, Abt Associates Inc., Cambridge Mass.

Messerlin, P.A. and G. Reed (1995), 'Anti-dumping Policies in the United States and the European Community', *Economic Journal* 105, pp. 1565–75.

Metcalfe, M.R. (2000), 'Environmental Regulation and Implications for the US Hog and Pork Industries', PhD. Dissertation, North Carolina State University.

Michalopoulos, C. (2000). 'The Role of Special and Differential Treatment for Developing Countries in GATT and the World Trade Organization', Policy Research Working Paper No. 2388, World Bank.

Milazzo, M. (1998), 'Subsidies in World Fisheries: A Re-examination', Discussion Paper No. 406, World Bank, Washington DC.

Mills, B.F. and D.E. Sahn. (1995), 'Reducing the Size of the Public Sector Workforce: Institutional Constraints and Human Consequences in Guinea', *Journal of Development Studies* 31, pp. 505–28.

Milner, C. and P. Wright (1998), 'Modelling Labour Market Adjustment to Trade Liberalisation in an Industrialising Economy', *Economic Journal* 108, pp. 509–28.

Minot, N. and F Goletti (1998), 'Export Liberalization and Household Welfare: The Case of Rice in Vietnam', *American Journal of Agricultural Economics* 80, pp. 738–49.

Morduch, J. (1994), 'Poverty and Vulnerability', *American Economic Review* 84, pp. 221–5.

Morduch, J. (1995), 'Income Smoothing and Consumption Smoothing', *Journal of Economic Perspectives* 9, pp. 103–14.

Morrissey, O. (1995), 'Political Commitment, Institutional Capacity and Tax Policy Reform in Tanzania', *World Development* 23, pp. 637–49.

Mosley, P. (1999a), 'Micro-macro Linkages in Financial Markets: The Impact of Financial Liberalization on Access to Rural Credit in Four African Countries', *Journal of International Development* 11, pp. 367–84.

Mosley, P. (1999b), 'A Painful Ascent: Obstacles to the Green Revolution in Africa', mimeo, University of Sheffield.

Mosley, P., J. Harrigan and J. Toye (1995), *Aid and Power: The World Bank and Policy-based Lending*, London: Routledge.

Mountford, A. (1997), 'Can a Brain Drain Be Good for Growth in the Source Economy?' *Journal of Development Economics* 53, pp. 287–303.

Mussa, M. (1986), 'The Adjustment Process and the Timing of Trade Liberalization', in *Economic Liberalization in Developing Countries*, edited by A.M. Choksi and D. Papageorgiou, Oxford: Blackwell.

Nadal, A. (2000), 'The Environmental and Social Impacts of Economic Liberalization on Corn Production in Mexico', Oxfam GB and WWF International, September 2000.

Narayan, D., R. Chambers, M.K. Shah and P. Petesch (2000), *Voices of the Poor: Crying out for Change*, New York: Oxford University Press for the World Bank.

Nash, J. and W. Takacs (1998), 'Lessons from the Trade Expansion Program', in *Trade Policy Reform: Lessons and Implications*, edited by J. Nash and W. Takacs, Washington DC: World Bank.

Nicolaides, P. (1989), 'The Problem of Regulation in Traded Services: The Implications for Reciprocal Liberalization', *Aussenwirtschaft* 44, pp. 29–57.

Nordström, H. and S. Vaughan (1999), 'Trade and the Environment', WTO Special Studies 4:109.

Nurkse, R. (1953), *Problems of Capital Formation in Underdeveloped Countries*, New York: Oxford University Press.

Obstfeld, M. and K. Rogoff (1996), *Foundations of International Macroeconomics*, Cambridge, Mass. and London: MIT Press.

Odii, M.A. (1997), 'Land Resource Use Efficiency of Rural Women Farmers under Alternative Tenurial Arrangements', *Journal of Rural Development and Administration* 29, pp. 1–9.

OECD Joint Group on Trade and Competition (1999), 'Competition Elements in International Trade Agreements: A Post-Uruguay Round Overview of WTO Agreements', OECD Note, OECD, Paris.

Otsuki T., J.S. Wilson, and M. Sewadeh (2001), 'A Race to the Top? A Case Study of Food Safety Standards and African Exports', Working Paper No. 2563, World Bank.

Oxfam (2000), *Cut the Cost, Patent Injustice: How World Trade Rules Threaten the Health of Poor People*, Oxford: Oxfam.

Oxfam-IDS (1999), *Liberalisation and Poverty*, Final Report to DfID, August 1999.

Paasman, B.R. (1999), 'Multilateral Rules on Competition Policy: An Overview of the Debate', CEPAL *Serie Comercio Internacional* 55.

Panagariya, A. (1999a), 'The Millennium Round and Developing Countries: Negotiating Strategies and Areas of Benefits', in Conference on Developing Countries and the New Multilateral Round of Trade Negotiations, Harvard University.

Panagariya, A. (1999b), 'TRIPS and the WTO: An Uneasy Marriage', mimeo, University of Maryland.

Panagariya, A. (2000), 'Evaluating the Case for Export Subsidies', World Bank Policy Research Working Paper 2276.

Panagariya, A. and D. Rodrik (1993), 'Political-economy Arguments for a Uniform Tariff', *International Economic Review* 34, pp. 685–703.

Perroni, C. and R. Wigle (1999), 'International Process Standards and North-South Trade', *Review of Development Economics* 3, pp. 11–26.

Peters, P.E. (1996), 'Failed Magic or Social Context? Market Liberalisation and the Rural Poor in Malawi', mimeo, Harvard Institute for International Development.

Pindyck, R., S. (1991), 'Irreversibility, Uncertainty and Investment', *Journal of Economic Literature* 29, pp. 1110–48.

Pitt, M. and M. Rosenzweig (1986), 'Agricultural Prices, Food Consumption and the Health and Productivity of Indonesian Farmers', in *Agricultural Household Models: Extensions, Applications and Policy*, edited by I. Singh, L. Squire and J. Strauss, Baltimore: John Hopkins University Press.

Poulton, C. (1998), 'The Cashew Sector in Southern Tanzania: Overcoming Problems of Input Supply', in *Smallholder Cash Crop Production under Market Liberalisation: A New Institutional Economics Perspective*, edited by A. Dorward, J. Kydd, and C. Poulton, Wallingford: CAB International.

Prebisch, R. (1950), *The Economic Development of Latin America and its Principal Problem*, Santiago: UNECLA.

Pritchett, L. (1996), 'Measuring Outward Orientation: Can it Be Done?' *Journal of Development Economics* 49, pp. 307–35.

Pritchett, L. and G. Sethi (1994), 'Tariff Rates, Tariff Revenue, and Tariff Reform: Some New Facts', *The World Bank Economic Review* 8, pp. 1–16.

Pritchett, L., A. Suryhadi and S. Sumarto (2000), 'Quantifying Vulnerability to Poverty: A Proposed Measure with Application to Indonesia', World Bank Policy Research Working Paper No. 2437, Washington DC: World Bank.

Putzel, J. (1998), 'Land Reform and Rural Poverty: Thinking about Lessons from Asia for Sub-Saharan Africa', Institute of Development Studies, Sussex.

Quisumbing, A.R. and J.A. Maluccio (2000), 'Intrahousehold Allocation and Gender Relations: New Empirical Evidence from Four Developing Countries', IFPRI FCND Discussion Paper 84.

Rama, M. and D. MacIsaac (1999), 'Earnings and Welfare after Downsizing: Central Bank Employees in Ecuador', *The World Bank Economic Review* 13, pp. 89–116.

Rausch, J.E. (1999), 'Networks versus Markets in International Trade', *Journal of International Economics* 48, pp. 7–35.

Rausch, J.E. and R.C. Feenstra (1999), 'Introduction to Symposium on 'Business and Social Networks in International Trade'', *Journal of International Economics* 48, pp. 3–6.

Ravallion, M. (1990), 'Rural Welfare Effects of Food Price Changes under Induced Wage Responses: Theory and Evidence for Bangladesh', *Oxford Economic Papers* 42, pp. 574–85.

Ravallion, M. (1998), 'Does Aggregation Hide the Harmful Effects of Inequality on Growth?' *Economics Letters* 61, pp. 73–7.

Ravallion, M. and B. Bidani (1994), 'How Robust is a Poverty Profile?' *The World Bank Economic Review* 8, pp. 75–102.

Ravallion, M. and D. Van de Walle (1991), 'The Impact on Poverty of Food Pricing Reforms: A Welfare Analysis for Indonesia', *Journal of Policy Modeling* 13, pp. 281–99.

Razin, A. and A.K. Rose (1992), 'Business-cycle Volatility and Openness: An Exploratory Cross-sectional Analysis', in *Capital Mobility: The Impact on Consumption, Investment and Growth*, edited by L. Leiderman and A. Razin, Cambridge: Cambridge University Press.

Reardon, T. (1997), 'Using Evidence of Household Income Diversification to Inform Study of the Rural Nonfarm Labor Market in Africa', *World Development* 25, pp. 735–47.

Reinert, K.A. (2000), 'Give Us Virtue, But Not Yet: Safeguard Actions under the Agreement on Textiles and Clothing', *World Economy* 23, pp. 25–55.

Renkow, M.. (2000), 'Poverty, Productivity and Production Environment: A Review of the Evidence', *Food Policy* 25, pp. 463–78.

Repetto, R. (1995), *Jobs, Competitiveness and Environmental Regulation: What are the Real Issues?*, Washington DC: World Resources Institute.

Rhee Y.W., B. Ross-Larson and G. Pursell (1984), *Korea's Competitive Edge: Managing the Entry into World Markets*, Baltimore: Johns Hopkins University Press for the World Bank.

Robilliard, A., F. Bourguignon and S. Robinson (2001), 'Crisis and Income Distribution: A Macro-micro Model for Indonesia', International Food Policy Research Institute and the World Bank.

Robilliard, A. and S. Robinson (1999), 'Reconciling Household Surveys and National Accounts Data Using a Cross Entropy Estimation Method', Washington DC: Trade and Macroeconomics Division, International Food Policy Research Institute.

Rodríguez, F. and D. Rodrik (1999), 'Trade Policy and Economic Growth: A Skeptic's Guide to the Cross-national Evidence', Centre for Economic Policy Discussion Paper No. 2143, London.

Rodrik, D. (1989), 'Credibility of Trade Reform: A Policy Maker's Guide', *World Economy* 12, pp. 1–16.

Rodrik, D. (1995a), 'Political Economy of Trade Policy', in *Handbook of International Economics*, edited by G.M. Grossman and K. Rogoff, Amsterdam: Elsevier.

Rodrik, D. (1995b), 'Trade and Industrial Policy Reform', in *Handbook of Development Economics*, edited by J. Behrman and T.N. Srinivasan, Amsterdam: Elsevier.

Rodrik, D. (1996), 'Labour Standards in International Trade: Do They Matter and What Do We Do About Them?', mimeo, Overseas Development Council.

Rodrik, D. (1997), *Has Globalization Gone Too Far?*, Washington DC: Institute for International Economics.

Rodrik, D. (1998), 'Why Do More Open Economies have Bigger Governments?' *Journal of Political Economy* 106 pp. 997–1032.

Rodrik, D. (1999a), 'Investment Strategies', in *The New Global Economy and Developing Countries: Making Openness Work*, edited by D. Rodrik, Washington DC: Overseas Development Council.

Rodrik, D. (1999b), *The New Global Economy and Developing Countries: Making Openness Work*, Washington DC: Overseas Development Council.

Roemer, M. and M.K. Gugerty (1997), 'Does Economic Growth Reduce Poverty? Technical Paper', CAER Discussion Paper No.5. Harvard Institute for International Development, Cambridge, Mass.

Rollo, J. and L.A. Winters (2000), 'Subsidiarity and Governance Challenges for the WTO: Environmental and Labour Standards', *World Economy* 23, pp. 561–76.

Romer, D. (1993), 'Openness and Inflation: Theory and Evidence', *Quarterly Journal of Economics* 108, pp. 870–903.

Romer, P. (1994), 'New Goods, Old Theory and the Welfare Cost of Trade Restrictions', *Journal of Development Economics* 43, pp. 5–38.

Romer, P. (1992), 'Two Strategies for Economic Development: Using Ideas and Producing Ideas', in *World Bank Annual Conference on Economic Development*, Washington DC: World Bank.

Rosenstein-Rodan, P. (1943), 'Problems of Industrialisation of East and South-east Europe', *Economic Journal* 53, pp. 202–11.

Ruttan, V.W. (2001), *Technology, Growth, and Development: An Induced Innovation Perspective*, New York and Oxford: Oxford University Press.

Sachs, J.D. (1999), 'Helping the World's Poorest', *The Economist*, 14 August, pp. 16–22.

Sachs, J.D. and A.M. Warner (1995), 'Economic Reform and the Process of Global Integration.' *Brookings Papers on Economic Activity* 1, pp.1–95.

Sadoulet, E. and A. de Janvry (1995), *Quantitative Development Policy Analysis*, Baltimore: John Hopkins University Press.

Safadi, R. and S. Laird (1996), 'The Uruguay Round Agreements: Impact on Developing Countries', *World Development* 24, pp. 1233–42.

Sahn, D.E. and A. Sarris (1991), 'Structural Adjustment and the Welfare of Rural Smallholders: A Comparative Analysis from Sub-Saharan Africa', *The World Bank Economic Review* 5, pp. 259–89.

Sahn, D.E., P.A. Dorosh and S.D. Younger (1997), *Structural Adjustment Reconsidered: Economic Policy and Poverty in Africa*, Cambridge: Cambridge University Press.

Sampson, G.P. (1999), *Trade, Environment, and the WTO: The Post-Seattle Agenda*, Policy Essay 27, Washington DC: Overseas Development Council.

Sapir, A. (1995), 'The Interaction Between Labour Standards and International Trade Policy', *World Economy* 18, pp. 791–803.

Sapir, A. (2000), 'Who's Afraid of Globalisation?', paper for the conference on 'Efficiency, Equity and Legitimacy: The Multilateral Trading System at the Millennium', June 2000, Harvard University.

Schiff, M. and A. Valdés (1992), *The Political Economy of Agricultural Pricing Policy Volume4: A Synthesis of the Economics of Developing Countries*, Baltimore: John Hopkins University Press.

Schiff, M. and A. Valdés (1998), 'Agriculture and Macroeconomy', in *Handbook of Agricultural Economics*, edited by B. Gardner and G. Rausser, Amsterdam: Elsevier.

Selden, T.M. and M.J. Wasylenko (1992), *Benefit Incidence Analysis in Developing Countries*, Washington DC: World Bank.

Sen, A. (1981), *Poverty and Famines*. Oxford: Clarendon Press.

Sen, A. (1993), 'Capability and Well-being', in *The Quality of Life*, edited by M. Nussbaum and A. Sen, Oxford: Clarendon Press.

Sen, A. and J. Dreze (1989), *Hunger and Public Action*, Oxford: Clarendon Press.

Serra, R. (1997), 'Fostering in Sub-Saharan Africa: An Economic Perspective', Centro studi 'Luca d'Agliano' and Queen Elizabeth House Development Studies Working Papers.

Sicular, T. (1995), 'Redefining State, Plan and Market: China's Reforms in Agricultural Commerce', *China Quarterly* No. 144, pp. 1020–46.

Singer, H.W. (1950), 'The Distribution of Gains Between Investing and Borrowing Countries', *American Economic Review* (Papers and Proceedings) 40, pp. 473–85.

Singh, A. (1994), 'Openness and the Market Friendly Approach to Development: Learning the Rights Lessons from Development Experience', *World Development* 22, pp. 1811–23.

Singh, A. (1996), 'The Post-Uruguay Round World Trading System, Industrialisation, Trade and Development: Implications for the Asia-Pacific Developing Countries', in *Expansion of Trading Opportunities to the Year 2000 for Asia-Pacific Developing Countries: Implications of the Uruguay Round and Adaptation of Export Strategies*, edited by UNCTAD, Geneva: UNCTAD.

Singh, A. and R. Dhumale (1999), 'Competition Policy, Development and Developing Countries', Trade Related Agenda, Development and Equity Working Paper 7, South Centre.

Singh, A. and A. Zammit (2000), 'The Global Labour Standards Controversy: Critical Issues for Developing Countries', mimeo, South Centre.

Singh, I., L. Squire and J. Strauss (1986), 'A Survey of Agricultural Household Models: Recent Findings and Policy Implications', *The World Bank Economic Review* 1, pp.149–79.

Sinner, J. (1994), 'Trade and the Environment: Efficiency, Equity and Sovereignty Considerations', *Australian Journal of Agricultural Economics* 38, pp. 171–87.

Spinanger, D. (1999), 'Textiles Beyond the MFA Phase-Out', *World Economy* 22, pp. 455–76.

Squire, L. (1991), 'Introduction: Poverty and Adjustment in the 1980s', *The World Bank Economic Review* 5, pp. 177–85.

Srinivasan, T.N. (2000), 'Developing Countries in the World Trading System: Emerging Issues', mimeo, Yale University.

Stevens, C., R. Greenhill, J. Kennan and S. Devereux (1999), 'Study of the Implications of Multilateral Agricultural Trade Agreements for the Ability of Developing Countries to Pursue Effective Food Security Policies', report for DfID and the Commonwealth Secretariat, Institute of Development Studies, Sussex.

Stewart, F. (1995), *Adjustment and Poverty: Options and Choices*, London and New York: Routledge.

Strasberg, P.J., T.S. Jayne, T. Yamano, J. Nyoro, D. Karanja and J. Strauss (1999), 'Effects of Agricultural Commercialization on Food Crop Input Use and Productivity in Kenya', Food Security II Co-operative Agreement, Michigan State University.

Strauss, J. (1986), 'Estimating the Determinants of Food Consumption and Caloric Availability in Rural Sierra Leone', in *Agricultural Household Models: Extensions, Applications and Policy*, edited by I. Singh, L. Squire, and J. Strauss. Baltimore: John Hopkins University Press.

Subramanian, A. (1990), 'TRIPs and the Paradigm of the GATT: A Tropical, Temperate View', *World Economy* 13, pp. 509–21.

Summers, L.H. (1999), 'Distinguished Lecture on Economics in Government: Reflections on Managing Global Integration', *Journal of Economic Perspectives* 13, pp. 3–18.

Swinnerton, K.A. (1997), 'An Essay on Economic Efficiency and Core Labour Standards', *World Economy* 20, pp. 73–86.

Ten Kate, A. (1992), 'Trade Liberalization and Economic Stabilization in Mexico: Lessons of Experience', *World Development* 20, pp. 659–72.

Tharakan, P.K.M. (1999), 'Is Anti-dumping Here to Stay?' *World Economy* 22, pp. 170–206.

Thirsk, W.R. (1997), *Tax Reform in Developing Countries*, Washington DC: World Bank.

Thomas, V. and Y. Wang (1998), 'Missing Lessons of East Asia: Openness, Education and the Environment', paper for the annual World Bank conference on 'Development in Latin America and the Caribbean', June 1998, Montevideo.

Thorbecke, E. and H. Jung (1996), 'A Multiplier Decomposition Method to Analyse Poverty Alleviation', *Journal of Development Economics* 48, pp. 279–300.

Timmer, P. (1997), 'How Well Do the Poor Connect To the Growth Process?' CAER Discussion Paper 17, Harvard Institute for International Development, Cambridge, Mass.

Townsend, R.M. (1995), 'Consumption Insurance: An Evaluation of Risk-bearing Systems in Low-income Economies', *Journal of Economic Perspectives* 9, pp. 83–102.

Tschirley, D., T.S. Jayne, M. Mukumbu, M. Chisvo, M.T. Weber, B. Zulu, R. Johansson, P. Santos and D. Soroko (1999), 'Successes and Challenges of Food Market Reform: Experiences from Kenya, Mozambique, Zambia and Zimbabwe', Food Security II Co-operative Agreement, Michigan State University.

Tybout, J.R. and M.D. Westbrook (1995), 'Trade Liberalization and the Dimensions of Efficiency Change in Mexican Manufacturing Industries', *Journal of International Economics* 39, pp. 53–78.

Tyers, R. and K. Anderson (1992), *Disarray in World Food Markets: A Quantitative Assessment*, Cambridge: Cambridge University Press.

Tyers, R. and R. Falvey (1989), 'Border Price Changes and Domestic Welfare in the Presence of Subsidised Exports', *Oxford Economic Papers* 41, pp. 434–51.

Tyler, G.J. and O. Akinboade (1992), 'Structural Adjustment and Poverty: A Computable General Equilibrium Model of the Kenyan Economy', Oxford: International Development Centre, Oxford.

UN (1991), *Barriers to Access of Rural Women to Land, Livestock, Other Productive Assets and Credit in Selected African Countries*, Addis Ababa: United Nations Economic Commission for Africa.

UNCTAD (1993), 'Environmental Management in Transnational Corporations: Report on the Benchmark Environmental Survey', Program on Transnational Corporations, UNCTAD, Geneva.

UNCTAD (1996), *The TRIPS Agreement and Developing Countries*, New York: United Nations.

UNCTAD (1999a), *Future Multilateral Trade Negotiations: Handbook for Trade Negotiators from Least Developed Countries*, Geneva: UNCTAD.

UNCTAD (1999b), *Report on the Role of Competition Policy for Development in Globalizing World Markets*, Geneva: United Nations.

UNCTAD and World Bank (1997), 'Strengthening the Service Infrastructure: Uganda', Expansion of Foreign Direct Investment and Trade in Services Paper, UN, New York, UNCTAD/ITE/IIT/Mics.5.

UNDP (1998), *Overcoming Human Poverty*, New York: United Nations.

UNDP (1999), *Globalization with a Human Face*, New York: United Nations.

UNESCO (2000), *Education for All 2000 Assessment: Statistical Document,* New York: United Nations.

US International Trade Commission (1995), *The Economic Effects of Anti-dumping and Countervailing Duty Orders and Suspension Agreements,* Washington DC.: USITC.

Valdes, A. and J Zietz (1980), 'Agricultural Protection in OECD Countries: Its Costs to Less-developed Countries', Research Report No.21, IFPRI, Washington DC.

Vamvakidis, A. (1999), 'Regional Trade Agreements or Broad Liberalization: Which Path Leads to Faster Growth?' *IMF Staff Papers* 46, pp. 42–68.

Van de Walle, D. (1993), 'Incidence and Targeting: An Overview of Implications for Research and Policy', in *Including the Poor,* edited by M. Lipton and J. Van der Gaag, Washington DC: World Bank.

Van der Hoeven, R. (1996), 'Structural Adjustment and Poverty: Review of Experiences in the 1980s', in *Economic Reforms and Poverty Alleviation in India,* edited by C.H. Hanumantha Rao and H. Linnemann, Sage Publications.

Wade, R. (1990), *Governing the Market: Economic Theory and the Role of Government in East Asian Industrialization.* Princeton: Princeton University Press.

Wang, Z. and L.A. Winters (2000), 'Putting 'Humpty' Together Again: Including Developing countries in a Consensus for the WTO', Policy Paper No. 4, Centre for Economic Policy Research, London.

Watal, J. (2000), 'Access to Essential Medicines in Developing Countries: Does the WTO TRIPs Agreement Hinder It?', mimeo, Institute for International Economics and Harvard Institute for International Development.

Whalley, J. (1975), 'How Reliable is Partial Equilibrium Analysis?' *Review of Economics and Statistics* 57, pp. 299–310.

Whalley, J. (1999), 'Special and Differential Treatment in the Millennium Round', *World Economy* 22, pp. 1065–93.

White, H. (1997), 'Poverty and Adjustment in Sub-Saharan Africa: A Review of the Literature', The Hague: Institute of Social Studies.

White, H. and A. Anderson (2000), 'Growth vs. Distribution: Does the Pattern of Growth Matter?' paper for the DfID White Paper *Eliminating World Poverty: Making Globalisation Work for the Poor.*

White, H., T. Killick, S. Kayizzi-Mugerwa and M. Savane (1999), 'Africa: Poverty Status Report', paper for the Special Programme on Africa.

WHO (1997), *Third Report on the World Nutritional Situation 1997,* Geneva: WHO.

Winters, L.A (1989), 'The So-called 'Non-economic' Objectives of Agricultural Support', OECD *Economic Studies* 13, pp. 237–66.

Winters, L.A. (1991), *International Economics,* London: Harper Collins Academic.

Winters, L.A. (2000a), 'Assessing the Efficiency Gain from Further Liberalization: A Comment', paper for the conference on 'Efficiency, Equity and Legitimacy: The Multilateral Trading System at the Millennium' June 2000, Harvard University.

Winters, L.A. (2000b), 'Trade and Poverty: Is There a Connection?' in Ben David, D., H. Nordstrom and L.A. Winters, *Trade, Income Disparity and Poverty,* Special Study No.5, Geneva: WTO.

Winters, L.A. (2000c), 'Trade Liberalisation and Poverty', Working Paper 7, Poverty Research Unit, Sussex.

Winters, L.A. (2000d), 'Trade Policy as Development Policy: Building on 50 Years' Experience', paper for the UNCTAD X High-level Round Table on 'Trade and Development: Directions for the Twenty-first Century', February 2000, Bangkok.

Winters, L.A. (2000e), 'Trade, Trade Policy and Poverty: What are the Links?', Discussion Paper No. 2382,Centre for Economic Policy Research, London.

Winters, L.A. (2001), 'Harnessing Trade for Development', paper for the conference on 'Making Globalisation Work for the Poor - The European Contribution', June 2001, Kramfors, Sweden.

Winters, L.A. and Z. Wang (1994), *Eastern Europe's International Trade*, London: Manchester University Press.

Wood, A. (1994), *North-South Trade, Employment and Inequality: Changing Fortunes in a Skill-driven World*, Oxford: Clarendon Press.

Wood, A. and Jordan, K. (2000) 'Why does Zimbabwe Export Manufactures and Uganda Not? Econometrics Meets History', *Journal of Development Studies*, 37, pp. 91–116.

Wood, W.C. (1996), *International Standards for Competition Law: An Idea Whose Time Has Not Come*, Washington DC.

Woolcock, S. (1995), 'The Trade and Labour Standards Debate: Overburdening or Defending the Multilateral System?' Economic and Social Research Council 4.

World Bank (1990), *World Development Report 1990: Poverty*, Washington DC: World Bank.

World Bank (1992), 'Trade Policy Reforms under Adjustment Programs', Operations Evaluation Department. World Bank, Washington DC.

World Bank (1993), *The Asian Miracle: Economic Growth and Public Policy*, Washington DC: World Bank.

World Bank (1996), 'China-container Transport Services and Trade: Framework for an Efficient Container Transport System', *World Bank Report*.

World Bank (1999a), 'Managing the Social Dimensions of Crises', mimeo, World Bank.

World Bank (1999b), 'Panama Poverty Assessment', mimeo, World Bank.

World Bank (1999c), *Poverty Trends and Voices for the Poor*, Washington DC: World Bank.

World Bank (1999d), *World Development Indicators*, Washington DC: World Bank.

World Bank (2000a), *Africa Can Claim the 21st Century*, Washington DC: World Bank.

World Bank (2000b), *Poverty Reduction and the World Bank: Progress in Fiscal 1999*, Washington DC: World Bank.

World Bank (2000c), *World Bank Progress in Poverty Reduction 1999*, Washington DC: World Bank.

World Bank (2001), *Attacking Poverty: World Development Report 2000/2001*, Washington DC: World Bank.

WTO (1998), 'Computer and Related Services', Background Note by the Secretariat, S/C/W/45 (98–2805), July 1998.

Xing, Y. and C. Kolstad (1998), 'Do Lax Environmental Regulations Attract Foreign Investment?' University of California, Santa Barbara, Working Papers in Economics 02/96.

Yang, G. and K. Maskus (1999), 'Intellectual Property Rights and Licensing: An Econometric Investigation', University of Colorado Working Paper.

Young, A.M. (2000), 'What Next for Labor Mobility under GATS',in *GATS 2000: New Directions in Services Trade Liberalization*, edited by P. Sauve and R.M. Stern, Washington DC: Brookings Institutions Press.

Zarrilli, S. (1999), 'WTO Sanitary and Phytosanitary Agreement: Issues for Developing Countries', mimeo, South Centre.

Zietz, J. and A Valdes (1989), 'International Interactions in Food and Agricultural Policies: Effects of Alternative Policies', in *Agricultural Trade Liberalisation: Implications for Developing Countries*, edited by I. Goldin and O. Knudsen. Paris: OECD.